The Nicest Kids in Town

AMERICAN CROSSROADS

Edited by Earl Lewis, George Lipsitz, George Sánchez, Dana Takagi, Laura Briggs, and Nikhil Pal Singh

The Nicest Kids in Town

American Bandstand, *Rock 'n' Roll,*
and the Struggle for Civil Rights
in 1950s Philadelphia

Matthew F. Delmont

UNIVERSITY OF CALIFORNIA PRESS
Berkeley · Los Angeles · London

University of California Press, one of the most
distinguished university presses in the United States,
enriches lives around the world by advancing
scholarship in the humanities, social sciences, and
natural sciences. Its activities are supported by the UC
Press Foundation and by philanthropic contributions
from individuals and institutions. For more information, visit www.ucpress.edu.

University of California Press
Berkeley and Los Angeles, California

University of California Press, Ltd.
London, England

Library of Congress Cataloging-in-Publication Data

Delmont, Matthew F.
    The nicest kids in town : American Bandstand,
Rock 'n' Roll, and the Struggle for Civil Rights in
1950s Philadelphia / Matthew F. Delmont.
        p. cm. — (American crossroads ; 32)
Includes bibliographical references and index.
ISBN 978-0-520-27207-1 (cloth : acid-free paper)
ISBN 978-0-520-27208-8 (pbk. : acid-free paper)
    1. Philadelphia (Pa.)—Race relations—History—
20th century.   2. African Americans—Civil rights—
Pennsylvania—Philadelphia—History—20th century.
3. Segregation—Pennsylvania—Philadelphia—
History—20th century.   4. Civil rights movements—
Pennsylvania—Philadelphia—History—20th century.
5. American Bandstand (Television program)
6. Minorities on television. I. Title.
    F158.9.N4D45 2012
    323.1196'073074811—dc23

                                    2011038775

Manufactured in the United States of America

20 19
10 9 8 7 6 5 4 3 2

Contents

Illustrations

Acknowledgments

I am fortunate to have received encouragement from family, friends, mentors, and colleagues for as long as I can remember. My mom, Diane Delmont, gets top billing because she has played the largest role in my life. Among many things, what I value most is that she taught me the importance of working hard every day and being nice to people. I could not ask for a more dedicated and caring parent.

My extended family have, each in their own way, shaped the person I have become. Thank you to Kaye Henrikson, Bobbie and Lindy Stoltz, Katie Stoltz, Terry Lick, Leari Jean and Jewel Anderson, Frank Bowman, my late aunt Joanne Tucker, Jason Tucker, Mel Wernimont, Nancy Wernimont, Nicole Wernimont and Ramses Madou, and Zach Wernimont for their love and support.

Thank you to all of my teachers, especially Mrs. Knox and Mr. Hauer at Burroughs Elementary School and Mike Byrne, Solfrid Ladstein, Michael Manning, Robert Slater, and Colonel (Ret.) John Gritz at Saint Thomas Academy. Thanks also to Tim Kelly whose generosity enabled me to attend Saint Thomas Academy. Thanks to Peter Lindsay for answering various questions about social theory as a sophomore at Harvard and to Adam Biggs for reading multiple drafts of my undergraduate senior thesis. I now understand much better how much work that entails.

While I did not end up working in marketing, Chris Clouser has been a generous and kind mentor.

I am blessed to have many good friends from different stages in life. Thanks especially to Jason Christopher, Doug Hoffert, Shawn Anderson, Tim Arnold, Victor Danh, Jake Ewart, Jake Lentz, Ken Miller, Cabral Williams, Paul Berens, Kevin Berry, John Foley, Peter Fritz, Dave Semerad, George Smolinski, Joe Wills, Kate Arnold, Kara Alexander, Sonia Berlin, Don Casey, Jessie and Ben Davis, Holly Eagleson, Emilie Ewart, Kara Hughes, Katie Monin, Sarah and Matt Sherman, Heather Stroud, Brian and Debra Ballentine, Dave Ben-Merre, and Keri Holt.

I thank Matt Garcia and Susan Smulyan for being excellent mentors and advisers, as well as helpful critics of my work. They saw this project grow from its earliest stages and were always supportive. I also learned a great deal about teaching from watching them; I try to put this into practice on a daily basis. It's safe to say that I would not have become the type of researcher or teacher that I am without them as role models. I also learned a lot from Lynne Joyrich and Carl Kaestle during our discussions for field exams and while working on my dissertation. Thanks to Evelyn Hu-Dehart for giving me a place to work at the Brown University Center for the Study of Race and Ethnicity in the Americas, and for her job advice. Thanks to James Campbell, Bob Lee, and Ralph Rodriguez for being friendly and supportive. Thank you to the staff at the Sheridan Center for Teaching and Learning, especially Rebecca More and Laura Hess, for helping me become a better teacher. Thanks to my graduate school colleagues in the department of American Civilization, especially Jin Suk Bae, Liza Burbank, Alma Carrillo, Tom Chen, Joe Clark, Erin Curtis, Sara Fingal, Caroline Frank, Gill Frank, Jim Gatewood, Morgan Grefe, Karen Inoyue, Jessica Johnson, Stephanie Larrieux, Eric Larson, Mireya Loza, Angela Mazaris, Gabriel Mendes, Ani Mukherji, Nicole Restaino, Mikiko Tachi, Gosia Rymsza-Pawlowska, Felicia Salinas, Margaret Stevens, Aslihan Tokgoz, Sarah Wald, Susanne Wiedemann, and Miel Wilson. Special thanks to Marcia Chatlain and Mario Sifuentez for being great office mates and friends in graduate school.

The Brown University Graduate School, Temple University Urban Archives, Philadelphia Jewish Archives Center, and Scripps College all provided financial support to defray research costs. Margaret Jerrido, Brenda Wright, John Pettit, and the other staff members at the Temple University Urban Archives were very friendly and helpful on several early mornings and late afternoons. The staffs at the Philadelphia City Archives, Philadelphia Schools District building, Philadelphia Jewish Archives Center, and African-American Museum in Philadelphia were also very generous with their time and expertise. Thanks to Terry Scott at West Philadelphia High School, Don Synder at South Philadelphia High School, and the librarians at William Penn High School, Northeast High School, and West Catholic High School for keeping their schools' yearbooks in safe places and for allowing me to look at them after their long school days. Thank you to everyone who took the time to talk to me about their memories of growing up in Philadelphia. Arlene Sullivan deserves a special thank you for putting me in touch with several other *American Bandstand* folks.

My editor at University of California Press, Niels Hooper, has been very supportive in bringing this project to print. Eric Schmidt, Kate Warne, Mary Francis, Hillary Hansen, Kim Hogeland and Caitlin O'Hara have also offered support at key stages. Thanks to Sybil Sosin for her careful copy editing. Thanks to George Lipsitz and Jay Mechling for offering comments on the draft manuscript that greatly strengthened this book. Thanks also to Josh Kun, Dan Horowitz, and Erika Doss for their support of my research.

Thank you to Tara McPherson, John Carlos Rowe, and Phil Ethington for organizing an engaging National Endowment for the Humanities/Vectors digital humanities seminar, and to all of the fellows who offered helpful suggestions as I prepared a digital companion to this book.

I've found, at Scripps College, an extraordinary place to teach American Studies. Thanks to Julie Liss, Rita Roberts, Sheila Walker, Bill Anthes, Nancy Neiman Auerbach, Hal Barron, Sid Lemelle, Mark Golub, Hao Huang, Eric Hurley, Amy Marcus-Newhall, Stu McConnell, Lily Geismer, Chris Guzaitis, Frances Pohl, Dan Segal, Diana Selig, Claudia Strauss, Cheryl Walker, and all my other colleagues at Scripps College and the Claremont Colleges. A special thanks to Cecilia Conrad, Michael Lamkin, and Lori Bettison-Varga for their early and consistent support.

Finally, thank you to Robert Scholes for teaching what turned out to be the most important seminar in my life. Numbers are not real, but if they were I would have to find a very large number to properly thank Jacque Wernimont for her love. I'll always associate this book with our summers in Philadelphia and the many happy memories before and after. We'll always have 4500 Springfield Avenue. A final thank you to Xavier Sebastian for arriving just before the deadline to submit these acknowledgments. Your timing is perfect and we love you greatly.

Introduction

In August 1957, teenagers across the country started watching teenagers in Philadelphia dance on television. Thanks to *American Bandstand,* the first national daily television program directed at teenagers, Philadelphia emerged as the epicenter of the national youth culture. The show broadcast nationally from Philadelphia every afternoon from 1957 to early 1964 and featured performances by the biggest names in rock and roll. In addition to these musicians, the local Philadelphia teenagers who danced on the show became stars. For the millions of young people across the country who watched the program every day on television, these Philadelphia youth helped to shape the image of what teenagers looked like.

More than fifty years after the show first broadcast, *American Bandstand*'s representations of youth culture remain closely linked both to the show's legacy and to larger questions about popular culture, race, segregation, and civil rights. *Billboard* magazine journalist Fred Bronson, for example, argues that *American Bandstand* was a "force for social good."[1] Bronson bases this claim on Dick Clark's memory that he integrated the show's studio audience when he became the host in 1957. "I don't think of myself as a hero or civil rights activist for integrating the show," Clark contends, "it was simply the right thing to do."[2] In the context of local and national mobilization in favor of segregation, underscored by widespread antiblack racism, integrating *American Bandstand* would have been a bold move and a powerful symbol. Broadcasting daily evidence of Philadelphia's vibrant interracial teenage culture would have offered viewers images of black and white teens interacting as peers at a time when such images were extremely rare. Clark and *American Bandstand,* however, did not choose this path, and the historical record contradicts Clark's memory of integration. Rather than being a fully integrated program that welcomed black youth, *American Bandstand* continued to discriminate against black teens throughout the show's Philadelphia years.

The real story of *American Bandstand* and Philadelphia in the postwar era is much more complicated than Clark suggests. It requires understanding not only how *American Bandstand* became racially segregated, but also how the show influenced and was influenced by racial discrimination and civil rights activism in the city's neighborhoods and schools. In telling this story, this book explores five main themes: first, how television and housing formed overlapping and reinforcing sites of struggle over segregation; second, how school officials in Philadelphia, like *Bandstand*'s producers, opposed meaningful integration while claiming to hold color-blind, nondiscriminatory policies; third, how *American Bandstand*'s decision not to integrate, while motivated by very real social and commercial pressures, was not inevitable; fourth, how *American Bandstand* used television production strategies to construct an image of national youth culture and encourage viewers and advertisers to see the show as the center of this imagined community; and finally, how *American Bandstand* is part of an ongoing struggle over how the history of racism and civil rights in the North is remembered.

TELEVISION AND HOUSING

The location of *American Bandstand*'s studio highlights how the everyday material reality of race in Philadelphia's neighborhoods intersected with televised representations of race. *Bandstand* broadcast from a studio in West Philadelphia during a period of intense struggles over racial discrimination in housing. Just blocks from *Bandstand*'s studio doors, groups of white homeowners like the Angora Civic Association organized to prevent black families from moving into West Philadelphia. The racial tensions around *Bandstand*'s West Philadelphia studio threatened to scare off the advertisers who were the show's lifeblood. Specifically, *Bandstand*'s producers sought to broadcast advertiser-friendly content to the show's viewers in Pennsylvania, New Jersey, Delaware, and Maryland. WFIL-TV called this four-state region "WFIL–adelphia" and emphasized the station's ability to help advertisers reach millions of these regional consumers. *Bandstand*'s producers wanted to make the show's representations of Philadelphia teenagers safe for television advertisers and viewers in WFIL–adelphia, and they decided to achieve this goal by not allowing black teenagers to enter the studio. Both WFIL and white homeowners associations justified their defense of racial segregation through a language of private property and profit that monetized and racialized space. The anti-integration sentiments of the homeowners associations, of white suburbanites, and of the advertisers eager to reach these viewers influenced *Bandstand*'s admission policies, while *Bandstand*'s daily broadcasts of its exclusively white studio audience disseminated these anti-integrationist views to a large regional audience. Looking at these overlapping forms of "defensive localism" in housing and television helps to explain when, how, and why *Bandstand* implemented racially discriminatory admissions policies. The policies, adopted during the show's early years as a local program (1952–1957), limited the range of racial representations the show presented to viewers when it went national in 1957. They also made *Bandstand* a target of protests by the black teenagers who were excluded from the show.

TELEVISION AND SCHOOLS

The Philadelphia teenagers who danced on, watched, or protested *American Bandstand* did so not just as media consumers, but also as students and citizens. Like *Bandstand*, high schools shaped the everyday experiences of young people in Philadelphia; and in their differential treatment of black students and their denials of discrimination, the Philadelphia school board's policies resembled those of *Bandstand*'s producers. *Bandstand*'s producers insisted that the show's admissions policy was color-blind but repeatedly denied admission to black teenagers; at the same time, the school board embraced antidiscrimination rhetoric while tracking black students into lower-level curricula and building schools in areas that exacerbated school segregation. Philadelphia's civil rights activists challenged the school board's claims of innocence with regard to school segregation and racial discrimination. Jewish civil rights leader Maurice Fagan and black educational activist Floyd Logan waged separate media campaigns, including television and radio broadcasts and newspaper articles, to call attention to the city's educational inequality. Fagan and Logan used these media outlets to make educational discrimination a front-page issue in Philadelphia. Fagan also worked to make Philadelphia a focal point for a national network of social scientists interested in prejudice and race relations by implementing the work of social scientists such as Gunner Myrdal and Kenneth Clark at the grassroots level and by partnering with school officials to distribute an array of antidiscrimination education materials.

While Fagan attempted to draw national attention to Philadelphia and introduced the language of intercultural education into the school curriculum, Logan used the schools' antidiscrimination rhetoric to call attention to the persistent discrimination against black students in the city's schools. Logan's educational activism took many forms: he investigated individual cases of discrimination on behalf of students and teachers; he collected information on school demographics and facilities to demonstrate inequality; he pushed the school board to take an official position on discrimination and segregation; and through his public letters and reports he served as an unofficial reporter on educational issues for the *Philadelphia Tribune,* the city's leading black newspaper. As the civil rights movement gained national attention, Logan used national events like the Little Rock school integration crisis to increase local awareness of Philadelphia's school segregation and educational inequality. By the early 1960s, the struggle over de facto segregation in the city's schools emerged from written demands and evasions into courtroom arguments and street protests. Logan's research and accumulated records on discrimination in the public schools provided the base of knowledge that the local National Association for the Advancement of Colored People (NAACP) branch and other civil rights advocates used to escalate the school segregation issue. Like their counterparts in cities in the North, Midwest, and West, Philadelphia's educational activists faced tremendous resistance to integration and educational equality from school officials who insisted that they did not discriminate on the basis of race. Unlike other case studies of de facto segregation, Philadelphia was also home to *American Bandstand,* and the city provides a unique example of how schools and television articulated similar visions of segregated youth culture.

TEEN TELEVISION AND MUSIC IN PHILADELPHIA

While *American Bandstand* elected to broadcast a segregated representation of youth culture, other Philadelphians used local television and music to different ends. *They Shall Be Heard,* a local teenage television program, dealt directly with Philadelphia's racial tensions at the same time that *Bandstand* implemented racially discriminatory admissions policies. Created by the Fellowship Commission, the city's leading civil rights coalition, *They Shall Be Heard* brought together teenagers of different races to discuss tensions in racially changing neighborhoods, such as West Philadelphia, at a time when *Bandstand*'s admissions policy prohibited such exchanges. *The Mitch Thomas Show,* a locally televised dance show similar to *American Bandstand,* was among the first television shows with a black host (it debuted fifteen years before *Soul Train*). Thomas's show highlighted the creative talents of black teenagers and brought images of these teens into Philadelphia homes. The show also offered a mediated space for interracial association and influenced many of *American Bandstand*'s dancers.

In addition to these local television programs, Georgie Woods, a leading rock and roll deejay, used music to advance civil rights in Philadelphia. Woods's civil rights activism developed out of his experience working with black teenagers as a deejay and concert promoter, as well as his concern about the lack of black television personalities and black-owned broadcast stations in the city. Woods used his radio show and concerts to raise money for the NAACP Legal Defense and Education Fund and to promote civil rights protests, drawing praise from Martin Luther King Jr. for his work. By merging his critiques of the media industry with civil rights work in support of the black teenagers who sustained his broadcast career, Woods offered a model for what music could achieve beyond commercial success.

Enormous social and commercial pressures encouraged *American Bandstand* to exclude black teenagers, but these alternative local examples suggest that *Bandstand*'s segregation was not inevitable. *American Bandstand*'s producers made a choice to pursue a commercial model for teenage television in an era when advertisers and television networks studiously avoided offending the racial attitudes of white viewers. *Bandstand*'s model of teen television emerged victorious, in large part, because federal broadcast policy gave advertising-supported network programs an advantage over local civic-oriented shows.

TELEVISION AND NATIONAL YOUTH CULTURE

The history of discrimination on *American Bandstand* is important because the program was the first television show to construct an image of national youth culture. Through a range of production strategies, *American Bandstand* encouraged the show's viewers, advertisers, and television affiliates to see it as the thread that stitched together different teenagers in different parts of the country into a coherent and recognizable national youth culture. From large markets like San Francisco and New Orleans to small towns like Lawton, Oklahoma, and Waukegan, Illinois, *American Bandstand* invited viewers to consume the sponsors' snacks and soft drinks along with the latest music and dances. More important, the program encouraged teenagers to imagine themselves as part of a national audience participating in the same consumption rituals at the same time. The central problem facing *American Bandstand*'s producers was that their show's marketability depended on both the creative energies of black performers and the erasure of black teenagers. Although *American Bandstand*'s music and dances were influenced by deejays Georgie Woods and Mitch Thomas and their black teenage fans, the image of youth culture *American Bandstand* presented to its national audience bore little resemblance to the interracial makeup of Philadelphia's rock and roll scene. As the television program that did the most to define the image of youth in the late 1950s and early 1960s, the exclusionary racial practices of *American Bandstand* marginalized black teens from this imagined national youth culture.

At the same time that *American Bandstand*'s producers excluded black teenagers from the program's studio audience, the show's image of youth culture moved ethnicity and gender to the foreground. Whereas television programs with ethnic characters like *The Goldbergs* and *Life with Luigi* were being replaced by (supposedly) ethnically neutral programs like *Leave It to Beaver* and *Father Knows Best,* because of its specific local context, *American Bandstand* offered working-class Italian-American teenagers from Philadelphia access to national visibility and recognition. Many of the show's regulars viewed *American Bandstand* as a welcoming space that provided a unique exposure for Italian-American teens. *American Bandstand* also recognized teenage girls for their interest in music and dancing and offered an after-school activity in an era when budget allocations limited the range of extracurricular activities available to young women in Philadelphia's public and parochial schools. *American Bandstand* became an integral part of the peer culture in the Italian neighborhoods of South Philadelphia, where many teens watched the show religiously.

TELEVISION, HISTORY, AND MEMORY

As the television program that helped to define teenage identity for a generation, *American Bandstand* is remembered by millions of people in the United States and internationally and is viewed as a powerful symbol of an era in American culture. Much of this memory rests on the belief that *American Bandstand* united a generation of viewers across lines of race, class, and region. While Dick Clark insists that he integrated *American Bandstand* in 1957, this book offers new archival documents, newspaper articles, and oral histories that demonstrate that *American Bandstand* continued to discriminate against black teenagers until the show left Philadelphia for Hollywood in 1964.

To understand the tension between Clark's memories and the historical record, this book examines how contemporary concerns may have influenced Clark's memories of *American Bandstand* in different eras. When *Soul Train* started winning viewers away from *American Bandstand* in the 1970s, for example, Clark emphasized *American Bandstand*'s role as a champion of black performers. Clark's memory of integrating the show also responded to music historians and critics who, writing in the wake of the civil rights movement, raised awareness of the frequent exploitation of black music artists by white producers. Writing in the 1990s and 2000s, Clark presented *American Bandstand* as part of the popular national history of the 1950s. Framed in this way, the supposed integration of *American Bandstand* becomes part of the national civil rights narrative. This approach evades the specific local history surrounding *American Bandstand*'s years in Philadelphia, as well as the antiblack racism in Philadelphia and nationally that motivated the show's discrimination.

American Bandstand is part of the civil rights story, but not in the way Clark suggests. Black teenagers contested *American Bandstand*'s segregation on several occasions, inspired by both the everyday discrimination they faced in Philadelphia and by national civil rights events like the Little Rock school integration crisis. Although they were not able to change the show's policies, the efforts of these black teens make clear that *American Bandstand*'s studio remained a site of struggle over segregation through the early 1960s. Yet, these stories of the black teenagers who made *American Bandstand* a civil rights issue are erased in Clark's popular histories of *American Bandstand*.

Because *American Bandstand* is so widely known, the show's images and themes have continued to circulate in popular culture well after the show's commercial peak. Two productions from the 2000s, for example, present stories of teen television, music, youth culture, and race relations in the *American Bandstand* era: the Emmy award–winning television drama *American Dreams* explores race relations in early 1960s Philadelphia on and around *American Bandstand*; and the musical film

Hairspray tells the story of the struggle over segregation on Baltimore's version of *American Bandstand*. *American Dreams* and the Broadway version of *Hairspray* both debuted shortly after September 11, 2001, and producers presented these productions as nostalgic stories about the *American Bandstand* era. While both *American Dreams* and *Hairspray* portray racial conflicts to raise the dramatic tensions in their respective stories, both productions manage these racial conflicts so as not to offend the fond remembrances of contemporary viewers. For viewers in the 2000s, *American Dreams* and *Hairspray* provide narrative proof that individual racial prejudice existed in the past, but was overcome through the racial tolerance of whites and the successful assimilation of African Americans. Rather than arguing that *American Dreams* and *Hairspray* are bad history, I am more interested in the ways *American Dreams* and *Hairspray* look to the *American Bandstand* era to tell stories about the past and present, and how these productions foreground narratives of white innocence and interracial unity that work against structural understandings of racism.

When viewed in the appropriate local and national contexts, this history of *American Bandstand* and postwar Philadelphia provides new insights on the immense resistance to civil rights and racial integration in the North, on the early use of color-blind rhetoric to maintain racially discriminatory policies, on the ways popular culture serves as a barometer of racial progress, and on the persistence of myths of white innocence that deny, disavow, or distort the history of racism in the civil rights era. Dick Clark's claims about the integration of *American Bandstand*, for example, exhibit the selective memory that historian Jacquelyn Dowd Hall has identified in the dominant narratives of the civil rights era. Against the distortions in many of these narratives, Hall suggests making civil rights "[h]arder to celebrate as a natural progression of American values. Harder to cast as a satisfying morality tale. Most of all, harder to simplify, appropriate, and contain."[3] Like the stories that Hall critiques, Clark's popular histories of the *American Bandstand* present segregation as a simple moral question of right or wrong, rather than as a deeply entrenched system of policies and customs with material consequences. Clark's claims of integrating the show not only overstate *American Bandstand*'s role as a force for social good; they also obscure the very reasons why integrating the show would have been noteworthy. Clark presents himself as the brave individual who broke down *American Bandstand*'s racial barriers, rather than describing the immense economic and social pressures that made segregation the safe course of action. In this way, Clark's memory of *American Bandstand* resembles the determined efforts of white homeowners to maintain neighborhood segregation while claiming to be innocent of racial discrimination. As historian Robert Self notes in his study of anti–open housing legislation in 1960s California, white resistance "rested simultaneously on both willful actions and a rhetoric of innocence" that "underscored the physical and social remove that were the privileges of . . . whiteness as well as the power of segregation to perpetuate racism and false consciousness among whites."[4] While Clark's investment in the rhetoric of racial innocence is widely shared, unlike the white suburbanites Self describes, Clark became an extraordinarily wealthy media personality by hosting one of the most popular television programs of all time, and his self-mythologizing popular histories of *American Bandstand* have circulated widely.

As Dick Clark's claims about integrating the show suggest, something is at stake in how we remember the history of *American Bandstand*. When I started research on this project, I believed, as Clark has claimed, that *American Bandstand* was fully integrated in the 1950s. I expected to contrast the show's integration with the segregation of Philadelphia's public schools and neighborhoods and explore how popular culture fostered interracial attitudes that challenged the existing racial order. The historical evidence ultimately led me to see how *American Bandstand* emerged from strong desires to protect racial segregation in both Philadelphia's neighborhoods and schools and also in local and national youth consumer culture.

Rather than a mythical history in which *American Bandstand* made a major contribution to desegregation, this book investigates how television, neighborhoods, and schools became segregation battlegrounds in postwar Philadelphia and how these sites produced racial difference within the burgeoning national youth culture. I tell this story by drawing on a range of textual, visual, and aural evidence both inside and outside of the archives, including letters, meeting minutes, speech transcripts, handbills, city government reports, grant proposals, census data, maps, newsletters, newspapers, magazines, editorial cartoons, high school yearbooks, photographs, television programs, radio scripts, films, songs, popular histories of *American Bandstand*, *American Bandstand* memorabilia, and twenty-one original oral histories with people who grew up in Philadelphia and attended, watched, and/or protested *American Bandstand*. Through these sources I explore the choices *American Bandstand*'s producers made in their specific contexts, the choices other Philadelphians made under similar circumstances, and the ongoing struggle over how this history of racial discrimination and antidiscrimination activism is remembered. From television producers and radio deejays to school officials and civil rights advocates, all of the people who make up this history understood the daily lives of teenagers and the representations of these lives as important sites in the struggle for racial equality in postwar Philadelphia. Thanks to *American Bandstand*, images of Philadelphia teenagers became meaningful for young people across the country. This book reveals how *American Bandstand* reinforced, rather than challenged, segregationist attitudes, and how this discrimination has been repeatedly disavowed over the past half century.

CHAPTER I

Making Philadelphia Safe for "WFIL-adelphia"

Television, Housing, and Defensive Localism in Bandstand's Backyard

Advertisers ... there's $6 Billions [sic] waiting for you in WFIL-adelphia. SELL ALL of America's 3rd market on WFIL-TV. You can really go to town—to hundreds of towns in the rich Philadelphia market—on WFIL-TV. .... Get the most for your money, the most people for your money. Schedule WFIL-TV.

—WFIL-TV call for advertisers, *Philadelphia Inquirer*, 1952

Do you like your home and neighborhood? Then why not protect them?

—Angora Civic Association flier

Throughout 1954, white and African American teenagers fought outside of WFIL-TV's West Philadelphia studio on an almost daily basis. Philadelphia experienced more than its share of racial tension in this era, but these teenager brawls stand out because they were sparked by a television program. WFIL-TV broadcast the popular, regionally televised teenage dance show *Bandstand* (which became the nationally televised *American Bandstand* in 1957). It broadcast *Bandstand* to parts of Pennsylvania, New Jersey, Delaware, and Maryland, a four-state region it called "WFIL-adelphia." In its calls for advertisers, WFIL emphasized the station's ability to help advertisers reach millions of these regional consumers.[1] WFIL-TV was a particularly lucrative advertising venue because it was part of Walter Annenberg's media empire, which also included WFIL radio, the

Philadelphia Inquirer, TV Guide, and *Seventeen* magazine, among other properties.

At the same time WFIL aimed to capitalize on its regional market, the area around the station's West Philadelphia studio became a site of intense struggles over racial discrimination in housing. Just blocks from *Bandstand*'s studio doors, white homeowners associations and civil rights advocates fought a block-by-block battle over housing. Groups of homeowners like the Angora Civic Association sought to prevent black families from moving into West Philadelphia. The racial tensions around *Bandstand*'s West Philadelphia studio threatened to scare off the advertisers who funded the show and forced *Bandstand*'s producers to take a position on integration. Fueled by the show's commercial ambitions, the producers chose not to allow black teenagers to enter the studio. By blocking black teens from the studio, *Bandstand*, like the white homeowners associations, sought to protect homes from the perceived dangers of integration.

The respective efforts of WFIL and the white homeowners associations to maintain segregated spaces constituted overlapping and reinforcing versions of "defensive localism," a term used by sociologist Margaret Weir and historian Thomas Sugrue to describe the way homeowners associations emphasized their right to protect their property values and the racial identity of their neighborhoods.[2] As historian David Freund has shown, white homeowners in the postwar era expressed a deeply held belief that black people posed a threat to white property values. This way of viewing race was significant, Freund argues, "because it allowed whites to address their racial preoccupations by talking about property instead of people."[3] In *Forbidden Neighbors*, his 1955 study of racial bias in housing, Charles Abrams noted the pervasiveness of this link between race and property values:

> Homeowners, home-builders, and mortgage-lenders seemed convinced that people should live only with their own kind, that the presence of a single minority family destroys property values and undermines social prestige and status. National and local real estate organizations were accepting these assumptions as gospel, as were popular magazines, college texts, and technical journals.[4]

As Abrams notes, the federal government and private mortgage lenders directed housing loans to maintain segregated housing markets. At the neighborhood level, white homeowners associations used covenants and violence to protect what they viewed as their right to live in racially homogenous neighborhoods. The term *defensive localism* is useful to understanding white mobilization for segregation because it links the monetization and racialization of space. As in other northern cities, anti-integration forces in Philadelphia seldom used explicitly racist language to defend their position. Rather, racial integration was rejected as a threat to property values. This logic applied not just to homeowners, but also to the television stations and advertisers that sought to reach them. Figured in this way, the pursuit of profit, in this case through home equity or advertising revenue, could be used as a defense of racial prejudice and de facto segregation. Indeed, while homeowners associations fought to protect their home investments by keeping their neighborhoods exclusively white, WFIL fought to protect the commercial prospects of the fledgling *Bandstand* by making the show's representations of Philadelphia teenagers "safe" for television viewers in WFIL-adelphia.

WFIL's description of its four-state broadcast area as WFIL-adelphia points to the fact that postwar television was both urban and regional, that it was both a physical site of production and a network of viewers and advertisers responding to televisual images. Media studies scholar Anna McCarthy describes this as television's capacity to be both "site-specific" and "space-binding."[5] These qualities were in tension for WFIL. The everyday actions in Philadelphia and the images broadcast across WFIL-adelphia influenced each other in important ways. The station and its advertisers wanted access to the population, spending power, and creative potential of the nation's third largest market without any of the perceived problems of broadcasting from an urban area with a racially diverse population. With *Bandstand*, WFIL resolved this tension by drawing on Philadelphia's interracial music scene to create an entertaining and profitable television show, while refusing to allow the city's black teenagers into the studio audience for fear of alienating viewers and advertisers. Like the white homeowners associations' concerns about property values, WFIL's version of defensive localism built on a belief that integration would hurt the station's investment in *Bandstand*. When WFIL's *Bandstand* broadcast images of white teens on a daily basis, it disseminated the anti-integrationist views held by homeowners associations across a large regional broadcasting area. This broad view of defensive localism, stretching from the local homeowners associations around WFIL's West Philadelphia studio to the station's racially exclusive admissions policies on *Bandstand*, illustrates how housing and television formed overlapping and reinforcing sites of struggle over segregation and how the everyday material reality of race in Philadelphia intersected with media representations of race in WFIL-adelphia.

HOUSING FIGHTS IN WEST PHILADELPHIA

WFIL opened its West Philadelphia studio at 46th and Market Street just before *Bandstand* debuted in 1952. The studio housed all of the station's radio and television operations and sat next to the Market Street elevated train that connected West Philadelphia with center city to the east and Upper Darby to the west.[6] While Market Street featured primarily storefronts, the area surrounding *Bandstand*'s West Philadelphia studio included a mix of residential housing, including two- and three-story row homes, three-story Victorian semidetached "twin homes," low-rise apartment complexes, and a smaller number of detached single-family homes. Although the area was less densely populated than South Philadelphia and North Philadelphia in the early 1900s, West Philadelphia experienced a period of rapid urbanization from 1910 through 1940; by World War II, the area housed almost 20 percent of the city's total population.[7] The racial demographics of the city, and especially the area around WFIL's West Philadelphia studio, were changing rapidly when *Bandstand* debuted.

Demographic figures convey the scope of racial change in Philadelphia in this era. From 1930 to 1960, the city's black population grew by three hundred thousand, increasing from 11.4 percent of the city's total population to 26.4 percent. The changes were similarly dramatic in West Philadelphia. The black population expanded in West Philadelphia after World War I and settled primarily in the area between 32nd and 40th Streets and from University Avenue to Lancaster. This eastern section of West Philadelphia, then called the "black bottom," expanded again in the 1940s and 1950s. Working-class blacks were drawn to the area because of strong neighborhood institutions and opportunities to rent apartments and houses denied them in other parts of the city. By the 1950s, the "black bottom" was a vibrant neighborhood of businesses and row homes, 15 to 20 percent of which were owned by black families.[8] Through the 1940s and 1950s, as many white residents moved to new suburban developments in other areas, West Philadelphia's black population continued to expand further west and north. The increase first occurred above Market Street, an area with many subdivided housing units and lower rents. Through the 1950s and 1960s, black families expanded to the west of the "black bottom" on the south side of Market Street, where homeownership opportunities were greater.[9] By 1960, the black population in West Philadelphia was the second largest in the city.[10]

These statistics, however, do not adequately convey the block-by-block struggle over housing. Racially discriminatory housing practices fueled the concentration of blacks in West Philadelphia and other neighborhoods. Private housing developers openly discriminated because they believed their white customers wanted segregated neighborhoods. As the former president of the Philadelphia Real Estate Board acknowledged, "most of the people when purchasing or renting homes place great value upon exclusiveness in terms of religion and ancestry, and particularly to color. These desires are in conflict with the basic concept of the open market."[11] Fair-housing advocate Charles Abrams also noted that builders could accommodate white home buyers' racial prejudice without raising the price of the home. "Unlike the tiled bathroom, venetian blinds, and television outlets," Abrams noted, "the promise of racial exclusiveness cost the builder nothing."[12]

These real estate practices severely limited the housing options for black Philadelphians. A 1953 Commission on Human Relations study of new private housing in the Philadelphia metropolitan area found that only 1,044 of more than 140,000 recently constructed units (less than 1 percent) were available to blacks.[13] From 1946 to 1953, only forty-five new homes were offered for sale to blacks. With their options limited by racially restrictive covenants and mortgage redlining, the other twenty thousand black families who became homeowners in this period bought secondhand houses at higher financing charges.[14] Historian Beryl Satter has shown how speculators profited by selling houses to African American on exploitative terms. "The reason for the decline of so many black urban neighborhoods into slums was not the absence of resources," Satter argues, "but rather the *riches* that could be drawn from the seemingly poor vein of aged and decrepit housing and hard-pressed but hardworking and ambitious African Americans."[15]

This widespread housing discrimination posed a challenge for the city's Commission on Human Relations (CHR). The city's voters passed a city charter in 1951 that established the CHR to administer antidiscrimination provisions in employment and public accommodations. The CHR's first annual report declared that, with support from the city's administration, the CHR's "substantial powers of investigation," and "strong community backing mobilized by the Fellowship Commission,"

TABLE I   PHILADELPHIA POPULATION BY RACE, 1930–1960

Year	Total	Total percentage change	White total	White percentage	White percentage change	Black total	Black percentage	Black percentage change
1930	1,950,961		1,728,417	82.6%		219,599	11.3%	
1940	1,931,334	-1.0%	1,678,577	86.9%	-2.9%	250,880	13.0%	14.2%
1950	2,071,605	7.3%	1,692,637	81.7%	0.8%	376,041	18.2%	49.9%
1960	2,002,512	-3.3%	1,467,479	73.3%	-13.3%	529,240	26.4%	40.7%

SOURCE: U.S. Census.

TABLE 2   PHILADELPHIA POPULATION BY RACE AND NEIGHBORHOOD, 1960

Neighborhood	White total	Percent	Black total	Percent	Total
South	217,699	74.5%	74,674	25.5%	292,373
North Central	101,296	32.9%	207,007	67.1%	308,303
North	345,345	88.3%	45,659	11.7%	391,004
Kensington-Northeast	444,196	98.3%	7,834	1.7%	452,030
Germantown- Roxborough	127,306	81.3%	29,335	18.7%	156,641
West, North of Market	83,205	42.1%	114,383	57.9%	197,588
West, South of Market	148,433	72.6%	56,140	27.4%	204,573
Total	1,467,480	73.3%	535,032	26.7%	2,002,512

SOURCE: Commission on Human Relations, "Philadelphia's Non-White Population 1960, Report no.1, Demographic Data," CHR collection, box A-621, folder 148.4, PCA.

the city had assembled the tools for an "effective attack on racial and religious prejudice and discrimination and for building rich and wholesome relationships among the racial, religious and nationality groups that make up America."[16] The creation of the CHR encouraged many Philadelphians to see their city as a leader in racial equality. At the same time, however, the CHR lacked the power to address housing or educational discrimination, and its case-by-case approach to employment discrimination was overwhelmed by the number of complaints received.[17] For its part, the Fellowship Commission, the city's leading civil rights coalition, prioritized fair employment legislation over fair-housing legislation before eventually lobbying the state to enact a narrowly tailored housing bill (excluding private sales of owner-occupied houses) in 1961.[18] Without fair-housing legislation, black residents in West Philadelphia and other neighborhoods continued to face a restricted housing market throughout the 1950s.

In addition to restrictive housing covenants, white homeowners organized in neighborhoods across the city in order to block what they viewed as the encroachment of black families in all-white neighborhoods. These groups emphasized their right to protect their property values and the racial identity of their neighborhoods. In West Philadelphia, the Angora Civic Association (ACA) sought to prevent black families from moving into the Angora-Sherwood sections of West Philadelphia, along Baltimore Avenue from 50th to 60th streets. The ACA resembled white homeowners' groups that mobilized to maintain segregated neighborhoods in Chicago, Detroit, Baltimore, Washington, D.C., Miami, Houston, Los Angeles, San Francisco, and elsewhere across the

| A Tale of Two Cities.

FIGURE 1. Philadelphia, "The Exemplary City of Human Relations," turns up its nose at Detroit, "The Cauldron of Race Hatred." This 1952 editorial cartoon questioning the appointment of Detroit's George Schermer to head Philadelphia's Commission on Human Relations captured the feeling that Philadelphia was a leading city in antidiscrimination laws and programs. December 30, 1952. Jerry Doyle / *Philadelphia Daily News*.

country.[19] These groups used a range of tactics to achieve their aims, including mob violence and physical and mental harassment. While the homeowners' groups were a nationwide phenomenon, the Angora Civic Association is noteworthy because of its proximity to the WFIL studio and because the group's founding coincided with *Bandstand*'s debut.

Starting in 1952, the ACA distributed fliers and held meetings encouraging its neighbors to exercise their rights as homeowners. A contemporary study of the racial change in this West Philadelphia neighborhood noted: "The entry of nonwhites appears to have come as a heavy shock to white residents, and a severe panic existed through 1954."[20] Indeed, the language in the association's meetings and fliers stressed the white homeowners' anxiety at the prospect of a racially changing neighborhood. One meeting notice invited residents in this section of West Philadelphia

[t]o discuss some very serious problems which are confronting your neighborhood NOW. One of these problems may be right in your block, or even as close as next door. At any rate one of them cannot be very far away. One thing we can assure you of is that they are not mythical or imaginary, but

very real, and will require very real concentrated and realistic attention if you want your neighborhood to remain as it now is.[21]

Another flier asked: "Do you like your home and neighborhood? Then why not protect them?"[22] Aware that members of the CHR and Fellowship Commission covertly attended their meetings, the homeowners' groups avoided racist epithets in favor of thinly veiled references to neighborhood "problems" and "undesirable" neighbors. In the ACA's view, keeping black families from buying houses in the neighborhood would protect both the racial identity of the neighborhood and the property values of the homes. Since homeownership represented a significant financial investment in this working-class and middle-class area, fears of blockbusting and panic selling fueled the ACA's economic anxiety. A meeting announcement warned: "If you are ready and willing to throw away thousands of $$$ for what you now have and own, then throw this notice away and don't read any further."[23] The ACA regularly drew between fifty and three hundred people to its monthly sessions, and as many as seven hundred attended its most popular meetings.[24] Although the historical evidence does not allow a close analysis of the association's membership, meeting records include names such as Petrella, DeRosa, Callahan, Vandergrift, Craig, Stahl, and Rabinowitz, suggesting that individuals from several white ethnic groups participated.[25]

At its best-attended meetings, the ACA invited leaders of similar white homeowners' groups from other parts of the city to share tactical ideas and offer support. The leader of the eleven-year-old Overbrook Improvement Co., for example, told the ACA of his group's success in keeping blacks out of the Overbrook neighborhood in the northwest section of West Philadelphia. The Overbrook group president, Harold Stott, recommended "putting pressure on real estate men, banks and mortgage companies," and he advised the ACA to raise money to buy houses in the neighborhood so that they could be resold to whites rather than blacks. While these homeowners' groups did not openly advocate violence, they suggested that white residents should try "psychological methods." These methods included repeated visits by white neighbors asking the "undesirable" family to move, vandalism of property, and threats of violence to dissuade black families from moving into the neighborhood and to convince those who did manage to buy houses to sell their homes to the corporation and move out.[26]

Throughout these meetings, the ACA, Overbrook association, and other groups stressed both the urgency and the legality of their cause.

DO YOU LIKE YOUR HOME AND NEIGHBORHOOD?
THEN WHY NOT PROTECT THEM?
THE
ANGORA CIVIC ASSOCIATION

is calling a meeting to discuss neighborhood problems
with its friends and neighbors regarding the changing
of Communities.

Let US talk facts about West Philadelphia and its future.

Let US talk about Money, People and Real Estate, and
what can happen to our investments and our way of life.

This is an opportunity for you to help protect your
home. Don't adopt the attitude that George can do it.
Only **YOU** can do it

Our organization is growing bigger and stronger. But
our association, like a chain, is only as strong as its
weakest link. Don't **YOU** be that weak link.

We plan to have guest speakers from the following
organizations who have neighborhood problems similar
to ours. Let us hear how **THEY** meet them.

Overbrook Improvement Co., Inc.—Overbrook Section
North Penn Civic Association—North Philadelphia.
Broomall Civic Association—Broomall, Pa.
Upper Darby Civic Association—69th Street Area.

If you are interested in your community's welfare and
your children's future come to the

ARCADE HALL, 5039 Baltimore Avenue

THURSDAY, NOVEMBER 18, 1954

8:00 P. M.

Admission — **FREE**   **What Can You Lose?**

FIGURE 2. The Angora Civic Association distributed
thousands of fliers like these to recruit community members to
its meetings. White homeowners' groups and civic associations from other neighborhoods attended these meeting to
show support and share tactics. November 18, 1954. Temple
University Libraries, Urban Archives, Philadelphia, PA.

"Help!! Help!!" proclaimed one meeting notice. "These are words we hear every day from the Property Owners of our Community. Our Association can render you this help *If You Want It!*" This notice ended with an ominous evaluation: "IT'S LATER THAN YOU THINK!"[27] This language resonated with similar appeals to antiblack prejudice in Philadelphia during and after World War II. Historian James Wolfinger has shown that Republican campaign brochures that circulated in Irish and Italian sections of West Philadelphia during 1944 used similar language to warn residents that "black domination" threatened their city. "Will you stand by and see our homes, schools and our entire neighborhood taken away from you and your children by a race stimulated by RUM—JAZZ—WAR EASY MONEY?" the pamphlet read. "Vote a straight Republican Ballot next Tuesday and save your salvation."[28] Additionally, fliers linked to a resurgent Ku Klux Klan in Philadelphia in the early 1950s urged white men to join forces for "the protection of homes and loved ones."[29] Despite appealing to racist sentiments, the white homeowners' groups defended their calls to action by asserting what they viewed to be their legal rights as truly American homeowners. The Overbrook group president told the 120 residents at the meeting that the members of the ACA "are 100% Americans. All they are asking is to keep the high standards of their own neighborhood and to pick their neighbors besides protecting their property. In doing this they are exercising their rights under the Bill of Rights and there certainly is nothing un-American about that."[30] This rights rhetoric cast the homeowners' groups as possessing an Americanness—and whiteness—threatened by black interlopers. As David Freund notes in his study of suburban Detroit, this language of property rights enabled whites to mobilize for segregation as homeowners, citizens, taxpayers, and parents while maintaining that they were not racist.[31] In his study of California's ballot initiatives, political scientist Daniel Martinez HoSang describes this rights rhetoric as central to a set of "norms, 'settled expectations,' and 'investments' [that] shape the interpretation of political interests, the boundaries of political communities, and the sources of power for many political actors who understand themselves as white." Like the "political whiteness" HoSang identifies in postwar California, white homeowners associations fought to protect "our neighborhoods," "our kids," "our property values," and "our rights," while claiming to be innocent of racism.[32]

These white homeowners' groups also directed their defensive localism and rights discourse toward the Fellowship Commission's civil rights work. The leaders of the Angora and Overbrook associations accused the Commission of forcing its integration agenda on blacks. Reporting on a Fellowship Commission meeting that he attended covertly, the Overbrook association president told the homeowners' groups that the "colored" people at the meeting "did not seem to be at all interested in housing [but] the 'Fellowship Boys' got up and agitated these people by saying to them that they had the right to move in to any street or any neighborhood in Philadelphia they wanted to."[33] The Overbrook president advised the association members: "You see that these Fellowship people are fellowship for them only—no fellowship for everybody."[34]

The homeowners associations also accused the Fellowship Commission of being involved in a "sinister conspiracy" with real estate agents who had reportedly convinced white homeowners to sell their houses to blacks, thereby "blockbusting" all-white neighborhoods. There is no evidence that the Fellowship Commission and real estate agents worked in concert, and, in fact, real estate brokers played a much larger role than the Commission in helping black families move into formerly all-white neighborhoods. Real estate agents had complex motives, but, in almost every case, racially changing neighborhoods presented brokers with substantial economic opportunities. Blockbusting real estate brokers looked for, and sometimes fostered, panic in racially changing neighborhoods and bought homes at below-market prices from panicked white sellers. They then placed advertisements in black newspapers touting these new homeownership opportunities.[35] The *Philadelphia Tribune*, the city's largest black newspaper, ran several such advertisements every week during the early and mid-1950s. A real estate advertisement from 1952, for example, advised readers to "Go West Young Man. Come to West Philadelphia." Another realty company promised that "we will secure homes for you in any neighborhood desired," while a company billing itself as "Phila.'s Most Progressive Office" listed different "West Phila. Specials" on a weekly basis.[36] These homes usually sold at a markup to black buyers looking for good quality homes. While these agents helped expand homeownership opportunities for the city's black residents, they also accelerated the tensions in racially changing neighborhoods like West Philadelphia, and many brokers made significant sums of money in the process.[37] For the white homeowners' groups, both blockbusting real estate agents and the Fellowship Commission represented outside agitators threatening the racial identity of their neighborhoods.

Since the CHR lacked the ability to prosecute cases of housing discrimination, the Fellowship Commission took a different approach. The

Commission believed that the best options were simultaneously to try both to win the ACA over by persuading it that its actions would only foster panic selling and to isolate the group by planning meetings and events to improve relations in the racially changing neighborhoods of West Philadelphia. The Fellowship Commission and its West Philadelphia chapter worked with the CHR and local Baptist and Catholic clergy to reach out to the homeowners' groups. A flier for the Fellowship Commission's first outreach meeting in 1954, under the headline "Let's All Pull Together," invited residents to talk "facts about West Philadelphia" concerning "money, people and houses for sale."[38] Illustrating the strength of the Commission's relationships with the city's Democratic Party, the city's district attorney and future mayor Richardson Dilworth spoke at the meeting. Fellowship Commission executive director Maurice Fagan also met with the ACA president privately, advising him that the Commission was concerned with the rights of religious and nationality groups as well as those of racial groups.[39] Fagan further told the ACA that the Commission would not object to "open and above board" civic associations. These efforts to influence the attitudes of white homeowners prefigured the CHR's 1958 series of "What to Do" kits that were distributed to residents in racially changing communities. Aimed at local leaders in areas like West Philadelphia, the "What to Do" folders included suggestions for local leaders on how to organize and conduct meetings to discuss the importance of communities working together to avoid panic selling and to ensure fair-housing practices. While the CHR distributed the kits widely in an attempt to meet the scale of racial change in the neighborhood, they did not lead to a substantial decrease in reports of community tensions over housing.[40]

In addition to these outreach efforts, the Fellowship Commission also sponsored neighborhood seminars to encourage community involvement in intergroup relations. Foremost among these efforts, the Commission worked with principals, teachers, and home and school associations to plan inter-playground fellowship events at the elementary schools in West Philadelphia.[41] These events were well attended and well received by many black and white parents and children in the area. The Fellowship Commission's efforts appear to have limited the growth of the ACA past 1955. Racial tensions in other West Philadelphia neighborhoods and other parts of the city, however, overwhelmed the Fellowship Commission's resources.[42] In his evaluation of the Commission's work in 1955, Fagan asserted:

New problems are developing faster than old ones are being solved because of the emphasis on cases instead of causes. With only 35 full-time workers in the entire city of Philadelphia, it is not possible . . . to do more than move from crisis to crisis, neighborhood to neighborhood, without staying put long enough to make an enduring difference.[43]

As Fagan noted, the depth of white resistance to racial integration overwhelmed the Fellowship Commission's educational strategy.

On the legislative front, the Fellowship Commission played an important role in passing the state's fair-housing bill, which was enacted in 1961. The Commission lobbied the forty-two member groups of the Pennsylvania Equal Rights Council to advance a narrow bill that covered new housing and housing transactions receiving government assistance, but excluded sales of owner-occupied homes such as those frequently purchased by blacks in racially changing urban neighborhoods.[44] While the Commission's fair-housing bill made political sense in an effort to get legislation through the Republican-controlled state senate, the bill's exemptions aligned with the view of property rights being advocated by the white homeowners' groups and weakened the credibility of the Commission's approach to civil rights.

The magnitude of the challenges facing the Fellowship Commission and other fair-housing advocates, however, was immense. Discriminatory federal housing policy and the business practices of the real estate industry blocked black families from most new suburban construction and managed the racial turnover of urban neighborhoods. Mortgage redlining treated black neighborhoods and black homeowners as investment risks, and this lack of access to credit limited the efficacy of open occupancy or fair-housing legislation for many African Americans.[45] Combining with these factors, white homeowners' groups and civic associations policed the boundaries of segregated neighborhoods and demonstrated what James Wolfinger calls "the limits imposed on liberalism from below."[46] In many cities and states, this resistance to integrated housing coalesced into organized opposition to fair-housing legislation. Most notably, in the 1964 election 65 percent of California voters approved Proposition 14, which sought to nullify the Rumford Fair Housing Act (the state Supreme Court declared Proposition 14 unconstitutional in 1966). As with the Angora Civic Association, supporters of Proposition 14, such as future California governor and U.S. president Ronald Reagan, portrayed fair-housing legislation as "forced housing" and as "an infringement of one of our basic individual rights."[47] As his-

torian Robert Self shows in his study of Oakland, this language of property rights appealed to a large cross section of white voters. "The numbers suggest that the resistance to desegregation in Oakland did not
come solely from an antiliberal white working class," Self argues, "but
arose equally among middle- and upper-class whites who understood
property rights as sacrosanct expressions of their personal freedom and
had little daily contact with African Americans."[48] Similarly, historian
Phil Ethington notes that in Los Angeles, the white neighborhoods most
geographically isolated from black communities were more likely to
vote to repeal fair-housing legislation.[49] While anti-fair-housing legislation did not become a ballot issue in Pennsylvania, a 1965 survey of residents in Philadelphia suburbs found that over 70 percent considered
"keeping undesirables out" to be a very important objective for local
government, rating it well ahead of "maintaining improved public services," "providing aesthetic amenities," and "acquiring business and industry."[50] Attempts to pass fair-housing legislation at the federal level
also encountered significant resistance. President Lyndon Johnson's aide
later recalled that when Johnson first tried to push a national fair-
housing bill through Congress in 1966, for example, the bill "prompted
some of the most vicious mail LBJ received on any subject."[51] When
Congress finally passed the 1968 Fair Housing Act in the wake of the
assassination of Dr. Martin Luther King Jr., the bill's weak enforcement
provisions did little to curb housing discrimination.[52]

Sociologist Jill Quadagno summarizes opposition to fair-housing legislation simply, arguing that "for many white Americans, property
rights superseded civil rights."[53] White mobilization for segregated
neighborhoods, in combination with discriminatory federal housing
policy, the business practices of the real estate industry, and the shortcomings of local and federal antidiscrimination policies in housing,
made residential segregation the norm in cities and suburbs around the
nation. As chapters 3 and 4 demonstrate, defenders of housing segregation laid the foundation for de facto school segregation. This residential
segregation emerged from and reinforced a belief that a neighborhood's
racial composition and property values were intertwined and mutually
constitutive. This way of viewing space informed everyday encounters
across the United States, and in Philadelphia it motivated white homeowners' groups like the Angora Civic Association to fight for segregation. This group was part of a larger national story, but it also reflected
and influenced racial attitudes locally, in *Bandstand*'s backyard.

INTEGRATION AND SEGREGATION IN YOUTH SPACES
IN WEST PHILADELPHIA

These everyday fights over segregation were not confined to housing. For the teens who appeared on *Bandstand* and for those who watched the program on television, different levels of racial integration and segregation were part of their daily experiences in youth spaces such as schools, parties, snack counters, and roller rinks. As more black families moved into previously all-white neighborhoods in West Philadelphia, for example, some youth spaces became integrated by virtue of the racially mixed neighborhoods in which they were located. At West Philadelphia High School (WPHS), black enrollment grew from 10 percent in 1945 to 30 percent in 1951.[54] Black students held leadership roles in the school, including class president, received class honors in the school yearbook (e.g., most popular, most likely to succeed, peppiest), attended school dances, and participated on the boys' track, basketball, and swimming teams; the girls' sports club; and the school newspaper.[55] Despite these signs of inclusion in the social life of the school, black students also encountered the anxieties of parents, teachers, administrators, and students who associated their presence with racially changing neighborhoods. In 1951, for example, George Montgomery, the newly appointed principal at WPHS, singled out working-class black students in an assembly after an incident in the school. The *Philadelphia Tribune* quoted Montgomery as telling the students: "Negroes have become more conspicuous in Philadelphia. There are [a] few intelligent Negroes in the city, there are some fine colored children. However, if you choose to class yourself with them, then it is up to you to go home and ask your parents to which class they prefer you to belong to, the lower or upper class of colored people."[56] Class differences among the black students at West Philadelphia, specifically the entrance of working-class students from the "black bottom" neighborhood, motivated at least some of this racial anxiety. Walter Palmer, who lived in the "black bottom" and graduated from West Philadelphia in 1953, recalled that most of his black and white classmates lived in the more prosperous "top" or western part of West Philadelphia. "We dressed differently, talked, walked, danced, and fought differently," Palmer remembered. "They were folks with better resources. They tolerated people like myself because they needed me to protect them outside of the school. We didn't get invited to their parties. We would invite them to ours, but they would be too afraid to come."[57] While it was far from a model of racial equality, in the early 1950s

FIGURE 3. Teens dancing at prom at West Philadelphia High School. Located three blocks from WFIL's studio, West Philadelphia High School was racially integrated when *Bandstand* debuted. *West Philadelphia High School Record*, 1953. West Philadelphia High School Archives.

WPHS was among the only high schools in the city that were neither 90 percent white nor 90 percent black (90 percent being the percentage the city's civil rights leaders would later use to define segregated schools).

Outside of school, informal youth gatherings at house parties and snack shops offered the possibility of interracial association. Dances in the small basements of row houses were a frequent social outlet for teens in West Philadelphia. Weldon McDougal, who grew up in a subdivided house on 48th and Westminster Avenue, in what he called the "top part" (or northwest side) of the "black bottom" neighborhood, remembered:

> In the neighborhoods, this is how it worked. I lived at 48th street. Somebody would say, "hey man, there's a dance on at Shirley's house tomorrow." On the way to Shirley's house which is maybe two blocks away, you could hear a party going on in another basement. So you go down there, and you know there some kids there dancing and having a good time. Well, anybody could come down there. And like I said, we lived next door to white guys and everything so they would come to the dances.

Between twenty and fifty teenagers, mostly black but some Italian and Irish teens from the neighborhood, squeezed into these basements to dance to their favorite R&B songs, and whatever other 45s they brought to the party. McDougall recalls that there were five or six of these local dances every Friday and Saturday in his West Philadelphia neighborhood.[58]

An After-School Snack . . . Eat At
JOE'S SNACK BAR
229 SOUTH 47TH STREET   Featuring Hoagies and Sausage

FIGURE 4. From 1954 to 1960, the proprietors of Joe's Snack Bar placed ads in West Philadelphia High School yearbooks featuring an integrated group of students from the school. *West Philadelphia High School Record*, 1955. West Philadelphia High School Archives.

In addition to weekend dances, young people hung out at a variety of lunch counters, soda fountains, and ice cream parlors in West Philadelphia. While historical evidence of the racial climate of these establishments is difficult to ascertain and surely varied based on proprietor and clientele, at least one attempted to welcome both black and white teenage customers. Joe's Snack Bar, located across the street from the West Philadelphia High School, placed advertisements in the school's yearbook every year from 1954 to 1960.[59] These ads stand out from those of the other shops and services that advertised to West Philadelphia students and their parents because every Joe's Snack Bar ad pictured the proprietors, a middle-aged white couple, happily serving an interracial group of students.

In contrast to the opportunities for casual and friendly interracial interactions at WPHS, basement parties, and some snack shops, other youth spaces were segregated by policy or by custom. Many popular social and recreational spaces used by young people, such as roller skating rinks, bowling alleys, and swimming pools, had segregated admissions practices that flouted the city's antidiscrimination policies. The Adelphia Skating Rink in West Philadelphia on 39th and Market Street, for example, operated as a club that required teens to be sponsored by members in order to be admitted. Using this policy, the rink's manager turned away any potential customers he deemed undesirable, including all black teenagers.[60] The discriminatory practices at the Adelphia, as well as at rinks in other sections of the city, drew the attention of the local branches of the American Civil Liberties Union (ACLU) and the National Association for the Advancement of Colored People (NAACP). Working in cooperation with adult members of the ACLU and NAACP, the teenage members of the Fellowship Club formed interracial teams to test the policies of the city's rinks. With the help of Fellowship Club's volunteer investigators, the ACLU and NAACP brought the skating rink issue to the Commission on Human Relations (CHR).

In spring of 1953, after receiving reports of discrimination at skating rinks, CHR officials met with the owners of Imperial and Adelphia, as well as four other rinks. The CHR secured written agreements from all of the rink owners to operate in accordance with the city's antidiscrimination policies.[61] Despite these agreements, when mixed groups of skaters from the Fellowship Club tested the rinks' policies, they continued to find evidence of racially exclusive signs and membership practices, and of managers encouraging segregated patronage. In further defiance of the city's antidiscrimination policies, rink operator Joe Toppi called the CHR before he opened the Imperial skating rink in West Philadelphia on 60th and Walnut Street to ask permission to operate the rink on a segregated basis. After being informed that this would be illegal, Toppi said he would not exclude anyone, but that he would do everything he could to influence white and black teens to come on different nights. With the rink set to open in early September 1953, Toppi posted signs at the rink and distributed fliers in West Philadelphia and South Philadelphia publicizing three "white nights" and three "sepia nights" a week. This practice immediately drew criticism from the black community in West Philadelphia, and on September 17 a group of black teenagers from the NAACP youth council picketed the rink.[62] This same group of teens gained admission on one of the white nights and reported that the white skaters were friendly and that no incidents occurred. Despite the efforts of these black teens, Toppi kept his signs up and continued encouraging white teens to skate on white nights and black teens to come on sepia nights until at least the following year.[63]

The strongest remedial powers at the CHR's disposal were public hearings, which it used for the first time in the skating rink discrimination cases. In the internal meeting where it decided to use public hearings, the CHR identified three purposes: First, it would give "the respondent an extra chance to comply before taking him to trial." Second, it would have a "good psychological effect [and] both the respondent and complainant would be more impressed by the power of the CHR." And third, the "hearing could be of tremendous community value." Whereas the CHR lacked the power to address many facets of discrimination in the city, it believed these youth cases would "strengthen the CHR" and show that the group was "coming of age," without forcing the group to test its authority by confronting the school board or business interests as it would in large-scale education or employment cases.[64] In May 1954, the CHR held public hearings charging the proprietors of two skating rinks in Northeast Philadelphia of failing to comply with city and state laws prohibiting discrimination in public accommodations or recreation. The CHR reached a settlement calling for the rinks to stop using membership cards and other discriminatory membership practices, and to post signs stating the new nondiscriminatory admissions policies.[65] While the agreement reduced the discriminatory practices at most rinks and the CHR did not hear another skating rink case, the Fellowship Club volunteers continued to find evidence of segregation at skating rinks and bowling alleys through the late 1950s.[66]

The CHR's public hearings on discrimination at skating rinks came just days before the U.S. Supreme Court handed down the first *Brown* decision on May 17, 1954, outlawing de jure racial segregation in education. Although the decision applied only to the southern and midwestern states in which schools were segregated by law, many civil rights advocates in Philadelphia expressed optimism that the decisions would force the city to address the de facto racial segregation of its schools. As chapters 3 and 4 demonstrate, however, the school board's independence from the city government insulated the schools from CHR investigations. The CHR's inability to check housing discrimination or address school segregation made small victories like the skating rink cases all the more important. Yet despite its attention to integration in these youth spaces, the CHR was wholly ineffective when faced with the segregation of *Bandstand*, the most visible youth space in Philadelphia. If the housing fights in *Bandstand*'s backyard of West Philadelphia were about the physical proximity of people of different races as neighbors, the struggles over segregation on *Bandstand* were about the potential for teenage social interactions, and televisual representations of these meetings, to disturb anti-integration sentiments among the viewing public.

CREATING WFIL-ADELPHIA

Broadcasting from West Philadelphia, WFIL could not ignore the battles over segregation taking place around its studio and across the city. The station, however, had a vested interest in not presenting visual evidence of these local fights to its regional viewers. Like the Angora Civic Association, WFIL viewed the station's neighborhood through the lenses of property values and race. Yet while the homeowners' groups fought over individual houses and blocks, WFIL's calculations included millions of homes in the Philadelphia region and the advertisers eager to reach this lucrative market. This meant that WFIL courted viewers not only in Philadelphia and the growing suburban counties outside of the city, but also those across a four-state broadcast region that included parts of Pennsylvania, New Jersey, Delaware, and Maryland. The station called this area "WFIL-adelphia," and in the early 1950s the station made this phrase the centerpiece of its marketing campaign. Radio and television broadcast signals, of course, do not conform to the geographic or political boundaries of cities, so WFIL was not unique in having a regional audience. WFIL's use of WFIL-adelphia to bring the station, city, and region together under one brand name, however, illuminates the station's approach to early television and is essential to understanding how *Bandstand* became segregated.

The WFIL-adelphia moniker was part of a larger campaign by Walter Annenberg's Triangle Publications to promote the Delaware Valley as a center for business and industry. In October 1952, the *Philadelphia Inquirer* (owned by Annenberg) featured an eighty-page pullout magazine on the growth and promise of "Delaware Valley, U.S.A." Aimed at the business community, the magazine's inside cover thanked more than eighty companies for their advertising support. The report, extolling the virtues of the Delaware Valley port and the region's "steel, oil, textile, auto manufacturing, electronic, and chemical" industries, recalled the nineteenth-century boosterism that helped draw industries to midwestern hubs like St. Louis and Chicago.[67] A full-page world map, for example, illustrated how "raw materials from at least 75 foreign countries funneled into Delaware Valley" port facilities, including cocoa beans and iron ore from Nigeria, marble from Italy, and lumber from Brazil. All routes on the map lead back to the Delaware Valley, the only site

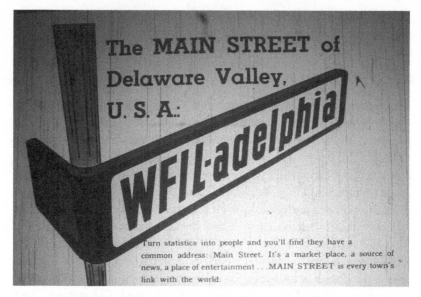

The MAIN STREET of Delaware Valley, U. S. A.: WFIL-adelphia

Turn statistics into people and you'll find they have a common address: Main Street. It's a market place, a source of news, a place of entertainment ... MAIN STREET is every town's link with the world.

FIGURE 5. WFIL pitched the station to potential advertisers as the best way to reach viewers not just in Philadelphia but across the Delaware Valley. October 13, 1952. Used with permission of *Philadelphia Inquirer*.

labeled in the United States. A large circle marks the region, covering the entire Eastern Seaboard.[68]

While the Delaware Valley–centric worldview was undoubtedly exaggerated, promoting the Delaware Valley as a place of "amazing, breathless growth" and the "greatest industrial area of the world" also helped to promote the value of Annenberg's media properties in the region.[69] Indeed, two full-page advertisements described WFIL as the best way to connect people and potential customer across the Delaware Valley (or WFIL-adelphia) region. WFIL promised advertisers that the television station would bring them "5,869,284 customers" across a "27-county area." The ads described these viewers in explicitly monetary terms: "Advertisers ... there's $6 Billions [sic] waiting for you in WFIL-adelphia. SELL ALL of America's 3rd market on WFIL-TV. You can really go to town—to hundreds of towns in the rich Philadelphia market—on WFIL-TV ... Get the most for your money, the most people for your money. Schedule WFIL-TV."[70] West Philadelphia may have been the station's physical home, but this vast regional WFIL-adelphia consumer market was what WFIL sold to *Bandstand*'s advertisers.

FIGURE 6. The WFIL-adelphia broadcast market included parts of Pennsylvania, New Jersey, Delaware, and Maryland. October 13, 1952. Used with permission of *Philadelphia Inquirer*.

These ads also cast WFIL-adelphia as the new "Main Street of Delaware Valley, U.S.A.":

Turn statistics into people and you'll find they have a common address: Main Street. . . . MAIN STREET is every town's link to the world. Today, thanks to electronic science, Main Street goes to the people. And from curb to curb of the Philadelphia Retail Trading area, the busiest Main Street is WFIL-adelphia. The population of this trading zone, as well as a vast area beyond, lives, works and shops in WFIL-adelphia. WFIL-adelphia is a market place—where America's leading advertisers sell their wares, via WFIL-TV.[71]

In describing WFIL-adelphia in this way, the ads reenvisioned the "resonant and symbolic location" of Main Street.[72] Historian Alison Isenberg has described how "varied downtown investors endeavored to make their own markets and to chart Main Street's future in order to protect and enhance their stakes."[73] Isenberg notes how local newspapers and regional news companies, like Annenberg's *Philadelphia Inquirer* and WFIL radio and television stations, had a vested interested in bolstering Main Street's advertising value and frequently sponsored the Main Street postcards that were ubiquitous in the early twentieth century.[74] "The 'place' . . . illuminated in the postcards was not a brick-and-mortar location," Isenberg writes, "but rather a territory within Americans' imaginations, a hopeful vision of urban commerce transformed."[75] WFIL's ads imagined the place of Main Street in similar ways. The ads did not make reference to a physical Main Street, but rather to the "5,869,284 customers" in homes dispersed across a "27-county area." With WFIL-adelphia, WFIL promised to use broadcast technology to further transform urban and regional commerce. If Philadelphia could no longer connect businesses, advertisers, and customers on Main Street, WFIL-adelphia would provide this safe and prosperous commercial space. (Disneyland, of course, also made use of this Main Street ideal to promote a suburban and racially homogenous alternative to urban and multiracial commercial spaces when it opened in 1955.)[76]

While not mentioned in the ads, the WFIL-adelphia viewers that WFIL promoted to advertisers lived in states that supported racial segregation by both law and custom. Both Maryland and Delaware maintained de jure segregated school systems until the *Brown* decisions and resisted court-ordered desegregation for another decade thereafter.[77] Interracial marriage was also illegal in both states until *Loving v. Virginia* in 1967.[78] For a station pitching itself as a regional Main Street, the existence of legal segregation in its broadcasting area offered a significant financial incentive to not upset anti-integration sentiment among viewers and advertisers. At the same time, the segregated housing policies in Pennsylvania suburbs also contributed to WFIL's understanding of WFIL-adelphia. The *Philadelphia Inquirer*'s pullout magazine on the Delaware Valley offered pictures and glowing profiles of housing developments under construction in Levittown and Fairness Hills, Pennsylvania, as evidence that the region was "booming."[79] These neighboring Bucks County developments had policies that prevented blacks from buying homes, making Levittown and Fairness Hills what Charles Abrams termed "closed cities."[80] While WFIL-adelphia attempted to reconstitute Main Street in an era of suburbanization, the decision to profile Levittown and Fairness Hills as exemplars of the Delaware Valley reemphasized that WFIL-adelphia would privilege the desires and attitudes of white suburban consumers.

In this way, WFIL-adelphia offers an example of how television helped reorganize urban and suburban spaces. As media studies scholar Lynn Spigel has suggested, many postwar commentators argued that television "would allow people to travel from their homes while remaining untouched by the actual social contexts to which they imaginatively ventured." Television could act as a space-binding tool to promote public culture among viewers living in detached single-family suburban homes, while also keeping "undesirable" people and topics out of the home. Spigel calls this a "fantasy of antiseptic electrical space."[81] WFIL-adelphia promised a version of "antiseptic electrical space" to both viewers and advertisers. To viewers, it offered the ideal of Main Street without upsetting their anti-integrationist attitudes. To advertisers, it offered access to a growing market of suburban consumers with disposable income. All the while, WFIL still needed Philadelphia—the economies of scale it provided, the size of its population, and the creative energies of its people—in order to promote WFIL-adelphia. The best place to see how WFIL navigated the conflicting demands of WFIL-adelphia is the show that became the station's most popular locally produced program, *Bandstand*.

BROADCASTING *BANDSTAND* TO WFIL-ADELPHIA

From its debut, *Bandstand*'s producers looked beyond Philadelphia to the potential profits available from advertisers and record companies eager to reach the largest possible television audience. In doing so they carved out a new position for a local television program in relation to the radio and record industries at a time when all three industries were undergoing significant changes. *Bandstand* debuted in a pivotal year in television's development into a national medium. Between 1948 and 1952, the number of television sets increased from 1.2 million to 15 million, and the percentage of homes with television increased from 0.4 percent to 34 percent.[82] More important, in April 1952 the Federal Communication Commission (FCC) lifted its freeze on television licenses, ending a four-year block on new licenses and making more frequency assignments available to a larger number of metropolitan areas.

Over the next three years, the number of television stations in operation increased from 108 in 1952 to 458 in 1955. By 1955, the most populous cities each had between three and seven stations, and the FCC believed that 90 percent of the nation's population lived in the broadcast range of at least two stations.[83]

Media consolidation increased as the FCC allocated new television licenses. Newspapers owned 69 percent of TV licenses in 1953, up from 33 percent when the freeze started in 1948. Multiple ownership also became much more common in television than in radio, where newspapers owned 20 percent and 32 percent of AM and FM radio stations, respectively, in 1953.[84] The FCC's decision to allow newspaper-television cross-ownership helped to ensure that television, like radio before it, would follow the commercial advertising model. With an increased number of potential viewers and a limited number of new licenses, VHF TV stations were extremely valuable. Lobbying FCC commissioners became commonplace, and newspapers were among the applicants most capable of assuring favorable licensing decisions.[85] Triangle Publications, owned by Walter Annenberg, who had inherited the *Philadelphia Inquirer* from his father in 1942 and had purchased WFIL radio in 1945, was among the media conglomerates to add a television station in 1948. Annenberg described the reasoning that pushed him into television to his biographer in 1996:

> I was willing to gamble that [WFIL-TV] wouldn't lose that much money. And it didn't cost me much. It operated in the red for only six months. But my instinct told me this was an opportunity. How could it fail? WFIL had authorization for television [grandfathered in by the FCC] and I knew Philadelphia was going to be entitled to three stations. I would have one of three in an area that served more than five million people. I knew the advertising potential. It had to be a bonanza![86]

As Annenberg liked to say, acquiring a television station only cost him a "three-cent stamp" to mail the license application, so the ratio of risk to reward was decidedly in his favor.[87] Annenberg expanded his investment in television by acquiring television magazines in several major cities and starting *TV Guide* in 1953. *TV Guide* combined television listings tailored to specific local markets with a wraparound national edition promoting television shows and personalities.[88] By 1959, Annenberg's Triangle Publications also owned television stations in Binghamton, New York; Altoona-Johnstown, Pennsylvania; Hartford-New Haven, Connecticut; Lancaster-Lebanon, Pennsylvania; and Fresno, California.[89] For

Bandstand, Annenberg's media empire provided advertising connections and expertise that helped to launch the show.

Through the early and mid-1950s, the increase in the number of channels expanded the total amount of airtime that stations needed to fill and left stations looking for profitable shows to broadcast in the daytime hours, when networks supplied affiliates with little if any programming. Like many other stations in the early 1950s, Philadelphia's WFIL filled its afternoon schedule with old movies, since ABC offered its affiliates no daytime programming and Hollywood leased only outdated movies to the perceived rival medium. These movies flopped, leaving WFIL with an afternoon slot to fill. Roger Clipp, the station's general manager, asked disc jockey Bob Horn to host an interview show, interspersed with filmed music shorts that had been collecting dust in WFIL's archives.[90] Horn already hosted a radio *Bandstand* program at WFIL; although his radio program was successful, like a number of prominent national radio personalities, he wanted to move from radio to television.[91] Radio comedians like Fred Allen, Milton Berle, Jack Benny, George Burns and Gracie Allen, Sid Caesar, and Bob Hope all moved to television in the early 1950s. Television networks viewed these radio personalities as established talent that would help the fledgling medium attract large national audiences and lucrative sponsors. In many cases, popular variety shows and sitcom programs were simply picked up from radio and reworked for television.[92] Like the national networks that signed these radio stars, WFIL viewed Horn as a dependable radio personality, and like these more widely known comedians, Horn viewed television as an exciting and potentially profitable endeavor.

The first televised version of Horn's *Bandstand* debuted in September 1952. Jazz musician Dizzy Gillespie, a friend of Horn's who happened to be in town, was the guest. Horn chatted with Gillespie for a few minutes about his current recordings and tour. Horn then turned to the camera to announce a film of Peggy Lee singing "Mañana." Subsequent shows continued in the same way, moving between Horn's interviews with whatever guests he could find and the films.[93] Despite Horn's talents as a disc jockey, this format proved unsuccessful. Determined to hold his television slot, Horn met with Clipp and station manager George Koehler and proposed to bring in a studio audience of teenagers and make their dancing the focal point of the program. Horn looked to Philadelphia's 950 *Club* (1946–55), where radio hosts Joe Grady and Ed Hurst invited local high school students to come to the show's center city studio and dance to the records they broadcast on their program.[94]

Horn combined this successful format with the name of his own successful radio show, *Bandstand*. WFIL's Clipp and Koehler gave *Bandstand* a second chance because the station wanted to add a show with low production costs that would attract teenagers, and the advertisers eager to reach teens, to WFIL's afternoon television lineup.[95]

Tony Mammarella, a talented producer at WFIL, joined Horn in readying *Bandstand* for its debut. As *Bandstand*'s producer, Mammarella prepared the set, managed the admission of the studio audience, acted as a liaison between sponsors and Horn, and served as an occasional cameraman and stand-in host. Working with a modest budget, Mammarella devised a set that looked like the inside of a record store using a painted canvas backdrop and a mock-up sales counter. Banners from neighborhood high schools hung on a canvas next to the record store set, and Mammarella installed wood bleachers at one side of the studio for seating. With a studio designed to resemble two teenage spaces—the record shop and the high school gymnasium—Horn's television *Bandstand* premiered on October 6, 1952, as a daily program broadcast in the Philadelphia area from 3:30 to 4:45 P.M.[96]

Thanks to a three-week promotional campaign and the proximity of three high schools—West Catholic High for Girls, West Catholic High for Boys, and West Philadelphia High—*Bandstand* had no trouble filling the studio to its two-hundred-person capacity. Only two blocks from the studio, the predominately Irish and Italian teenage girls who attended West Catholic High for Girls became the most consistent visitors to *Bandstand*. Teenage boys from West Catholic High for Boys were nearly as close, as were boys and girls from West Philadelphia High School, a public school that enrolled mostly Jewish and black students. Teens from other schools and neighborhoods also visited *Bandstand* shortly after its debut, and teens from South and Southwest Philadelphia became some of the most visible stars of the program.

The production format Horn and Mammarella established in *Bandstand*'s first days remained largely unchanged during *Bandstand*'s local years. During the broadcasts, Horn introduced records, and the cameras focused on the teenagers dancing. At the midway point in the show, Horn yelled "We've got company" and introduced that day's musical guest, who would lip-sync his or her latest record.[97] On its first day, as it would in its first two years, *Bandstand* featured music primarily from white pop singers such as Joni James, Georgia Gibbs, Frankie Laine, Connie Boswell, and Helen O'Connell. In an era before black rhythm and blues crossed over to mainstream white audiences, and "rock and roll" was not yet a household term, this selection of artists reflected what most radio stations played. Jerry Blavat, who became a regular on *Bandstand* and went on to become an R&B deejay in the Philadelphia area, remembers being exposed to both white pop music and black R&B as a teenager in an Italian section of South Philadelphia:

> When I was a kid at 12 or 13 years old, I lived in a neighborhood where there was always music. And I would hear my aunts and my uncles playing the Four Aces, the Four Lads, Frankie Laine, and Rosemary Clooney. And then all of the sudden I turned on a television show in 1952 and I see kids dancing to this music. But I also hear rhythm and blues. "Sh-Boom" by the Chords and "Little Darling" by in those days the Gladiolas, before "Little Darling" was remade by the Crew Cuts. And this music hit my ear even though I was listening to my aunts and uncles play the pop music of the day.[98]

While hip teenagers like Blavat were becoming familiar with R&B through jukeboxes and records, *Bandstand*'s white pop songs proved popular with many of the city's young people. By the show's first anniversary, *Bandstand* fan club membership neared ten thousand local teenagers, and the Philadelphia edition of *TV Guide* praised the show as "the people's choice" (both *Bandstand* and *TV Guide*, of course, were part of Annenberg's Triangle Publications).[99] In outlying neighborhoods, where young people could not make it to the show's studio, *Bandstand* annexes were set up in firehouses and other public buildings where teenagers gathered to watch the show on TV and dance. By the start of 1955, the show was the top-rated local program in its time slot, and tens of thousands of teenagers had attended a *Bandstand* show at WFIL's studio.[100]

The teenagers who visited *Bandstand* came not only from Philadelphia, but also from across the wider WFIL-adelphia area. Pennants along the studio wall featuring the names of high schools and towns outside of Philadelphia reminded television viewers (and advertisers) of *Bandstand*'s geographic scope, as did a daily roll call during which teens in the studio audience gave their names and high schools. The show also featured a character called Major Max Power (a man dressed in a dark military-styled uniform with a large *MP* on his chest) who appeared weekly to tell host Bob Horn (and the studio and television audiences) about new viewers seeing the program.[101] With each of these features, *Bandstand* made reference to the WFIL-adelphia market and to the show's ability to deliver a large regional viewing audience to advertisers.

Although *Bandstand* was not always on the cutting edge of new music, Philadelphia was a "breakout" city where producers would test records before distributing them nationally. Producers looked to Philadelphia

FIGURE 7. Bob Horn, the original host of *Bandstand*, interviews audience members during the daily roll call. This segment, along with the pennants displayed in the background, reminded viewers of the show's large regional audience. *The Official 1955 Bandstand Yearbook.*

because of its proximity to New York, where many of the record companies were located, and because it was the third largest city in the United States in the early 1950s, with more residents than St. Louis and Boston combined. Philadelphia's racial and ethnic makeup also made the city a productive place to test new music and find musical talent. The city's black and Italian residents lived in close proximity in many neighborhoods, and despite significant tensions over housing and education, musical styles and tastes often overlapped. These interracial music exchanges made Philadelphia a thriving market in which to test new R&B and rock and roll music.[102]

From its earliest days, *Bandstand*'s producers viewed the show as a regional program with the potential, given Philadelphia's clout as a test market, to influence the music played on pop radio stations across the country. The decentralization of the recording and radio industries made the show even more valuable as a platform for artists and record labels to reach larger audiences. Through the 1950s, a number of small record labels and local radio stations emerged to challenge the major record firm oligopolies and national radio networks. This decentralization occurred for four reasons. First, in 1947 the FCC approved a large backlog of applications for new radio stations. As a result, many independent stations emerged, doubling the number of radio stations in most markets. Second, the advent of smaller, lighter, and more durable 45 rpm records (as opposed to delicate 78s) made it possible for smaller companies to ship records across the country. Third, after television took much of the entertainment talent and national advertising spending away from radio, radio stations focused on local markets and turned to records as inexpensive forms of programming. And finally, these smaller record firms and radio stations thrived by marketing to distinct segments of the audience, including the teenage market that grew in size, had more access to music through cheap and compact transistor radios, and gained recognition among marketers through the 1950s.[103]

Taken together, these changes profoundly affected the range of music available to consumers via records and radio. For example, the four largest record firms—RCA, Columbia (CBS), Capitol, and American Decca (MCA)—held an 81 percent market share of hit records in 1948, but by 1959 this share declined to 34 percent. The four radio networks (CBS, NBC, ABC, and Mutual Broadcasting System) that vied for a share of the total national radio audience in 1948 gave way to more than one hundred autonomous local markets by the end of the 1950s.[104] Many of these radio stations followed the network standard and programmed news alongside vocal and orchestral popular music. A smaller number of stations looked for attention-catching records that would attract teenage listeners. These radio stations turned to the recently founded companies that recorded R&B rather than the big band swing and crooners still favored by the major labels. These stations first emerged in cities with sizable black populations, like Philadelphia's black-oriented WHAT-AM, and there were at least fifty other R&B stations across the country by 1960.[105]

Compared to these radio stations, *Bandstand* was conservative in its musical selection. While *Bandstand* sampled watered-down covers of black R&B records by white artists in the early 1950s, radio shows in other cities introduced teenagers to a variety of original R&B records. While these radio R&B shows caused some controversy, radio continued to have more freedom than television to play new music by black artists because the stations broadcast later at night and did not feature visual images. Foremost among these radio outlets, Memphis's WDIA, the first radio station programmed by blacks for a black audience, and Alan Freed's popular *Moondog* radio show in Cleveland and later New York played original R&B songs produced by small independent record companies.[106] Audiences for these radio shows varied based on the demographics of the areas in which they broadcast, but most attracted young people across racial, class, and spatial lines.[107]

Bandstand was among the first television programs to join these radio broadcasters and record producers as an important promotional platform for music. For example, the Three Chuckles, a white Detroit-based group, drove all the way to Philadelphia to perform on *Bandstand* in 1953. The group performed "Runaround," which at the time was a local hit released on Boulevard, a small Detroit label. Fueled by sales of the song in Philadelphia, major label RCA Victor released "Runaround" nationally, and it became a hit in 1954.[108] On television's power as a promotional tool in this era, jazz trumpeter and trombonist Kirby Stone told *Down Beat* magazine, "We could have knocked around in clubs for 10 years and never have been seen by the number of people who have seen us on television. One night on TV is worth weeks at the Paramount."[109] Even though *Bandstand* was not yet broadcast nationally, it offered recording artists exposure far beyond the show's point of origin in West Philadelphia.

With its regional and national influence, *Bandstand* was at the leading edge of the emerging relationship among television, radio, and the music industry. *Bandstand* was not the only local television show to create a niche in this changing media landscape, and by 1956 nearly fifty markets had television dance shows similar to *Bandstand*.[110] However, with a broadcast signal that reached parts of four states, positive publicity from Walter Annenberg's media properties such as the *Philadelphia Inquirer* and *TV Guide*, and daily musical guests, *Bandstand* was the most influential of these locally televised music shows. Before Alan Freed brought his popular radio shows and concerts to television in 1956, and before Ed Sullivan broadcast Bo Diddley in 1955 and Elvis Presley in 1956, Bob Horn's *Bandstand* had grown into a local show with national influence, making it the most important television venue in this era for artists and producers looking to reach a large audience. This success, however, came at a price for the black teenagers in the West Philadelphia neighborhood around *Bandstand*'s studio. While the program started playing black R&B by 1954, the show also implemented admissions policies that had the effect of excluding black teens. While the producers' racial attitudes may have contributed to these policies, their desire to create a noncontroversial advertiser-friendly show did more to encourage the policies. For *Bandstand*, reaching teenage consumers across WFIL-adelphia took priority over providing a space that would be open to all teens in its backyard of West Philadelphia.

"OBSERVERS NOTE A LACK OF NEGRO PARTICIPATION"

Over the course of *Bandstand*'s local production history (September 1952 to July 1957), teens who visited the studio or watched the show experienced it first briefly as an integrated space and later, after changes to the admission policy, as a segregated space. When it started in 1952, *Bandstand* admitted teenagers on a first-come first-served basis. Weldon McDougal, who attended West Philadelphia High School, remembered that although *Bandstand* did not yet play the R&B music he liked, he had no trouble getting into the show in 1952 and 1953:

> West Philly [High School was] so close to *Bandstand*. *Bandstand* used to start at 2:45. West Philadelphia at the time, we used to get out at 2:15. When Bob Horn was there, I'd rush over there and it was first-come first-served. So I'd go in there and dance, until they started playing all of this corny music. Then there weren't many black guys who would go over there. I was considered corny going over there. I was just seeing what was happening. It wasn't like I wanted to be on television, because I didn't care after awhile.[111]

As the show's popularity increased, however, *Bandstand* adopted admission policies that, while not explicitly whites-only, had the effect of discriminating against black teenagers. In 1954, *Bandstand* selected a group of twelve white teenagers to serve as the show's "committee." Committee members enforced the show's dress code (a jacket or a sweater and tie for boys, and dresses or skirts for girls) and were tasked with maintaining order among the other teens on the show.[112] In the *Bandstand* pecking order, the committee members were followed by studio regulars and by periodic visitors to the show. The committee members exercised considerable sway over who would be admitted on a regular basis, and, by 1954, *Bandstand* required everyone but the committee members and the regulars to send a letter to WFIL in advance to request admission to the show on a specific day.[113] In practice, this admissions policy resembled the discriminatory membership policy of the skating rinks outlined earlier. Teens who gained admission to *Bandstand* after 1953 did so in one of two ways. Some teens were in the same social peer group as the show's committee and regulars, who by 1953 came mostly from Italian neighborhoods in South Philadelphia or West Catholic High School (which was predominantly Irish and Italian). Other teenagers had to plan their visits weeks or months in advance and request tickets. This became a common practice for teens who lived in Allentown, Reading, and other cities and towns outside of Philadelphia. These teens became familiar with the show from television and from the record hops in the areas around Philadelphia that Bob Horn hosted with the *Bandstand* regulars. These areas included growing suburban counties with small black populations, such as Delaware County (7 percent black population in 1950), Montgomery County (4 percent), and Bucks County (less than 2 percent).[114] Given that the outlying areas had fewer black residents, the teens who traveled to visit the show were predominately white. For black teens who lived only a few blocks from the studio, the advance notice aspect of the admission policy further marginalized them from the show. As a result of these admissions policies, *Bandstand's* audience became almost all-white by the end of 1954.

The admission policies appealed to the producers' commercial goals for the program. By encouraging teenagers from outside the city to attend the show, *Bandstand* further established its popularity with WFIL-adelphia. Inviting teens from this regional area to watch the show, request tickets, and write fan letters strengthened *Bandstand's* ability to persuade advertisers to sponsor the show. Here again, *Bandstand's* producers marketed the program to the largest possible regional audience, appealing to those teens in the four-state broadcast area rather than the local teenagers in *Bandstand's* West Philadelphia neighborhood.

Bandstand's producers also adopted the new admissions policies to minimize the potential for racial tension among teenagers outside the studio. Yet while the producers hoped that distributing admissions passes in advance would make it easier to control the crowd of teenagers, the policy had the opposite effect. It provided black teenagers with an opening to protest their exclusion from the show. West Philadelphia teen Walter Palmer, for example, organized other black teenagers to test the show's admissions policies. "*Bandstand* was segregated," Palmer recalled. "There were white kids from all of the Catholic schools, but no black kids. West Catholic was on 46th, and they were always there; our school [West Philadelphia High School] was on 47th [and we could not go]." After graduating from West Philadelphia High School, Palmer remembered that "I engineered a plan to get membership applications, and gave them Irish, Polish, and Italian last names. They mailed the forms back to our homes and once we had the cards we were able to get in that day." Palmer's plan successfully undermined *Bandstand's* admission policies, but that day, and other times when black teens attempted to gain admission to the studio, they frequently dealt with violence from white teens. While Palmer recalls that he and his peers from the "black bottom" held their own in these fights, he remembered there were "all-out race riots outside the studio."[115] In their attempts to challenge *Bandstand*'s racially discriminatory admissions policies, black teens faced verbal and physical harassment that further marked *Bandstand* as a site restricted to white teenagers.

Concerned that racial tensions would threaten *Bandstand*'s image as a safe place for teenagers and scare off advertisers, WFIL sought help from the Commission on Human Relations (CHR) to calm the tensions among teenagers waiting in line. A May 1954 CHR case update, titled "WFIL-TV v. Negro and White Teen Agers," states: "Plans for admittance for teen agers as guests of the *Band Stand* program have been ineffective and conflicts have arisen principally on the part of those teen agers who could not gain admittance."[116] In other words, *Bandstand* implemented a racially discriminatory policy, and then asked the city's antidiscrimination agency to address the resulting protests. The *Philadelphia Tribune* reported that Horn assured the CHR that "the only preference shown was the case of special out-of-town groups visiting the studio" and that teens "who adhered to the policy of proper dress and conduct were readily admitted, without regard to the race."[117] Nominally nondiscriminatory, this policy gave *Bandstand* the flexibility to exclude black teenagers. Concerns about the potential for race riots among teens strengthened the producers' policy of admitting only committee members, regulars, and those who requested cards of admission rather than admitting teens on a first-come first-served basis. A second CHR report on intergroup tensions in recreation facilities in March 1955 makes clear the outcome of this policy:

> Police reported that disorderly behavior of teenagers at Bob Horn's *Bandstand* program, where the audience participate in the show by social dancing, had resulted in the absence of Negroes from attendance. The management denied having a discriminatory policy, and CHR had little upon which to base a case of discrimination. Observers note a lack of Negro participation.

The report went on to state that young women from the mostly black William Penn High School in North Philadelphia had raised "the question of elimination of Negro youth" from *Bandstand*, and that the CHR saw a need for "broad planning to effect integration of this activity for high school youth."[118] There is no evidence that the CHR ever undertook such efforts to integrate *Bandstand*, and available pictures of the show from 1955 and after reveal that the show remained segregated.

Interestingly, *Bandstand*'s inclusion of black R&B music increased at the same time that the show limited the admission of black teenagers. The

FIGURE 8. Photos in the *Bandstand* yearbook, oral histories, and Philadelphia Commission on Human Relations files indicate that by 1955 *Bandstand* became a space for white teenagers. *The Official 1955 Bandstand Yearbook.*

R&B breakthrough on *Bandstand* came in the summer of 1954 with "Sh-Boom" by the Chords, a black vocal harmony group from New York. Following the common practice of radio stations at the time, Horn initially played a copy of the song by the Crew Cuts, a white group that often covered black R&B songs. The show's regulars complained that the Crew Cuts' song was not the real version and persuaded Horn to test the Chords' version on the show's rate-a-record segment. After the Chords' record received a high rating, Horn agreed to play the original.[119] The introduction of R&B and rock and roll progressed slowly on *Bandstand*, and R&B artists like the Chords and the Red Tops continued to share airplay with white crooners like Tony Bennett and Vic Damone. By late 1955 and 1956, though, Horn's playlist influenced, and was influenced by, the rise in prominence of R&B and rock and roll, and included not only white singers like Bill Haley and His Comets and Elvis Presley, but also black performers like Little Richard and Frankie Lymon and the Teenagers.

Still, by 1955 teenagers had local knowledge that *Bandstand* was primarily a space for white teenagers. Lee Andrews, Weldon McDougal's friend who attended West Philadelphia's Bartram High School with his vocal group the Hearts and also lived in one of West Philadelphia's black neighborhoods, told historian John Jackson in a 1993 interview that there was "'always some reason black kids couldn't get into' the WFIL studio. It may have been because they did not have a membership card, or perhaps they did not meet the dress code, but for whatever reason, 'everybody began to understand [that] this is a show for white people.'"[120] Similarly, when asked if the show was integrated, Jerry Blavat, a South Philadelphia native who was one of the show's best dancers and became the leader of the show's committee of regulars from 1954 to 1956, recalled: "Well, there was no integration back then. And I guess sponsor-wise . . . you have to understand it was white television back then in the 1950s, because dollar-wise, advertisers were not beaming into the black community."[121] Reporting on the drunk driving arrest that cost Horn his job, the *Philadelphia Tribune* also noted the show's segregation: "The news of Horn's arrest came as a distinct shock, both to the hundreds of white parents whose children have appeared on the show and to countless Negro parents, who have sought in vain to have Horn consider their children on his televised 'Bandstand.'"[122] For Philadelphia teenagers, then, *Bandstand* as both a local dance space and as a regional television show became a site for white youth, and television viewers across WFIL-adelphia saw evidence of *Bandstand*'s segregation on a daily basis.

While other scholars have called attention to the ability of music and dance in the early rock and roll era to promote intercultural exchange, the local years of *Bandstand* demonstrate that the show's potential to serve as a space for changing racial attitudes was circumscribed by its regional commercial goals and discriminatory admissions practices.[123] *Bandstand* connected many of the city's white teenagers with music performed and influenced by black artists, but at the same time, the show became almost totally segregated by its third year as a local program. This contradiction highlights the importance of examining media within its local context. Philadelphia teens, like teenagers across the country, found meaning and value in R&B and rock and roll music, and in the presentation of music on television. They did so, however, in social spaces that often divided them on the basis of race. While *Bandstand* was not the only youth space that practiced racial discrimination, the impact of its discrimination was unique because the show reached a large television audience in Philadelphia and WFIL's four-state broadcasting region. Through this WFIL-adelphia broadcast platform, *Bandstand* influenced the styles and attitudes of teenagers in ways that strictly neighborhood youth spaces could not. In electing to play black R&B music on television, *Bandstand* took a risk that was repaid handsomely as the show's regional and national commercial influence expanded. In electing to take the segregationist side of the local fights occurring over housing, schools, and youth spaces, *Bandstand* obfuscated the neighborhood changes taking place outside of its studio doors.

In disseminating this anti-integration vision, *Bandstand* reinforced the defensive localism practiced just blocks from the studio by white homeowners. Both WFIL and white homeowners associations justified segregation by foregrounding financial interests, and this simultaneous monetization and racialization of space provided a foundation for the maintenance of de facto segregation. *Bandstand*'s version of defensive localism sought to maximize advertiser revenue by shielding regional television viewers from images of young people of different races dancing and socializing. For white homeowners associations and those who sought to protect their racial privilege by moving to suburban developments that excluded blacks, property values trumped black civil rights. The actions of WFIL and the homeowners associations did not need to be coordinated to be mutually influential. Groups like the Angora Civic Association fostered hostile racial attitudes in *Bandstand*'s backyard. These local housing fights, combined with WFIL's expressed commitment to give advertisers access to regional viewers in segregated suburban developments like Levittown and Fairness Hills, made it profitable for *Bandstand* to adopt racially discriminatory admissions policies. At the same time, *Bandstand*'s policies further entrenched segregation as a custom in the Philadelphia area. De facto segregation in the North was maintained through a series of everyday decisions like these, rather than strictly through a set of laws. *Bandstand*'s anti-integration stance was hardly unique in Philadelphia in this era, as the analysis of school segregation in chapters 3 and 4 makes clear. Within this system of de facto segregation, *Bandstand* conveyed an anti-integrationist perspective to a large television audience in a way that local supporters of segregation could not. In making Philadelphia safe for WFIL-adelphia,

Bandstand helped to normalize the racist attitudes and policies that limited black access to housing, education, and public accommodations. As chapters 6 and 7 examine, the number of teenagers and adults who viewed *Bandstand*'s exclusively white image of youth increased far beyond WFIL-adelphia when *American Bandstand* started broadcasting nationally in 1957. *Bandstand*'s position on integration, however, was not a given. By looking at *They Shall Be Heard*, a local teenage television program produced by the Fellowship Commission, the next chapter demonstrates that *Bandstand*'s producers could have selected a path other than segregation.

CHAPTER 2

They Shall Be Heard

Local Television as a Civil Rights Battleground

For years, the Fellowship Commission has been anxious to get into TV regularly, feeling that it is probably the most effective medium for forming desirable attitudes.

—Maurice Fagan, Executive Director of the Philadelphia Fellowship Commission and host of *They Shall Be Heard*, 1952

They Shall Be Heard is a road not taken. While *Bandstand* introduced Philadelphia teenagers to new popular music, dances, and fashion styles, another local program used television to educate teenagers about intercultural issues. Produced by the Fellowship Commission, *They Shall Be Heard* (1952–53) gathered a group of teenagers for a weekly televised discussion about racial and religious prejudice. Unlike *Bandstand,* which adopted admissions policies that excluded black teenagers, *They Shall Be Heard* brought together students of different racial, religious, and ethnic backgrounds. As *Bandstand* marked television as a place restricted to white teenage consumers, *They Shall Be Heard* introduced its audience to ideas and discussions beyond the limited boundaries of *Bandstand*'s commercial entertainment.

While *Bandstand*'s producers defined local television by the scope of WFIL's consumer market, the Fellowship Commission's vision for local television focused on the Philadelphia city limits. As Philadelphia's leading interracial and interreligious civil rights coalition, the Fellowship Commission worked through the late 1940s and 1950s to secure antidiscrimination laws and improve race relations in the city.[1] The Commission also worked closely with the school board to implement intercultural education materials designed to introduce students to the histories of different racial and religious groups and to counter stereotypes. Maurice

Fagan, the executive director of both the Fellowship Commission and the Jewish Community Relations Council, led the group's education program (Fagan's work on educational issues is discussed in greater detail in chapters 3 and 4). By the early 1950s, the Fellowship Commission enjoyed a close relationship with the school board, but it still lacked a connection to most neighborhoods and schools. Fagan articulated his concerns about these shortcomings in a speech to the Commission's members. "We are still far too middle class in our contacts and program," Fagan advised the group. "We too rarely reach either the upper or lower economic groups and neighborhoods. We are too dependent upon public relations techniques to reach the rank and file members of the groups we contact. We need to find ways to personalize and decentralize our activities." Fagan went on to suggest a way the group could address this issue. "Radio and television stations offer us more time than we are prepared to use well," he noted, "but we haven't even begun to work out ways of using television for educational purposes."[2] With these community relations goals in mind, Fagan and the Fellowship Commission approached *They Shall Be Heard* with optimism about television's potential to reach viewers, especially in the racially changing neighborhoods in which they lacked contacts.

The Fellowship Commission was one of a number of public and private agencies (e.g., DuPont, the Ford Foundation, the Fund for the Republic, and the AFL-CIO) that sponsored civic-oriented programs across the country in television's early years. These groups, media studies scholar Anna McCarthy has shown, looked to television as a tool to shape viewers' "conduct and attitudes" toward "rational civic practice."[3] The businessmen, labor leaders, social reformers, and public intellectuals who organized these efforts held differing ideas about good citizenship, but all saw television as a strategy of governance. The shows, McCarthy notes, did not always work as intended, and the groups "often discovered a profound discrepancy between the effects they hoped to achieve and the responses of their viewers."[4] The programs, moreover, frequently addressed viewers as problems to be fixed. As media studies scholar Ien Ang has argued in the context of British broadcasting, producers of public service programs, like commercial programs, frequently view their audience from "above" or "outside" as "objectified categories of others to be controlled." Whether addressing consumers or citizens, Ang suggests, television producers cannot stop "struggling to conquer the audience."[5] Like these efforts to shape citizenship, the Fellowship Commission looked to television for ways to engage and influence Philadelphians. The program it created, however, consciously tried to avoid the paternalistic tone common to public service programs. To address viewers as citizens without condescending to them, *They Shall Be Heard* deemphasized expert opinions in favor of unscripted discussions among "ordinary" teenagers. Fagan, in his role as moderator, sat off camera, encouraging viewers to focus on the young discussion participants. *They Shall Be Heard*'s producers sought to mitigate the power differential inherent in civic-oriented programming by respecting their audience's ability to be active participants in a televised discussion rather than passive viewers of a televised lecture.

Contrasting *They Shall Be Heard* and *Bandstand* illuminates the advantages enjoyed by the commercial model for teenage television. Unlike *They Shall Be Heard,* which relied on a voluntary goodwill agreement between a network affiliate and the school system, *Bandstand* could count on advertisers eager to reach potential consumers in "WFIL-adelphia." This inequity was owing to television's development along the advertising-supported model of radio. As noted in chapter 1, in the postwar years the FCC allocated television licenses along the narrow VHF band, with most of the licenses going to established media companies that already owned newspapers and/or radio stations. The two major networks, NBC and CBS, dominated these VHF stations, with ABC gaining affiliates over the course of the 1950s. This left little space for educational television or other noncommercial stations, and when they did develop, most were assigned to the UHF band, which viewers could not receive without special equipment. Commercial stations made only token attempts to serve the public interest, and the FCC did little to hold these stations accountable. Government decisions, therefore, facilitated the dominance of commercial television and made the survival of civic-minded discussion programs like *They Shall Be Heard* tenuous.

Bandstand and *They Shall Be Heard* both debuted in October 1952, but their different understandings of local television led them to address their audiences in different ways and sent the shows on divergent trajectories. *Bandstand* addressed its audience as consumers and asked them to buy products, while *They Shall Be Heard* addressed its audience as citizens and asked them to reject prejudice. *Bandstand* succeeded and expanded because it was profitable; WFIL produced it inexpensively, and advertisers supported the show because it allowed them to reach the valuable teenage consumer demographic. *They Shall Be Heard* became a brief television experiment because it relied on the cooperation of television stations for airtime and because the Fellowship

Commission was unable to establish a link between *They Shall Be Heard*'s "hearts and minds" approach to prejudice and the concurrent efforts undertaken by the Commission and other civil rights advocates to uproot structures of racial discrimination. The Fellowship Commission's antidiscrimination message was simply a harder sell than *Bandstand*'s pop music and bubblegum. Although *They Shall Be Heard* ran for only twenty-seven episodes and reached only a fraction of the number of viewers that *Bandstand* did, it offers an alternative model in which television's power to educate and challenge citizens took priority over television's power to persuade consumers.

GETTING *THEY SHALL BE HEARD* ON TELEVISION

In their desire to explore the opportunities offered by television, Maurice Fagan and the Fellowship Commission built on earlier successes with radio broadcasts and film discussions. As did *Americans All, Immigrants All*, a national radio program about immigrant contributions produced by the Bureau for Intercultural Education in the 1940s, the Fellowship Commission's *Within Our Gates* brought Philadelphians radio profiles of famous men and women of different racial, religious, and national backgrounds every Sunday morning from 1943 to 1952 on WFIL-radio.[6] The school board recommended *Within Our Gates* for out-of-school study, and copies of recordings and scripts were made available to the city's schools.[7] In addition, the Fellowship Commission maintained a library of short filmstrips and feature-length films on topics related to intercultural relations. The Commission made these films available to teachers in the school system, and from 1948 to 1952 it offered bus service that transported school groups to the Fellowship building, where a Commission member led a discussion of the films.[8] During 1951 alone, the Commission counted fifty-eight school classes and more than fifteen hundred students that used the free bus service to visit the library. Approximately twenty thousand people saw one of the Commission's films or filmstrips in schools or community meetings.[9]

In both title and content, *They Shall Be Heard* drew inspiration from *They Learn What They Live* (1952), a study of prejudice in children co-sponsored by the Fellowship Commission.[10] Conducted from 1945 to 1948 in Philadelphia's public schools, the study received national attention for its findings about the early age at which young people develop racial awareness and prejudice.[11] The study was part of a larger movement that encouraged schools to incorporate intercultural educational materials and perspectives into the classroom.[12] Fagan and the Fellowship Commission were familiar with much of this work, but they were less concerned with the academic debates over intercultural education than they were with developing strategies for accessing and reducing prejudice in Philadelphia's schools. The Fellowship Commission's long-held interest in new approaches to intercultural education led it to *They Shall Be Heard*.

Drawing on these experiences, in October 1952 the Fellowship Commission brought its intercultural education ideas to a larger audience with a televised discussion with junior and senior high school students. In contrast to *Bandstand*'s solid financial backing by WFIL and Walter Annenberg's Triangle Publications, *They Shall Be Heard* aired on Philadelphia's NBC affiliate (WCAU-TV) through a system of voluntary cooperation between the station and the city's public, private, and parochial school systems. Under this goodwill agreement, commercial stations would donate time for community and educational programming. This cooperation worked better in Philadelphia than in any other city, with all of the city's television stations providing time to the schools in the early 1950s. In her 1953 study of educational and community television across the county, for example, Jennie Callahan noted that Philadelphia was home to the "the largest community activity in educational television in the country."[13] The viability of *They Shall Be Heard* and other community and educational programs, however, depended on the willingness of commercial stations to continue providing airtime. Indeed, the cooperation that brought *They Shall Be Heard* to television was short-lived, and the show did not return in the fall of 1953. Although the program ran for only twenty-seven episodes, *They Shall Be Heard* represented the Fellowship Commission's most ambitious and innovative intercultural educational endeavor.

For this television program, the Fellowship Commission brought together students of different racial, religious, and ethnic backgrounds. To recruit students for the show, the Commission relied on the strength of its relationships with the public, private, and parochial school systems. Each of the three school systems recommended four students for each weekly program, drawing primarily from students in the schools' Fellowship Clubs. The group of twelve students changed every week, so that over the course of the show's run, more than three hundred students participated.[14]

The Fellowship House, an organization distinct from the Fellowship Commission run by Marjorie Penny, cofounder of the Commission,

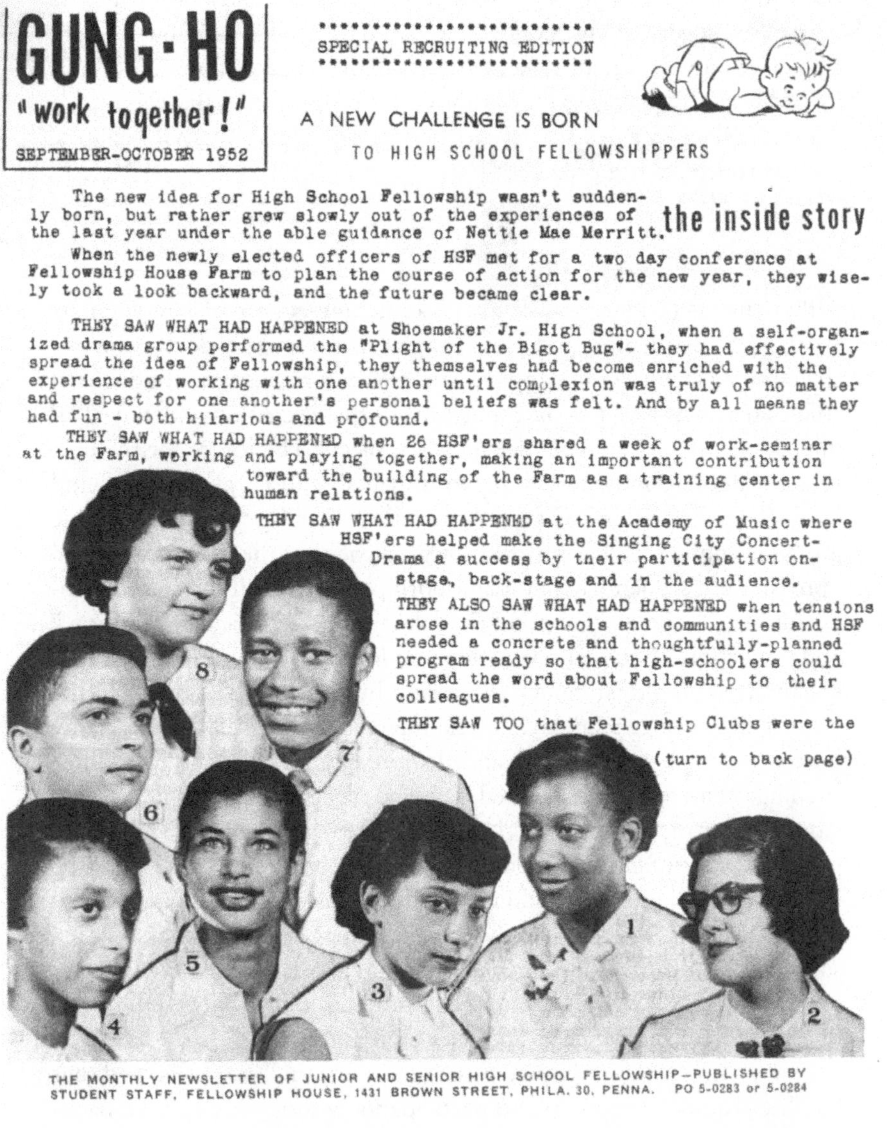
GUNG-HO

"work together!"

SEPTEMBER-OCTOBER 1952

SPECIAL RECRUITING EDITION

A NEW CHALLENGE IS BORN

TO HIGH SCHOOL FELLOWSHIPPERS

the inside story

The new idea for High School Fellowship wasn't suddenly born, but rather grew slowly out of the experiences of the last year under the able guidance of Nettie Mae Merritt.

When the newly elected officers of HSF met for a two day conference at Fellowship House Farm to plan the course of action for the new year, they wisely took a look backward, and the future became clear.

THEY SAW WHAT HAD HAPPENED at Shoemaker Jr. High School, when a self-organized drama group performed the "Plight of the Bigot Bug"- they had effectively spread the idea of Fellowship, they themselves had become enriched with the experience of working with one another until complexion was truly of no matter and respect for one another's personal beliefs was felt. And by all means they had fun - both hilarious and profound.

THEY SAW WHAT HAD HAPPENED when 26 HSF'ers shared a week of work-seminar at the Farm, working and playing together, making an important contribution toward the building of the Farm as a training center in human relations.

THEY SAW WHAT HAD HAPPENED at the Academy of Music where HSF'ers helped make the Singing City Concert-Drama a success by their participation on-stage, back-stage and in the audience.

THEY ALSO SAW WHAT HAD HAPPENED when tensions arose in the schools and communities and HSF needed a concrete and thoughtfully-planned program ready so that high-schoolers could spread the word about Fellowship to their colleagues.

THEY SAW TOO that Fellowship Clubs were the

(turn to back page)

THE MONTHLY NEWSLETTER OF JUNIOR AND SENIOR HIGH SCHOOL FELLOWSHIP—PUBLISHED BY STUDENT STAFF, FELLOWSHIP HOUSE, 1431 BROWN STREET, PHILA. 30, PENNA. PO 5-0283 or 5-0284

FIGURE 9. High School Fellowship Clubs brought together students of different racial, religious, and ethnic backgrounds. The students pictured in this club newsletter are among those who would have participated in *They Shall Be Heard*. September-October 1952. Temple University Libraries, Urban Archives, Philadelphia, PA.

coordinated the high school Fellowship Clubs. The Fellowship House relied on teachers at the high schools to sponsor Fellowship Clubs as extracurricular activities. At the time *They Shall Be Heard* debuted, eight of the twenty-one public high schools had active Fellowship Clubs. In addition to appearing on the show, young people in the Fellowship Clubs challenged the discriminatory practices of recreational facilities, such as roller-skating rinks.[15]

WATCHING TEENAGERS TALK

Although the producers did not make a kinescope of *They Shall Be Heard,* letters, memos, and photographs reveal a great deal about the structure of the program. Fagan, who was a former high school social studies teacher, served as the moderator of the discussion and played an important role in choosing the show's subjects. The topics for the programs ranged from issues related to students' schools, peer groups, and families to discussions of prejudice against racial, religious, or ethnic groups. Among this diversity of topics, episodes of the show considered "problems of students with foreign-born parents," "fair educational opportunities," "the atomic bomb," "color prejudice," "social rejection," and "rejection of students with high or low I.Q."[16] As the moderator, Fagan attempted to stimulate discussion by relating these topics to the lives of the teenage students. For example, in a show that asked "How far can personal liberty be extended?" the discussion focused on "hot-rodding." The teenagers debated whether special roads should be provided for car racing, whether their personal liberties conflicted with the potential emotional and economic costs to their parents should they be injured, and whether hot-rodding could be considered a religiously prohibited form of suicide.[17] As this example suggests, the show's discussions of prejudice and interracial issues sometimes took a backseat to topics that Fagan believed would capture and maintain the interest of the show's teenage panelists and television audience.[18]

Along with these unscripted discussions, Fagan also emphasized that the discussions be accessible to participants without any specific background knowledge in the subject. Here, Fagan contrasted *They Shall Be Heard* to *Quiz Kids,* a popular radio program in the 1940s and 1950s. Fagan informed a magazine editor that *They Shall Be Heard* "is not a 'Quiz Kid' program designed to present how much these youngsters know about a particular subject or even how bright they are. It is intended primarily to indicate how a group of fairly typical youngsters think about current human relations issues."[19] One student who participated in the program appreciated this approach and wrote to Fagan to encourage him to "continue this pattern of choosing subjects that will reveal the emotions and thoughts of students rather than their aptitudes and specific abilities."[20]

While Fagan exercised control over the show's subjects and provided the participants with discussion tips during the pre-show warm-up, he minimized his role as moderator during the broadcast itself. The Fellowship Commission's experience with film discussions influenced this decision to downplay the moderator's speaking role and emphasize the discussion among teenagers. For Fagan, discussion was an effective educational technique for two reasons. First, he thought it made students more amendable to intercultural attitudes. "Film-discussions," he argued in a 1947 issue of *Education* magazine, "are vastly superior to speeches or straight teaching because the children find the facts for themselves and probably will accept them more readily and retain them more permanently." Second, Fagan felt that discussion allowed educators to "spot pupils who are thoroughly democratic and others who are bigoted," and to address "preventative" or "curative" intercultural work accordingly.[21] The role of the moderator of *They Shall Be Heard*, therefore, was to facilitate exchanges that would reveal the opinions and attitudes of the participants without dominating the discussion. Fagan reiterated both of these points in a letter to a viewer who expressed concern with his muted role as moderator. "You must remember," he told the viewer,

> that these discussions are unrehearsed and, therefore, that youngsters will say things with which many or all of us may disagree but that the whole purpose of the programs is to bring such viewpoints out in the open where their faults could be shown and better ones could be developed. Since an important part of the program is to promote a free exchange of opinions . . . it is therefore important that these young people should not feel we are dominating their thinking or asking them in advance to agree with our thinking.[22]

In another letter, Fagan emphasized that "We take every pain to make sure that the moderator does not lecture, does not dominate the discussion with his own facts or views and does not manipulate the discussion."[23] *They Shall Be Heard* also used film clips and skits to stimulate discussion of racial prejudice. In each program, after Fagan explained the topic of discussion, he introduced either a film segment or a dramatic skit in which the students participated. For the former, the producers relied on the Fellowship Commission's library of films with intercultural themes. Using films on the undemocratic nature of racial discrimination, such as *Brotherhood of Man* and *Home of the Brave,* the producers selected scenes that presented the episode's subject provocatively.[24] In episodes that featured skits, the producers selected four or five students during the warm-up period. Students did not memorize lines, and Max Franzen, the Fellowship Commission's director of radio and television, admitted that "the skits were anything but professional jobs."[25] Nevertheless, these skits were central to exploring the themes of each show. For example, in an episode on fair educational opportunities, four students discussed their ambitions for college education. The dramatic tension in the brief skit flowed from the disappointment of one student who could not afford to go to college and of another who was turned down because of his race.[26] In this and other episodes, after introducing the film or skit, Fagan attempted to stay out of the discussion and encouraged the students to ask questions of each other.

This discussion format, Anna McCarthy notes, was popular among local civic groups that sponsored public service programs. "The act of *watching* the act of *having* a discussion," McCarthy suggests, "was a form of directive training, showing audience members appropriate and inappropriate forms of civic conduct."[27] Similarly, Fagan hoped that the discussions on *They Shall Be Heard* would influence the attitudes of teenage participants and television viewers and spark similar conversations among teenagers outside of the studio. By letting "average" teens talk through their ideas and concerns, moreover, the show challenged the custom of featuring well-known personalities or experts, which was emerging as the standard practice of television interview and discussion programs in this era. On nationally televised news programs like Edward R. Morrow's *See It Now* (1951–58) and variety talk shows such as *Arthur Godfrey Time* (1952–59) and *The Today Show* (1951–present), the hosts acted as central figures who interviewed major newsmakers and entertainers.[28] On NBC's *Youth Wants to Know* (1951–63), a national public affairs program broadcast from Washington, D.C., that most closely resembles *They Shall Be Heard,* local high school students asked questions of prominent guests (John Kennedy, Richard Nixon, Eleanor Roosevelt, Jackie Robinson, James Michener, Estes Kefauver, and Joseph McCarthy all appeared on the show during its first five years).[29] Unlike *Youth Wants to Know,* which made the famous guests the focal points of each episode, the producers of *They Shall Be Heard* distinguished their program from a typical news interview show by not providing detailed information on the students' backgrounds or qualifications for appearing on the show. This lack of information prompted a letter from the editor of *Exhibitor* magazine, who complained that the program would have been "far more interesting had each of the participants been identified as to name, [grade], and school. In that way, those listening could have known the background of the students and could have tied it in with the viewpoints which they presented."[30] Fagan replied that the WCAU-TV producers, whom he felt were more "qualified to judge what makes for good television," made the decision to omit this information, but that he felt that background information would "negate our purpose, which is to free the school from any embarrassment or endorsement of the views expressed and to give the youngsters the feeling that they can give their frank opinions as individuals."[31] This anonymity was in stark contrast to *Bandstand*'s roll call segment, in which teens introduced themselves by name and school. *They Shall Be Heard*'s decision to omit this information, when combined with the rotating cast of participants, helped to encourage the audience to see the students as "typical youngsters." The *Exhibitor* editor, however, remained unconvinced by Fagan's views:

> I still feel that there could have been more background information as to the youngsters, yourself, and the purpose of the program before it started. While it may be that you wish to avoid the usual and stereotyped that one sees in similar evidence on television these days, I do believe that for the most part television audiences are not accustomed to too great a change, and that they should be weaned gradually from standardized techniques.[32]

As this letter suggests, *They Shall Be Heard* was experimenting with a discussion format that was controversial in the early history of television.

THEY SHALL BE HEARD AND BANDSTAND

The production strategies and set design of *They Shall Be Heard* also emphasized discussion as the most important theme of the show. The show opened with an announcer introducing the program over filmed footage of crowd scenes in different countries. As these international scenes faded out, the camera focused on the group of students seated in a tight semicircle on chairs, stools, and the floor in a living room setting.[33] Regarding this arrangement, one student wrote to Fagan to complain that the participants were "packed together" and that those who sat on the stools sometimes felt awkward because they did not know what to do with their hands. Fagan replied that the students were seated closely together so that as different students spoke, the crew could quickly shift the camera and microphones.[34]

The show's living room setting and seating arrangements are notable for two reasons. First, many scholars have written about how television producers constructed programs around an imagined nuclear family in a home setting.[35] *They Shall Be Heard* borrowed the image of a living room, but rather than a breadwinning father and homemaking mother, the program filled the space with teenagers. *Bandstand,* in contrast, combined two popular teenage spaces, the gymnasium and the record shop. And unlike *Bandstand* host Bob Horn, who stood at a podium and came across as an easygoing school principal and a disc jockey, Fagan, in his role as moderator, sat off camera until the final wrap-up. While this arrangement aligned the viewer with both the camera and the moderator, in focusing almost exclusively on teenagers, *They Shall Be Heard* reworked a setting that was fast becoming a familiar television design. Second, in terms of seating, the technological limitations of early television (e.g., the large immobile cameras and crane microphones) actually promoted the physical proximity that the producers desired. It helped the Fellowship Commission to literally bring together young people from different racial, religious, and national backgrounds.

Through the production techniques of studio audience participation, seating arrangements, unscripted segments, and close-up shots, Fagan emphasized the spontaneity of live television on *They Shall Be Heard.* As media scholars like Jane Feuer and Rhona Berenstein have examined, television producers and performers have consistently emphasized the medium's liveness, immediacy, and intimacy.[36] For Fagan and the Fellowship Commission, the spontaneity of live discussion was central to *They Shall Be Heard*'s pedagogical potential. During the warm-up session, Fagan's Fellowship Commission colleague Max Franzen explained, "students are acquainted with the procedures of the program and begin to explore some of the points of the particular subject. We try not to exhaust the discussion during the warm-up period but try to discover the points on which the students are conversant and have ideas." Franzen hoped that this method would produce "spontaneity rather than 'conditioned' responses."[37] One teenage participant appreciated this plan, writing "I believe that your plan of not telling the participants exactly what they will discuss, although it adds to their nervousness, assures the onlookers that the views expressed by the speakers are unbiased."[38] In addition, a participant from West Catholic High School offered that he "liked the way in which the show was presented without scripts since it gave the

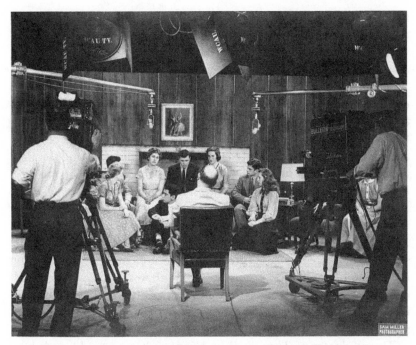

FIGURE 10. Teenagers participating in discussion in the living room set on *They Shall Be Heard*. Maurice Fagan, seated with his back to the camera, tried to downplay his role as moderator. 1952. Temple University Libraries, Urban Archives, Philadelphia, PA.

teenagers a chance to state their opinions on topics which directly concern them."[39]

In this format the discussion sometimes strayed from the topic, a point that drew a letter of complaint from the editor of *Exhibitor* magazine. In his reply, Fagan justified this discussion technique, arguing "It seems to me that many important ideas were advanced by the youngsters even though the discussion might not have had the well-rounded, pat character of rehearsed programs or programs where the youngsters were primed in advance with the wisdom of others." "Would you agree," Fagan asked, "that even if the end result is not a polished intellectual one that the basic purpose of presenting fresh, uncoached viewpoints is in itself a contribution of the first order?" Among the show's contributions, he argued, was that it enabled the "public [to] see 'how youngsters think' rather than just 'what they think.' "[40] For Fagan, the live televised discussions gave teenagers a chance to think through issues and express their ideas, and offered viewers a chance to see the thought processes in action. In both cases, *They Shall Be Heard* used spontaneity to address viewers as citizens and create the possibility for pedagogy through discussion.

Bandstand also emphasized the spontaneity of live television, but it did so to encourage viewers to develop a participatory consumer relationship with the program. *Bandstand* addressed viewers as part of a club that came together every afternoon to share in the consumption of music and sponsors' products. The teens in the studio influenced, and stood in for, the thousands of other teenagers watching the live program at home in the WFIL–adelphia region. In contrast to the discussions *They Shall Be Heard* encouraged, *Bandstand* emphasized the opinions of teenagers as a form of market research. Individual teenagers expressed their opinions of a given song or performer during the rate-a-record segment, while the studio audience registered its group opinion through the level of energy in dancing or applause. Appropriate to the show's focus on music and dancing, the studio was not designed for periods of sustained talking. In this way, *Bandstand* situated studio audience members as consumers and addressed its television audience in the same way.

The producers of *They Shall Be Heard* and *Bandstand* tuned their respective modes of address to adults as well as teenagers. In the case of *They Shall Be Heard*, the show aired Friday mornings at 10:30 A.M. during its first two months, a time at which most teenagers would be in school. Thanks to the school board's radio and television department's participation in the production, the program was listed for in-school viewing. Many schools did not have televisions, however, and individual teachers could decide whether to include the program. One of the participants on the show commented on this problem in a letter to Fagan "I think it would be better if the program could be seen by the girls and boys whom it would concern. That's all of us. They can't see it, so there isn't much sense in giving helpful solutions to problems. I think it would be better if it was held about 4 o'clock in the afternoon."[41] In his reply, Franzen assured the student that people were watching the show:

> I don't think you need to feel discouraged about the program not reaching people who will be helped by the ideas that the students have. We know there are many school classes that have the opportunity to tune in the program every Friday morning since it is listed by the public school system for in-school listening. We are even more thrilled to be able to reach parents, since we believe that the ideals, ideas and thinking of young people have an important effect on them.[42]

In December 1952, the producers' optimism about the audience increased when WCAU moved the show to a more coveted time slot, Sunday afternoons at 2:30 P.M., because WCAU thought it was a "strong program for family listening hours."[43] Fagan expressed his enthusiasm for this new time in a letter to a former participant of the show: "We are very pleased to be able to reach a much larger audience, particularly more young people who will be able to see it at that hour."[44] In a letter to WCAU staff, Fagan also noted that in providing an opportunity for "family units" to view the program,

> [they] were correcting one of the major weaknesses of many intergroup relations programs. That weakness is that the children are reached separately from their parents instead of simultaneously and thus some children may develop a smug or superior attitude and may even clash with their parents about particular issues. Family listening permits the adults and youngsters to view together and discuss together, to grow together.[45]

While the Fellowship Commission believed that young people held more malleable views on race and presented the most open audience for antiracist messages, it viewed parents as important influences on teenagers' racial attitudes, and believed that reaching both teens and adults together as citizens was a critical part of *They Shall Be Heard*'s goal of fighting prejudice.

Adults also made up a key portion of *Bandstand*'s television audience, but in this case parents figured as consumers of the show's entertainment and advertising rather than as local neighbors and citizens. The 1955 *Bandstand* yearbook, for example, depicts different family combinations in front of a television console under the heading, "The family enjoys 'Bandstand' at home, too." The yearbook continues:

> Whether young-in-age or young-at-heart, "Bandstand" viewers at home are just as ardent fans of the program as the teen-agers dancing "On camera" in the studio. . . . In fact, the program is so popular that Mom finds it difficult to leave the TV set when she's doing the family ironing. . . . Even Dad (if he's lucky) gets to enjoy the show, too, as sign-off isn't until 5 P.M.[46]

In the course of one paragraph, the yearbook assured potential advertisers that in addition to a devoted teenage following, *Bandstand*'s television audience included a profitable number of adult viewers. In this image of the audience, the yearbook called upon gender norms in relation to television viewers (e.g., the young housewife watching television while performing domestic chores in the home, and the father coming home from work early to sneak a peak at afternoon programming) that were a common trope for television producers and commentators in this era.[47] When *Bandstand*'s producers prepared to pitch the show to ABC for national broadcast in 1957, they continued to emphasize the profitability of these additional adult viewers and consumers.[48]

On May 10, 1953, after a twenty-seven-episode run, *They Shall Be Heard* went on summer hiatus. This happened in part because of the difficulty of getting students during the summer, but more so because WCAU aired Philadelphia Phillies baseball games in the afternoons during the summer months. In the spring of 1953, Franzen expressed hope that the station would be interested in resuming the program in the fall.[49] To encourage WCAU to resume the program, Clarence Pickett, the president of the Fellowship Commission, wrote directly to the station president. After thanking him for the valuable airtime and production assistance, Pickett detailed the contributions WCAU made by airing this series:

> First, a unique TV discussion format was developed. Second, it was a fine example of the cooperative efforts of the principal educational agencies of our city. Third, many boys and girls from different walks of life were given an opportunity to meet and consider current problems together. Fourth, it was a courageous presentation of significant educational material. And finally, as far as our own particular field is concerned, the program made a significant contribution to intergroup understanding.[50]

Pickett sent similar letters to the superintendents of the school systems and stressed the importance of cooperation among the public, private, and diocesan schools.

Just before the start of the 1953 school year, Fagan followed up on Pickett's letter by writing to Margaret Kearney at WCAU. Fagan reiterated the contributions of the show and emphasized the importance of broadcasting contentious intercultural education topics. "It took courage," he wrote, "for you and WCAU to risk a program which treated such highly controversial matter and which risked presentation with so little rehearsal." Fagan also reminded Kearney that the Fellowship Commission had cooperated with WCAU to minimize the potential controversy in the discussions:

> [I]n each of our planning periods you emphasized the need for sympathetic presentation of the viewpoints to be criticized so that the appeal of the program would be "to see the light" rather than to read out of society those who were unable so far "to see the light" as we think it should be seen. Thus, strongly antagonistic opinions were presented in a friendly, democratic spirit and the young people obtained experience in how to differ without being

disagreeable. They also learned the importance of getting as many view-points as possible before making up their minds.[51]

Despite these appeals, the show did not return to WCAU in the fall of 1953. Most likely, as television airtime had become more profitable, WCAU elected to reduce its voluntary cooperation with the school system, or shifted its goodwill time to the less lucrative late morning or early afternoon weekday hours. In addition, the policy of the schools' television broadcasting department, which distributed evaluation reports to the schools for comments and suggestions on programs, was to "plan series which will be acceptable to all the school systems receiving them for in-school viewing."[52] As such, pressure not to renew *They Shall Be Heard* might also have come from school personnel who vetted the school television lineup. In either case, after *They Shall Be Heard* was canceled, the broadcasts produced in cooperation between the city's commercial television stations and the schools were more didactic, featuring science, language, and musical instruction.

Philadelphia's school television program remained the largest in the country and was in its sixth year when *They Shall Be Heard* debuted. The schools continued to produce or coproduce fifteen television shows, including *R Is for Rhythm*, a music presentation for grade school students, and *How Is Your Social IQ?* an etiquette program aimed at high school girls.[53] The Fellowship Commission, however, no longer played a role in these productions, and none of the broadcasts broached potentially controversial topics.

In addressing their respective viewers as consumers and citizens, *Bandstand* and *They Shall Be Heard* were a small part of larger struggle over how consumership and citizenship would be related in the postwar era. Historians Lizabeth Cohen and Charles McGovern have suggested that American identities as "citizen" and "consumer" became linked in the decades before World War II.[54] Organized consumer movements pushed policy makers to see participation in the consumer economy as an essential part of full citizenship. "By the end of the depression decade," Cohen notes, "invoking 'the consumer' had become an acceptable way of promoting the public good, of defending the economic rights and needs of ordinary citizens."[55] In the postwar "consumers' republic," Cohen argues, this connection of citizenship and consumership underscored a belief that a prospering mass consumption economy could foster social egalitarianism and democratic participation. Private consumption became equated with civic duty itself and shaped many parts of postwar American life. Backed by federal policies and public and private investment, these consumer desires shaped where Americans lived, shopped, and went to school.[56]

Bandstand's model of teen television, one focused on the purchasing power of youth, fit neatly into the ethos of postwar consumer citizenship. *Bandstand* invited viewers to the new Main Street of WFIL–adelphia to participate in a consumption community every afternoon. *Bandstand* reminded viewers they were part of this community by repeating the names of the neighborhoods, cities, and towns represented in the studio audience and television audience. This community, however, did not ask viewers to do anything beyond continuing to watch the show and purchase the sponsors' products. *Bandstand* expanded on this shared experience of consumption to become a national commercial success as *American Bandstand*.

The Fellowship Commission, in contrast, wanted *They Shall Be Heard* to be a "public sphere," a space in which to stimulate debate and influence public opinion.[57] Specifically, the Fellowship Commission hoped to increase support for its civil rights message and to persuade viewers to reject racial prejudice and discrimination in housing, education, and employment throughout Philadelphia. The Commission never believed that a television show could resolve all of these problems, but it thought that giving teenagers an opportunity to participate in public discourse on community relations was one way to influence the opinions of people in neighborhoods experiencing changing racial demographics.

Bandstand's model of teen television emerged victorious, in large part, because federal broadcast policy gave advertising-supported programs an advantage over civic-oriented shows. As a result, *Bandstand* broadcast for ten hours a week to the four-state WFIL-adelphia area, whereas *They Shall Be Heard* relied on a system of voluntary cooperation to access the airwaves for just one hour a week. *Bandstand* and *They Shall Be Heard* illustrate, in microcosm, how television contributed to the elevation of consumer culture over civic life.

They Shall Be Heard broke new ground in the field of intercultural education and was among the Fellowship Commission's most innovative attempts to counter racial prejudice in Philadelphia. *They Shall Be Heard*'s cancellation dealt a blow to the Fellowship Commission's anti-discrimination work, but the group redoubled its efforts to improve race relations and end educational inequality in Philadelphia's public high schools. As chapters 3 and 4 show, Maurice Fagan, black educational activist Floyd Logan, and other civil rights advocates confronted the expansion of de facto school segregation. These activists faced the challenge of making de facto school segregation a visible issue in Philadelphia, a challenge compounded by the loss of a television forum like *They Shall Be Heard* in which to articulate these concerns.

CHAPTER 3

The de Facto Dilemma

Fighting Segregation in Philadelphia Public Schools

What has been called by certain groups "de facto segregation" in some schools has not been the result of policy by The
Board of Public Education. [T]he record of the progress of
the Philadelphia Public Schools in the integration movement
is among the best, if not the best, of those of the great cities
of the Nation.

—Allen Wetter, Superintendent of Philadelphia Schools in "For Every
Child: The Story of Integration in the Philadelphia Public Schools,"
October 1960

When the Philadelphia School Board published "For Every Child: The
Story of Integration in the Philadelphia Public Schools" in 1960, it was
the latest and most public rejoinder to the civil rights advocates who criticized the board for failing to address school segregation throughout the
1950s. As school officials continued to issue statements of their progress
on integration, however, the city's public schools grew more racially segregated. Philadelphia illuminates the dilemma posed by de facto school
segregation. While many educational activists used the term *de facto segregation* to describe the discriminatory practices of schools outside the
South, for school board officials *de facto* meant that segregation was the
product of market forces and private decisions beyond their control. Casting de facto segregation as "innocent segregation" allowed school officials
to claim that they had no legal responsibility or power to address it.

The de facto dilemma—visible school segregation with no means of
legal redress—became the defining challenge for civil rights advocates in
the North, Midwest, and West in the 1950s and 1960s. As in Philadelphia, educational activists in Boston, Chicago, Milwaukee, New York,

and other cities fought recalcitrant school officials to secure equal education for black students.[1] In the 1960s, the de facto dilemma also emerged as the dominant roadblock to school integration in the South. While school segregation has traditionally been understood through the dichotomy of de facto and de jure segregation, recent work on Charlotte, Atlanta, Mississippi, and other southern locales suggests that a broad spectrum of white politicians, school officials, and grassroots parents groups took up the language of de facto segregation to justify their inaction on school integration.[2] Rather than public displays of massive resistance, these southern moderates and elites voiced rhetorical support for integration and allowed token black students in white schools, but opposed the methods necessary to integrate schools. The de facto explanation crossed regional lines, providing opponents of school integration a color-blind rhetoric to defend the continuation of segregated education.

Historian Matthew Lassiter describes this de facto rational as the "suburban blueprint on school desegregation" that emerged in the late 1960s.[3] In this view, private housing choices caused segregated schools, and any resulting racial inequality was beyond the scope of governmental responsibility. This way of explaining away school segregation ignored the role of government agencies in supporting residential segregation, as well as the role of school zoning polices and construction practices in creating and maintaining segregated schools. Since the 1970s, the Supreme Court and many lower courts have embraced this view of schools as innocent victims of natural residential segregation, adopting what American studies scholar George Lipsitz calls an "epistemology of ignorance" dependent on the distortion, erasure, and occlusion of the clear and consistent evidence of racially discriminatory policies in education.[4] The de facto rationale, therefore, came to justify a theory of white innocence with regard to school segregation. While the de facto rationale eventually undercut desegregation efforts across the country, educational activists in Philadelphia were among the first to encounter the dilemma it posed.

Unlike other case studies of de facto segregation, Philadelphia was also home to *American Bandstand,* and the city provides a unique example of how schools and television articulated similar visions of segregated youth culture. For black teenagers and civil rights advocates, the city's public schools, like *Bandstand,* became sites of struggle over how to prove and overturn racially discriminatory policies. In their differential treatment of black students and their denial of charges of discrimination, the Philadelphia school board's policies resembled those of

Bandstand's producers. *Bandstand*'s producers, for example, insisted that the show's admissions policy was color-blind, while the school board embraced antidiscrimination rhetoric without committing itself to affirmative steps towards integration. This rhetoric obscured the fact that *Bandstand* consistently excluded black teens from the show's West Philadelphia studio and the school system tracked black students into lower-level curricula. Moreover, while *Bandstand*'s producers took the segregationist side of neighborhood fights over integration in order to present a safe image of youth culture to advertisers, the school board contributed to these neighborhood racial changes only in one direction by building schools in areas that exacerbated de facto school segregation. If *Bandstand* made television an important site of struggle over segregation and the representation of youth culture, Philadelphia's civil rights advocates made public schools sites of struggle over segregation and the daily experiences of young people.

The fight against Philadelphia's school segregation gained momentum in the 1950s thanks to Maurice Fagan of the Fellowship Commission and Floyd Logan of the Educational Equality League. Fagan served as the executive director of the Fellowship Commission, Philadelphia's leading interracial civil rights coalition, and was a major figure in the city's Jewish civil rights community. Fagan was part of a generation of Jewish community workers who turned to intergroup relations as a tool to fight prejudice and keep postwar anti-Semitism at bay.[5] Logan founded the Educational Equality League with fifteen other black citizens in 1932 at the age of thirty-two and was Philadelphia's leading advocate for black students and teachers in the public schools in the 1940s and 1950s. In attempting to reform education in Philadelphia, where the school board was largely isolated from political debates and public opinion and educational issues received little newspaper coverage, Fagan's and Logan's first challenge was to make educational discrimination an issue that resonated with citizens beyond the neighborhood level.[6] Fagan worked to make Philadelphia a focal point for a national network of social scientists interested in prejudice and race relations. He implemented the work of social scientists such as Gunner Myrdal, Kenneth Clark, and Gordon Allport at the grassroots level by partnering with school officials to distribute an array of antidiscrimination education materials. His commitment to addressing prejudice at an individual level, however, prevented Fagan from working to change the school policies that contributed to de facto segregation.

While Fagan attempted to draw national attention to Philadelphia and introduced the language of intercultural education into the school curriculum, Logan used the schools' antidiscrimination rhetoric to call attention to the persistent discrimination against black students in the city's schools. Logan's educational activism took many forms: he investigated individual cases of discrimination on behalf of students and teachers; he collected information on school demographics and facilities to demonstrate inequality; he pushed the school board to take an official position on discrimination and segregation; and through his public letters and reports he served as an unofficial reporter on educational issues for the *Philadelphia Tribune*, the city's leading black newspaper. As the civil rights movement gained national attention, Logan also used events like the Little Rock school integration crisis to call attention to Philadelphia's school segregation and educational inequality. Logan's research and accumulated records on discrimination in the public schools also provided the base of knowledge that the local NAACP branch and other civil rights advocates used to escalate the school segregation issue in the early 1960s. Confronted by Logan and his fellow educational activists, the school board pointed to its adoption of the intercultural educational materials provided by Fagan and the Fellowship Commission as evidence of antidiscrimination progress. The school board played the city's civil rights advocates against each other, adopting the language of intercultural education and declaring success on the question of integration to avoid making the tangible policy changes that would promote integration. Logan's struggle to prove the existence of school discrimination and the school board's manipulation of Fagan's intercultural educational achievements highlight the difficult challenges northern civil rights advocates faced in fighting school segregation.

MAKING PHILADELPHIA THE CAPITAL OF INTERCULTURAL EDUCATION

Set against the backdrop of persistent employment and housing discrimination, schools were not a top-tier issue for most of Philadelphia's civil rights advocates in the 1950s. Breaking racial barriers in the labor and housing markets required considerable resources, and despite making slow and fitful progress on these fronts, the outlook for addressing school discrimination was even less promising. The challenge of fighting discrimination in the schools stemmed largely from the institutional inertia of the city's school board. Many historians have argued that Progressive Era campaigns to "take the schools out of politics" were veiled attempts by elites to take control of school boards away from the ethnic and working-class communities that controlled urban boards in the early twentieth century.[7] While Philadelphia was part of this larger trend, its school board was even more removed from community groups and voters than in other major cities. Unlike cities in which school board members were selected by mayors or chosen in elections, Philadelphia's fifteen-member board of education was selected by a panel of judges, and members could be reappointed for six-year terms as long as they chose to serve. In New York, Chicago, Baltimore, and San Francisco, mayors appointed school board members, while in Los Angeles, Detroit, Cleveland, St. Louis, and Boston members were selected in nonpartisan elections. Only in Washington, D.C., and Pittsburgh, among other major cities, were school boards appointed by a panel of judges as they were in Philadelphia.[8]

In practice, the panel of judges appointed candidates selected by the city's political parties, alternating between Democratic and Republic appointees. Although members were nominally independent from political influence, a 1967 study by City University of New York researchers contended that the school board was "conservative and closely aligned with the city's political leadership" and included "members of the Philadelphia business community who were less concerned with educational policy than they were with avoiding controversy and limiting school expenditures to acceptable levels."[9] School district business manager Add Anderson supervised these expenditures and pleased both political parties by keeping school tax increases as low as possible. Anderson controlled more than two hundred patronage jobs and wielded enormous influence until his death in 1962.[10] The school board setup also insulated the district from investigations by the Commission on Human Relations (CHR), the city's discrimination watchdog group, and isolated the schools from public opinion during Philadelphia's era of civic reform in the early 1950s.[11] "The board is a removed aristocracy, twice removed from popular control," CHR chairmen George Schermer told a reviewer from the U.S. Commission on Civil Rights in 1962. "Its members sit on Olympus, insulated by a board of judges, and insensitive to the popular demands of the school public."[12] A civic groups' description also conveyed the school board's secrecy and insularity:

> The afternoon meetings of the Board of Public Education in Philadelphia are formal and brief, and attendance by the public is limited. Decisions are reached in executive session; discussions of programs rarely take place in public view although wide differences of opinion exist among board members on some issues. The printed minutes of the Board's meetings contain routine adminis-

trative details. In one recent instance where controversy erupted in a public meeting of the board, all reference to the dispute was further expunged.[13]

All of this made the work of civil rights advocates who prioritized the issue of discrimination in schools, like Fagan and Logan, more urgent and difficult.

Confronted with a school board isolated from the daily experiences of the city's students and parents, Fagan worked to strengthen the Fellowship Commission's relationship with the schools in order to implement intercultural educational materials and programs into the curriculum. The Fellowship Commission's relationship with the school system dated back to the Commission's founding in 1941. The first chairman of the Fellowship Commission, William Welsh, was also an assistant superintendent of schools, and Fellowship Commission vice chairmen Tanner Duckrey served as an assistant to the Department of Superintendents, the first African American to serve in this capacity.[14] The Commission started its first school project in September 1944. In this Early Childhood Project, the Fellowship Commission worked with the public schools and consultants from the Bureau for Intercultural Education, a national organization of progressive educators led by William Kilpatrick of Columbia University. The Fellowship Commission and the Bureau for Intercultural Education sought to find a scientific basis for showing that children's attitudes could change, and that teachers who were not experts in intercultural educational methods could help bring about this change.[15] The results of this research were published in 1952 in *They Learn What They Live,* the eighth in a series of ten books produced by the Bureau on Intercultural Education from 1943 to 1954 in its Problems of Race and Culture in American Education series.[16]

The Early Childhood Project received attention in education journals, as well as in Philadelphia newspapers and national newspapers and magazines. The *Philadelphia Evening Bulletin* praised the research for offering "concrete, scientific proof that brotherly love isn't a nebulous out-dated ideal, not even in these tense times."[17] The *New York Times* called the project "pioneer research" that revealed that young children bring to school "definite feelings about race, awareness of religious differences and of the significance of 'we're rich' or 'they're poor.'"[18] More important, the Early Childhood Project helped to establish Philadelphia as a leading national site for intercultural education, and it helped the Fellowship Commission solidify its friendly working relationship with the school system. By 1947, George Trowbridge, chairman of the Fellowship Commission, told those gathered at the annual meeting that "Undoubtedly the most encouraging evidence of successful results in 1946 is to be found in our relationships with the Philadelphia School System."[19] Between the completion of the project in 1948 and the publication of the final report in 1952, the Fellowship Commission continued to strengthen this relationship by organizing intercultural leadership seminars for teachers, principals, and parents and by developing new intercultural education materials as curriculum supplements.

Building on the positive reception to the Early Childhood Project from educational scholars across the country, Fagan believed that this national community of social scientists could be the key to addressing discrimination in Philadelphia's schools. To this end, Fagan dedicated a majority of his time between 1952 and 1954 to developing an ambitious Ford Foundation proposal he believed would further establish Philadelphia as a leader in antidiscrimination education. The proposal called for a thirteen-year plan in which the Fellowship Commission would work with a group of leading social scientists to use Philadelphia as a "laboratory on intergroup relations." The Fellowship Commission proposed to establish eight field offices to study community relations in segregated and integrated neighborhoods. In the central component of this study, human relations experts would follow young people in different neighborhoods from kindergarten through high school. They hoped to examine the development of intergroup attitudes, including whether and how intergroup contact in neighborhoods affected the intercultural education being offered in the schools. Fagan and his colleagues also hoped to use the grant to experiment with new uses of television, building on their teenage television program *They Shall Be Heard*, to "personalize" intercultural education messages.[20] Although the Ford Foundation rejected the six-and-a-half-million-dollar proposal, the request clearly outlines the Fellowship Commission's thinking on intercultural relations in this period.[21] In its focus on ascertaining and changing prejudiced attitudes, the Fellowship Commission's approach to this study mirrored the work of academics who, in the wake of Gunner Myrdal's *An American Dilemma* (1944), published widely on prejudice and social relations, including publications that influenced the *Brown* decision.

Myrdal's thirteen-hundred-page book argued that racism contradicted America's democratic ideals and that the racial dogma that supported racial oppression could be uprooted through education. The Carnegie Corporation, the project's sponsor, had previously paid little attention to domestic race issues, focusing instead on financing educational projects in British colonies in Africa.[22] Carnegie trustees proposed a study of the "Negro problem" in 1935 largely out of concern for rising racial tensions.[23] They picked Myrdal, a Swedish economist with little familiarity with American race relations, to bring an "entirely fresh mind" to the subject. For Carnegie Corporation president Frederick Keppel, this meant breaking with both the "old regime of the South" and the "traditions of the abolitionist movement."[24] Following this directive, Myrdal presented facts about racial violence and oppression in a way that would be palatable for the broadest possible audience. "Myrdal's genius," sociologist Stephen Steinberg argues, "was to dispense only as much medicine as the patient was willing to swallow."[25] Myrdal's book was politically safe because he emphasized moral persuasion rather than specific policies or legislation to challenge racial structures. While Myrdal's anti-prejudice framework helped to delegitimize racism, *An American Dilemma* also obscured frameworks for understanding racism as a result of structural power inequalities.

In contrast, African American historian Rayford Logan (no relation to Floyd Logan) edited *What the Negro Wants*, a collection of fourteen essays including contributions from W. E. B. Du Bois, A. Philip Randolph, Mary McLeod Bethune, and Langston Hughes. Published the same year as *An American Dilemma*, the essays in *What the Negro Wants* focus on the need for African Americans to push for full economic, political, legal, and social equality. These opinions were initially deemed too controversial to print by the editor who commissioned the study. After Logan threatened to take the manuscript to another press and consult an attorney, the editor agreed to publish the book, provided that it contained an introduction disassociating himself from the essays. "What disturbed Mr. Couch [the editor] more than anything else," Logan later wrote, "was the virtual unanimity of the 14 contributors in wanting equal rights for Negroes."[26] Logan's contribution to the collection, "The Negro Wants First-Class Citizenship," clearly outlined six fundamental civil rights demands: "Equality of opportunity; Equal pay for equal work; Equal protection of the laws; Equality of suffrage; Equal recognition of the dignity of the human being; and Abolition of public segregation."[27] Unlike Myrdal, Logan and his fellow essayists framed racism in terms of power and the unequal allocation of resources and life chances. They welcomed education and moral persuasion as tools to fight prejudice, but recognized that these tools alone were insufficient in fighting structural racism. *What the Negro Wants* influenced postwar civil rights activists, but it lacked both the Carnegie Corporation's prestigious imprint and the politically safe message that helped to elevate *An American Dilemma*. Myrdal's anti-prejudice framework became the dominant model for understanding racial problems in this era, and his book shaped the way many political leaders, courts, journalists, and local organizations like the Fellowship Commission talked about racism.[28]

Working in the shadow of Myrdal, Fagan hoped to use social science methods to move beyond "trial and error" approaches to antidiscrimination work by establishing a "sound and scientific basis" for a new "science of intergroup relations."[29] Not coincidentally, several professors of psychology and sociology reviewed drafts of the Fellowship Commission's Ford Foundation proposal and submitted letters of support for the project, including Otto Klineberg and R. M. MacIver of Columbia, Ira Reid of Haverford College, and Gordon Allport of Harvard University, who called the proposal "brilliant and audacious."[30] In submitting this proposal, the Fellowship Commission believed that Philadelphia could provide a model for other cities to follow in dealing with rapidly changing neighborhoods and schools.

Yet while the Fellowship Commission was drawing up plans to use Philadelphia as a national laboratory for community relations, the city's schools grew more segregated. The tension between the Fellowship Commission's ambitions and the city's changing educational situation came out in the group's first meeting to discuss the Ford proposal. Florence Kite, a Society of Friends representative on the Fellowship Commission, questioned Fagan about the intercultural school programs he hoped to make citywide. "What is the point of working on an intercultural human relations program in the high schools . . . when some of our local Philadelphia high schools are segregated?" Kite asked. Kite further questioned Fagan about the utility of intercultural programs "when there is no opportunity for the students to meet other students who are not of their own group, within a given high school." Fagan replied:

> *Both* programs are important, the one of breaking down the pattern of segregated schools where they exists [sic], and, at the same time, affording opportunities in the interim for students from such a homogenous school to mix with students from other groups in such organizations as High School Fellowship, for example. We must find some way of doing both at the same time—for we dare not abandon either approach.[31]

Fagan argued for this dual approach in 1952, but through the mid- and late 1950s the Fellowship Commission dedicated more resources to, and had more success with, its intercultural education programs. Fagan and the Fellowship Commission illustrate, at a local level, the limitations of focusing strictly on education to eliminate prejudice. The Fellowship Commission's strategic decision to focus on prejudiced attitudes rather than the school board's zoning or building policies meant that the burden of fighting de facto desegregation in the city's schools fell almost entirely to Floyd Logan.

FIGHTING DISCRIMINATION AT THE NEIGHBORHOOD LEVEL

While Fagan and the Fellowship Commission worked to make Philadelphia a locus of activity for intercultural educators, Floyd Logan was almost two decades into his work on behalf of black teachers and students. Born in Asheville, North Carolina, Logan attended segregated schools from elementary school through high school. Logan moved to Philadelphia in 1921, where he worked with the U.S. Customs Bureau and later the Internal Revenue Service. In 1932, Logan and fifteen other black Philadelphians founded the Educational Equality League (EEL) with the goals of obtaining and safeguarding "equal education opportunities for all people regardless of race, color, religion, or national origin" and bringing "about interracial integration of pupils, teachers, and other personnel."[32] Logan worked on the issue of employment discrimination against teachers through the late 1930s and the 1940s, and although progress was slow, he helped to secure the merger of racially segregated teacher eligibility lists and helped a small number of black teachers make inroads into junior and senior high schools.[33] During this time, Logan was the EEL's president, spokesman, and chief researcher, and he dedicated himself full-time to this unpaid work when he retired with a government pension in 1955.

Working from his home in West Philadelphia, Logan wrote thousands of letters requesting statistical information from the school board, notifying school and city officials of discrimination encountered by black students and teachers, and reminding officials of promises and policies they had failed to implement.[34] Logan worked occasionally with the Fellowship Commission, the NAACP, the Urban League, and other civil rights advocates, but he was the only one who dedicated himself full-time to educational issues. Logan's work on behalf of black students in these years reveals the inequities of a public school system that, as a result of discriminatory housing practices, the school board's school construction decisions, and the school board's unwillingness to implement affirmative policies for integration, grew more segregated throughout the decade.

Logan first turned his attention to the segregation of students in public schools in November 1947 when he called the first of two conferences with leaders of local civil rights organizations, including the Philadelphia NAACP, the Philadelphia Council of Churches, and the National Conference of Christians and Jews. The members met with school officials to express their "deep concern over the alarming growth of predominant[ly] colored schools in Philadelphia." They also discussed possible legal suits "testing the legality of the practice of segregation on the basis of race in our public schools," but they did not make any progress on this front in the subsequent three years.[35] In early 1951, however, Logan seized on a visiting committee's report on the majority-black Benjamin Franklin High School to lobby for the replacement of its outdated facilities and limited curriculum. In taking up this high school case, Logan addressed the educational level in which black students encountered the widest spectrum of educational discrimination.

Between 1900 and 1950, high school enrollments increased dramatically. Nationally, the percentage of fourteen- to seventeen-year-olds in high school grew from 10 percent in 1900 to 51 percent in 1930 and to 76 percent in 1950. Graduation rates also increased, with the percentage of seventeen-year-olds who completed high school rising from 6 percent in 1900 to 29 percent in 1930 and to 59 percent in 1950.[36] These statistics, however, belie the disparities in the quality of education among Philadelphia's high schools in this era. Among the city's twenty-one high schools, for example, two were application-only academic high schools (Central High School of Philadelphia and Philadelphia High School for Girls), and three were vocational schools (Bok, Dobbins, and Mastbaum). In addition to these official designations, many schools held unofficial reputations related to the racial, ethnic, religious, and socioeconomic characteristics of their neighborhoods and student populations. These reputations were a mix of personal experience, anecdotes, and rumor, but they had real implications for the quality of education offered at different schools. As the U.S. Supreme Court found in *Green v. New Kent County School Board* (1968), racially identifiable schools, where residents knew which schools were "white" schools and which were "black" schools, were a barrier to a unitary school district offering real equality of opportunity.[37] In Philadelphia, schools with bad reputations had difficulty attracting experienced teachers and therefore had a larger number of substitute teachers. These schools were also more likely to lose academically talented students who transferred to schools with better reputations. In addition, if the students who remained at these schools did not score well on IQ tests, administrators were more likely to follow the tenets of life adjustment education and assign students to modified nonacademic curricula. Given the discrimination blacks faced in the city's housing market and the racial prejudice that informed the unofficial reputations of schools, black students were much more likely to attend high schools offering watered-down courses, such as Franklin.

Located in the lower North Philadelphia area, Franklin opened as an all-boys school in 1939. The school occupied a structure built in 1894 to house Central High School, one of the city's two prestigious academic high schools, which moved to the Olney area above North Philadelphia in 1936. In the years after World War II, Franklin operated a daytime high school as well as an evening Veterans School, offering accelerated college preparatory courses and refresher courses for World War II veterans. This Veterans School enrolled more than ten thousand men and women from 1945 to 1955, half of whom continued on to college or technical school.[38]

The students attending Franklin during the day, over 95 percent of whom were black, were not as fortunate. While the school attended to the education of veterans, allocating school board funds to cover library materials and offer supplies not covered by the Veterans Administration, the regular day students attended one of the most poorly funded high schools in the system. In April 1951, a visiting committee from the Middle States Association of School and Colleges catalogued the shortcomings of the school. The committee members noted that Franklin had the worst attendance record in the city and that only 20 to 30 percent of the students who started school in tenth grade graduated. Although the visiting committee made few direct criticisms of the board, the members did criticize what they viewed to be the school board's policy of grouping students with low IQ scores in one school.[39] Logan raised this criticism throughout the 1950s, but the school board, following educational thought of this era, continued to place students in different curriculum tracks based on their IQ scores, junior high school grades, and teacher recommendations.

Illustrative of this educational practice at Franklin was Operation Fix-up. In this program, students went to an "outdoor classroom" built in an alley between row homes in South Philadelphia at Eighteenth and Cleveland Streets to learn about home repairs and home maintenance. With supervision and direction from the Redevelopment Authority and the Citizen's Council on City Planning, the students helped to lay concrete, hang doors, and repair brick outhouses to be used as trash can shelters, among other tasks.[40] Explaining the motivation for Operation Fix-up, Franklin principal Lewis Horowitz told the *Philadelphia Evening Bulletin*:

> We realized that many of our boys would never learn about proper lighting, furnishing, sanitation and the like from their home surroundings. We also suspected that many had not the ability to become workmen in the skilled trades which required long years of training. So we decided to shift the emphasis in our instruction to make it more realistic.[41]

Horowitz's belief in educating "nonacademic" students for the jobs available to them agreed with the tenets of life adjustment education, an outgrowth of the vocational education movement that enjoyed national popularity among high school educators from 1945 to the early 1950s.[42] Historian Herbert Kliebard describes life adjustment education as conveying the "social message" that "each new generation needed to internalize the social status quo."[43] Indeed, with black students and workers blocked from the skilled trades because of discrimination in the school's union-sponsored apprenticeship classes, life adjustment education reinforced discriminatory employment practices.[44] At best, then, this education provided students with training for unskilled construction jobs. At worst, the program increased the education gap between these students and those at other high schools, while normalizing slum clearance and providing urban renewal interests with free labor. In either case, Franklin was unique among Philadelphia high schools in offering this curriculum option.

The poor conditions at Franklin did not come as a surprise to Logan or to black teenagers and parents in the Franklin school community. However, the Middle States report offered Logan an opportunity to bring more attention to the inequities of segregated education. Logan wrote letters to the *Philadelphia Tribune* and the *Philadelphia Inquirer*, and both papers ran articles quoting the visiting committee's description of Franklin as a "Jim Crow school."[45] Building on this publicity, Logan next organized a conference on the "Democratization of Philadelphia Public Schools." On October 15, 1951, forty civic and cultural organizations, including the NAACP, black fraternities and sororities, and the Jewish Community Relations Council, met at the Fellowship Commission building to discuss how to break down segregation in the public schools. Discussing issues of zoning, teacher placement, and curriculum, the groups started to draw up resolutions to present to the school board. Logan and his colleagues recommended that the board state its policy with regard to integration, that teachers be assigned based on qualifications rather than race, and that intercultural ideals expressed in curriculum publications be implemented in zoning and put into practice in the classroom. These recommendations remained the focal points of Logan's work for the next decade.[46]

Only three days after these resolutions were drafted, an incident at West Philadelphia High School (WPHS) broadened the scope of Logan's critique of the public schools and increased his sense of the urgency of bringing these policy recommendations to the board. The principal at West Philadelphia High School, George Montgomery, singled out the schools' black students and blamed them for increased crime in the school and the city.[47] At a pep rally before the afternoon football game the next day, black students, who made up 30 percent of the student body, protested the principal's remarks by sitting silently. That same day, a group of parents met with the principal to discuss his remarks. Among these parents were Granville Jones, a black Democratic state representative whose three children attended WPHS, and the Reverend E. Luther Cunningham, the treasurer of the NAACP branch and a board member of the Fellowship Commission, whose daughter was present at the assembly. In addition to these black leaders, other parents sent letters of concern to Floyd Logan and the NAACP asking them to address this issue with the school board. "I have written to most of the papers and done all I can at the present," one parent wrote. "This is not right because we help to pay [the principal's] salary too. Is this supposed to be where all are created equal and where ours as well as theirs die in wars for this country?"[48] On October 26, representatives of the NAACP and the EEL met the school superintendent Louis Hoyer. "In a very few moments [the principal] has created a segregated school. . . . He has set aside one group of the student body to be looked at with contempt as a [minority] group," Walter Gay Jr., an attorney representing the EEL, told the superintendent.[49] The Reverend Jesse Anderson, a member of the Fellowship Commission and the minister of the West Philadelphia Episcopal parish, pointed out the gap between the school board's intercultural rhetoric and the principal's comments. "A goodly segment of the authorities, principals and teacher of this school system . . . have been getting away with literal murder in their handling of minority groups," Anderson said. "I fail to see how you reconcile the inept racial attitude and expression of the principal with the beautiful pamphlets entitled

'Democracy in Action,' 'Living Together,' and 'Openmindedness.' "[50] Gay and Anderson concluded by asking for Montgomery's resignation. Superintendent Hoyer said that he regretted the principal's comments, but that he would need to meet with Montgomery before he could make a decision.

In November 1951, the education committee of the NAACP and the EEL met to develop a plan to rid Philadelphia schools of discrimination. On December 15, at a second meeting with members of the school board, the committee from the NAACP and the EEL offered a plan for improvements at WPHS. The committee requested that Montgomery be removed, citing a loss of confidence of parents, students, and the community. They asked that black teachers be integrated into the school's all-white faculty. Arguing that the primary job of the public school was "to teach the children of *all* the people," the committee also called for an end to watered-down classes for black students deemed by teachers to be "slum" children. Finally, the committee requested that specific steps be taken to improve "human relations" at WPHS, including in-service courses in intercultural education for administrators and teachers, community meetings for parents, adult education courses in intercultural education, the integration of black pupils into extracurricular activities at the school, and the organization of a fellowship club for students.[51] As would become the pattern in the school board's dealings with Logan, an official response was deferred until a later date.

Having not received a decision by the end of the 1952 school year, Logan appeared before the school board again on June 10. Gladys Thomas, the Philadelphia NAACP's education director, and Dr. Marshall Shepard, a Baptist minister from West Philadelphia, represented the EEL. Logan reiterated the EEL's requests for a policy on integration, for further integration of teachers at the senior high school level, and for zoning to promote desegregation. To emphasize his request that Franklin should be closed and replaced with a new building, Logan recounted that on a recent visit to the school's auditorium, "it seemed more like the auditorium of a backwoods Southern school than part of a Philadelphia high school, and . . . the board should be ashamed to maintain a high school in that condition." Moreover, he argued, bringing more equality to the schools would "deprive the Communists of their main source of propaganda and strength."[52] Following Logan, Shepard criticized the board for requesting more facts on discrimination in the schools, after Logan had already distributed a twenty-point list of statistics on segregation the previous year. "It [is] most unnecessary for us to tell the Board what it already [knows]," Shepard stated directly.[53] Again, the board referred the EEL's proposals to its policy committee for further study.

Following the meeting, Walter Biddle Saul, an attorney and the president of the school board, invited Logan and the other EEL members to an off-the-record conference with a smaller group of school officials. Saul opened the meeting by telling Logan that the EEL was wrong to refer to any schools as segregated schools. Saul further contended that "colored schools were such because of population," that Logan "could not expect the schools to compel children to attend schools where they do not live," that "state law requires the Board to accord to parents the right to send their children to schools of their choice," and that many black parents favored having this option.[54] Logan countered by arguing that Saul's critiques did not meet the "serious study and consideration" promised by the board. Logan's minutes from the meeting suggest that Saul conceded this point and appointed the school board's policy committee chairwoman to study these "undemocratic problems" (Logan's minutes also note the incongruity of Saul's appointing a committee to study the problems that he had earlier declared not to exist).[55] Before the close of the meeting, Saul stressed that he was opposed to the EEL's publicizing these issues. Similarly, the school's policy chairwoman said that the study would take at least four to five months, during which she hoped that her committee would not be under "too much pressure" from the EEL.[56]

While he waited for the completed report, Logan sent the committee more examples of discrimination in school zoning, classroom practices, and administrative appointments. After nine months, the school committee informed Logan that it had finished the report and invited him and other EEL members to a meeting on June 24, 1953. Logan later told the *Philadelphia Tribune*: "Though we were not overly optimistic of the investigation, we nevertheless felt that it would be at least fair."[57] After two years of waiting for the school board to take action on his evidence of discrimination in the schools, Logan was deeply disappointed with the report submitted by the committee. The report directly contradicted each of the points the EEL had raised: The school committee argued that the board's teacher policies were in accord with the city's Fair Employment Practices Ordinance, that there was no evidence of racial gerrymandering of district boundaries, that race was not a consideration in student transfers, and that white students were not transported by school bus to avoid majority black schools.[58] After outlining these points, the committee went on to argue that the problem of integration was made "very much more acute and more difficult by the recent large Negro migration into Philadelphia," and that black leaders had a responsibility to orient these "new Negro citizens to urban life and acceptable community behavior." In addition to faulting black migrants for segregation, the school's policy committee praised the school's curriculum committee for undertaking "various projects to alleviate prejudice and neighborhood racial tensions through its courses on 'Living Together' and 'Open-Mindedness.'"[59]

For Logan, the problem with the committee's report was that it was unwilling either to recognize the trend toward racial segregation in the schools or to recognize that the school board could take any steps to stem this trend. As Logan wrote to the chairwoman of the committee after the disappointing meeting, "we must sound a note of warning on the dangerous trend toward predominant and all colored schools. Many possibilities exist for reducing this trend and they should be explored. Specifically the Board must adopt a policy of planned mixing of as many students as population distribution will permit."[60] As he frequently did in his correspondence with school officials, Logan followed this recommendation with an appeal for the schools to live up to their antidiscrimination rhetoric. "Adoption by our Board of such democratic policies," Logan wrote, "will put into practice our excellent intercultural courses [and in] this way we will be living 'democracy,' as well as teaching it."[61] As the school year began in 1953, Logan and his fellow educational activists in the EEL and NAACP finished a two-year encounter with the school board, in which time they saw little progress. Despite his frustration over the school board's delays and refusal to address the policies that contributed to segregation, Logan continued to petition for an official policy on integration and pressed school officials to hold to their promise of building a new Franklin High School.

By 1953, the Philadelphia school board had crafted a solid defense for de facto segregation. First, it argued that segregated schools were the result of segregated housing patterns, over which it had no control. The naturalness of housing segregation became the centerpiece of the de facto rationale school officials in the North, Midwest, and West used to claim innocence with regard to school segregation. The de facto rationale replaced massive resistance in the South and has informed court decisions on school segregation since the early 1970s. This fiction of voluntary housing choice imposed an extremely difficult challenge for groups contesting school segregation. As desegregation expert Gary Orfield contends:

> The school districts, which try to use housing as a justification for school segregation, often have the money to create what appears to be plausible evidence that local segregation is a product of choice by minority and white families, not discrimination. The plaintiffs usually lack the money to prove the history of housing discrimination. They cannot document the vicious cycles that led to those "choices." They often lack the expertise to attack the validity of flawed survey data assessing the issues of guilt and remedy. Some courts adopt as facts what are speculative interpretations of misleading data used for inappropriate purposes.[62]

Although the NAACP did not file a lawsuit against school segregation in Philadelphia until 1961, Logan started gathering evidence in the late 1940s that he hoped would prove that racial segregation and unequal schools existed and were the result of official policy. Like Logan, educational activists in Boston, Los Angeles, New York, Chicago, and other cities faced off against school boards that maintained racial segregation while also denying its existence.[63] The Philadelphia School Board thwarted the work of Logan and his fellow civil rights advocates by delaying action on proposals, holding off-the-record meetings, appointing internal committees to study the problem, and publishing reports that contradicted the evidence offered by critics.[64] Outside the sight of the mainstream press and most citizens, these exchanges took place between a small group of school officials and the civil rights advocates who refused to let the issue be ignored. Without making any public statements favoring segregation, the school board honed a de facto rationale to avoid taking actions to integrate the schools.

In addition to holding up residential segregation to explain school segregation, the Philadelphia school board also argued that it was being especially proactive in creating better racial attitudes among its students. The schools' anti-prejudice curriculum efforts, it argued, were far more progressive than those found in other cities and constituted a sufficient response to the racial change in the city's schools. Here, the school board co-opted the antidiscrimination rhetoric that Fagan and the Fellowship Commission were working to implement. The ease with which the school officials embraced intercultural education and sidestepped integration highlights the limits of the Fellowship Commission's educational approach to discrimination. As Logan made increasingly vocal demands for the school board to address school segregation, much of the Fellowship

Commission's energy went into the Ford Foundation proposal and related intercultural education programs. The Fellowship Commission assigned the task of developing a position on segregated schools to its Fair Education Opportunities Committee, headed by Nathan Agran of the Jewish Community Relations Council and Walter Wynn of the Urban League (the committee's minutes note that Fagan attended the majority of the monthly meetings, but that Logan attended only twice in a three-year period). The committee dedicated meetings in January and February 1953 to the question of segregated schools, citing segregated housing and pupil transfers from "mixed" schools as primary causes.[65] The committee only discussed the issue periodically over the next two years, focusing more attention on removing discriminatory quotas in college and professional school admissions, and later on pushing for a city community college.

Beyond allocating time to other forms of educational discrimination, the school board's rejection of Logan's proposals in 1953 influenced the Fellowship Commission's shift of attention to admissions quotas. "The Executive Committee decided about two years ago to postpone approaches to the School System on the matter of 'one-group' schools," Fellowship Commission chairman David Ullman noted in April 1955.[66] Fagan and the other members of the Fellowship Commission were reluctant to jeopardize their close relationship with the public schools. When Fagan wrote to the new president of the school board Leon Obermayer in 1955 to request support for the Ford proposal, for example, he proclaimed that "The Fellowship Commission has demonstrated over the past fourteen years that it will not usurp the prerogatives of the educator and that it can be and is one of the staunchest champions of the School System."[67] While this approach allowed the Fellowship Commission to influence the classroom experience in many schools through intercultural education seminars and materials, it also meant that the largest civil rights organization in Philadelphia, during its most influential period, failed to address one of the most significant civil rights issues in the city. More insidiously, the school board took up the Fellowship Commission's antidiscrimination language to reject Logan's calls for an affirmative policy on integration. Even before the Supreme Court's *Brown* decision led southern politicians and segregationists to develop their strategies for massive resistance, the Philadelphia school board used a combination of tactics to position itself as antidiscrimination while supporting policies that contributed to de facto schools segregation.

BUILDING A SEGREGATED SCHOOL SYSTEM

The school board's refusal to develop a policy on de facto segregation was based on the claim that school segregation was a housing-related development beyond the board's control. Despite this assertion, the school board's construction decisions after World War II exacerbated segregation in the city's schools and made Logan's work even more difficult. Of the twenty-two new elementary, junior high, and senior high schools built after World War II, all but three were built in either new suburbanizing white neighborhoods on the city's outskirts or in expanding black neighborhoods. As a result, school site selection was the determining factor in creating one-group schools that were almost all white or all black.[68]

These school placement decisions followed logically from governmental policies, initiated during the New Deal, that facilitated residential segregation in private and public housing. In Philadelphia's private housing market, less than 1 percent of new construction was available to black home buyers in the 1950s.[69] These racially distinct housing markets, supported by government dollars and abetted by the lack of federal and local antidiscrimination oversight on housing, provided the foundation for the de facto rational for segregated schools. White homeowners and renters who expected to live in racially homogeneous neighborhoods saw their preferences reflected in the school construction decisions. For black parents, new construction relieved school overcrowding, but given the school board's history of second-class treatment of majority-black schools, siting schools in mostly black neighborhoods was a mixed blessing.

A leading concern for black parents and educational activists like Logan was that students at majority black schools would receive a lower quality of education than that available at majority white schools. Their concerns were well founded because the racial demographics of schools were an important factor in determining the curricular options available to students. The most glaring examples of the relationship among school construction, de facto segregation, and school curriculum are Northeast High School, Thomas Edison High School, and Franklin High School. The students at the all-boys Northeast High School attended one of the best public schools in the city. The school opened in 1905, but the school's history dated to the 1890s when it operated as the Northeast Manual Training School. With a focus on engineering rather than a strictly academic curriculum, the school became the second most prestigious public school for young men in Philadelphia, trailing only Central High School.[70] By the early 1950s, the school had a well-developed alumni network that raised money to provide college loans to students and awards for championship sports teams.[71] In the fifty years since the school opened at Eighth Street and Lehigh Avenue in North Philadelphia, the racial demographics of the neighborhood changed from majority white to a mix of white ethnic groups and black residents. As a result, unlike many other schools in the city, Northeast's student body in the mid-1950s was evenly divided between black and white students.

All of this changed in February 1957. Halfway through the school year, two-thirds of the teachers and a number of students left the school at Eighth and Lehigh for a new Northeast High in the fast-growing suburban neighborhoods at the edge of the city. The school board and Northeast's alumni started discussing the new high school in the early 1950s, but for most of the teachers and students left behind at the old school (renamed Thomas Edison High School), the move happened abruptly. Almost overnight, the school's name, most experienced teachers, and alumni network disappeared. The black and working-class white students who attended Northeast High School as sophomores and juniors in 1955 and 1956 were left to graduate from Thomas Edison High School when the new Northeast High opened in February of their senior year. The students left behind at Edison selected "hiatus" as their senior yearbook theme. This yearbook also showed that the new Northeast High secretively moved the school's athletic trophies. While the yearbooks of the previous graduating class described the trophy case as "the symbol of the greatness of our school," the "hiatus" seniors used before and after pictures of the full and empty trophy case to depict the loss of the most visible daily evidence of the school's history.[72]

The Northeast section of Philadelphia expanded rapidly in the 1940s and 1950s, with new tract homes, shopping centers, and industrial parks replacing farmland. Almost all of the area's population increase came from white families, many of whom moved from racially changing neighborhoods in other parts of the city. The Northeast's small number of black residents lived in sections that dated back over a hundred years, but other black and Chinese American families who sought to move into the Northeast section were met with protests by white homeowners.[73] Real estate agents turned away several black families who sought to move to Northeast neighborhoods in the late 1950s, claiming that they "were not accepting any colored applicants" or that they had been "instructed not to sell to anyone . . . that might disturb

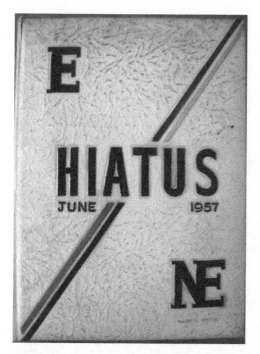

FIGURE 11. The students who attended Northeast High School as sophomores and juniors were left to graduate from Thomas Edison High School when the new Northeast High School opened in February of their senior year. They selected "hiatus" as their yearbook theme. June 1957. Philadelphia School District Archives.

the neighborhood."[74] In addition, historian Guian McKee has shown how the Northeast benefited from Philadelphia's industrial renewal program, which decentralized the city's industry by building and renovating industrial areas. New industrial parks in the Northeast were not accessible by subway, trolley, or commuter rail, and McKee argues that "this orientation towards automobile transportation reinforced preexisting patterns of employment discrimination."[75] The racial segregation of Northeast High, therefore, followed housing and employment discrimination and was not the result of innocent private decisions.

The case of Edison and Northeast reflected the growing divide between public schools in affluent neighborhoods and those in working-class and poor communities. Although both schools were technically in the same school system, Northeast represented a process of suburbanization within city lines. The U.S. Supreme Court ruling against cross-district metropolitan desegregation plans in *Milliken v. Bradley* (1974), and the continued defense of de facto segregation by courts, politicians, and parents, meant that this school inequality became commonplace nationally. Educational scholar Jeannie Oakes describes this process of providing already advantaged students with more advantages as a process

FIGURES 12 AND 13. Before and after pictures depict the loss of the school's trophies and history. The prior class's yearbook described the trophy case as "the symbol of the greatness of our school." June 1957. Philadelphia School District Archives.

of "multiplying inequalities" that facilitates and rationalizes "the inter-
generational transfer of social, educational, and political status and
[constrains] social and economic mobility."[76] Northeast High's enrollment criteria made this transfer of privilege explicit. The school board
limited enrollment in the new high school to students from this suburban Northeast area, and two-thirds of the first fifteen hundred students
at the school transferred from Olney High School, Lincoln High School,
and Frankford High School, which were also between 97 percent and
99 percent white.[77] Among students from the old Northeast High (Edison High School), only those whose grandfathers were alumni of the
school could transfer. This policy left the working-class black and white
students at Edison High School to be taught by inexperienced and substitute teachers. While the new Northeast High School was built in a
sprawling campus style that resembled suburban schools being built in
Pennsylvania and New Jersey, Edison students were left with the aging
building formerly occupied by Northeast High.[78]

Neither Northeast's alumni nor the school board ever explicitly mentioned school segregation as the motivation for building the new Northeast High School. William Loesch, an alumnus of the school and banker
who sat on the school board, had lobbied school administrators to consider building a new Northeast High since Central High School received
a new building in 1939.[79] The alumni association advanced this campaign in 1954 when it met with Add Anderson, the school board's business manager, who controlled the budget for new school construction. In
approving the plans for a new Northeast High, Anderson cited the need
for a high school to serve the growing population in the "Greater Northeast" section of the city.[80] Commenting on school construction in 1962,
school superintendent Allen Wetter also argued that "population" and
"cost" were the main considerations, and that "the segregation issue was
no factor at all in the making of . . . recommendations for new schools."[81]
In letters and phone calls with Floyd Logan, moreover, both Anderson
and Wetter continued to insist that the school's building policy was
color-blind and that school segregation was a housing-related development beyond the school's control.[82] The case of Northeast High belies
these claims. By choosing to build a new high school in the suburban
section of the city, the school board created a school that enrolled
99 percent white students through the mid-1960s. The drastically dis-
similar racial demographics at Northeast High and Edison High were
indicative of the growing segregation in Philadelphia's public high
schools in these years. By 1961, while the total high school population

was 34 percent black, four schools were over 90 percent black, and seven schools were over 90 percent white.[83] Despite the race-neutral rhetoric, the school board's construction decisions built and maintained de facto segregated schools like Northeast High.

In building the new Northeast High, the school board not only exacerbated school segregation; it also left students at Edison High with a limited range of course offerings. Whereas the school once offered a full range of academic, commercial, and trade courses, the students at Edison were channeled into lower-level vocational courses like paper hanging, painting, simple woodwork, and upholstery.[84] These limited curricular options were commonplace at majority-black high schools in the city, where school officials used IQ tests to determine the appropriate tracks for students. One such school, Franklin High, provides an important counterpoint to the experience of the new Northeast High.

After five years of pressure from Logan, the school board started construction on a new Franklin High School in 1955. Although construction on Northeast High and Franklin started in the same year and both new buildings cost $6 million, the types of education offered within these buildings differed dramatically. While the students at Northeast High took college preparatory courses and commercial courses that would prepare them for employment, most students at Franklin were offered the same watered-down vocational options as students at Edison. Logan tried to address these inadequacies before the board released architectural plans for the new building.[85] As the new high school building neared completion in September 1959, Logan, along with the Reverend William Ischie and the Reverend Leon Sullivan, pastor of Zion Baptist Church in North Philadelphia, met with school board members to demand that students at this new building not receive the same unequal education offered to students for years at Franklin.[86] Wetter again dismissed Logan's demands, arguing that Franklin was not districted on a racial basis and that it was the policy of the schools to gear course instruction to the capacity of the students, as determined by IQ tests.[87] Using this policy, the school board rated Franklin High as a "minus" school because the average student IQ score was twenty points below the city average. The plus and minus ratings were unpublished, but in his research Logan learned that the school board listed most all-black and majority-black schools in the minus category.[88] These IQ-based ratings dictated that the curriculum available to students at Franklin High would be different from that at Northeast High. Across the school system, this curriculum differentiation most often meant that administrators tracked

TABLE 3   PERCENTAGE OF BLACK STUDENTS IN PHILADELPHIA HIGH SCHOOLS BY DISTRICT, 1956–1965

Percentage of Black Students in Philadelphia High Schools by District, 1956–1965

	1956	1957	1958	1959	1960	1961	1962	1963	1964	1965
District 1										
Bartram	27%	30%	32%	35%	41%	45%	48%	48%	49%	56%
West Philadelphia	68%	73%	79%	85%	92%	97%	98%	97%	99%	99%
District 2										
Franklin	90%	91%	93%	91%	91%	91%	93%	96%	94%	96%
Girls' High	26%	22%	19%	16%	16%	18%	18%	18%	20%	22%
William Penn	91%	93%	95%	95%	96%	95%	97%	95%	96%	97%
District 3										
South Philadelphia	15%	16%	17%	15%	16%	17%	19%	24%	31%	40%
Bok Voc. - Tech.	66%	66%	71%	71%	75%	78%	81%	83%	86%	89%
District 4										
Gratz	84%	86%	93%	96%	95%	99%	99%	99%	100%	99%
Overbrook	52%	48%	46%	48%	50%	54%	54%	57%	62%	73%
Dobbins Voc. - Tech.	30%	31%	35%	39%	41%	45%	43%	44%	45%	46%
District 5										
Edison	48%	52%	54%	56%	52%	58%	54%	61%	67%	72%
Kensington	39%	43%	42%	45%	46%	42%	40%	43%	47%	50%
Mastbaum Voc. - Tech.	3%	3%	3%	3%	4%	4%	4%	5%	5%	6%

(*continued*)

TABLE 3 (*continued*)

	Percentage of Black Students in Philadelphia High Schools by District, 1956–1965									
	1956	1957	1958	1959	1960	1961	1962	1963	1964	1965
District 6										
Central	5%	5%	6%	6%	6%	6%	7%	7%	8%	10%
Germantown	33%	33%	32%	32%	35%	41%	41%	44%	50%	63%
Roxborough	4%	4%	4%	4%	5%	4%	4%	4%	6%	11%
Wissahickon Farm	9%	12%	13%	19%	13%	17%	14%	15%	19%	32%
District 7										
Frankford	3%	3%	3%	3%	3%	3%	3%	3%	3%	5%
Olney	0%	1%	1%	1%	2%	3%	4%	7%	10%	20%
District 8										
Lincoln	1%	1%	1%	1%	1%	1%	1%	1%	1%	2%
Northeast	NA	1%	1%	1%	1%	1%	1%	1%	1%	1%
Total	30%	30%	30%	39%	32%	34%	34%	36%	39%	48%

SOURCE: Philadelphia Board of Education, Division of Research, "A Ten-Year Summary of the Distribution of Negro Pupils in the Philadelphia Public Schools, 1957–1966," December 23, 1966, FL collection, Acc 469, box 23, folder 6, TUUA; "Number of Negro Teachers and Percentage of Negro Students in Philadelphia Senior High Schools, 1956–1957 [n.d.]," FL collection, Acc 469, box 14, folder 10, TUUA.

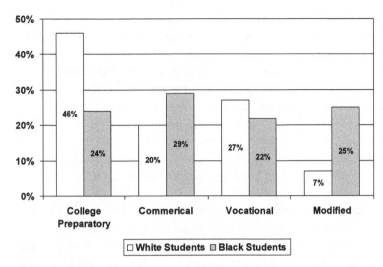

CHART I
SOURCE: William Odell, "Educational Survey Report for the Philadelphia Board of Public Education," February 1965, Philadelphia School District Archives.

black students into courses that limited their prospects for future employment and higher education.[89]

Aware of the dangers of racialized tracking, Logan continued to press Wetter regarding the academic reorganization of Franklin. "In approving the expenditures of more than $6,000,000 for creation of the new Benjamin Franklin High School," Logan wrote, "it is evident that the Board of Public Education had in mind an improved type of high school, not only in building and facilities, but in curriculum, student body, and so forth. . . . Otherwise, if the status quo is maintained, the expenditure of such a large sum of money will not be justified."[90] Logan's concern was prescient. Months before the school board officially dedicated the new building in May 1961, the first class of students to attend classes in the new building prepared for graduation. Only 21 of the 151 students (14 percent) who started three years earlier graduated.[91] Echoing the growing literature on the low educational achievement of "culturally deprived" minority children in urban schools, the *Philadelphia Evening Bulletin* placed the blame for this low graduation rate on the school's student body. The *Bulletin's* editorial argued that Franklin's students came from "'migrant families' . . . newly arrived from the Deep South," that many grew up in "homes in which there never has been a recognized father or husband," and that in Franklin's "sanitary halls, under the authority of its educated and gentlemanly faculty, some students experienced their only real contact with civilization."[92] Logan criticized the *Bulletin's* attempts to blame Franklin's students in a letter to Wetter and several newspapers. In the letter, Logan also reminded Wetter of his promise to reorganize and expand the curriculum at Franklin to include programs in mathematics, science, and foreign language, and to publicize these changes to the community in a brochure.[93] In the fall of 1961, as a result of Logan's years of work and a citywide increase in academic guidance programs at mostly black high schools, the board introduced new curriculum options at Franklin, and graduation rates at the school increased slowly through the early 1960s.

The limited educational opportunities available to black and working-class students at Edison and Franklin were not anomalies, but rather were in line with the school board's curriculum tracking policies. Although the school board publicly stated that IQ tests, not race, were the criteria for this tracking, race often came to stand in as evidence of the limited potential of students in majority-black schools. In a letter describing Edison High to a member of an outside evaluation committee, for example, Wetter wrote: "because the population of the school is about half Negro there are many slow learning pupils."[94] Whether through test scores or assumptions about performance made by teachers and counselors, administrators disproportionately tracked black students into lower-level programs. Drawing on her two decades of research, Jeannie Oakes shows that tracking labels, once affixed to students, are difficult to overcome and shape how teachers view students, as well as how students view their peers and themselves. "Because public schools are governmental agencies," Oakes argues, "tracking is a governmental action that classifies and separates students and thereby determines the amount, the quality, and even the value of the government service (education) that students receive."[95] The school board's decision to build schools in parts of the city where they were guaranteed to be one-group schools, such as Northeast and Franklin, was a double injury for black students because racially isolated schools maintained de facto segregation and naturalized curriculum tracking on the basis of race.

Logan's fight to equalize curricular options in mostly black schools ran up against the national push for high schools to group young people based on standardized test scores and to focus attention on the highest scoring teenagers. James Conant's nationally published reports on education, *The American High School Today* (1959) and *Slums and Suburbs* (1961), were at the forefront of this push for more testing and tracking.[96] While Conant was a prolific writer and speaker on educational issues during and after his tenure as president of Harvard University from 1933 to 1953, *The American High School Today* and *Slums and Suburbs* reached a broad popular audience. Funded by the Carnegie Corporation and published by McGraw-Hill, the reports were treated as news stories rather than academic reports. To this end, a meticulously planned media campaign accompanied Conant's work and garnered favorable stories in *Life, Look, Newsweek, Time,* and *U.S. News and World Report.*[97] In these nationally published reports, Conant endorsed more extensive standardized testing that would enable counselors to precisely identify students' abilities and guide them to appropriate courses of study. Through this method, he suggested, the comprehensive high school could remain true to its meritocratic mission by fine-tuning the process of curriculum differentiation. While he emphasized the benefits of curriculum differentiation for students at all ability levels, the majority of Conant's recommendations focused on improving the quality of education offered to "gifted" students.

Conant's reports had influence because they were timely and pragmatic. His first report was published in the wake of the launch of the Soviet Sputnik space satellite in October 1957. Concerned that the United States was losing the cold war because of a failing school system, Congress passed the National Defense Education Act (NDEA) in 1958. The NDEA allocated millions of dollars to improve science, math, and foreign language training and to better educate gifted students. In this context, Conant's recommendations to expand ability grouping, increase the number of counselors, and emphasize the training of gifted students largely overlapped with the educational practices already in place at high schools across the country.[98] In addition to endorsing the existing practices of guidance and grouping, Conant also avoided the controversial subject of integration in *The American High School Today*. When he addressed the issue in *Slums and Suburbs,* he argued that improving vocational programs should take precedence over integration: "Antithetical to our free society as I believe *de jure* segregation to be, I think it would be far better for those who are agitating for the deliberate mixing of children to accept *de facto* segregated schools as a consequence of a present housing situation and to work for the improvement of slum schools."[99] As was the case with Conant's other educational recommendations, many school officials embraced his position on segregation because it required little immediate action. In Philadelphia, the educational status quo Conant endorsed meant that teenagers would continue to attend high schools that were both highly segregated and rigidly differentiated in terms of curricular options and access to college.

The post-Sputnik emphasis on testing and tracking dovetailed with the national discourse of cultural deprivation. From the late 1950s through the end of the 1960s, educators and social scientists published books and articles and held conferences and seminars on the topic of cultural deprivation. They sought to examine, explain, and remedy the lagging academic skills of low-income students and students of color in urban schools. While cultural deprivation research influenced policy makers and professional educators and reached a wide popular audience, the term acquired its strength from its vagueness. Some commentators, like Conant, used *cultural deprivation* as a synonym for *slum*, and called for larger and better staffs and more money for schools in these areas.[100] Other researchers used the term to describe what they called the "cultural differences" between racial and socioeconomic groups.

The Research Conference on Education and Cultural Deprivation, held at the University of Chicago in June 1964, for example, gathered over thirty leading social scientists and received financial support from the U.S. Office of Education. The authors of the conference report noted that they used the term "culturally disadvantaged or culturally deprived because we believe the roots of their problem may in large part be traced to their experiences in homes which do not transmit the cultural patterns necessary for the types of learning characteristic of the schools and the larger society."[101] While the report's recommendations laid the groundwork for school breakfast and lunch programs and Head Start preschool education for low-income children, the authors offered few specific ideas regarding curricular guidelines, materials, or methods to improve academic performance. Moreover, the report's emphasis on the deficits of low-income students omitted any discussion of the students' talents or recommendations for structural changes to schools.[102]

As the conference report influenced federal educational policies, Frank Riessman's *The Culturally Deprived Child* (1962) was being widely used in teacher preparation programs and was reaching a broad popular audience. Riessman, a professor of education and psychology at New York University, contended that the number of culturally deprived children in the nation's largest cities had increased from one in ten in 1950 to one in three in 1960. "Effective education of the 'one in three' who is deprived," he argued, "requires a basic, positive understanding of his traditions and attitudes."[103] Riessman critiqued educators for seeking to make low-income students into "replicas of middle-class children" and encouraged teachers to develop an "empathetic understanding" of "culturally deprived" students.[104] Yet, as Riessman sought to refocus the approach of schools to educating low-income students, he also implied that "lower-class culture" and "middle-class culture" were clearly defined and delineated ways of life.[105]

While these cultural deprivation researchers differed in their recommendations, their cultural approach to educational performance allowed other commentators to use students' backgrounds as a deterministic explanation for academic failure. The Philadelphia school board, for example, picked up cultural deprivation theories in its curricular recommendations. Emphasizing that "everyone is different," a 1962 Philadelphia public school report outlined curriculum plans for three groups of students: a college preparatory course for the "academically talented," commercial and vocational curricula for "student[s] who will enter the world of work" after graduation, and a modified course for "slower learning" or "culturally deprived" students.[106] Philadelphia's schools, therefore, remained devoted to tracking in the early 1960s and continued to disproportionately track black students away from the academic programs and into the modified curriculum.

Despite this racialized tracking and the increased number of segregated schools, the school board continued to be proactive in its insistence that it did not discriminate against black students or support segregated schools. A 1960 report prepared by Wetter, "For Every Child: The Story of Integration in the Philadelphia Public Schools," made this point emphatically. While Logan and other civil rights advocates began discussing potential legal action to force the board to address de facto segregation, Wetter praised the board's early adoption of intercultural education materials as evidence of progress on integration. "As early as 1943," Wetter recounted, "the Superintendent of Schools led the way for the development of a comprehensive program in human relations."[107] Here again, the school board manipulated the Fellowship Commission's intercultural education efforts to deflect criticism and delay action on school segregation. Wetter also contended that "what has been called by certain groups 'de facto segregation' in some schools has not been the result of policy of The Board of Public Education," but that "the record of progress of the Philadelphia Public Schools in the integration movement is among the best, if not the best, of those of the great cities of the Nation." The Philadelphia school board refused to back down from the de facto rationale that school segregation was the result of private housing decisions for which the board had no power or responsibility.

In the 1950s, civil rights advocates who fought educational discrimination in Philadelphia's public schools met far more defeats than victories. The work of Maurice Fagan, Floyd Logan, and the numerous activists and parents who challenged prejudice and inequality in schools is instructive for what it reveals about the challenges of fighting de facto school segregation. Black Philadelphians and their allies faced a de facto dilemma that has emerged as the fundamental barrier to integrated and equal education in the half-century since *Brown*. Everyone could see that schools were becoming more racially segregated, and there was substantial evidence that these racially separate schools were not equal. Yet foes of de facto segregation, in Philadelphia and elsewhere, lacked legal redress.

Logan and Fagan challenged discrimination on a student-by-student and school-by-school basis, while also looking beyond the neighborhood level to change school board policies. Their tactics helped to secure new school buildings, introduce intercultural educational materials in the curriculum, and, to a limited extent, expand curriculum programs at majority-black schools. Their efforts were overwhelmed, however, by discriminatory housing policies that produced residential segregation and the school board's refusal to admit that its school construction, zoning, and transfer policies contributed to segregation, or that it should take any affirmative steps to address this segregation. While these educational advocates struggled to change school policy, as the next chapter shows, they also waged a media battle to convince their fellow Philadelphians that the city operated a segregated school system that needed to be restructured.

CHAPTER 4

From Little Rock to Philadelphia

Making de Facto School Segregation a Media Issue

The only thing we did wrong was to let segregation stay so
long.
—Protestors at Philadelphia NAACP picketing a school construction
site, May 1963

In her introduction to *Freedom North*, historian Jeanne Theoharis contends that in "history textbooks, college classrooms, films, and popular
celebration, African American protest movements in the North appear as
ancillary and subsequent to the 'real' movement in the South."[1] Such histories, Thomas Sugrue suggests, "are as much the product of forgetting as
of remembering."[2] Thanks to work by Theoharis, Sugrue, Komozi Woodard, Martha Biondi, Matthew Countryman, and many other historians,
the story of civil rights in the North is no longer a footnote. Calling attention to northern civil rights struggles was also a cause for concern for
Philadelphia activists in the 1950s and 1960s. National news coverage, as
well as Philadelphia newspapers and television stations, paid far more
attention to school segregation in the South than to similar stories in
northern cities. This media coverage laid the groundwork for the historical amnesia regarding northern civil rights. At the same time, however,
Philadelphia's civil rights activists tried to use the media to make de facto
segregation an issue that the school board could not avoid. Black educational activist Floyd Logan, for example, found the widest audience for
the issue of Philadelphia's school segregation in the wake of the integration crisis at Little Rock's Central High School in the fall of 1957.

The coverage of the Little Rock crisis in Philadelphia's print and
broadcast media raised the profile of the city's own educational issues to
a higher level than in the previous two decades. Logan took advantage

of this opportunity to secure the school board's first statement on non-discrimination and to foreground school segregation as an issue to be taken up by the city's civil rights advocates. Three years before Little Rock, Logan tried to raise awareness of de facto segregation following the first *Brown* decision in May 1954. Logan sent telegrams to city and state school officials requesting immediate compliance with the decision. In his message to the city school board, Logan argued that "the time is opportune for the Philadelphia School district to redistrict in such a manner as to effect integration of its 10 all-colored schools and its many predominantly colored schools." Similarly, Logan called Pennsylvania governor John Fine's attention to the existence of segregated schools in Philadelphia and other parts of the state and asked him to ensure that Pennsylvania would "conform to the momentous decision of the United States Supreme Court."[3] Logan's attempts to link the *Brown* decision with segregation in Philadelphia went unnoticed in the mainstream press. Unlike the month of front-page coverage Little Rock received in Philadelphia's newspapers, the *Brown* decision was quickly summarized in the *Philadelphia Evening Bulletin* and the *Philadelphia Inquirer* as a southern case.

Without an ongoing story line, these mainstream papers covered the *Brown* decision for only two days. Only the *Philadelphia Tribune*, the city's leading black newspaper, continued to discuss school segregation in Philadelphia and Logan's work to eradicate it. In addition to his lobbying of politicians and school officials, his advocacy for black students and parents, and his research on the schools' practices and policies, Logan essentially functioned as the *Tribune*'s education reporter in these years. Logan played a central role in the network that circulated news of civil rights issues. His collection of information on the Philadelphia schools and his persistent requests for action by school officials enabled the *Tribune* to make the city's school segregation a recurring topic at a time it received little attention in the white press.[4] Logan also worked as an amateur archivist, keeping detailed records of his correspondence with school officials (records that provide the foundation for this and the previous chapter). Using the visibility of Little Rock as leverage, Logan helped the school segregation issue in Philadelphia reach a larger audience in the black community and set the stage for larger protests in the early 1960s.

SCHOOL SEGREGATION AS A MEDIA EVENT

While the *Brown* decisions came and went quietly from Philadelphia newspapers and broadcast media, the struggle over integration in Little Rock was on the front page of the *Philadelphia Evening Bulletin* and the *Philadelphia Inquirer* for over twenty-five days in September and October 1957.[5] School segregation conflicts in Virginia, Tennessee, and Texas also became front-page stories.[6] In addition to print media, Philadelphia's CBS affiliate, WCAU-TV, sent reporter Ken Mayer to Little Rock to track what WCAU-TV called "the nation's newest and most threatening powder keg."[7] The Little Rock crisis also received nightly coverage on national television news, and was followed by a large national audience of viewers that journalist Daniel Schorr described as "a national evening séance."[8] As historian Taylor Branch has argued, "[t]he prolonged duration and military drama of the siege made Little Rock the first on-site news extravaganza of the modern television era."[9] Television news established its legitimacy in the late 1950s in large part by covering civil rights stories like Little Rock. Unlike *American Bandstand* and other entertainment programs that pursued a national audience by avoiding controversy, television news relied on the visuality and topicality of certain racial incidents to establish its authority to frame national issues for a national audience.[10]

At the same time, media coverage of Little Rock and other cases of "massive resistance" in the South presented racism and school segregation as a uniquely southern problem. Launched in 1956 by U.S. senator Harry Byrd of Virginia, *massive resistance* described a group of student placement and school funding laws designed to maintain southern school segregation in defiance of federal court orders. Although not all southern whites supported these policies, massive resistance gained broad and vocal support among diehard segregationists and many southern politicians. The pro-segregationist views underlying massive resistance were put into action by white mobs who harassed and threatened black students who sought to attend formerly all-white schools across the South, including in cities such as Charlotte, Nashville, and, most famously, Little Rock.[11] Racial violence in small southern towns also made its way into American living rooms. As legal scholar Peter Irons notes, "most white Americans learned about mob violence in town like Cilton (TN), Manfield (TX) and Sturgis (KY) from television news reports."[12] For most of the 1950s and early 1960s, these arch-segregationist politicians, white mobs, and public confrontations were absent from the northern fight

FIGURE 14. WCAU-TV advertised "on the scene" reports
from Little Rock with newscaster Ken Mayer. September 11,
1957. *Philadelphia Evening Bulletin.*

over school integration, and the less visible causes of de facto school segregation did not receive the same level of media scrutiny. This media in-
visibility made school segregation in northern cities like Philadelphia
much more difficult to fight.

Nevertheless, local events linked Little Rock to Philadelphia. Just
days after Arkansas governor Orval Faubus ordered the Arkansas National Guard to stop nine black students from enrolling at previously
all-white Central High School, rumors of a shooting in South Philadelphia sparked racial tensions among teenagers. The Philadelphia police
commissioner attributed these tensions in part to Little Rock, and the
Philadelphia Inquirer criticized the perception that racial tensions were
exclusively a southern story.[13] The events at Little Rock's Central High
School also motivated black teenagers in Philadelphia to challenge the

FIGURE 15. The *Philadelphia Inquirer* noted the connection between Little Rock and racial tensions among teenagers in South Philadelphia. October 2, 1957. Hugh Hutton / *Philadelphia Inquirer.*

discriminatory admissions policies at *American Bandstand,* whose broadcast studio was located in West Philadelphia.[14]

The long shadow of Little Rock helped open the door, albeit slightly, for public discussions of local school segregation issues in Philadelphia. While national media coverage of Little Rock portrayed the "Little Rock Nine" in sympathetic terms vis-à-vis the white mob they encountered outside the school, the local mainstream media attention given to Philadelphia's de facto school segregation was more ambivalent. On one hand, the Philadelphia story was less clear than Little Rock, and, at least until the early 1960s, it lacked the characters and images of the southern story. On the other, southern civil rights stories were safe for Philadelphia media in ways that local issues were not. Reading and watching stories about Little Rock required Philadelphians to form opinions, but did not necessarily require them to take action in their own city. In contrast, raising the specter of integration in Philadelphia forced citizens to consider changes to their schools, and mainstream newspapers and televisions stations were keenly aware that their audiences did not universally support civil rights activism in the city.

Still, Logan believed that building public awareness of de facto segregation was an essential step in forcing the school board to take action. In Philadelphia, as in cities from New York to Los Angeles, Little Rock influenced newspapers outside the South to examine race issues in their own cities.[15] Little Rock prompted the *Philadelphia Inquirer,* for example, to run the first school segregation story in the Philadelphia mainstream press, a joint interview with school superintendent Wetter and Charles Shorter, executive secretary of the Philadelphia branch of the NAACP. In his first public comments on the question of school segregation, Wetter argued that Philadelphia's school board was doing its best to address integration. "I sincerely believe that our record of carrying on a full program of integration in Philadelphia is as fine as that found in any city across the America," Wetter told the *Inquirer.*[16] To rebut this claim, Shorter raised several of the issues to which Logan had called attention in the previous years, including school construction policies and student transfer policies. Wetter conceded: "We haven't gone as far as we'd like to. . . . But I think that we're on the right track."

Although it was far from a promise to take action to address de facto segregation, Logan mailed the article to state officials, writing that "the interview establish[es] beyond reasonable doubt, the racial patterns as they exist with respect to pupils and teachers in our local school system."[17] As the *Philadelphia Tribune* ran frequent stories on the struggle over school segregation in the South, Logan pressed the Philadelphia school issue over the next year through repeated appeals to Wetter and state educational officials.[18] Logan asked these officials to address boundary lines, student transfers, and teacher assignments. Logan escalated his appeals in February 1959 when he organized a group of black educational activists, including representatives from the Philadelphia NAACP, the *Philadelphia Tribune*, and several African American churches, who presented the school board with a petition outlining demands to implement nondiscriminatory policies. In a brief supporting this petition, Logan wrote: "For 26 years the Educational Equality League has been striving for interracial integration of Philadelphia public schools. In the beginning, we, too, favored the gradual approach. But today we are certain that we have advanced far beyond the gradual stage."[19] Despite his exasperation with the delays of the board, Logan was still forced to wait while the board considered his petition. Finally, on July 8, 1959, the school board unanimously adopted an official policy barring racial discrimination in the city's public schools. The resolution, drafted by *Philadelphia Tribune* publisher E. Washington Rhodes, the only black member of the school board, outlined a color-blind policy, but did not address the affirmative steps requested by Logan:

> WHEREAS the Board of Public Education seeks to provide the best education possible for all children; and
>
> WHEREAS the Educational Equality League and other organizations have requested the adoption of written policies for full interracial integration of pupils and teachers:
>
> Be it resolved, That the official policy of The Board of Public Education, School District of Philadelphia, continues to be that there shall be no discrimination because of race, color, religion, or national origin in the placement, instruction and guidance of pupils; the employment, assignment, training and promotion of personnel; the provision and maintenance of physical facilities, supplies and equipment; the development and implementation of the curriculum including the activities program; and in all other matters relating to the administration and supervision of the public schools and all policies related thereto; and,
>
> Be it further resolved, That notice of this resolution be given all personnel.[20]

While Logan described the press coverage generated by the policy as one of his "major accomplishments," the school board's policy did not spell out specific actions with regard to school boundaries, school construction, or student assignments to promote integration.[21] By stating that nondiscrimination "continued to be" the policy, moreover, the board sought to absolve itself of having ever supported discriminatory policies.[22] Complicating the issue for Logan and his colleagues was that by 1960 even the board's limited rhetorical commitments to antidiscrimination policies and programs raised concerns among white Philadelphians that civil rights groups exercised undue influence in the schools.

The Fellowship Commission was the first to feel the backlash against civil rights advocates working in the schools. As it built its relationship with the schools throughout the 1940s and 1950s, the Fellowship Commission did not call public attention to its school efforts. The hostile reception the group received when working on housing issues, especially among working-class and middle-class white communities that feared the influx of black families into their neighborhoods, convinced Fagan and his colleagues of the difficulty of persuading people to hear the Fellowship Commission's antidiscrimination message.[23] A 1956 update on its educational seminars, for example, noted the importance of not "push[ing] the reluctant too hard and too early." The report also noted that the Fellowship Commission responded to early fears that the group "might want to barge into classrooms" or "meddle in school affairs," by foregoing its typical publicity campaign.[24] The increased media and community attention to education in the wake of Little Rock, therefore, made the Fellowship Commission's intercultural education ideas and language more important to the school system's public presentations, while it also jeopardized the Fellowship Commission's actual work in the schools.

This disjuncture between the school system's public embrace of antidiscrimination language and actual classroom practices came to the forefront when the schools considered adding intercultural education materials to the high school curriculum in 1960. The textbook controversy that followed effectively ended the Fellowship Commission's work in the public schools. In February 1960, following a wave of anti-Semitic vandalism in the Philadelphia area, Fagan met with David Horowitz, associate superintendent in charge of community relations.[25] Fagan requested that a survey of textbooks be conducted to probe their treatment of the Nazi era in Germany, as well as issues of civil rights, housing, religious freedom, immigration, hate movements, and intergroup relations. Fagan suggested that the school board hire a sociologist to conduct the survey, but instead Horowitz conducted the initial review, which he submitted to the Fellowship Commission along with copies of the textbooks in question and a copy of the board's new guide to the American History and Government course.[26] This new course of study, prepared after the Fellowship Commission's survey request, included a unit on the maintenance of good intercultural relations. As topics to investigate in the intercultural relations section, the guide listed "persecution of minority groups in Hitler's Germany; Immigration laws affecting people of Asian origin and the McCarran-Walter Immigration Act; the Fair Employment Practices Commission; and Jim Crow racial restrictions and efforts to end segregation in the schools."[27] While this course guide marked the first time intercultural education was included in the official school curriculum, as opposed to in seminars or supplementary pamphlets, the guide noted that the time allotted to the units "should be determined by the need of the individual school."[28]

After reviewing these materials, Fagan wrote to Horowitz to praise the intercultural relations unit as "excellent" and to thank him for the school's prompt review of the textbooks. While Fagan was pleased that none of the textbooks contained "derogatory or prejudiced references," he criticized the textbooks for omitting historical facts related to the Nazi era, for the absence of nonwhite people in illustrations, and for the "bland" treatment of civil rights. Fagan recommended that the school system advise textbook publishers of these shortcomings and request improvements.[29] On July 5, 1960, Fagan presented these recommendations at a press conference that included Horowitz, Helen Bailey of the school's curriculum committee, and two other school representatives. The two sides differed on what the schools could ask of the publishers. Fagan thought that the schools shared responsibility for advising publishers when textbooks needed improvement, while Horowitz thought this was beyond the function of the school system. The meeting, nevertheless, ended cordially. The school representatives agreed to hold an annual meeting every fall with the social studies department heads and a group of concerned citizens led by the Fellowship Commission. The Fellowship Commission also agreed to write to the National Education Association and national intergroup agencies requesting that similar textbook studies be conducted in other cities, with the hope that publishers would be more likely to respond if several cities pressed for textbook changes.[30]

While this meeting was not noticeably different from the moderate demands the Fellowship Commission made of the schools in the past, the textbook survey sparked a controversy regarding the authority of the Fellowship Commission to advise the public schools. On July 6, the day after the meeting, the *Bulletin* announced that the school board planned to add a unit on intercultural relations to the high school's social studies classes in the fall.[31] While the Fellowship Commission's textbook survey in February 1960 influenced the school's decision to develop these units in the following month, the *Bulletin* article gave the impression that the school board drafted the unit as an immediate response to the prior day's meeting. The newspaper exploited this confusion in an editorial on July 10, 1960, titled "Indoctrination Course." "Within 24 hours," the editorial charged:

the educators announced that next fall . . . pupils will be instructed on Jim Crowism, on efforts to end school segregation, on slums and housing, on the importance of city planning. How they will be instructed will be the fascinating thing to see. In accordance with the strong beliefs of the Fellowship Commission? In accordance with the equally strong and often quite different beliefs of the taxpaying parents whose schools these are?[32]

Superintendent Wetter responded with a letter published in the following Sunday's paper. Wetter wrote to assure readers that "no new courses were developed in 24 hours to meet deficiencies cited in the Commission's report," and that the materials in intercultural relations and urban renewal had been in preparation for several months.[33]

Wetter's letter, however, ran below a second *Bulletin* editorial that criticized him for "knuckling under" to the wishes of the Fellowship Commission. The editors pointed out what they viewed as a conflict between the beliefs of the Fellowship Commission and those of other city residents:

Moderation, even in instructing against bigotry, is the point of the matter. The Fellowship is sincere and well within its rights in espousing a rapid end to what it believes to be evil—housing segregation, for example. Yet, many a kindly citizen would be astonished to find that by the Fellowship's indices he would be ruled a bigot. The public schools belong to all Philadelphians. Many of these owners of the schools would deem it wrong if they were used as told to speed social progress under an extreme definition thereof.[34]

The readers' letters that the *Bulletin* choose to publish as "evidence that moderation is the wise course" point to a mounting segregationist backlash to the Fellowship Commission and its moderate civil rights work. One reader wondered by "what authority [the Fellowship Commission] have become judges of school textbooks," and argued that "the taxpaying public is sick to death of narrow-minded bigots . . . seeking undeserved privileges." Another reader, calling the Fellowship Commission "propaganda artists," noted that "they'll have fewer and fewer children to deal with as the free-thinking opposition continues removing to the suburbs in search of more independent schools."[35] Portraying themselves as taxpayers willing to move to the suburbs to avoid the encroachment of civil rights "propaganda artists," these letter writers used the rhetoric of private property rights similar to the white homeowners' groups that fought against neighborhood integration.[36] This language also anticipated the antibusing activists who described "neighborhood schools" being unfairly threatened by "forced busing."[37] In the case of the textbook controversy, making sections on the Holocaust and Jim

Crow optional parts of the school curriculum prompted charges of indoctrination from the city's largest newspaper and many of its readers.

In his reply to these editorials, Fagan said that the Fellowship Commission had no problem with the editors recommending moderation, noting that the Fellowship Commission had been charged with being too moderate for its position on fair housing legislation. "Our criticism . . . is not leveled at moderation," Fagan offered, "but rather at those who are so frightened by the label 'controversial' that they not only avoid but oppose efforts to explore all sides of such controversies." Fagan concluded by asking, "Is it really too much to call for social studies textbooks to deal forthrightly and fairly with the pros and cons of the issues affecting the security, rights, liberties, opportunities, relationships and responsibilities of all racial, religious, and ethnic groups?"[38]

Despite the controversy caused by the *Bulletin* editorials, the new units on intercultural education and urban renewal entered the curriculum in the fall of 1960. Through 1961, Fagan corresponded with Horowitz regarding errors and misstatements in the textbooks and met with the heads of the social studies departments to discuss additional intercultural resources for these units. The textbook controversy, however, ended the close relationship between the Fellowship Commission and the school system. Isolated from the public schools, Fagan and the Fellowship Commission turned its attention to a campaign to establish a community college in Philadelphia.[39]

Unlike the highly visible integration crisis in Little Rock, the school segregation crisis in Philadelphia played out in letters, policy statements, newspaper articles, and editorials rather than on school steps or television screens. Like Fagan's often co-opted intercultural education initiatives, the heightened profile of Philadelphia's segregation problem, which Floyd Logan had worked so long to foster, was a mixed blessing. Publicity made more people aware that school segregation was not strictly a southern issue, but left open the question of how and by whom this issue should be addressed. Logan's position, that the school board should implement affirmative policies to promote integration, gained popularity among many civil rights advocates, but received little citywide publicity and was not enough to effect change in the school board's policy. The school board sidestepped Logan's demands by co-opting the Fellowship Commission's antidiscrimination rhetoric and refusing to commit to any specific actions to address integration. Despite the school board's caution regarding the question of integration, even these limited intercultural efforts prompted critiques of the school board by citizens who viewed intercultural education as a form of civil rights propaganda. By the early 1960s, the struggle over segregation in the city's schools emerged from written demands and evasions into courtroom arguments and street protests.

SCHOOL PROTESTS AND BACKLASH

In recognition of Logan's fight against de facto segregation, the *Philadelphia Tribune* named him the paper's Man of the Year for 1959. In the tribute to Logan, the paper contrasted his modest means with his accumulated research on educational discrimination:

> Floyd Logan has little money. He receives no salary. He lives in an apartment and maintains himself from a small pension he receives from the Federal Government, after long years of service. . . . Yet, he has more information at his fingertips about the school system than most highly paid executives. His bulging files contain complete records of every step made to advance the cause of equality in public education.[40]

Although the school board refused to implement his demands, Logan provided the knowledge and experience on which later educational advocates would draw. Taking up Logan's lead, by the early 1960s Philadelphia's schools became an important target for a coalition of black civil rights activists. Like Logan, these activists pushed the school board to address de facto segregation at the city level, while they also lobbied against educational discrimination in individual neighborhood schools. Unlike Logan, this new wave of educational activists had the resources to bring litigation against the school system and had a larger basis of support organized among the city's black churches, civic groups, and neighborhoods. Moreover, unlike the Fellowship Commission's interracial coalition building or Logan's largely solitary work, the new educational activists increasingly looked to intra-racial mass protest techniques to secure equal educational opportunities for black students. In their protests, these community members encountered a school board that continued to deny the existence of bias, as well as increasingly vocal opposition from predominantly white sections of the city.

Logan played a supporting role on educational issues throughout the 1960s, though not entirely of his choosing. The Philadelphia branch of the NAACP, which had been an inconsistent ally on educational issues through the 1950s, began to play a more significant role in fighting school segregation.[41] Logan and the NAACP worked together briefly in an attempt to force state officials to establish legal requirements to act affirmatively for integration. Logan initiated a strategy to change the state law governing school enrollment boundaries and presented his argument to the Governor's Committee on Education in 1960. "If Pennsylvania really wants interracially integrated public schools with respects to pupils, and teachers," Logan argued,

> it must amend Section 1310 of the School Laws of the State by specifically regulating the wide discretionary powers of pupil assignments, including transfers [that] will not result in perpetuation of present racially segregated schools, and the creation of other all and predominantly [sic] white or Negro schools. . . . Also, a flexible system of districting for pupil enrollment should be devised in which representatives of the general community should be given a voice.[42]

Following this meeting, the Governor's Committee on Education recommended that the state pass a "fair educational practices law . . . banning discrimination on account of race, color, or creed" and that it conduct a study of the school boundary lines and student transfer policies throughout the state.[43] The state officials also scheduled an initial meeting with Wetter, Logan, and representatives from the Philadelphia NAACP for April 1961.

After years of the Philadelphia NAACP's sporadic activity on the local educational front, Charles Beckett, the branch's recently appointed education committee chairman, met with Logan several times in 1960 and 1961. As Beckett reported to his colleagues, "Years of proficient research, investigation and forthright presentation made to official bodies have provided [Floyd Logan] with a storehouse of knowledge and information invaluable to the community and state within which and for which [he] has labored so effectively."[44] The NAACP, however, was also preparing to file a lawsuit against the schools and canceled a scheduled meeting with state and local school officials because the organization felt it "would serve no purpose."[45] Logan considered the cancellation "shocking" and reminded school officials and the NAACP of his work on school issues. "In the first place, it was the Educational Equality League which made the original request for a state investigation," Logan argued. "Hence, we do not feel that such a feeling on the part of the NAACP, justifies the cancellation of the scheduled meeting."[46] Cecil B.

Moore, a lawyer and community activist who had lost the previous two elections for NAACP branch president, supported Logan's stance:

> We are anxious to have the investigation proceed as expeditiously as possible by methods which will effectively implement desegregation without regard to any position taken by the NAACP. . . . [W]e should proceed now as several years may elapse between the commencement and certainly successful termination of imminent litigation, whereas the practices of which we complain may continue during those years, with their attendant harmful effects on the education of a large majority of Negro pupils.[47]

The cancellation of the meeting delayed the start of the state's study of school boundaries, but, more important, it created a rift between Logan and the NAACP's leadership that limited the effectiveness of both parties.

In June 1961, the Philadelphia branch of the NAACP filed a lawsuit in the U.S. District Court for the Eastern District of Pennsylvania, charging the Philadelphia Board of Education with discriminating against black students and teachers by not providing and maintaining a racially integrated school system. The NAACP brought the case, *Chisholm v. Board of Public Education,* on behalf of black students at Emlen elementary school in the northwest section of the city. Parents and community members in this area had raised questions for the previous five years regarding the boundary lines and student transfers that made Emlen almost all-black while the neighboring Day school was almost all-white. The case was among the first northern school desegregation cases and came just months after *Taylor v. Board of Education* (1961), in which a federal judge found gerrymandering of school district lines in New Rochelle, New York, to be unconstitutional. The New Rochelle case did not rule on de facto segregation, but it prompted a flurry of legal activity against school districts in the North, Midwest, and West before the Supreme Court's decision in *Keyes v. School District No. 1* (1973), which found evidence of unconstitutional segregation in Denver and expanded desegregation requirements outside the South.[48] Leon Higginbotham, who led the Philadelphia NAACP's legal team and was the branch president when the *Chisholm* suit was filed, recalled the difficulty of proving de facto segregation in a 1991 interview with Anne Phillips:

> What was . . . insidious was that you had declarations by the school board saying that they opposed segregation . . . so that therefore you could not try what I call a "document case" in the traditional sense where you have what we call in evidence "a smoking gun." . . . So what we tried to do is determine: How do you set up a case to demonstrate to a court that the way in which boundaries are chosen [is] not a matter of pure coincidence? . . .

[T]here was enough if I thought that I had to go to trial as a trial lawyer that I would be able to establish and to discover questions of policy which [went] back a half-century almost, at which time there's just no doubt that there was discrimination in the system. And, therefore, the whole argument in the northern cases would be that after you have established a prima-facie case of administrative policies, intentionally designed to preclude integration of students, that is the equivalent of [de jure segregation].[49]

The challenges Higginbotham and his colleagues encountered in pursuing this case were similar to those Logan had met over the previous decades; that is, they needed to extract evidence of educational discrimination from a school board that insisted it did not discriminate. Gary Orfield has shown that foes of de facto segregation in other northern and western cities faced similar barriers to litigation. "The lower courts," Orfield argues,

> would act only when the NAACP could provide incontrovertible proof of intentional, broad discrimination by school boards. Finding such evidence about the intentions of past school board members was almost impossible. Although they may have been well aware of racial patterns and of the racial implications of their zoning, site selection, transfer policy, and other decisions, they rarely discussed them in public. A clear pattern of decisions that had intensified segregation usually emerged, but they were not the kind of thing explicitly noted in the board's minutes.[50]

The Philadelphia school board, which operated largely outside of public view and assiduously avoided controversy by publishing only administrative details in its minutes, proved an especially difficult target.[51]

Compounding this legal challenge, by the time a judge heard the case in early 1963, the NAACP's local leadership was in flux. Higginbotham resigned in 1962 to accept an appointment to the Federal Trade Commission in the Kennedy administration. In the election to replace Higginbotham, Cecil Moore won the NAACP branch presidency thanks to his popularity in black working-class neighborhoods and his promises to take the branch in a more militant direction. In addition to Higginbotham, who was co-counsel on the case, all but one of the twenty-four lawyers working on the case pro bono left because of the controversy and political alliances within the branch.[52] Due to the lingering tension over the canceled meeting, moreover, the original legal team did not take full advantage of Logan's research materials and lacked the funds to conduct new surveys of school boundary, student transfer, and teacher placement policies. One of the outgoing members of the legal team, William Lee Akers, wrote to Moore regarding the challenges this case presented. "I do not believe that any lawyer who has a day to day practice or employment can do justice to the case," he wrote. "I would be pleased to continue to assist in this case but am firmly resolved that I will not go to the poorhouse by attempting to carry this monster on my own shoulders. . . . This is most unfortunate and is not what the case and the Association deserve, but I have no choice."[53] By spring 1963, Isaiah Crippens was the only attorney remaining on the case. Without a team to conduct the necessary research, Crippens agreed to wait until two committees on school segregation appointed by the school board filed their reports.[54]

If the NAACP's traditional legal approach to educational discrimination was threatened by branch politics and a lack of funds, it was also increasingly out of step with the mass protest strategies favored by black leaders and community members frustrated by the persistent inequality in the city's schools. Cecil Moore, the newly elected NAACP branch president, became the most prominent of these local protest leaders. As historian Matthew Countryman describes, Moore positioned himself "as a local version of Malcolm X, the only black leader in the city unwilling to censor his words and actions to conform to white liberal sensibilities."[55] Moore helped build this reputation by organizing a picket at a junior high school construction site in the predominantly black Strawberry Mansion section of North Philadelphia. The protest was a continuation of more than a month of protests over labor discrimination at city-sponsored construction projects, and started just days after Moore and the Philadelphia NAACP organized a rally at City Hall to support the civil rights demonstrators who were attacked in Birmingham, Alabama.[56]

The pickets at Strawberry Mansion Junior High linked employment discrimination in school construction with the issues of school segregation and school-sponsored apprenticeship programs that discriminated against blacks. Like the schools' site selections for Northeast High School and Franklin High School, the Strawberry Mansion site ensured that the school would be segregated as soon as it opened. That the skilled union workers building the school were almost exclusively white was largely a result of the exclusion of black students from apprenticeship classes. These classes used public school space and resources to train future union workers. The unions selected the students who could participate in the classes, and first preference was usually given to sons and nephews of union members. In other cases, ethnic associations and neighborhood churches and clubs provided apprentices for larger unions. In almost all cases, the family and social networks that fed these apprenticeship programs excluded blacks from the building trades.[57] To protest these conditions, the NAACP began picketing the school site on May 24. Small groups of protesters arrived at the construction site every morning, and they were joined each afternoon by teenagers and blue-collar workers who came from their schools and work sites, respectively. As they walked around the entrance to the construction site, protestors shouted, "The only thing we did wrong was to let segregation stay so long."[58] Taking up the theme of this protest chant, the *Philadelphia Tribune*'s editorial page noted that although a state law prohibiting discrimination in school construction was passed fourteen years earlier, "There was no effort made by anyone to enforce it, despite the fact that it is generally agreed that there has been and continued to be discrimination against Negro skilled labor."[59] Among the hundreds of picketers were black laborers assigned to work on the school site who refused to cross the picket line. "This is a false democracy when qualified colored people can't get a job building schools for their own kids," one worker told the *Tribune*.[60] This combination of employment discrimination against adults and educational discrimination against young people motivated protestors to stay on the picket line for a week.

After the fifth and most violent day of clashes between protestors and police, the school board and construction leaders agreed to the NAACP's demand that five black skilled workers be hired at the site and that a joint monitoring committee be appointed to increase black employment in skilled trades. In negotiations prompted by the protests, the school board also agreed to close apprenticeship programs that excluded black students. At the time, the Strawberry Mansion pickets were the largest mass protest against educational discrimination in the city's history. Although they did not force the school board to take action to address school segregation, the protests provided black leaders with another strategy to use against the school board's delays. "The old procedures of quiet protest have been abandoned for open demonstration," the *Tribune* declared in an editorial on the importance of education to civil rights.[61] The threat of protests, and media coverage of these protests, became a key tool as Moore and other black activists continued to fight the school board through the summer of 1963.

In addition to these mass protests, Moore and the NAACP continued to pursue a legal victory over school segregation in the *Chisholm* case. Judge Harold Wood set September 15, 1963, as the date by which the schools and the NAACP would have to come to an agreement to avoid going to trial. The school's nondiscrimination committee had prepared a plan for desegregation in advance of the deadline, but Walter Biddle Saul, a former school board president and the school board's counsel for the *Chisholm* lawsuit, refused to file the document with the court. Filing a plan for desegregation, Saul argued, would constitute an admission that the school segregation existed, which he insisted was not the case.[62] In response, Moore and the 400 Ministers, a group of clergy who led a successful selective patronage campaign against local companies with discriminatory hiring practices, threatened to organize direct action protests and student boycotts if the board did not adopt an acceptable policy.[63]

The tension between these activists and the school board increased when Judge Wood ordered the board to adopt a desegregation plan that included changes in school feeder patterns to further integration. Wood also granted a continuance in the case, meaning that it would not go to trial as long as both parties submitted a progress report every six months. The *Tribune* portrayed this decision as an unmitigated victory, declaring: "Parents of children across the city raised their voices in a chorus of 'hallelujahs,' as the Board of Education accepted unconditionally the demands of the NAACP for a desegregated school system."[64] The desegregation plan included reviews of school boundaries and school building programs and agreements that the board would modify its boundary policies and building site selection to foster desegregation. In total, the plan committed the school board to take many of the affirmative steps toward integration long encouraged by educational advocates.

Rather than overturning de facto segregation, however, the judge's order sparked another round of delays by the school board, protests by civil rights advocates, and counterprotests by segregationist antibusing groups. In the first protest following the order, black parents joined Moore and the NAACP in pickets at Meade Elementary School in North Philadelphia after the principal announced plans to address overcrowding by busing students to another segregated school. In addition to the school protests, the NAACP led pickets at the Board of Education building, the home of the school principal, and the homes of superintendent Wetter and Robert Poindexter, one of two black members of the school board. Moore promised to keep the pickets going until students at the overcrowded school could transfer to an integrated school. "We've learned that you can't believe what the Board says it's going to do," Moore told the *Tribune*.[65] After a student boycott kept half the students out of classes for one day, Moore successfully negotiated the transfer with school officials.[66] Building on this victory, Moore warned that the school board would face larger protests if it continued to delay desegregation efforts:

"Be it in the courts, the streets, or the ballot box, the NAACP will integrate the schools. If they're going to be stubborn, we'll show them that what we accomplished at the Meade School and at 31st and Dauphin sts. [Strawberry Mansion Junior High construction site] was only a petty example of what they can expect in the future."[67] As the school board filed progress reports that retreated from its earlier desegregation plans, these mass protest tactics became increasingly important to civil rights advocates.

The struggle over school desegregation in Philadelphia peaked in 1964. As required by the continuance in the *Chisholm* case, the school board filed a progress report in January announcing plans for limited student busing. A second report in April laid out plans to realign the boundaries of half of the city's elementary schools.[68] In both cases, the plans were designed to relieve overcrowding first and secondarily to foster integration. The plans drew criticism from both civil rights advocates and antibusing groups. Isaiah Crippens, the NAACP's attorney in the *Chisholm* case, dismissed the first report as a "public relations gimmick, a hoax, a linguistic swindle."[69] Many black parents also doubted the school board's intentions and, with the assistance of Moore and the NAACP, protested boundaries and overcrowding at two schools.[70]

The school board's reports also prompted parents in several predominately white neighborhoods to form groups to oppose the proposed busing and boundary changes. Speaking at meetings throughout the city, Joseph Frieri, the leader of the Parents' and Taxpayers' Association of Philadelphia, the largest of these antibusing groups, argued for the importance of neighborhood schools. Rather than busing or boundary changes, Frieri argued, the schools should focus on remedial training for low-income black children whom, he claimed, were culturally deprived. Members of another antibusing group dramatized Frieri's concerns by carrying a coffin symbolizing the death of the neighborhood school into a school committee meeting.[71] Mayor James Tate and City Council President Paul D'Ortona joined these parents in attacking the school board's plan for limited busing. D'Ortona claimed that busing would increase juvenile delinquency and leave students "prey to moral offenders." D'Ortona also toured white sections of the city delivering these arguments and urged white citizens to "storm City Hall" to defend neighborhood schools.[72]

In supporting segregation by sounding warnings about culturally deprived and delinquent black youth, these antibusing leaders identified black students as the problem with Philadelphia's schools. This line of argument built on a magazine article, published earlier that year, that attacked Philadelphia public schools and black students. Published in *Greater Philadelphia Magazine,* a magazine marketed to members of the Philadelphia business community, "Crisis in the Classroom" claimed to be an inside report on the Philadelphia school system. *Greater Philadelphia Magazine* reporter Gaeton Fonzi worked for just six days as a substitute teacher and spent a month talking with administrators and teachers. Fonzi's statement of concern for the state of education in Philadelphia's schools fixed blame on unprepared, unruly, and violent black youth. The teachers of these students, he argued, were "living a professional lie, refusing to admit, even to themselves, that what they face daily is the impossible task of trying to reach human beings who don't want to be reached." In Fonzi's view, "culturally deprived" black students were synonymous with the public schools, and were at the root of the schools' problems. "The great bulk of the Philadelphia public school system is composed of an economically deprived, socially-suppressed class of adolescent who has been environmentally conditioned to a life that is without hope or ambition," Fonzi wrote. He continued:

> The Philadelphia public school system is, in other words, a Negro system. But it is more than that: it is a ghetto system overburdened with the intellectual, moral and economic remnant of society. The private and parochial schools have siphoned off the cream of Philadelphia's school-age population, both Negro and white. The children who go to the public school system are those who have no where else to go.[73]

Fonzi went on to degrade black teachers "recruited from hole-in-the-wall type Southern Negro state colleges" and to call the Philadelphia public schools "the most obscene institutions in the city."[74] Echoing attacks on welfare that gained strength in the mid-1960s, Fonzi described the visit of a truancy officer to a poor neighborhood in order to criticize a mother of seven on public assistance and to ask "what sort of behavior can be expected from a child who doesn't know what a father is or whose older sister is a whore?"[75] In this attack, Fonzi singled out William Penn, a majority-black all-girls school in North Philadelphia, as an example of what he felt was wrong with Philadelphia's public schools. Noting the school's "Code of Behavior" (Do act like young ladies at all times. Don't use profane or foul language.), he scoffed: "How ridiculous such minimum middle-class standards seem in contrast to actual behavior not only at William Penn but in most of the schools. Young ladies? Dozens drop out each year because of pregnancy."[76] Fonzi further described the success of small groups of students in counseling and motivation programs as "diamonds in a pile of manure."[77]

In its coverage of the story, the *Philadelphia Tribune* reprinted Fonzi's article, followed by a two-part rebuttal by Floyd Logan. Logan likened the article to those authored by "Southern racist writers" who sought to "denigrate the image of the Negro child, his mental ability, character, health, home and family background, even his birth, in order to emphasize his unassimability into predominately white schools."[78]

While it is tempting to dismiss Fonzi's article as the thoughts of an isolated bigot, his criticisms of black students came at the peak of the struggle over school segregation in Philadelphia. Against civil rights activists who pushed the school board to take affirmative steps to integrate Philadelphia's schools, Fonzi's racist article provided rhetorical support for antibusing protestors who contended that black students were culturally deprived and would benefit from remedial education rather than integration.[79]

Logan and Moore rebutted the claims of these antibusing leaders. In response to Mayor Tate's intervention into the busing plan, Logan resigned his position on the Mayor's Citizens Advisory Committee on Civil Rights.[80] Taking a more vocal position on desegregation than he had in the 1950s, Logan told the *Tribune*: "All this business about asking white people if they want colored children in 'their schools' is nonsense. We're talking about law, not opinion polls. The School Board must have the courage to do what is right regardless of opposition from either whites or Negroes."[81] In a speech at a NAACP meeting, Moore extended Logan's critique to the subject of the neighborhood school: "The only difference between a segregationist like Paul D'Ortona and one like Gov. Wallace is that one uses 'neighborhood rights' and the other 'states rights' to disguise his basic desire to keep the Negro enslaved."[82] Moore's statements highlighted the concept of neighborhood schools as one of the most powerful ideas available to officials and citizens who opposed desegregation efforts. The neighborhood schools concept tapped into sentiments that led white homeowners in Philadelphia and other cities to organize groups to "defend" their neighborhoods from what they perceived to be the threat of black migration.[83] The discourse of neighborhood rights also resembled the freedom of choice rhetoric used in southern school districts after civil rights advocates challenged massive resistance laws in federal court. Matthew Lassiter argues that antibusing groups in Charlotte crafted an "identity politics of suburban innocence that defined 'freedom of choice' and 'neighborhood schools' as the core elements of homeowner rights and consumer liberties."[84] By maintaining segregation in both housing and schools, these groups, in Philadelphia and elsewhere, sought to preserve localized forms of racial privilege. Like the school board's antidiscrimination rhetoric, moreover, holding up neighborhood schools as an ideal allowed school officials, politicians, and citizens to adopt a color-blind ideology and avoid integration without publicly supporting segregation.

Respect for the neighborhood school concept also underscored the Lewis Committee's report on school integration required by the *Chisholm* case. Appointed by the school board, the Lewis Committee was an interracial group of community representatives interested in integration. The report affirmed the committee's "unanimous belief in the principal of integrated public education," but outlined preconditions for reorganizing schools to achieve full integration that would have been difficult for even the most optimistic integration advocate to envision. The committee recommended:

> First the community as a whole and especially those people living in predominantly white neighborhoods must be convinced that the very existence of the city and their own enlightened self-interest depend on their acceptance of integration as the modern and satisfactory pattern for life—in housing, in jobs, and in education. . . . The second fundamental need to be realized before integration of the schools on a wide basis can take place successfully is to improve the educational achievements of the schools themselves.[85]

The Fellowship Commission's limited success in persuading people to embrace anti-prejudice ideals made the first requirement seem far-fetched, while the years of neglect of majority-black schools like Franklin made the second equally unrealistic. The report concluded with suggestions for integration that the schools might implement at an undetermined future date, and recommended that the busing of white children to foster integration be given "no further consideration." Instead, the committee suggested additional compensatory and remedial education for students in underperforming schools, primarily black and Puerto Rican youth. Set in the context of protests and counterprotests over what the schools could and should do to address school segregation, the Lewis Committee's report sided with the segregationist antibusing groups and absolved the school board of taking any affirmative steps to promote integration.

The fight over educational discrimination in Philadelphia's schools continued after the Lewis Committee report, but the school board would not make any serious moves toward desegregation after 1964. Maurice

Fagan and the Fellowship Commission celebrated the opening of the Community College of Philadelphia after a fifteen-year legislative and public relations campaign. The Community College opened doors to higher education for a large number of students.[86] Floyd Logan continued to work on educational issues, focusing on the schools near his home in West Philadelphia (the new West Philadelphia High School gymnasium was named after Logan in 1979).[87] Cecil Moore continued to be the most prominent and outspoken black leader in Philadelphia. On the educational front, Moore tried to reopen the *Chisholm* case in 1966 to get a ruling, but his request was denied. Moore also led an eight-month protest of Girard College, a boarding school for fatherless boys that excluded black youth. Although Girard College was unaffiliated with the public schools, the school's ten-foot stone walls made it a highly visible symbol of racial exclusion in North Philadelphia. Protests at the school in the summer of 1965 provided an outlet for the anger felt by black teenagers and received extensive coverage from the *Philadelphia Tribune*.[88]

In addition to the Girard College protests, Moore played a supporting role as a younger generation of Black Power activists organized high school student protests in the summer and fall of 1967.[89] A decade after Little Rock, the educational inequalities in Philadelphia's de facto segregated schools became a very public issue. These protests prompted negotiations among students, parents, community activists, and school officials that led to a larger role for black community members in the governance of majority-black schools, including black-only student groups in the schools and black studies courses. At the same time, police commissioner Frank Rizzo capitalized on white opposition to these school protests and the school reform efforts when he was elected mayor on a strong anti–civil rights platform in 1971.[90] At the start of the 1970s, Philadelphia's schools were among the most racially segregated in the country, with 93 percent of black students attending majority-black schools and one in twenty attending all-black schools.[91]

On the legislative front, the Pennsylvania Human Relations Commission issued an order in 1970 requiring five state public school districts to develop plans to balance the racial composition of students in their schools. The Philadelphia school board challenged the Human Relations Commission's authority to act in the absence of de jure segregation. The case that emerged, *School District of Philadelphia v. Pennsylvania Human Relations Commission* (1972), was the first of eleven cases stretching over almost forty years. In the wake of U.S. Supreme Court's decision in *Milliken v. Bradley* (1974), which held that desegregation plans could not extend into suburban school districts unless multiple districts had deliberately engaged in segregated polices, the Pennsylvania Commonwealth Court allowed the school board to submit a voluntary plan for integration that did little to lower the number of racially identifiable schools. The Human Relations Commission conceded that with students of color making up the majority of the public school population, racially integrating the school system was not feasible. By the 1990s, the school board submitted a plan to the court that said little about racially isolated schools, focusing instead on general educational reform efforts. The school desegregation case ended in 2009 when the Commonwealth Court judge accepted the school district's five-year strategic plan that was approved by the Human Relations Commission and the educational advocacy groups representing the defendant. The plan, *Imagine 2014*, outlined several goals, including the school district's commitment to increase the compensation for teachers in low-performing schools, to allow low-performing schools to select teachers without regard to seniority, and to institute weighted student funding within five years to increase the resources available at low-performing schools.[92] While unnoted in the school board's press release, in making this plan for the future of Philadelphia schools, the school board also echoed the past. *Imagine 2014* reiterated the demands for improved educational opportunities for low-income students and students of color made by Floyd Logan and his fellow educational activists over the previous six decades.

Underlying Floyd Logan's quest to make de facto school segregation a media issue was faith that publicizing educational inequality would compel the school board to take action. In this view, the *Brown* decisions and Little Rock provided openings in which to make school segregation a relevant issue for all Philadelphians. As political theorist Danielle Allen has argued, images from Little Rock "forced a choice on U.S. viewers" regarding their "basic habits of interaction in public spaces" as citizens, and that many "were shamed into desiring a new order."[93] While Little Rock raised questions of citizenship for Philadelphians, the local import of this national civil rights story was far less clear. Counter to Logan's hopes, as Philadelphia's school segregation became more highly visible, the school board, politicians, and white parents became more adamant about protecting the status quo at the expense of integrated education and equal educational opportunities for black students. Ultimately, Logan did not overestimate the importance of media publicity so much as he underestimated the extent of entrenched white resistance to integration.

The failure of school integration in Philadelphia made other spaces of intercultural exchange among teenagers more important. Radio programs, concerts, record hops, talent shows, and television shows dedicated to rock and roll became important sites of youth culture in the 1950s. In some cases, these youth spaces allowed teens to interact with cultural productions and peer groups across racial lines. At other times, youth spaces rearticulated the ideals of racial segregation. The next chapter examines the emergence of rock and roll in Philadelphia and the deejays and teenagers who shaped the city's youth culture.

CHAPTER 5

The Rise of Rock and Roll in Philadelphia

Georgie Woods, Mitch Thomas, and Dick Clark

The masses of African Americans who have been deprived of educational and economic opportunity are almost totally dependent on radio as their means of relating to the society at large. . . . Television speaks not to their needs, but to upper middle class America. . . . No one knows the importance of [radio deejay] Tall Paul White to the massive nonviolent demonstrations of the youth in Birmingham in 1963; or the funds raised by Purvis Spann for the Mississippi Freedom Summer Project of 1964; or the consistent fundraising and voter education done for the Southern Christian Leadership Conference and the Civil Rights Movement by Georgie Woods, my good friend in Philadelphia. . . . In a real sense, you have paved the way for social and political change by creating a powerful cultural bridge between black and white. . . . I salute you.

— Martin Luther King Jr., keynote address, National Association of Radio and Television Announcers Convention, Atlanta, 1967

Starting in 1957, millions of teenagers across the country tuned into *American Bandstand* every afternoon to watch Philadelphia teenagers dance to the most popular music of the day. The history of *American Bandstand,* however, starts not on national television, but with the rise of rock and roll in Philadelphia through radio, concerts, record hops, talent shows, and local television. Like youth across the country, Philadelphia teenagers found meaning in rock and roll, but they did so in ways that were mediated by deejays who sought to capitalize on the music's popularity with youth. At the same time, these deejays introduced young people to the music that helped form their teenage communities. Attending to the local roots of rock and roll, and the deejays who led this development, highlights the complex mix of commerce and community in the growth and popularization of rock and roll. In addition to showing how *American Bandstand* emerged from a fertile musical culture in Philadelphia, this local perspective also makes it clear that the show's particular mix of commerce and community was not the only available option.

This chapter begins and ends with Georgie Woods, a leading rock and roll deejay who also advanced civil rights in Philadelphia. Woods's civil rights activism developed out of his experience working with black teenagers as a deejay and concert promoter as well as his concern about the lack of black television personalities and black-owned broadcast stations in the city. Woods used his radio show and concerts to raise money for the NAACP legal defense fund and to promote civil rights protests, in which he also participated. Woods drew praise from Martin Luther King Jr. for his work. By merging his critiques of the media industry with civil rights work in support of the black teenagers who sustained his broadcast career, Woods offered a model for what music could achieve beyond commercial success. In addition to Woods, black deejay Mitch Thomas hosted a locally televised dance show that drew black teenagers from across the Philadelphia region and was watched by teenagers across racial lines. *The Mitch Thomas Show* was among the first television shows with a black host (it debuted fifteen years before *Soul Train*). Thomas's show highlighted the creative talents of black teenagers and brought images of these teens into Philadelphia homes. The show also offered a mediated space for interracial association and influenced many of *American Bandstand*'s dancers.

Rock and roll developed in Philadelphia thanks largely to Woods, Thomas, and their teenage audiences. Dick Clark tapped into this excitement for rock and roll, first as a radio deejay, and later as the host of *American Bandstand*. Clark acknowledged that Woods's and Thomas's programs influenced the music and dance styles on his show. A talented cultural producer in his own right, Clark guided *Bandstand* from a local program to a national show with lucrative sponsorships. Woods, Thomas, and Clark all capitalized professionally on young people's interest in rock and roll. The three differed, however, in their visions of what music meant to Philadelphia's teenagers. For Woods, music became a way to raise money for and awareness of civil rights. For Thomas, music offered a safe leisure space for teenagers and, through his television show, made black youth culture more visible. For Clark, music was the best way to appeal to, and become famous among, the growing youth demographic. As three of the people who did the most to shape Philadelphia's rock and roll scene, the careers of Woods, Thomas, and Clark demonstrate how rock and roll became big business, but also how it was capable of being something more.

As the quotation from Dr. King at the start of this chapter suggests, Woods was part of a generation of radio deejays who played important roles in local black communities across the country. Deejays like "Tall Paul" Dudley White in Birmingham; Purvis Spann, Herb Kent, and Wesley South in Chicago; Spider Burks in St. Louis; Johnny Otis and Magnificent Montague in Los Angeles; and Jocko Henderson in Philadelphia and New York raised money and recruited members for local and national civil rights organizations, serving as what historian William Barlow calls the "media nerve centers of the civil rights movement."[1] Black deejays played important community roles, more so than their white counterparts, because local radio remained the most important form of media among black consumers. Advertisers looked to black deejays to sell products, and by 1963 there were over eight hundred "black appeal" stations, most of them white-owned.[2] These commercial interests were important for black deejays like Woods, but they were only part of the story. Through their actions, both inside and outside of the broadcast studio, many black deejays were "local people" in the sense that historians Jeanne Theoharis and Komozi Woodard use the term. That is, they exhibited "a sense of accountability and an ethical commitment to the community" that went beyond economic gain.[3] Martha Jean "the Queen" Steinberg, who broadcast in Memphis and Detroit, recalled that the mission of black deejays was "to serve, to sell, to inform, to entertain, and to educate our community."[4] The localism of black radio, therefore, both constrained and enabled black deejays. Georgie Woods would never get a shot at national television like Dick Clark, but he would forge relationships with his community of local listeners that enabled him to use music to advance the struggle for civil rights.

GEORGIE WOODS'S ROCK 'N' ROLL SHOW

While Bob Horn's televised *Bandstand* still played white pop music and copies of black rhythm and blues songs performed by white artists, deejays like Georgie Woods and Mitch Thomas started playing rhythm and blues music and calling it "rock 'n' roll."[5] Woods and Thomas held rock and roll concerts in large arenas and hosted record hops at skating rinks and recreation centers in addition to their daily radio shows. Vocal harmony groups in the city's black neighborhoods, moreover, performed at these neighborhood shows and developed singing styles that influenced and were influenced by what they heard on the radio. Beyond the walls of *American Bandstand*'s studio, then, black broadcasters and teenagers made Philadelphia a vibrant rock and roll scene.

While radio was the most important medium for the development of rock and roll in Philadelphia, Georgie "the Guy with the Goods" Woods became the city's most prominent black broadcaster. Woods was born in rural Barnett, Georgia, in 1927, the ninth of eleven children. Like many black families in the area, Woods's family faced consistent threats from the Ku Klux Klan, culminating when the Klan burned a cross in his family's yard. While his father continued his work as a preacher in Georgia, Woods's mother moved the family to Harlem in 1936 to escape this racial violence and to find better employment and educational opportunities. After his mother died, Woods dropped out of high school at fourteen to work, and later spent two years in the army before returning to New York City. Woods got his start in radio with WWRL, a black-oriented station in New York, and came to Philadelphia's WHAT in 1953 after one of its deejays quit.[6]

Although Woods was less experienced than WHAT's other popular black deejays, Doug "Jocko" Henderson and Kae Williams, he distinguished himself by pitching his show to teenagers. Influenced by the popularity of Alan Freed's radio program in New York, Woods started describing his program as "rock 'n' roll," a black slang term that Freed brought into the mainstream. Freed's large interracial rock and roll audiences impressed Woods. In January 1955, for example, Woods described these interracial audiences in his weekly column in the *Philadelphia Tribune*, "Rock and Roll with Georgie Woods":

> There is a change taking place in the music industry of America, especially in the so-called rhythm and blues field. Today, as never before, white teenagers are buying rhythm and blues tunes. Reason—the younger generation is away from the old idea that rhythm and blues music is strictly for Negroes. In this writer's opinion, Rock and Roll music is the rhythm of America and there are many who will agree. Here's an example of how the change in taking place. In New York City a disc jockey by the name of Allan [sic] Freed . . . plays only rock and roll music and yet he has more white listeners than Negro listeners. . . . [H]e gave an affair at the St. Nick's arena and . . . it went like this: The affair was a complete sellout—30,000 strong for both shows at $2.00 per, and

FIGURE 16. Georgie Woods with his teenage fans at a record hop at Imperial Roller Skating Rink in West Philadelphia. Woods staked his claim as Philadelphia's "King of Rock 'n' Roll" through his radio show and his stage shows. October 12, 1954. Used with permission of the *Philadelphia Tribune*.

each nite there were more whites in attendance than Negroes. . . . A change for the better is taking place and I for one can't see any wrong in that change.[7]

For Woods, *rock and roll* did not refer to a new type of music, but rather to a larger consumer market for rhythm and blues music. Already a popular radio personality, Woods started billing himself as the "King of Rock 'n' Roll" and organized his first rock and roll stage show at the Met in North Philadelphia in April 1955. This first concert was followed by shows in Center City at the Academy of Music and the Mastbaum Theater.[8] Each of these shows featured a mix of rhythm and blues singers like LaVern Baker, big bands like the Buddy Johnson Orchestra, and vocal harmony groups such as the Roamers. More important for Woods, each concert sold out. The Academy of Music show, the *Philadelphia Tribune* reported, "was packed and jammed with over 5,000 yelling, screaming high school students."[9] Woods used his radio show to promote these concerts, and this cross promotion prompted a dispute with station management that led him to leave WHAT and sign with the rival black-oriented station WDAS.[10] He maintained his popularity after switching stations, and with each of the concerts Woods established himself as the leading rock and roll personality in Philadelphia.[11]

As he promoted these large stage shows, Woods also hosted smaller dances and concerts in the city's majority black neighborhoods. Although teens paid only twenty-five or fifty cents to attend the record hops and one or two dollars for the larger concerts, these events helped to supplement Woods's radio salary of twenty-five dollars a week.[12] Beyond this financial motivation, the concerts and record hops also established a closer relationship between Woods and his teenage audience. Woods recalled that "anyplace where a number of people could gather, we [held a dance]. It wasn't just one special place . . . we used playgrounds, gyms or auditoriums to do the dances."[13] Combining recorded music, live performances, and dancing, these neighborhood events were "community theaters," which music scholar Guthrie Ramsey describes as central to the cultural experience and memory of black music.[14] As rock and roll was starting to take off nationally, these local concerts and record hops established black community spaces as the local sites through which this music could be experienced. These events often featured vocal harmony groups made up of teenagers from the neighborhood.[15] A North Philadelphia group called the Re-Vels, for example, performed frequently at the Richard Allen Community Centre in its neighborhood.[16] Weldon McDougal, who lived in West Philadelphia and sang with the Philadelphia Larks, remembered that these talent shows provided a rare opportunity to venture into other neighborhoods:

> You didn't go to too many different neighborhoods to go to any dance. Because again, they didn't want you to mess with their girls. You had to have a good reason [to go]. Like the Larks, we'd sing in community centers and also we would sing in talent shows in other parts of the city, like in North Philly at the Richard Allen projects, which I lived in [when I was younger]. So when they said they had a talent show over there, I said "oh man, let's go over there" . . . now here I am from West Philly going to the Richard Allen projects, and we didn't have cars so we caught the trolley. And we'd get off and walk on over there. And lo and behold here comes a gang. And they said, "What are y'all doing around here?" And we said, "We're in the talent show." And they said, "Y'all can't sing. The best group in the world is the Re-Vels." They lived in the Richard Allen projects. And they said, "We gonna kick your ass if y'all can't out sing the Re-Vels." They said, "sing something." So then I broke out, and they said "man, y'all sound pretty good." And they said "listen, we're gonna come to the talent show, but I don't think y'all can sing as good as the Re-Vels." And what it really was, these guys, they liked us, so we weren't in danger of getting beat up. But they still didn't like us enough to beat the Re-Vels, so they would come to the talent show and they'd be hollering and screaming. It was exciting you know?[17]

Like the Re-Vels and the Larks, several other singing groups formed among teenagers in the city's black neighborhoods. These vocal harmony groups were part of "the forgotten third of rock 'n' roll."[18] Stuart Goosman, Robert Pruter, and Philip Groia have shown that vocal harmony took off in Baltimore, Washington, D.C., Chicago, Los Angeles, and New York as it did in Philadelphia. These singing groups, usually comprising blue-collar young men from urban neighborhoods, drew from pop, blues, and novelty songs to create a smooth form of R&B that reached national popularity with groups like the Orioles, Clovers, Cadillacs, Cardinals, Flamingoes, and Moonglows. At the local level, vocal harmony groups practiced on street corners, in school hallways, in recreation centers, and in any available neighborhood space. Many groups became famous in their communities without ever recording an album.[19] The *Philadelphia Tribune* ran pictures and stories about local groups such as the Guy Tones, the Dreamers, the Opals, Ronald Jones and the Classmates, and the Satellites.[20] At a time when discrimination limited educational and employment opportunities for black youth, and stories on juvenile delinquency appeared frequently in the mainstream press, these "local teens make good" articles highlighted music as a productive activity that could lead to a career and financial success. Indeed, several recreation centers and church groups also put on talent shows for teenagers as a way to curb juvenile delinquency and gang violence.[21] While most vocal groups only performed at neighborhood showcases, several groups signed recording contracts and released singles, while other individuals, like Weldon McDougal, used their music experience to go into music promotion or production.[22] Regardless of their level of commercial success, each of these groups contributed to the development of rock and roll in Philadelphia.

MITCH THOMAS, TELEVISION PIONEER

If Georgie Woods became the most prominent rock and roll personality in Philadelphia and teenage singing groups and their fans provided the energy that fueled the music's growth in the city's neighborhoods, Mitch Thomas brought black rock and roll performers and teenage fans to television. Born in West Palm Beach, Florida, in 1922, Thomas's family moved to New Brunswick, New Jersey, in the 1930s. Thomas graduated from Delaware State College and served in the army before becoming the first black disc jockey in Wilmington, Delaware, in 1949. In 1952, Thomas moved to a larger station (WILM) that played music by black

FIGURE 17. The Re-Vels was one of the most popular teenage vocal harmony groups in Philadelphia, with twelve fan clubs including over a thousand members. May 19, 1956. Used with permission of *Philadelphia Tribune*.

R&B artists. By early 1955, Thomas also had a radio show on Philadelphia's WDAS, where he worked with Woods and Jocko Henderson. When a television opportunity opened up in Thomas's home market of Wilmington, Thomas got the call over these better-known Philadelphia-based radio hosts.[23]

The Mitch Thomas Show debuted on August 13, 1955, on WPFH, an unaffiliated television station that broadcast to Philadelphia and the Delaware Valley from Wilmington.[24] The show, which broadcast every Saturday, featured musical guests and teens dancing to records. In its basic production the show resembled *Bandstand* (which at the time was still a local program hosted by Bob Horn) and other locally broadcast teenage dance programs in other cities. *The Mitch Thomas Show* stood out from these other shows, however, because it was hosted by a black deejay and featured a studio audience of black teenagers. Otis Givens, who lived in South Philadelphia and attended Ben Franklin High School, remembered that he watched the show every weekend for a year before he finally made the trip to Wilmington and danced on the show. "When I got back to Philly, and everyone had seen me on TV, I was big time," Givens recalled. "We weren't able to get into *Bandstand*, [but] *The Mitch Thomas Show* gave me a little fame. I was sort of a celebrity at local dances."[25] Similarly, South Philadelphia teen Donna Brown recalled in a 1995 interview: "I remember at the same time that *Bandstand* used to come on, there used to be a black dance thing that came on, and it was *The Mitch Thomas Show. . . .* And that was something for the black kids to really identify with. Because you would look at *Bandstand* and we thought it was a joke."[26] The *Mitch Thomas Show* also became a frequent topic for the black teenagers who wrote the *Philadelphia Tribune*'s "Teen-Talk" columns. Much in the same way that national teen magazines followed *American Bandstand,* the *Tribune*'s teen writers kept tabs on the performers featured on Thomas's show, and described the teenagers who formed fan clubs to support their favorite musical artists and deejays.[27] The fan gossip shared in these columns documented the growth of a youth culture among the black teenagers whom *Bandstand* excluded. It was one of these fan clubs, moreover, that in 1957 made the most forceful challenge to *Bandstand*'s discriminatory admissions policies.[28] Although many of these teens watched both *Bandstand* and Thomas's program, as *Bandstand* grew in popularity and expanded into a national program, *The Mitch Thomas Show* was the only television program that represented Philadelphia's black rock and roll fans.

WPFH's decision to provide airtime for this groundbreaking show was influenced more by economics than by a concern for racial equality. Eager to compete with *Bandstand* and the afternoon offerings on the other network-affiliated stations, WPFH hoped that Thomas's show would appeal to both black and white youth in the same way as black-oriented radio.[29] The station's bet on Thomas was part of a larger strategy that included hiring white disc jockeys Joe Grady and Ed Hurst to host a daily afternoon dance program that started at 5 P.M., after *Bandstand* concluded its daily broadcast.[30] While *The Grady and Hurst Show* broadcast five times a week, it was the weekly *Mitch Thomas Show* that proved to be the more influential program.

Drawing on Thomas's contacts as a radio host and the talents of the teenagers who appeared on his show, the program helped shape the music tastes and dance styles of young people in Philadelphia. In a 1998 interview for the documentary *Black Philadelphia Memories,* Thomas recalled that "the show was so strong that I could play a record one time and break it wide open."[31] Indeed, Thomas's show hosted some of the biggest names in rock and roll, including Ray Charles, Little Richard, and the Moonglows. Thomas's show also featured several vocal harmony groups from the Philadelphia area.[32] Like Woods, Thomas promoted large stage shows in the Philadelphia area as well as small record hops at skating rinks.[33] In a 1986 interview with the Wilmington *News*

FIGURE 18. Mitch Thomas debuts on WPFH in Wilmington, Delaware. From 1955 to 1958, *The Mitch Thomas Show* broadcast the creative talents of black teenagers and influenced the dance styles on *Bandstand*. August 6, 1955. Used with permission of *Philadelphia Tribune*.

Journal, Thomas remembered that these events were often racially integrated: "The whites that came, they just said, 'Well I'm gonna see the artist and that's it.' I brought Ray Charles in there on a Sunday night, and it was just beautiful to look out there and see everything just nice."[34] The music and dance styles on his show also appealed to the white teenagers who danced on *American Bandstand*.[35] Because the show influenced *American Bandstand* during its first year as a national program, teenagers across the country learned dances popularized by *The Mitch Thomas Show*.

Despite its popularity among black and white teenagers, Thomas's show remained on television for only three years, from 1955 to 1958. The failure of the station that broadcast *The Mitch Thomas Show* underscores the tenuous nature of unaffiliated local programs like Thomas's. Storer Broadcasting Company purchased WPFH in 1956.[36] Storer frequently bought and sold stations, and, at the time of the WPFH acquisition, Storer also owned stations in Toledo, Cleveland, Atlanta, Miami, and Portland, Oregon. Storer changed WPFH's call letters to

WVUE, and hoped to move the station's facilities from Wilmington closer to Philadelphia. The plan faltered, and the station suffered significant operating losses over the next year.[37] Thomas's show was among the first victims of the station's financial problems. While advertisers started to pay more attention to black consumers in the 1950s, a product-identification stigma lingered throughout the decade, preventing many brands from sponsoring black programs.[38] WVUE canceled *The Mitch Thomas Show* in June 1958, citing the program's lack of sponsorship and low ratings compared to the network shows in Thomas's Saturday time slot.[39] Shortly after firing Thomas, Storer announced plans to sell WVUE in order to buy a station in Milwaukee (FCC regulations required multiple broadcast owners to divest one license in order to buy another). Unable to find a buyer for WVUE, Storer turned the station license back to the government, and the station went dark in September 1958.[40] The manager of WVUE later told broadcasting historian Gerry Wilkerson: "No one can make a profit with a TV station unless affiliated with NBC, CBS or ABC."[41] As Clark and *American Bandstand* celebrated the one-year anniversary of the show's national debut, local broadcast competition brought *The Mitch Thomas Show*'s groundbreaking three-year run to an unceremonious end. Mitch Thomas continued to work as a radio disc jockey through the 1960s, until he left broadcasting in 1969 to work as a counselor to gang members in Wilmington.[42]

Thomas's short-lived television career resembled the experiences of African American entertainers who hosted music and variety shows in this era. *The Nat King Cole Show* (1956–57) failed to attract national advertisers and lasted only a year. Before Nat King Cole, shows hosted by black singers Lorenzo Fuller (1947) and Billy Daniels (1952) and the variety program *Sugar Hill Times* (1949) also fared poorly. Among local programs, the *Al Benson Show* and Richard Stamz's *Open the Door Richard* both had brief periods of success in 1950s Chicago. Two other local dance programs featuring black teens proved more successful than *The Mitch Thomas Show*. *Teenage Frolics*, hosted by Raleigh, North Carolina, deejay J. D. Lewis, aired on Saturdays from 1958 to 1983, and Washington, D.C.'s *Teenarama Dance Party*, hosted by Bob King, aired from 1963 to 1970. Most famously, *Soul Train* started broadcasting locally from Chicago in 1970 before being picked up for national syndication from 1971 to 2006. Fifteen years before *Soul Train*, however, Mitch Thomas brought the creative talents of black teenagers to television.[43]

Georgie Woods viewed Thomas's breakthrough television show as a first step in securing more black-oriented, black-produced, and black-owned media. As Woods grew in popularity through the 1950s, he became increasingly vocal about these goals. Starting with these critical appraisals of the media industry, Woods used his platform as a broadcaster to become a prominent civil rights activist in the early 1960s. Woods's early work as Philadelphia's "king of rock and roll" made this later work possible. As Woods's radio show and concerts continued to attract larger audiences, rock and roll thrived in Philadelphia. Teenage vocal harmony groups and their fans kept the music going at the neighborhood level, and Mitch Thomas highlighted the talents of these musical artists and teenage dancers every Saturday afternoon. On the eve of *Bandstand*'s national debut in 1957, the television show was part of the local development of rock and roll in Philadelphia, but the most influential performances took place outside of *Bandstand*'s television studio.

THE EMERGENCE OF DICK CLARK AND
AMERICAN BANDSTAND

As Georgie Woods and Mitch Thomas helped popularize rock and roll, Dick Clark broke into radio broadcasting in Philadelphia. Clark was born in the upper-middle-class town of Bronxville, New York, in 1929 and graduated from Syracuse University with a major in advertising and a minor in radio broadcasting. After graduation, Clark worked as a radio announcer in Utica, New York, for one year before landing an interview with Philadelphia's WFIL with the help of family connections.[44] Clark started at WFIL in 1952 and hosted the radio version of *Bandstand* from 1954 to 1956. Bob Horn hosted the successful locally televised version of *Bandstand* during these years. Horn's tenure at *Bandstand* ended abruptly in June 1956 when police arrested him for drunk driving during the city's monthlong campaign against DWIs. Rumors also linked Horn to a vice ring that lured teenage girls to participate in pornographic photo sessions. Fearing the possibility of a scandal, WFIL fired Horn for causing an "embarrassment to the station."[45]

Producer Tony Mammarella replaced Horn on a temporary basis, but WFIL's general manager favored Clark as the new host. The twenty-six-year-old Clark debuted on *Bandstand* on July 9, 1956. In the wake of the allegations against Horn, WFIL emphasized Clark's "all-American boy" image. WFIL's managers also hoped that Clark's wholesome persona would keep *Bandstand* from being tainted by the anti–rock and roll protests that took place across the country in 1955 and 1956.

Much of this anti–rock and roll sentiment was fueled by overt racism and fears of miscegenation. Asa Carter, leader of the white supremacist North Alabama Citizens Council, garnered attention from national news media for his campaign to ban rock and roll, which he described as an NAACP plot to "mongrelize America." Members of Carter's North Alabama Citizens Council jumped on stage and attacked Nat King Cole at a concert in Birmingham in 1956 and also picketed a concert featuring the Platters, LaVern Baker, Bo Diddley, and Bill Haley with signs reading, "NAACP says integration, rock & roll, rock & roll," "Jungle Music promotes integration," and "Jungle music aids delinquency." While Carter and his white citizens' council received the most attention, segregationists across the South picketed rock and roll concerts, and city officials in Alabama, Louisiana, Arkansas, and Virginia passed regulations prohibiting interracial concerts and dances. In the West, a white supremacist group in Inglewood, California, published fliers with pictures of young black men and white women dancing, with captions reading "Boy meets girl . . . 'be-bop style,' and "Total Mongrelization."

As the rock and roll controversy escalated, city councils ranging from Jersey City to Santa Cruz and San Antonio banned rock and roll performances, and radio stations in Pittsburgh, Chicago, Denver, Lubbock, and Cincinnati refused to play rock and roll. These protests received national coverage in magazines like *Time, Newsweek, Life,* and *Look,* as well as major newspapers like the *New York Times.* While many of these articles expressed bemusement that a musical fad would generate so much attention, all of the articles conceded that the rhetoric against rock and roll was widespread.[46]

In addition to fears about racial mixing, rock and roll also faced criticism stemming from the moral panic surrounding juvenile delinquency in the mid-1950s. Juvenile delinquency garnered attention from both Washington and Hollywood in the postwar era and became a front-page issue in communities around the country. A wide range of critics argued that mass media, especially comic books, Hollywood films, television crime shows, and rock and roll music, incited young people to violence and illegal behavior. These disparate critiques from social reformers, psychologists, religious leaders, and politicians coalesced into a national issue when the Senate Subcommittee to Investigate Juvenile Delinquency held widely publicized hearings from 1954 to 1956. The Senate hearings led to

FIGURE 19. WFIL-TV advertisement for Dick Clark and *American Bandstand*. WFIL looked to Clark to put at safe face on teenage music. October 7, 1957. Used with permission of *Philadelphia Inquirer*.

no direct action, but they amplified the public furor over youth behavior and encouraged the public to fix blame on the media. Hollywood profited from and further escalated the moral panic surrounding juvenile delinquency with films like *Rebel without a Cause* (1955) and *Blackboard Jungle* (1955), the latter of which featured Bill Haley and His Comets' "Rock around the Clock" over the opening credits. Although these were "social problem" films aimed primarily at adult audiences, Hollywood producers took note of the teenager moviegoers who embraced stories of rebellious youth and produced a slew of rock and roll themed films, such as *Rock around the Clock* (1956), *Shake, Rattle, and Rock!* (1956), *The Girl Can't Help It* (1956), *Rock, Rock, Rock!* (1956), and *Don't Knock the Rock* (1957). Incidents of minor violence at screenings of these films contributed to the public discourse that linked rock and roll with juvenile delinquency.[47]

When Dick Clark took over *Bandstand* in the summer of 1956, then, rock and roll faced widespread and well-organized opposition. Clark defended the music because he saw that the future of *Bandstand*, and his own career trajectory, could be jeopardized by the criticism against rock and roll. He was not, however, a dedicated rock and roll fan when he took over the show. In his 1976 autobiography, Clark admitted: "I really didn't understand the music Horn played on 'Bandstand.' When I took over . . . I don't think I knew more than one or two tunes on the music list that afternoon."[48] Producer Tony Mammarella selected most of the music in Clark's first month on the *Bandstand*.[49] What Clark lacked in musical knowledge, however, he made up for with a desire to succeed financially. "I listened to the kids and let them tell me what they liked," he remembered. "I knew that if I could tune into them and keep myself on the show I could make a great deal of money."[50] In addition to the show's teens and Mammarella, Clark sought a musical education from Georgie Woods and two other deejays at the city's two black-oriented radio stations, Hy Lit and Jocko Henderson. Clark recalled that Georgie Woods "was my line to the black music market. Many records played on 'Bandstand' came on first as hits that were brewing on WDAS."[51] While he immersed himself in a crash course on rock and roll, Clark also developed relationships with established and up-and-coming record labels, disc jockeys, distributors, promoters, managers, and singers in Philadelphia and across the country.[52] As the radio and recording industries grew more decentralized in the mid-1950s, Clark's connections strengthened *Bandstand*'s status as a vital center in the music industry.

At the same time he established himself in the music business, Clark and WFIL's executives negotiated with ABC to pick up *Bandstand* as a national program. In 1957, ABC was the country's third major network, with fewer local network affiliates than NBC or CBS. In an effort to compete with the larger networks, whose programs mostly appealed to older audiences, ABC executives opted to develop programs targeted at younger viewers.[53] As historian Christopher Anderson has argued, ABC's "counter-programming" against the larger networks started in 1954 when the network partnered with independent producer Walt Disney to develop the *Disneyland* series. *Disneyland,* which featured Disney films, behind-the-scene footage from the Disney studio, and virtual tours of the new Disneyland amusement park, fit ABC's desire to encourage "habitual viewing" of weekly shows rather than the expensive spectaculars offered by the other networks. As Anderson notes, "ABC's programming strategy was built on the belief that television's fundamental appeal was less its ability to deliver exotic events, than its promise of a familiar cultural experience."[54] In a 1957 interview with *Television* magazine, ABC executive Leonard Goldenson outlined this counter-programming strategy. "Whatever audience is not watching at any given time makes for new possibilities," he noted. "We are not trying to take away audiences from CBS and NBC. . . . We are trying to carve our own network audience, to create new audiences."[55] This corporate strategy made *Bandstand* and its loyal audience of teen viewers, both of which came with low production costs, an attractive addition for ABC.

To sell *Bandstand* to ABC, WFIL executives sent a kinescope of the show to the network, and Clark met with ABC executives in New York. The WFIL team outlined *Bandstand*'s sales pitch most clearly in *The Official Bandstand Yearbook 1957*. The yearbook was ostensibly a memento for the show's fans, but WFIL also distributed it to potential sponsors. On the yearbook's final page Clark delineated, for both sponsors and ABC, the reasons why *Bandstand* provided a sound commercial investment. "For nearly five years now, BANDSTAND has come to you each weekday afternoon over WFIL-TV," he wrote. Clark continued:

> For the hundreds of youngsters who come to the studios each day, and the millions of "youngsters" of all ages who watch television, we hope BAND-STAND continues to be an entertaining and enjoyable experience.
>
> Our effort is dedicated to bringing young men and women together in a friendly atmosphere, and to provide wholesome entertainment for a few hours each afternoon.
>
> Because everyone who watches BANDSTAND is a part of the show, I know you will be as happy as I am to learn how successful the program is. It is, for example, the most-viewed program in Philadelphia daytime television; it has been copied by scores of stations across the country; it has a larger audience at its time period than all the stations combined in Detroit, Washington, Los Angeles, or Seattle.[56]

Set next to a head shot of a young, neatly groomed Clark in a jacket and tie, this summary presented *Bandstand* as having successfully tapped into the lucrative teenage market without being pulled into the controversies that surrounded rock and roll. Clark and WFIL pitched the show in relation to a specific demographic (teenagers) and a specific day part (afternoon), both of which resonated with ABC's niche market strategy. All of this appealed to ABC, as did WFIL's promise to deliver the program for no charge other than the expense of transmitting *Bandstand* from Philadelphia to the network feed.[57] After this extensive lobbying by Clark and WFIL executives, ABC decided to give the show a trial national broadcast run under the name *American Bandstand*.

American Bandstand debuted nationally on August 5, 1957, from 3 to 4:30 P.M. across forty-eight of ABC's affiliate stations (viewers in Philadelphia received an extra sixty minutes of *Bandstand*, as the program continued to broadcast locally from 2:30 to 3 and from 4:30 to 5:00 P.M.). The show maintained several of the basic production elements established during the Bob Horn era. Dick Clark introduced records, and the camera followed teenagers as they selected partners to dance. Two or three times during the show, Clark would introduce singers or groups who would lip-sync their latest hits. The production was so familiar that the *Philadelphia Inquirer*'s review of the national debut noted that *American Bandstand* was "pretty much the same dance-disc-and-din mixture as before."[58] National press reviews were less generous. *Billboard* magazine praised Clark, but complained that "the bulk of the 90 minutes was devoted to colorless juveniles trudging thru early American dances like the Lindy and the box step to recorded tunes of the day." The premiere succeeded as a "sociological study of teenager behavior," the article continued, but failed as "entertainment."[59] The *New York Times* reviewer J. P. Shanley shared this dim view of the show's entertainment value. "Viewers who are much beyond voting age are not likely to derive much pleasure from 'American Bandstand.' . . . Those who have been voting for quite a few years may, in fact, find [the program] to be something of an ordeal," Shanley commented. Shanley, who also praised Clark, took note of the show's dress code: "The girls wore pretty gowns and the boys were dressed conservatively. There were no motorcycle jackets and hardly a sideburn in the crowd." *American Bandstand*, Shanley concluded, was "almost identical" to a locally broadcast televised dance program hosted in New York by disc jockey Ted Steele.[60] Similarly, *Washington Post* critic Lawrence Laurent compared *American Bandstand* to Milt Grant's televised dance show for D.C. teens. Laurent bemoaned the number of television shows aimed at teenagers and hoped that the trend would pass.[61] George Pitts, the reviewer from the *Pittsburgh Courier*, a leading black newspaper, was equally dismissive. He compared the program to dance shows hosted by local deejays Clark Race and Chuck Brinkman, and summarized *American Bandstand* as "The kids screamed and chomped gum. Dick Clark giggled and sold more gum."[62] As these reviews suggest, *American Bandstand* was not an immediate hit among adult critics, and the show's music and dancing format was similar to that of locally broadcast television shows in other cities.

While *American Bandstand* failed to impress these critics, it received support from other important backers. *TV Guide*, which like WFIL-TV was owned by Walter Annenberg's Triangle Publications, published favorable reviews of the show in September and October 1957. Among teen magazines, *Seventeen* (another Triangle Publications property), *Teen*, and *16 Magazine* quickly ran stories featuring Dick Clark and *American Bandstand*'s teenage regulars. The program also proved to be an immediate ratings success for ABC. Nielsen ratings showed that 20 million viewers watched *American Bandstand* during the first week, and new stations were signing up to carry the show. By September, the number of affiliates carrying the show had increased from forty-eight to sixty, and ABC added *American Bandstand* to its schedule on a permanent basis.[63]

THE RISE AND DECLINE OF *AMERICAN BANDSTAND*'S INFLUENCE ON POPULAR MUSIC

When Clark and *American Bandstand* came to national television, they benefited from and contributed to the restructuring of key media industries. In the early 1950s, the record and radio industries started to decentralize, and a number of small record labels and local radio stations emerged.[64] When Clark took over *Bandstand* in 1956, hit records were made on a city by city (or market by market) basis. Major record companies and large independent labels in New York, Chicago, and Los Angeles had local promotion men whose job was to get their records played on local radio in smaller markets. Cincinnati's independent King Records, for example, had a network of thirty-three branch offices across the country.[65] Record companies would track which records were "breaking" (getting airplay and selling well) in different cities, and these popular records would then be pushed across the country. Record companies considered Philadelphia a "break-out" market that could influence national distribution, but records that were hits on smaller independent labels in cities like Cleveland or Minneapolis could also shape Philadelphia's playlist.

When ABC started broadcasting *American Bandstand* nationally in 1957, the show reshaped this city-by-city method of song promotion. Whereas recording artists and record promoters formerly needed to make numerous appearances at local radio stations and concerts across the county to increase record sales, daily airplay on *American Bandstand* or a single guest appearance could instantly help move a record up the charts.[66] The power of *American Bandstand* as a distribution channel and promotional vehicle of new music was not lost on record companies. Eager to get their artists booked on the show, record distributors often reimbursed the program for the appearance fee paid to the artist. Describing this kickback system in a 1988 interview, Clark recounted: "Artists would come on the show, and the record company would allegedly pay them for their performance [to satisfy union requirements]. We'd pay for maybe half the people who came on, and when our money ran out, we'd say 'We'll book them and you'll pay them.' It wasn't illegal, nor was it immoral."[67] While these reimbursements fell on the right side of the law, record companies also frequently gave disc jockeys money, gifts, or song-writing credits in exchange for playing certain records. These business practices, called "payola," were an outgrowth of song-plugging, a music business tradition that dated to Tin Pan Alley publishing companies in the early twentieth century. While not new, payola emerged as a major scandal in 1959 when the congressional investigation into rigged television quiz shows turned its attention to the music business.[68]

The rise in popularity of teen music, such as rock and roll and R&B, fueled the payola scandal. The politicians involved in the investigation hoped to impress their constituents during an election year by uncovering corruption in the music business. Encouraging these politicians to investigate teen music was the American Society of Composers, Authors, and Publishers (ASCAP), which was in a struggle against rival song/performance-licensing agent Broadcast Music, Inc. (BMI). To strengthen its case, the ASCAP songwriters hired Vance Packard, media critic and author of *Hidden Persuaders,* who argued that "the rock and roll, hillbilly, and Latin American movements were largely engineered, manipulated for the interests of BMI, and . . . that the public was manipulated into liking rock and roll."[69] The unpredictability of the market for rock and roll and R&B records was also a theme in contemporary press coverage of the new teen music. "The rock 'n' roll business is crazy," *Life* reported just before the payola scandal. "Anyone—*anyone*—can record and press 5,000 records for $1,200. So there now are more than 1,500 little pop records companies who press almost any song or sound that comes along and hope the lightening will strike." This article went on to quote a record executive who lamented: "Anyone who thinks he can pick what the kids'll want next, his orientation is in Cloudsville."[70] One of the payola subcommittee's tasks, then, was to clarify how the record industry worked. These politicians, however, struggled to distinguish among the various financial investments and incentives that connected record companies, deejays, and playlists.

Clark was the only disc jockey with a national audience, and the subcommittee was especially interested in his business endeavors. The hearings revealed that Clark had an interest in thirty-three music-related companies and that he owned copyrights to 160 songs, 143 of which he received as gifts. Music industry witnesses called by the subcommittee testified to giving Clark copyrights to songs or paying him consulting fees to receive more spins on *American Bandstand*. Defending himself from these allegations, Clark told the subcommittee, "I have never taken payola. . . . I followed normal business practices under the ground rules that then existed."[71] Here and throughout the hearings, Clark adopted a narrow definition of payola as an explicit agreement to play a particular record in return for a specified payment. Robert Lishman, chief counsel for the house subcommittee, argued that this definition was "phrased in such careful legal draftsmanship as to let him do the substance of the wrong and avoid the consequence."[72] To convince the subcommittee that *American Bandstand* did not artificially manipulate the popularity of records, Clark paid Computech, a New York data processing firm, to conduct a study of the number of times *American Bandstand* played each record. The firm then compared the "popularity scores" for the Clark-affiliated records to those that were not linked. Not surprisingly, the report concluded that Clark did not favor records in which he had an interest. In his 1976 autobiography, Clark recalled Computech as a successful diversion. "I spent $6,000 creating the biggest red herring I could find," he recalled, "something that would shift the Subcommittee's attention away from my scalp."[73] This misdirection prevented the subcommittee from noting, as historian John Jackson has calculated, that over half of the records produced by Clark-affiliated companies were played on *American Bandstand*, including many that never appeared on *Billboard*'s top 100. While the subcommittee focused on *American Bandstand*'s ability to make any record into a hit, it failed to see that records in which Clark had a financial interest received an inordinately high percentage of spins relative to competitors.[74]

In addition to probing the connection between Clark's financial interests and *Bandstand*'s playlist, the subcommittee expressed its animus to teenage music generally, asking Clark why he did not play more songs by "Frank Sinatra, Bing Crosby, Perry Como, and other established stars, instead of building up unknown names." Clark replied that Sinatra and the older generation of singers did not appeal to his teenage audience.[75] In pointing to his teenage audience as a defense of his choice of records, Clark reiterated an argument he used earlier to dismiss critics of the show. "Unlike the legitimate theater, television doesn't live or die by the critics," he told the *Saturday Evening Post* in the first year of the payola investigations. "I'm not putting on my show for them. My only aim is to please the people at home who watch."[76] Similarly, in March 1960, a month before he testified to the subcommittee, Clark told an interviewer: "I don't set trends. I just find out what they are and exploit them. . . . Like any businessman, the desires of my customers must come first."[77] Presenting himself in the subcommittee hearings and popular press as the unbiased servant of the teen consumer market, Clark distanced himself from the charges of influence and reified the existence of the teen market as an entity to be served.

Despite the evidence presented in the hearings, Clark successfully deflected the subcommittee's charges. Clark had to divest himself of his numerous financial interests in music publishing and record manufacturing firms, but the subcommittee only reprimanded him. Clark's clean image and cool demeanor helped him weather the payola scandal, but more important, ABC president Leonard Goldenson and Walter Annenberg, both of whom had an investment in *American Bandstand*'s continued success, stood behind Clark during the hearings and helped rebuild his image afterward. When the payola scandal started to develop, ABC asked the network's music-related employees to sign an affidavit stating that they had not received payola in any form and that they did not possess interests in any record companies. When *American Bandstand* producer Tony Mammarella received the affidavit, he admitted receiving monetary payments from several record companies and, opting to maintain these financial interests, resigned. Alan Freed, whose radio show broadcast on WABC in New York, refused to sign the affidavit for risk of perjuring himself by saying he had never taken payola. In contrast, ABC allowed Clark to draft and sign his own affidavit with a more narrow definition of payola than the affidavit circulated company-wide. As part of this negotiation with ABC, Clark agreed to divest himself of his numerous financial interests in music publishing and record manufacturing firms. ABC supported Clark's statement of innocence and played up Mammarella's payola confession. The network issued press releases before and after the hearings reiterating their support of Clark, and in his testimony, Goldenson defended his network's star. *TV Guide,* which like *Bandstand*'s Philadelphia home WFIL was part of Walter Annenberg's Triangle Publications, ran a story after the hearings titled "Guilty Only of Success," which reported the outpouring of support for Clark from *American Bandstand* fans.

The payola investigations derailed the careers of several major disc jockeys, including Freed and Tommy Smalls, Jack Walker, and Hal Jackson in New York; "Jumpin" George Oxford in Oakland; Tom Clay in Detroit; and Joe Smith in Boston. These deejays, both black and white, lacked the high-profile support that Clark enjoyed. *American Bandstand* made Clark the only national deejay, and while this celebrity made Clark a target for the payola subcommittee, it also gave him more clout with ABC than other deejays had with their local stations.[78]

While the payola investigation threatened Clark's career, the scandal actually strengthened *American Bandstand's* position in the pop music business in the early 1960s. After the payola scandal, disc jockeys held less power in selecting their own playlists, and in their place station program directors reduced the range of songs stations played. The tightening of playlists was abetted by the shift in radio ownership from individual local stations to chain owners who held station licenses in multiple markets. Entering the 1960s, these chain owners adopted a Top 40 radio strategy that called for stations to limit their programming to forty mainstream market pop singles, and to play the top ten songs in the heaviest rotation. While this Top 40 concept proved financially successful for the chain owners, it centralized and homogenized radio by catering to listeners' current tastes and limiting the willingness of stations to play unknown music.[79]

American Bandstand contributed to, and thrived in, this atmosphere of sameness. The program featured a number of singers, signed to local record labels, who sounded very much alike. Bobby Rydell and Charlie Gracie on Cameo-Parkway, Fabian and Frankie Avalon on Chancellor, and Freddie Cannon on Swan all appeared regularly on *American Bandstand* and had hit records in the late 1950s and early 1960s. In addition to these Philadelphia label stars, Paul Anka (ABC-Paramount), Bobby Darin (Atlantic), and Johnny Tillotson (Cadence) also scored hit records with tame rock and roll songs in a crooning style.[80] Like Clark, these white "teen idols" presented a sanitized version of rock and roll designed to sell records while avoiding the connections to race and sex that fueled opposition to rock and roll. Clark also had financial interests in many of these artists. Before he divested his formal recording interests during the payola hearings in early 1960, Clark had an interest in Swan and was reported to have interests in Cameo and Chancellor. After divesting, Clark maintained close connections with the directors of these Philadelphia labels and negotiated exclusive performances of their artists on *American Bandstand*.[81]

Reflecting on the commercial dominance of the these artists, music historians Steve Chapple and Reebee Garofalo have called the period from 1958 to 1963 "the lull in rock," in which "Philadelphia Schlock" filled the vacuum left by "hardline rock 'n' rollers" like Elvis Presley, Buddy Holly, Little Richard, Jerry Lee Lewis, and Chuck Berry."[82] Similarly, R&B historian and critic Peter Guralnick described this era as the "treacle period" in which "rock 'n' roll died."[83] While the promotional power of *American Bandstand* and the show's primary audience of teenage girls certainly helped these teen idols sell lots of records, the program also offered a wider variety of music than was available on Top 40 radio. From 1958 through 1963, *American Bandstand* hosted R&B vocal groups like the Coasters, the Revels, the Drifters, and the Impressions; early girl groups like the Shirelles; rockabilly and country-influenced artists like Brenda Lee, Johnny Cash, Conway Twitty, and Patsy Cline; and Motown artists such as Mary Wells and Smoky Robinson and the Miracles; as well as R&B and soul pioneers like James Brown and the Famous Flames, Marvin Gaye, and Aretha Franklin.[84] If *American Bandstand* helped push Philadelphia Schlock up the charts in this era, it also exposed viewers to a wider range of music than did Top 40 radio. Still, like Top 40 radio, *American Bandstand* showcased and marketed new records and neglected veteran R&B musicians who helped create rock and roll, like T-Bone Walker, Big Mama Thornton, LaVern Baker, and Bo Diddley. The payola scandal contributed to this homogenization of popular music, and the predominance of teen idols on *American Bandstand* marked rock and roll and the youth consumer culture surrounding it as white.

American Bandstand lost much of its power as a new music venue in August 1963, when ABC moved the show from weekdays to Saturday afternoons. As the network affiliates began to tire of the format, the show lost its hold on the local markets that were central to its daily success. Clark later recalled that affiliated stations "got greedy and took the time back to put their own material on where they got 100 percent of the revenue. . . . As two or three stations grab it off, you get less clearance, therefore you get less ratings, and it's an endless cycle. You eventually get cancelled."[85] Most often, stations turned to syndicated reruns of network sit-coms, westerns, or adventure series.[86] In Philadelphia, for example, WFIL filled the weekday afternoon slot with *Major Adams—Trailmaster* and syndicated reruns of *Wagon Train*. Responding to ABC's reduction of *American Bandstand*'s airtime, Clark increased his focus on other television opportunities. In late 1963, Clark's desire to expand his television career led him to California to host a game show called *The Object Is*. Although the show was short-lived, the move precipitated *American Bandstand*'s move from Philadelphia to Los Angeles. In February 1964, *American Bandstand* made its debut in Los Angeles, where it would broadcast weekly until 1989.[87] Even after the show went off the air, Dick Clark worked to maintain *American Bandstand*'s commercial visibility through televised anniversary specials, books and music box sets, and the NBC drama *American Dreams* (2002–2005). *American Bandstand*'s successful seven-year run as a daily program in Philadelphia and its remarkable longevity made it part of the cultural memory of millions of viewers.

GEORGIE WOODS, ROCK AND ROLL, AND CIVIL RIGHTS

Shortly before he decamped for the West Coast, Dick Clark narrated a short booster film called *Song of Philadelphia*. Designed to promote the city as a destination for tourism and business, the film juxtaposed images of the history of Philadelphia, including Independence Hall, the Liberty Bell, and Betsy Ross's house, with contemporary scenes of the new metropolis, such as skyscrapers, the science museum, and, of course, *American Bandstand*.[88] Not surprisingly, this fourteen-minute advertisement for the "quaint" and "majestic" city of Philadelphia made no mention of the civil rights protests that were growing larger and more publicized in the city, or of the deejay who played a leading role in these protests. When *American Bandstand* wrapped up its run in Philadelphia in 1964, deejay Georgie Woods was more successful than ever and was in the process of using music to advance civil rights. Woods's civil rights activism developed out of his experience in working with black teenagers as a deejay and concert promoter as well as his concern about the lack of black television personalities and black-owned broadcast stations in the city. Woods used his radio show and concerts to raise money for the NAACP Legal Defense and Education Fund and to promote civil rights protests, in which he also participated. By merging his critiques of the media industry with civil rights work in support of the black teenagers who sustained his broadcast career, Woods offered a model for what music could achieve beyond commercial success.

Although Woods's concerts were popular when they started in 1954, they took off in the late 1950s and became part of the fight against juvenile delinquency. With his drawing power and the chance for artists to perform on *American Bandstand* while they were in Philadelphia, Woods's concerts attracted some of the biggest names in rock and roll. Woods's March 1958 ten-day show at the Uptown Theater in North

Philadelphia, for example, featured Chuck Berry, while Sam Cooke head-lined his April 1958 show at the Arena in West Philadelphia.[89] The Up-town was part of an informal network of black theaters that hosted concerts in the East and Midwest, including New York's Apollo Theater, Washington, D.C.'s Howard Theater, Baltimore's Royal Theater, Detroit's Fox Theater, and Chicago's Regal Theater. The *Philadelphia Tribune* esti-mated that sixty thousand people attended the Uptown concerts and noted that "the long waiting lines of teenagers outside the theater—sometimes more than a block long—are visible proof of the magic draw-ing power of Georgie Woods, the 'King of Rock and Roll.'"[90] Woods built on this success with two more shows in 1958 and four in 1959, all multiple-day shows at the Uptown. In addition to enhancing his stature as a broadcaster, Woods believed that these concerts helped curb juvenile delinquency. Woods told the *Tribune:*

> Many of the teenagers who patronize these shows find in them an outlet for their emotions. And while previous single shows have been attended by as many as 30,000 teenagers we have never had any serious trouble. This proves, as far as I am concerned, that there might be less delinquency if there was more healthy entertainment such as that offered by our shows.[91]

With this commitment to music as a way to reduce juvenile delin-quency, Woods and deejay Mitch Thomas also hosted dances at the El-mwood skating rink in Southwest Philadelphia and the Carmen skating rink in the Germantown section of the city.[92] Although some white teenagers attended Woods's Uptown and Elmwood events, black teens made up the majority of the audiences. Woods used his celebrity to pro-vide healthy social activities for teens and built on the work of local black churches and community organizations that had a long-standing concern with delinquency.[93]

In addition to his well-received concerts, Woods also used his column in the *Philadelphia Tribune* to critique the lack of black representation in the media industry. More specifically, Woods raised the question of why, after the cancellation of Mitch Thomas's show, there were no black dee-jays on television in Philadelphia. Woods started by noting that "Teen-agers have won the hearts of advertisers," and that these teens "have said that the time is ripe for a DJ on one of the TV channels here."[94] As evi-dence Woods cited Sandra Williams, a North Philadelphia teen who was collecting one thousand signatures asking for the addition of a black deejay to one of the local television stations. Woods wrote that these teens viewed Dick Clark as "the most," but that they preferred the music played on Woods's WDAS over *American Bandstand*. Woods concluded by asking his readers to join these teens in a letter-writing campaign to television stations: "It is my feeling, as I have previously stated, that the Negro population in this city warrants a Negro on the staff of a TV station, whether it be DJ or in some other capacity."[95] Woods continued to make his case in subsequent columns. Outlining the millions of dollars black Philadelphians spent on food, household goods, apparel, and other products and services, Woods asked why more black personalities were not hired to advertise these products.[96] "Television, like radio, is only able to exist because of advertising in America," Woods wrote. "There can be no question that capable men and women, with tan skins, and some who have that one drop of colored blood in their veins, are available and what they don't know about TV they can be taught."[97] Woods concluded:

> It is our contention that there is many a Negro who can sell soap, cosmetics, beer, automobiles, food or anything else just as well as a white person can. All he asks is a chance. Begin to flood the TV stations here, folks, and advise them the time is RIPE for a Negro to be engaged.[98]

Woods peppered these columns with notes on the lack of black technicians at the city's television stations and black-oriented radio stations.[99] Neither these columns nor the letter-writing campaign produced immediate changes in the city's media industry, but Woods continued to look for opportunities to establish a foothold in television. He eventually got his shot at television in 1965 with a dance program called *Seventeen Canteen,* which broadcast locally for two years on WPHL, a new station in which he held a small ownership stake.[100]

These critiques of the media industry came at the same time as Woods became more involved in Philadelphia's growing civil rights movement. Although Woods had participated in NAACP membership drives since 1955, it was Cecil B. Moore's campaign for NAACP branch president in 1962 that drew him fully into civil rights work.[101] As Woods recalled in a 1996 interview with radio historian and producer Jacqui Webb:

> I got into civil rights because there was discrimination against black people everywhere, and I felt it personally. Then I met Cecil Moore and he asked me to join in some pickets and demonstrations and things like that, and I'd go on the air and tell people where I was going to be demonstrating, and a mob of people would show up and I had a microphone and I was directing people. When school let out I had all the kids in town listening to me. When school got out all the teenagers came and got into the pickets lines because I was there demonstrating for our rights.[102]

FIGURE 20. NAACP Philadelphia branch president Cecil B. Moore (far right) presents singer Jackie Wilson (left) and deejay Georgie Woods (center) with awards for their support of local NAACP's activities. September 10, 1963. Used with permission of *Philadelphia Tribune*.

Moore's demands for black leaders who were in touch with black working-class communities echoed Woods's critique of the lack of black leadership in the city's media. After Moore's election, Woods became the vice president of the Philadelphia branch of the NAACP and used his talents as a concert promoter to help raise money for the NAACP. Woods held his first fundraising concert at the Uptown Theater on May 14, 1963. Singers Jackie Wilson and Linda Hopkins, comedian Bill Cosby, and other acts performed to a sold-out crowd of two thousand people in an atmosphere the *Philadelphia Tribune* said had "the flavor of an old-fashioned, 'down home' revival."[103] The show raised $60,000 for the local branch and provided Moore and Woods with an opportunity to urge fans to support the NAACP.

The concert came days after Moore and the Philadelphia NAACP organized one of the city's largest civil rights demonstrations to support the Birmingham civil rights movement. Moore made a provocative comparison between Philadelphia and Birmingham in his speech at the concert: "Personally, I can't see much difference between a Philadelphia policeman and a Ku Klux Klansman in Birmingham. The only difference is the geographic location."[104] Focusing on employment discrimination in Philadelphia, Moore went on to detail differences in pay for white and black construction workers. Moore noted that white construction workers were paid $200 and asked the crowd: "They want to pay your daddies and husbands $75 a week. We aren't going to put up with that are we?" Moore concluded his speech by asking for support for the upcoming pickets of city construction sites, which developed into a weeklong picket at the Strawberry Mansion Junior High School construction site in North Philadelphia. Woods praised Moore's words and actions, calling him "a leader who has the nerve to point his finger in the white man's face and tell him when he's wrong. That's the only reason Cecil Moore is criticized. He's criticized because he stands up for the Negro."[105] In addition to his fundraising and words of support, Woods also participated in the NAACP's school construction protest two weeks later.[106]

Woods expanded his civil rights activism over the next two years, supporting the NAACP with fundraising concerts, using his radio show to publicize issues and protests, and participating in pickets. In fall 1963, for example, Woods and Nat King Cole headlined a memorial and protest rally in Center City following the bombing of the 16th Street Baptist Church in Birmingham that killed four young girls.[107] Woods also hosted a Freedom Show in March 1964 to raise money for the NAACP Legal Defense and Education Fund and the Opportunities Industrialization Center, a North Philadelphia job training center run by the Reverend Leon Sullivan.[108] Held at the Convention Hall in West Philadelphia, the concert featured Sam Cooke, Jerry Butler, the Shirelles, Martha and the Vandellas, and comedian Jackie "Moms" Mabley.[109] The concert raised $30,000, and the *Tribune* estimated that fourteen thousand people filled the hall, with another five thousand waiting outside.[110] Woods hosted a second Freedom Show on March 23, 1965. In the weeks leading up to the show, Woods traveled to Selma, Alabama, to protest the attacks on civil rights marchers by state and local police. Civil rights activists in New York, Dallas, Washington, D.C., Nashville, Boston, San Francisco, and other cities organized sympathy protests against racial violence in Selma.[111] In Philadelphia, Woods led four thousand marchers from the Uptown Theater down Broad Street to City Hall, where they were joined by Moore, comedian Dick Gregory, and eight thousand other marchers. Almost all of the marchers were black, and many were teenagers from the city's public high schools, whom, the *Tribune* reported, "frequently left the main body of demonstrators to stage their own demonstration, featuring freedom 'war chants,' hand-clapping and rock 'n' roll-type singing."[112]

Woods marched in a blue denim workman's jumpsuit rather than his usual silk suit and explained to the *Tribune* reporter, "This is a day for walking, not talking."[113] The Freedom Show following the protest march raised another $30,000 for the NAACP. The *Philadelphia Tribune* praised Woods's accomplishments, calling him "a true champion of the civil rights offensive in Philadelphia."[114]

As historian William Barlow has shown, black deejays like Woods played an important role in mobilizing turnout for civil rights protests. Among civil rights organizations, Martin Luther King Jr. and the Southern Christian Leadership Conference worked to cultivate a network of black radio hosts across the country. In addition to Woods, Nat Williams in Memphis, Louis Fletcher in Nashville, Hot Rod Hulbert in Baltimore, Mary Mason in Philadelphia, and many others kept listeners abreast of local and national civil rights developments, interviewed civil rights leaders, and encouraged meeting attendance. In addition to providing a broadcast platform for civil rights information, deejays were well known and respected members of their communities who could move thousands of people to attend rallies.[115] For these broadcasters, the localism of radio made it the ideal medium for organizing grassroots actions. Woods used radio to this end in the mass protest organized by Moore and the NAACP at Girard College, a North Philadelphia boarding school for fatherless boys that, by rule of the founder's will, excluded black youth. As historian Matthew Countryman describes, for Moore "the goal of desegregating Girard College was ... less important than finding a protest target that would attract the black youth of North Philadelphia, and in particular the teenage members of the area's street-corner gangs, to join the NAACP picket line in front of [Girard's] ten-foot walls."[116]

Woods contributed to the Girard protest by leading marches of young people to the picket line and recruiting other teenagers through his radio and stage shows.[117] With Woods's help, civil rights activists picketed Girard every day from May 1 to December 18, 1965. Moore suspended the protests after two attorneys appointed by Governor William Scranton filed a lawsuit in federal court to overturn Girard's will.[118] On May 19, 1968, the U.S. Supreme Court ruled that Girard College could no longer admit only white students.[119]

Although the Girard victory was largely symbolic and did not impact the de facto segregation in the city's public schools, the protests at Girard mobilized anger among black Philadelphians over persistent racial inequality in the city. With Woods as one of the leading organizers, the protests also exposed many black teenagers to activism for the first time.

Kenny Gamble, for example, remembered that in his early twenties he became more aware of discrimination through the Girard protest. Gamble attended West Philadelphia High School, just blocks from the *American Bandstand* studio. As an aspiring singer, Gamble brought coffee and records he cut in penny arcade recording booths to Woods at the WDAS studio.[120] In a tribute to Woods's civil rights work, Gamble wrote:

> The public school system didn't teach us anything about our culture or our heritage or anything like that. So the Girard College demonstrations sort of opened my eyes to discrimination. . . . I felt good that Georgie Woods was there because this was somebody that I knew. . . . And when they were talking about how Girard College would not admit Black people, and how racist Stephen Girard and his whole system had been, it really opened my eyes up. From that day on I started to be more aware.[121]

By the end of the Girard protest in 1965, Gamble and his musical partner Leon Huff had started their first record label. With the help of writer-producer Thom Bell, Gamble and Huff became one of the leading R&B production teams of the late 1960s, and they founded Philadelphia International Records in 1970 as an upstart competitor to Motown. The soul-funk "Philadelphia Sound" they developed featured gospel-inspired vocals and narrative lyrics over tight rhythm tracks and lush string and horn arrangements.[122] Like Motown, Philadelphia International scored crossover hits on the R&B and pop charts in the early and mid-1970s with songs like "If You Don't Know Me by Now" by Harold Melvin and the Blue Notes, "Back Stabbers" and "Love Train" by the O'Jays, and "I'll Be Around" by the Spinners.[123] With his radio show at WDAS, Woods helped to break many of Gamble and Huff's songs, and helped to reassert Philadelphia's status within popular music.[124]

In 2009, Philadelphia dedicated the stretch of Broad Street in front of the Uptown Theater as Georgie Woods Boulevard, and a mural of Woods appears on the side of the building. These acknowledgements honor how Woods used his radio show and concerts to popularize rock and roll and R&B and how, in turn, he used this popularity to fight for civil rights and more black voices in media. While Mitch Thomas did not become an activist of Woods's stature, Thomas's television show broke ground as one of first televised dance show for black teenagers. *The Mitch Thomas Show* also made black youth culture visible at a time when black teens were excluded from *American Bandstand*. Despite their roles as rock and roll pioneers, neither Woods nor Thomas is well known outside of Philadelphia.

Dick Clark, in contrast, became one of the most successful entrepreneurs in music history. Clark's breakthrough moment was when ABC turned *Bandstand* into the nationally televised *American Bandstand*, making Clark the only national rock and roll deejay. Like Clark, Woods and Thomas sought to capitalize professionally from the popularity of rock and roll, but unlike Clark, Woods and Thomas remained focused on Philadelphia's local music scene and their local communities of fans. For Woods and Thomas, segregated local markets marked the opportunities and limits of their careers, and activism followed from these close community ties. Clark's understanding of the local community of fans was necessarily complicated by the fact that his show broadcast not just to Philadelphia, but also to Portland, Peoria, and dozens of other media markets as well. He had unique access to a nation of young consumers that he leveraged to great profit. With *American Bandstand*, commerce and community mixed at a national scale, and the next chapter explores the national youth culture that emerged in the process.

CHAPTER 6

"They'll Be Rockin' on Bandstand, in Philadelphia, P.A."

Imagining National Youth Culture on
American Bandstand

Cause they'll be rockin' on Bandstand
In Philadelphia P.A.
Deep in the heart of Texas
And 'round the Frisco bay
Way out in St. Louis
And down in New Orleans
All the cats wanna dance with
Sweet little sixteen.

— Chuck Berry, "Sweet Little Sixteen," 1958

It was no accident that Chuck Berry made reference to *American Bandstand* when he released "Sweet Little Sixteen" in January 1958. Berry made his national television debut on *American Bandstand* in 1957, and including these lyrics helped ensure that this new song would receive ample airtime on the program. Indeed, Dick Clark later recalled "Sometimes we heard a hit the first time we played the record—Chuck Berry's 'Sweet Little Sixteen' was like that."[1] Berry's song reached number two on the Billboard chart and stayed on the chart for sixteen weeks, thanks in large part to its frequent exposure on Clark's show. Less obvious than his references to Philadelphia and *American Bandstand*, Berry's nods to teens dancing in Texas, San Francisco, St. Louis, and New Orleans underscored a point that *American Bandstand* called attention to every afternoon—the existence of a national youth culture. As the show sought to establish itself as a national program, it pointed to its local fans and television affiliates in different parts of the country as evidence of its national reach. In helping viewers and advertisers imagine a national youth culture, *America Bandstand* promoted the idea that teenagers were united in their simultaneous consumption of television and rock and roll. This chapter examines how, through a range of production strategies, *American Bandstand* encouraged the show's viewers, advertisers, and television affiliates to see the program as the thread that stitched together different teenagers in different parts of the country into a coherent and recognizable national youth culture.

In exploring how *American Bandstand* producers articulated this vision of national youth culture, this chapter builds on Josh Kun's notion of "audiotopia" and Benedict Anderson's concept of "imagined communities." Kun uses the concept of audiotopia to describe how "music functions like a possible utopia for the listener, that music is experienced not only as sound that goes into our ears and vibrates through our bones but as a space that we can enter into, encounter, move around in, inhabit, be safe in, learn from."[2] *American Bandstand* adds a visual component to Kun's formulation. Teenagers tuned into *American Bandstand* to watch other teenagers dance to records, to see musical artists perform, and to try out the latest dance moves in their own living rooms. *American Bandstand*'s daily images encouraged teenagers to imagine themselves as part of a national audience enjoying the same music and dances at the same time. *American Bandstand* offered its viewers a teenage television audiotopia every afternoon. This televised audiotopia was most pronounced for the Italian-American teenagers who were prominently represented on the show. For them, *American Bandstand* made their neighborhood peer culture an integral and visible component of the national youth culture. The show's ongoing segregation, examined in the next chapter, makes it clear that this televisual audiotopia was not equally available to all viewers.

American Bandstand also adds a visual component to Anderson's theory of imagined communities. Anderson highlights newspapers as one of the ways that people first understood (or imagined) themselves as part of a community without face-to-face contact with other members of this community. He describes the "extraordinary mass ceremony" of the "almost precisely simultaneous consumption" of newspapers. The importance of this consumption ritual, Anderson argues, is that

> each communicant is well aware that the ceremony he performs is being replicated simultaneously by thousands (or millions) of others of whose existence

he is confident, yet of whose identity he has not the slightest notion. Furthermore, this ceremony is incessantly repeated at daily or half-daily intervals throughout the calendar. What more vivid figure for the secular, historically clocked, imagined community can be envisioned? At the same time, the newspaper reader, observing exact replicas of his own paper being consumed by his subway, barbershop, or residential neighbours, is continually reassured that the imagined world is visibly rooted in everyday life.[3]

As was the case with the newspapers in Anderson's example, teenagers watched *American Bandstand* simultaneously with little face-to-face knowledge of the millions of other viewers watching the show. Unlike newspapers, however, as a television program *American Bandstand* visualized this imagined community through its studio audience, viewer letters, and maps, and by consistently addressing its viewers as part of a national audience. As political scientist Diana Mutz notes, "[w]hat media, and national media in particular, do best is to supply us with information about those beyond our personal experiences and contacts, in other words, with impressions of the state of mass collectives."[4] *American Bandstand* used its production techniques and mode of address to offer teenagers daily evidence that the imagined national youth culture was "visibly rooted in everyday life." *American Bandstand*'s popularity and profitability flowed from its ability to get viewers, advertisers, and television affiliates to imagine a national youth culture with the show at the center.

In an era when advertisers "discovered" teenagers, *American Bandstand* offered daily access to the largest market of young consumers. Almost every minute of *American Bandstand* was dedicated to selling products. From paid advertisements for consumer goods to promotions of records and musical guests (also often paid for by record promoters), the show presented its viewers with a host of messages every day. The show urged teenagers to drink Seven-Up and Dr. Pepper, snack on Rice-A-Roni and Almond Joy, buy records by the newest hit-makers and carry these records in an *American Bandstand* case, read about the show's regulars in publications like 'Teen magazine, wear the same "Dick Clark American Bandstand" shoes as these dancers, learn new dances from the *American Bandstand* yearbook, and apply Clearasil to their pimples. This was an extraordinarily high level of promotional activity, even by the standards of commercial television. By representing the show's teenagers consuming all of these products, *American Bandstand* constructed a national youth culture centered on simultaneous consumption. By inviting viewers to participate in the same consumption rituals as the studio audience,

American Bandstand encouraged teens across the country to identify with each other.

American Bandstand established Philadelphia as the locus of this national youth culture, and it drew extensively from the creative abilities of the city's youth. Some of these contributions were well documented, others obscured. On the one hand, Italian-American teens figured prominently in the show's image of youth culture. Many of the show's regular dancers and local fans hailed from working-class Italian-American neighborhoods, and they later remembered *American Bandstand* as providing them with unique exposure. On the other hand, the program's racially discriminatory admissions policies remained in place. With the program broadcasting nationally, black teens were erased not just from the "WFIL-adelphia" regional market, but also from the national youth culture *American Bandstand* worked to build. While the next chapter examines the struggles over segregation surrounding the program, this chapter shows how *American Bandstand* became established as the afternoon site of the nation's youth.

PRODUCING NATIONAL YOUTH CULTURE

When ABC decided to take *Bandstand* national in 1957, dozens of local markets already had or would soon start their own teen dance shows. Like *Bandstand*, programs such as *The Milt Grant Show* in Washington, D.C., *The Buddy Deane Show* in Baltimore, *High Time* in Portland, Oregon, *The Clay Cole Show* in New York, *Dewey Phillips' Pop Show* in Memphis, Clark Race's *Dance Party* in Pittsburgh, Robin Seymour and Bill Davies's *Dance Party* in Detroit, Phil McClean's *Cleveland Bandstand*, Jim Gallant's *Connecticut Bandstand*, and David Hull's *Chicago Bandstand* cost little to produce and provided their stations with opportunities to capitalize on the profitable teenage demographic.[5] A sales pitch for *The Milt Grant Show* highlights the commercial appeal of these locally televised teen dance shows. Speaking directly to the camera, Grant addresses potential sponsors:

> Gentleman, I'm about to offer you the best television buy in the world. I'm Milt Grant, the producer and emcee of *The Milt Grant Show* and record hop here in Washington . . . we have a winner that can win for you and your client . . . you see the ingredients are sure fire. First of all, we have the top records of our day. Then we have big named stars . . . and we have a studio audience of seventy sampling for your clients' products. Some of our clients

are Motorola, Pepsi-Cola, [and] the Music Box store . . . our commercials
are thoroughly integrated with the program content. We have a winner and
it's growing. . . . Gentleman, here is the combination of sales, showmanship,
audience, and price that makes the Milt Grant Show the best television buy
in the world.[6]

While clearly hyperbolic, Grant's pitch is indicative of how local deejays and television stations sold their dance shows to potential sponsors. To distinguish *American Bandstand* from these local programs,
every aspect—from the show's title, introduction, and set design, to
Dick Clark's banter before playing records—provided advertisers, record producers, and viewers with evidence of the program's national
reach. For fans of the locally produced *Bandstand*, the most obvious
change when ABC started broadcasting the program nationally was the
title, *American Bandstand*. (The show continued to use both names
while it broadcast from Philadelphia, using *American Bandstand* for
the national ninety minutes, and *Bandstand* for the opening and closing
thirty-minute segments that were only broadcast locally). By calling the
show *American Bandstand*, the program's producers offered both an
accurate acknowledgment of the affiliates broadcasting the program
and an ambitious evaluation of the national audience they hoped would
tune in. For viewers in other parts of the country, many of whom were
already familiar with their own locally broadcast dance shows, the title
immediately announced *American Bandstand* as the national offering.

In addition to the name change, through its new introduction and
set design *American Bandstand* encouraged viewers to imagine themselves as part of a national audience of television viewers. Each show
opened with the camera focused on teenagers dancing in the studio to
"Bandstand Boogie," a big band swing style instrumental written especially for the show. The camera would pull back to reveal a large cut-
out map of the continental United States made out of blue-glittered
cardboard. With the teenagers now pictured as dancing inside this national map, the producers superimposed the show's title at the center.[7]
Using this technique, within the first minute of each program *American Bandstand* depicted its studio audience as literally dancing across
the nation.

American Bandstand's studio design also integrated this national perspective. Across from Clark's podium sat a second map of the United
States featuring the call letters of each of the local television stations
carrying the show. This map, which was visible periodically during each

FIGURE 21. *American Bandstand* opening credits, with teens dancing behind a cut-out cardboard map of the United States and the show's title superimposed at the center. Producers sought to remind viewers and advertisers about the national reach of *American Bandstand* in order to differentiate it from dozens of similar shows broadcast locally across the country. 1957–1958. Used with permission of dick clark productions inc.

show as the camera tracked teens dancing around the studio, served as a reminder of the program's national reach. More important, Clark frequently walked over to the board to make direct references to cities and stations in other parts of the country. "Let's go over to the *Bandstand* big board to see which stations we are going to check today," Clark announced in a typical episode in December 1957.[8] With the camera focused in tight close-up on the map, Clark informed viewers that Frankie Avalon's "De De Dinah" was topping the record charts in Buffalo, New York (home of affiliate WGR); Cleveland, Ohio (WEWS); Akron, Ohio (WAKR); and Youngstown, Ohio (WKST).[9] In another show that same week, Clark highlighted stations in San Francisco (KGO); Stockton, California (KOVR); Fresno, California (KJEO); and Decatur, Illinois (WTDP) before introducing Sam Cooke's "I Love You for Sentimental Reasons."[10] Built into the structure of each show, this affiliate map of the United States offered TV stations, advertisers, and viewers evidence that *American Bandstand* was a national program. With this national map of television stations, *American Bandstand* encouraged viewers to imagine a nation of audience members watching along with them.[11] Within a broadcast medium that repeatedly sought to generate a sense of a national culture, *American Bandstand* stood out for its insistent and geographically specific reminders that viewers were part of a national television audience.

FIGURE 22. Dick Clark talks with teens visiting *American Bandstand* from Los Angeles. *American Bandstand*'s studio featured a large map that included the call letters of each local affiliate that carried the show. *American Bandstand Yearbook, 1958.*

The *American Bandstand Yearbook, 1958* reiterated this ideal of a national audience with a station map featuring thirty-four teenage viewers from twenty-one different states. The yearbook showed WFIL-TV's signal reaching in concentric circles across the United States, and told advertisers and fans that these "friends from around the country" were "at 'American Bandstand' too." This national map motif expanded on the WFIL-adelphia theme that WFIL originally used to sell the station's four-state regional broadcast area. The photos of these teen viewers resembled headshots in a typical high school yearbook, but rather than representing a single city or town, the yearbook gathered teens from Fort Wayne, Buffalo, Salt Lake City, and New Orleans into a national cohort of teenage consumers. Despite this regional diversity, the fans highlighted in the yearbook reiterated *American Bandstand*'s white image of national youth culture.[12]

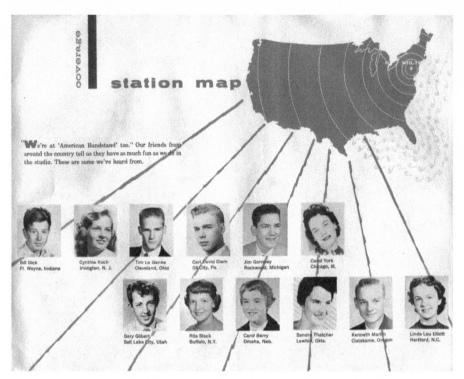

FIGURE 23. The *American Bandstand Yearbook, 1958,* picked up the station map theme to feature thirty-four teens from twenty-one different states. The fans highlighted in the yearbook also reiterated the white image of national youth culture constructed by *American Bandstand. American Bandstand Yearbook, 1958.*

Even when the station map was not pictured on the screen, Clark made frequent references to affiliated stations and markets when he presented records, introduced audience members from out of town, and opened viewer mail. In different programs, Clark told viewers about the popular records in Boston (WHDH) and Detroit (WXYZ), welcomed twin teenage girls from Minneapolis (WTCN) to the audience, and read a fan letter from Green Bay (WFRV).[13] By integrating the station call letters in this way, Clark emphasized the national reach of *American Bandstand* while also providing affiliates with brief advertisements that raised their local profiles. In an era when local NBC and CBS affiliates as well as independent stations could elect to carry individual ABC programs, these affiliate advertisements were critical to the commercial success of *American Bandstand* and the network. Since Clark and

ABC's network executives worked on a market-by-market basis to increase the number of affiliates carrying the show, these station announcements also offered a warning to stations that considered dropping the show. On the December 17, 1957, show, for example, Clark read a letter from Aida, Oklahoma, that relayed news that the local affiliate (KTEN) threatened to replace *American Bandstand* with a locally produced dance program. Teenagers in Aida, the letter continued, protested by writing to the station to demand that KTEN keep *American Bandstand* on the air. The protests proved successful, and Clark thanked the teenagers for their efforts. Using less than a minute of broadcast time, Clark provided viewers across the country with a tutorial on how to compel affiliates to continue broadcasting the program. Moreover, these station announcements identified teenagers in different parts of the country as television consumers linked to both a specific market and the national market.

Out of these local markets *American Bandstand*'s map created a vision of a national market of teenage consumers that advertisers and record producers sought to reach. Although the teenage consumer market began developing in the decades before World War II, in the 1950s marketers and the popular press emphasized the discovery of a previously untapped market of teenage consumers.[14] In 1956, for example, the *Wall Street Journal* described the nation's 16 million teenagers as a "market that's getting increasing attention from merchants and advertisers." Estimating that teens spent between $7 and $9 billion annually, the article described how advertisers were turning to teenage-market researchers to help them win the brand loyalty of these customers at an early age.[15] Foremost among these researchers, Eugene Gilbert generated many of the statistics that fueled the interest in the teenage market. Starting in the early 1940s, Gilbert, who called himself the "George Gallop of the teenagers," hired a network of high school students to conduct market research among their peers. By the late 1950s, Gilbert wrote a syndicated newspaper column, "What Young People Think," and published *Advertising and Marketing to Young People* (1957), encouraging marketers to develop specific strategies to reach teens.[16] Gilbert's *Advertising and Marketing to Young People* opens with charts emphasizing that the postwar baby boom had made eight- to eighteen-year-olds the fastest growing age demographic in the country. The size of the youth market, combined with young people's willingness to try new products, made an "unbeatable selling formula" in Gilbert's estimation. "Just look at youth!," Gilbert advised readers:

No established pattern.... No inventory of treasured, and to many an adult's way of thinking, irreplaceable objects. Youth ... is the greatest growing force in the community. His physical needs alone constitute a continuing and growing requirement in food, cloths, entertainment, etc. It has definitely been established that because he is open-minded and desires to learn, he is often the first to accept new and forward-looking products.[17]

Gilbert's statements of fact about the youth market were part of the midcentury growth of surveys about "average" Americans. In attempting to "reveal the nation to its members," historian Sarah Igo contends, these "social scientists were covert nation-builders, conjuring up a collective that could be visualized only because it was radically simplified."[18] Gilbert's writings on the youth market were influential because he provided pages of data on the consumer preferences of youth, thereby transforming millions of individual teens and pre-teens into a market niche. As evidence of a company eager to reach young consumers, Gilbert could have cited ABC's attempt to outflank the larger networks by targeting teenage viewers with programs like *American Bandstand*. For his part, Clark echoed Gilbert's descriptions of teens as a large, but underserved, consumer market. "It's been a long, long time since a major network has aimed at the most entertainment-starved group in the country," Clark told *Newsweek* in December 1957. "And why not? After all, teen-agers have $9 billion a year to spend."[19] While Gilbert generated interest in teenagers as lucrative consumers, *American Bandstand* provided Clark with a platform to put Gilbert's ideas into practice.

In this wave of attention focused on teenage consumer culture, *American Bandstand* stood out for the way that it showed teens using the sponsors' products. When buying time on *American Bandstand,* sponsors like 7-Up, Dr. Pepper, Clearasil, and Rice-A-Roni also bought interaction between their products and the show's teenagers. For example, after the opening shot of teens dancing behind the cut-out map of the United States in one 1957 episode, the camera focused on a 7-Up sign and bottles of the soda placed next to Clark at his podium. Clark read a letter from a viewer in Schenectady, New York, who sent him a bottle opener because he was unable to open a bottle of 7-Up in a previous show. After thanking the viewer for her letter and the gift and commenting on his thirst, Clark took an exaggerated swig of the soda. The camera cut to teenagers in the studio audience who asked for drinks of their own, which Clark promised to deliver after a short commercial. After a one-minute cartoon advertisement for 7-Up, the camera returned to a live shot of Clark handing out bottles of 7-Up from a cooler to an eager group of audience members. As Clark introduced "Get a Job" by the Silhouettes, the camera stayed focused on teens drinking 7-Up and milling about near the cooler through the first fifteen seconds of the song. Throughout the song, the cameras cut away from shots of teens dancing to return to the teenagers drinking 7-Up. All told, this 7-Up promo lasted nearly five minutes and was only the first of several in that episode.[20]

These interpolated commercials, which were common in radio and television shows in this era, provided *American Bandstand*'s viewers with daily visual evidence of teenagers' eagerness to consume products.[21] While such a message appealed to marketers looking to expand sales, images of teenagers as consumers also encouraged the home audience to join in by buying the sponsor's products. The show's advertisements focused on soft drinks and snacks—Popsicles, Mounds, Almond Joy, Dr. Pepper, and Welch's grape juice all advertised on the show—all of which were aimed at teenage viewers and their parents in the after-school hours.[22] *American Bandstand*'s afternoon broadcast time was also less expensive for sponsors. In 1958, these advertisers paid $3,400 per half hour compared to $30,000 to $45,000 for a half hour on a live music show in the evening.[23] For this bargain rate *American Bandstand* offered sponsors an unusually deep level of interaction with teenagers in the studio audience and those viewing at home.

To recruit sponsors, ABC also drew on market research suggesting that many housewives watched the show. The network sent a press release proclaiming "Age No Barrier to *Bandstand* Beat" to local affiliates and sponsors, and during the broadcast Clark encouraged "You housewives [to] roll up the ironing board and join us when you can."[24] By appealing to both the advertising industry's traditional view of housewives as archetypal consumers and the new interest in teenage consumers, Clark and ABC positioned *American Bandstand* to be as attractive as possible to advertisers.[25] In turn, these advertisers ensured the show's sustainability.

American Bandstand's productions strategies also encouraged viewers to participate in the show by taking an interest in the show's regulars and by learning dance steps. An October 1957 *TV Guide* review called attention to the show's camera techniques: "[T]hanks to some camera work by director Ed Yates that would do credit to any TV spectacular there isn't one of these amateur and largely anonymous supporting players who isn't worth watching."[26] While teens danced in the studio, the show's camera operators made frequent use of two types of shots. First, during slow dances they used extended close-ups on the couples' faces that provided viewers with an intimate look at which teens were dancing together. In turn, the show's regulars would jockey to dance in front of the cameras so they could be seen on television. Arlene Sullivan, who along with Kenny Rossi made up one of the show's most popular couples, remembered that "it got to the point where the regular kids wanted to be on camera all the time, so Dick Clark would turn off the red light so we were supposed to not know which camera was on. But we always knew where the camera was. We were hams." Asked how she knew which camera was on without the red light, Sullivan recalled, "Oh, you knew. You knew how they were focusing. And then Dick Clark would start to say, if he thought we were in front too long, 'OK, Arlene and Kenny in the back, Franni in the back, Carole in the back.' He wanted to give the other kids a shot."[27] Despite Clark's prodding, the regular dancers were on camera enough to become celebrities to the show's viewers and teen magazine readers. *Teen* magazine, for example, told readers they were "swamped with requests to do a story on the kids from *Bandstand*" and subsequently featured six cover stories on *American Bandstand* between 1958 and 1960, with profiles of current and former *Bandstand* regulars like Pat Molittieri, Kenny Rossi, and Arlene Sullivan. *Teen* also published two eighty-page special issues for teens to read more about the show's dancers.[28] Daily television exposure and celebrity-style coverage in teen magazines made *Bandstand*'s regulars into what would later be called reality television stars. These nonprofessional performers became, as *Teen* put it, the "most famous unknown[s] on TV today."[29] *American Bandstand*'s use of extended close-ups, coupled with numerous magazine profiles, invited viewers to follow along with the dating and style choices of the show's regulars and provided viewers with information about another form of consumption.

When the cameras were not holding tight close-ups of the regulars' faces, they were often focused on dancers' feet. These close-ups on the dancers' feet highlighted yet another product viewers could buy, Dick Clark American Bandstand Shoes. Teenagers could purchase shoes in the style popularized by the show's dancers. In another sign of the Dick Clark's quest to maximize profits, these shoes were advertised to black teenagers in the *Philadelphia Tribune* at the same time black teenagers were being turned away from the show's studio audience.

These below-the-knee shots, ranging between fifteen seconds and a minute in duration, also captured the teenagers' dance steps during

FIGURE 24. Thanks to daily exposure on *American Bandstand*, the show's regular dancers became teen stars. Pat Molittieri and other regulars were featured in "My Bandstand Buddies" published by '*Teen* magazine. 1959.

fast songs such as "At the Hop" by Danny and the Juniors and "Great Balls of Fire" by Jerry Lee Lewis, and during group dance songs such as "The Stroll" by the Diamonds. Along with dance instruction diagrams in the show's yearbooks and in teen magazines, these close-ups provided viewers with tutorials on the show's dance steps and identified *American Bandstand* as the best source of information about "new" dances. The 1958 *American Bandstand Yearbook* emphasized this point on a page titled "a new dance every day": "'The Chalypso,' 'The Walk,' 'The Stroll'—the list of new dances you've seen first on 'American Bandstand' just seems to grow each day. How do they get started? Well, if you ask some of the guests at the program, 'They just

the newest shoe sensation
for teens and pre-teens!

**DICK CLARK
AMERICAN
BANDSTAND
SHOES**

Regular
$8.95

• ALL COLORS
• ALL SIZES

NOW ... $5⁰⁰

Pliner's

Famous for Fine Junior Footwear

NORTH PHILADELPHIA	GERMANTOWN	OXFORD CIRCLE
5725 N. Broad St.	64 W. Chelten Ave.	6411 Castor Ave.
BALA - CYNWYD	CITY LINE CENTER	JENKINTOWN	AMBLER
79 City Line Ave.	7632 City Line Av.	435 York Rd.	48 E. Butler Pike

FIGURE 25. This advertisement for "Dick Clark American Bandstand Shoes" ran in the *Philadelphia Tribune,* the city's leading black newspaper, at the same time black teenagers were excluded from *American Bandstand.* September 13, 1960. Used with permission of *Philadelphia Tribune.*

happen.' "[30] Despite the suggestion that "new dances have 'just grown' on the program," most of these dances did not originate on *American Bandstand.* Rather, many of the dances originated at local teen dances or were performed by the black teenagers on *The Mitch Thomas Show.*

Ray Smith, who attended *American Bandstand* frequently and has done research for one of Clark's histories of the show, remembers that he and other white teenagers watched *The Mitch Thomas Show* to learn new dance steps. Describing the "black Bandstand," Smith recalled:

First of all, black kids had their own dance show, I think it was on channel 12, but one of the reasons I remember it is because I watched it. And I remember that there was a dance that [*American Bandstand* regulars] Joan Buck and Jimmy Peatross did called "The Strand" and it was a slow version of the jitterbug done to slow records. And it was fantastic. There were two black dancers on this show, the "black Bandstand," or whatever you want to call it. The guy's name was Otis and I don't remember the girl's name. And I

FIGURE 26. Close-up shot of dancers' feet from *American Bandstand* episode (ca. 1957–58). These tight camera shots emphasized the program as the place to learn about new dances and encouraged viewers at home to follow along. Used with permission of dick clark productions inc.

always was like "wow." And then I saw Jimmy Peatross and Joan Buck do it, who were probably the best dancers who were ever on Bandstand. I was talking about it to Jimmy Peatross one day, when I was putting together the book, and he said, "oh, I watched this black couple do it." And that was the black couple that he watched.[31]

These white teenagers were not alone in watching *The Mitch Thomas Show*. Smith's experience of watching the show supports Mitch Thomas's belief that "[*American Bandstand* teens] were looking to see what dance steps we were putting out. All you had to do was look at 'Bandstand' the next Monday, and you'd say, 'Oh yeah, they were watching.'"[32] They were watching, for example, when dancers on *The Mitch Thomas Show* started dancing the Stroll, a group dance where boys and girls faced each other in two parallel lines, while couples took turns strutting down the aisle. Thomas remembers that the teens on his show "created a dance called The Stroll. I was standing there watching them dancing in a line, and after a while I asked them, 'what are y'all doing out there?' They said, 'that's The Stroll.' And The Stroll became a big thing."[33]

The Stroll was actually a new take on swing-era line dances, and while the teens on *The Mitch Thomas Show* did not invent the Stroll, they, along with young fans of black R&B in other cities, were among the first young people in the country to perform the new version of the dance.[34] The

modern

"a new dance every day"

"The Bunny Hop," "The Chalypso," "The Walk," "The Stroll"—the list of new dances you've seen first on "American Bandstand" just seems to grow each day. How do they get started? Well, if you ask some of the guests at the program, "They just happen."

Entire new dances have "just grown" on the program. "The Circle Dance" created a lot of excitement as it developed from jitterbugging and we're sure you can see it owes a debt to square dancing. "The Stroll" is another dance that can be traced all the way back to those courtly dances of long, long ago. Now "The Stroll" is even being taught in dancing classes throughout the nation.

Wonder what the big dance will be next year? Whatever it is, you'll be sure to see it first on your program, "American Bandstand."

1. One of the most famous of "American Bandstand's" new dances, "The Stroll."
2. Second step, side by side up the aisle.
3. Everybody has a turn.
4. It's fun—and it's sweeping the country . . .

FIGURE 27. *American Bandstand* teens demonstrate their version of the Stroll. *American Bandstand Yearbook, 1958.*

Stroll was inspired by R&B artist Chuck Willis's song "C.C. Rider," itself a remake of the popular blues song "See See Rider Blues," which was first recorded and copyrighted by Ma Rainey in the 1920s and was subsequently recorded by dozens of others artists. Following Willis, a string of other R&B songs were produced based on the dance. By late 1957, the Diamonds, a white vocal group that frequently recorded cover versions of black R&B songs, released "The Stroll," a song made specifically for the dance. Dick Clark was a friend of the Diamonds's manager, Nat Goodman, and told him: "if we could have another stroll-type record, you'd have yourself an automatic hit."[35] The Diamonds' version outsold the others largely because *American Bandstand* played the song repeatedly. In addition to helping move the Diamonds's version of the song up the charts, the frequent spins also falsely established *American Bandstand* as the originator of the dance. The show offered viewers instruction on how to do the Stroll by showing close-ups on the dancers' feet during the dance.[36] The show's yearbook offered fans of more explicit instruction on the dance.

All this emphasis on *American Bandstand* as the birthplace of the Stroll upset some of the teenagers on *The Mitch Thomas Show*. Thomas later recalled that Clark was gracious when he complained to him about *American Bandstand* taking credit for the dance. "I called Dick Clark and told him my kids were a little upset because they were hearing that the Stroll started on 'Bandstand' " Thomas remembered. "He said no problem. He went on the show that day and said, 'Hey man, I want you all to know The Stroll originated on the Mitch Thomas dance show.' "[37] While Clark was courteous in this instance in acknowledging the creative influence of *The Mitch Thomas Show* on *American Bandstand*, the television programs remained in a vastly inequitable relationship. *The Mitch Thomas Show* broadcast to the Delaware Valley on an independent station that was not affiliated with one of the three major networks. *American Bandstand*, on the other hand, reached a national audience of millions with the financial backing of advertisers, ABC, and Walter Annenberg's media assets. The question of the Stroll's origins remained contentious because such new dances were one of the many products that *American Bandstand* sold to viewers. The appropriation of these creative energies contributed to the frustration felt by black teens who were denied admission to the show. The dance styles perfected by the black teenagers on *The Mitch Thomas Show* did reach a national audience, but the teens themselves were not depicted as part of the national youth culture *American Bandstand* broadcast to viewers.

ITALIAN-AMERICAN TEENS AND WHITENESS ON *AMERICAN BANDSTAND*

At the same time that *American Bandstand*'s producers excluded black teenagers from the program's studio audience, the show's image of youth culture moved ethnicity to the foreground. Whereas television programs with ethnic characters like *The Goldbergs, Life of Riley*, and *Life with Luigi* were being replaced with supposedly ethnically neutral programs like *Leave It to Beaver* and *Father Knows Best*, because of its specific local context, *American Bandstand* offered, in particular, working-class Italian-American teenagers from Philadelphia access to national visibility and recognition.[38] Many of the show's regulars viewed *American Bandstand* as a sort of televised audiotopia, a welcoming space that provided a unique exposure for Italian-American teens.

Arlene Sullivan recalled feeling like an outsider in her predominately Irish neighborhood in Southwest Philadelphia. "I was very shy growing up," Sullivan remembered. "A lot of kids were light eyed and red hair and blonde hair. I was really the only kid in the neighborhood who was kind of dark. I was half Italian and half Irish, but I really looked more Italian than I did Irish. And I always really felt like I was different from them." In contrast, Sullivan felt that "being on *Bandstand* of course you meet up with everybody, and you tended to see the love that they have for you. And especially for me, I just embraced them all, because they liked me. I was just surprised, because I was such a loner. And having all of these people like me."[39] Sullivan became one of the show's best-known dancers and appeared on the cover of *Teen* in 1959.

Frank Spagnuola, who grew up in an Italian section of South Philadelphia and danced on *American Bandstand* from 1955 to 1958, felt that the program introduced teens in other parts of the country to Italians: "When you say Italian, everybody in Philadelphia knew Italians, and in Reading [Pennsylvania], they knew about Italians, they didn't have any there, but they knew about them. But in the South they never saw an Italian, so this was a big thing. Dark hair, little darker [skin], it was a big thing."[40] Sullivan's dance partner, Ken Rossi, shared this view. In an interview conducted for one of Clark's histories of the program, Rossi recalled that "[Arlene and I] both had that ethnic look, dark wavy hair and all that. . . . I think a lot of people in the viewing audience had never really been exposed to this kind of ethnic concept."[41]

These recollections resonate with the 1961 findings of sociologist Francis Ianni, who suggested that "while there is not the same hostility and social distance that existed for the second generation teen-ager, Italo-Americans are still considered to be 'different,'" and as a result, the Italian-American teenager "does not participate as an equal in teen-age culture."[42] While Spagnuola and Rossi may overstate the lack of Italian-Americans in other states, the predominance of these teens would have been unique for most viewers of *American Bandstand* outside of the three major centers of Italian immigration (New York, Chicago, and Philadelphia). Television, in this case, transcended population patterns, bringing images of white ethnic teens into homes across the country.

In order to fully understand the significance of representing national youth culture through images of Italian-American teens, it is important to pay attention to what historian Thomas Guglielmo calls the distinctions between race and color before World War II, and between race and ethnicity in the postwar era. From the late nineteenth century through the mid-twentieth century, Guglielmo argues that Italian immigrants and their offspring experienced prejudice based on their perceived difference from Anglo Saxon, Nordic, or Celtic "races," but they were never systematically denied the institutional and material benefits of their "color" status as whites. As the definition of *race* shifted in the World War II era to refer to large groups such as "Caucasians," "Negroes," and "Orientals," Americans of Italian descent became an ethnic group, and many Italian-Americans began to organize around a white identity.[43] Guglielmo concludes: "In the end, Italians' firm hold on whiteness never loosened over time. They were, at different points, criminalized mercilessly, ostracized in various neighborhoods, denied jobs on occasion, and alternately ridiculed and demonized by American popular culture. Yet, through it all, their whiteness remained intact."[44] While Guglielmo focuses on Chicago, available evidence from Philadelphia supports his argument. Italian-Americans did face incidents of housing and educational discrimination in Philadelphia, but these incidents were neither as sustained nor as systematic as the discrimination against the city's black and Puerto Rican residents.[45] While the visibility of Italian-American teens was unique within the late 1950s television landscape, it served primarily to alleviate ethnic rather than racial prejudice. Italian-American teenagers did not need *American Bandstand* to become "white," but the show did help to cement their racial status.

The recognition *American Bandstand* offered to working-class Italian-American teenage girls and other girls across the country is also significant. *American Bandstand* recognized teenage girls for their interest in music and dancing and offered an after-school activity in an era when budget allocations limited the range of extracurricular activities available to young women in Philadelphia's public schools. *American Bandstand* became an integral part of the peer culture in the Italian neighborhoods of South Philadelphia, where many teens watched the show religiously. Like other teens across the country, they talked about the program's regulars, music, and fashions with friends during school, and they looked to the show to learn new steps that they could use at local dances, or to see which steps the show's regulars had picked up from these same local dances. Unlike most other viewers, however, several of the show's teenage regulars and musical guests came from their high schools or neighborhoods, offering a unique perspective on the show's local and national popularity. In each of these respects, *American Bandstand* became part of the daily lives of teenagers. Anita Messina, for example, remembers *American Bandstand* being an important point of connection among her friends at Southern High School. Asked how often she watched the show, Messina recalled:

> Every day. It was like bible. You'd run home from school, because then you became interested in the dancers, they became like your friends. "Oh so and so is dancing with this one, he was dancing with this other one for three days, I wonder if they broke up?" It was just like a way of life, if they were wearing something you had to go out and buy it. "Oh they had this kind of top, we're going to buy that kind of top." And Dick Clark, whatever records he put on, we had to go out in buy the records. It was big. It was really important to all of us to watch that show. . . . Usually everybody would go home after school to watch *American Bandstand*, and then they'd come out. I can't remember too many of my friends not watching *American Bandstand*. It was a big part of our lives in my age group. It was a topic of conversation. If you saw something on *Bandstand* you'd go to school the next day and talk about it. "Did you hear what Dick Clark said? Did you see Frannie Giordano? Did you see that this one was dancing with that one?" If they did a new dance, "did you see the dance they did?" It was really big.[46]

The televisual boundaries of *American Bandstand* were also blurry for Messina and her friends. For example, when Messina entered and won the show's contest to meet actor Sal Mineo, she remembers: "When my name came on it was like blood curdling screams. . . . And the next thing you know, because you live in the city, you heard screaming all down the block because everyone was watching it on TV. And there are like fifty kids banging on the door." Messina's friend and classmate Carmella Gullon also remembered *American Bandstand* as an integral part of the lives of teenage girls in her neighborhood. "Oh, god yeah, everybody [watched it]," Gullon remembered.

> You'd come home from school and you'd watch it on television and you'd dance. If your girlfriends were there you would dance with your girlfriends, and if not you'd dance with your banister. . . . That's what kids did. And I think girls more than guys. And the guys we knew were real good dancers, but I think more so girls, that's just what they did.[47]

Messina's and Gullon's recollections speak to *American Bandstand*'s power to shape the consumption decisions and interests of teenage girls. More important, however, in the context of their peer groups, *American Bandstand* was important because it reflected their interest in music and dancing. These music-centered peer relationships resemble what musicologist Christopher Small calls "musicking" to describe the

totality of a musical performance. "The act of musicking," Small suggests, "establishes in the place where it is happening a set of relationships, and it is in those relationships that the meaning of the act lies."[48]
Television enabled *American Bandstand* to connect teenagers across the
country, and at the same time, local teens in places like South Philadelphia felt intimately connected to this musical venue.

American Bandstand was especially important for Messina and Gullon because in the years they attended Southern High School (1958–61),
the school offered only a limited number of after-school activities for
girls. Darlina Burkhart, a friend of Messina's who was in the same graduating class, remembered that while the Southern football team and other
boys' sports teams were a big deal, "there was nothing like that for
girls."[49] Messina recalled, "My extracurricular activity was finding the
closest dance to go to."[50] These dances, held at churches, school gymnasi-
ums, social clubs, and recreational centers, were frequent gathering places
for teens on both weeknights and weekends. Neighborhood churches in
South Philadelphia, such as Bishop Neumann and St. Richard's, hosted
small dances, and St. Alice's in suburban Upper Darby (just outside West
Philadelphia) hosted some of the largest dances, with more than two
thousand teens filling the church's social center on Friday and Sunday
nights.[51]

While the white teens at these dances shared an interest in rock and
roll and R&B, class and ethnicity sometimes divided them. Gullon recalled one such incident:

> We went to a dance in Upper Chichester in our senior year, and the suburbs
> were a lot different from South Philly. We went into the dance with high
> heels and teased hair and crinoline. And everybody there was flat hair, very
> collegiate . . . and we were in there and we were dancing and we just made
> up a dance and everybody started to follow us, and it was a lot of fun. We
> had a great time. But we were just so different looking when we went in
> there. We didn't realize how different we would be until we went there. We
> stuck out like sore thumbs. Even when we went to St. Alice's [in Upper
> Darby] . . . you didn't really mingle with the [kids] from other schools.[52]

This clash in dress and hair styles between working-class and lower-
middle-class teens from South Philadelphia and their wealthy and
upper-middle-class suburban peers highlights the heterogeneity among
different local peer groups in the Philadelphia area.

In its pursuit of a national audience, however, *American Bandstand*
relied on the creative energy of Italian-American teens in constructing

the show's image of youth culture. While the styles *American Bandstand* allowed young people to wear were more conservative than those teens selected for neighborhood dances, by providing a daily television spotlight for music and dancing, *American Bandstand* validated the extracurricular activities valued by these working-class teenage girls from South Philadelphia. With *American Bandstand*, market formation and identity formation occurred simultaneously. The marketability of Italian-American teens and young women helped the show cultivate a national youth culture, while it also offered these teens a way to connect with their local peers and a way to imagine themselves as part of a national youth culture in which working-class Italian-American teens played a central role. *American Bandstand*, of course, was invested in selling products, not ethnic pride or gender equity, but the particular images through which the show sold youth culture elevated some teens while they also obscured others.

In its seven years as a network program broadcast from Philadelphia, *American Bandstand* encouraged viewers, advertisers, and television stations to view the show as the epicenter of American youth culture. From WFRV in Green Bay to KOVR in Stockton, California, the program offered daily reminders to viewers that teens across the country were watching *American Bandstand*, drinking the same sodas, eating the same snacks, and doing the same dances to the same music. In this way, *American Bandstand* played a crucial role in cultivating a market of teenage consumers. Building an image of national youth around simultaneous consumption proved very profitable for *American Bandstand*, as well as for the advertisers, record producers, and television stations that sought the attention of teenage consumers.

If the teenagers *American Bandstand* portrayed every afternoon provided the basis for an imagined national youth culture in the late 1950s and early 1960s, this imagined national youth culture, in turn, provided the template for the way the show would be remembered in subsequent decades as a televised audiotopia that defined a generation. In cultivating a national youth culture, *American Bandstand* also provided the raw material for generational memories. Black teens, however, were largely absent from this imagined national youth culture. As the next chapter demonstrates, *American Bandstand*'s producers maintained the show's discriminatory admissions policies during its years in Philadelphia. As a result, the television program that did the most to define the image of youth in the late 1950s and early 1960s, an image that continued to represent the era in later decades, marginalized black teens. Black teenagers protested the program on several occasions, but these civil rights challenges are not part of the popular history of *American Bandstand*. The daily broadcasts that established *American Bandstand* as the heart of national youth culture also inaugurated an ongoing struggle over how and by whom the show's relationship to segregation is portrayed.

CHAPTER 7

Remembering *American Bandstand,* Forgetting Segregation

There was one important change that [producer] Tony
[Mammarella] and I made in 1957. Up until that time, the
dancers on Bandstand had one thing in common—they were
all white. . . . So in 1957, we were charting new territory.
I don't think of myself as a hero or civil rights activist for
integrating the show; it was simply the right thing to do.

—Dick Clark, *Dick Clark's American Bandstand*, 1997

American Bandstand was also a force for social good.

—Fred Bronson, *Dick Clark's American Bandstand 50th Anniversary*,
2007

More than fifty years after the show first broadcast, *American Bandstand*'s representations of youth culture remain closely linked both to
the show's legacy and to larger questions about popular culture, race,
and civil rights. Since the late 1970s, Dick Clark has claimed that he
integrated the show's studio audience when he became the host in
1957. The problem is, Clark's memory runs counter to the historical
record. Black teenagers contested *American Bandstand*'s racially discriminatory admission policies on several occasions, inspired both by
the everyday discrimination they faced in Philadelphia and by national
civil rights events like the Little Rock school integration crisis. Although
they were not able to change the show's policies, their efforts make it clear
that *American Bandstand*'s studio remained a site of struggle over segregation through the early 1960s. The disjuncture between the evidence of

American Bandstand's segregation and Clark's claims that he integrated the show underscore the vexed relationship between history and memory.[1] Clark's memories of *American Bandstand*'s integration differ from archival materials, newspaper accounts, video and photographic evidence, and remembrances of people who were excluded from the show or witnessed this exclusion. This chapter uses this cluster of sources to evaluate the veracity of Clark's memories and to examine when and why Clark developed an alternative history of the show, and what this alternative history obscures.

Clark's popular history of *American Bandstand*, articulated in books and interviews, suggests two explanations. First, Clark initially made reference to the show's integration in 1976, when *American Bandstand* was competing for performers, viewers, and advertisers with *Soul Train*, which featured a predominately African American studio audience. Recalling *Bandstand*'s integration in this context, this memory sought to establish *American Bandstand*'s history of support for black music and culture. Second, Clark frequently presents *American Bandstand* within the context of the popular national history of the 1950s (e.g., the development of the national civil rights movement, the growth of television and rock and roll, and suburbanization). Framed in this way, the supposed integration of *American Bandstand* becomes part of the national civil rights narrative. This approach evades the specific local history surrounding *American Bandstand*'s years in Philadelphia, as well as the antiblack racism in Philadelphia and nationally, that motivated the show's discrimination. *American Bandstand* is part of the civil rights story, but not in the way Clark suggests. This chapter starts by examining the black teenagers whose protests made the show's admission policies a civil rights issue, and then explores how Clark developed a popular history of *American Bandstand* that erased these stories.

THE HISTORY OF SEGREGATION ON *AMERICAN BANDSTAND*

Like other young people across the country, black teenagers identified with different aspects of *American Bandstand*. Joan Cannady, who was the first black student to attend Germantown Friends High School in the northeast section of Philadelphia, remembers watching the program to hear black music that was not played at parties with her white classmates. Cannady recalled that the teens featured on *American Bandstand* did not resemble her white peers at Germantown Friends or the teens she knew through the black middle-class social group, Jack and Jill: "I saw *American Bandstand* as an Italian or Catholic school thing, and therefore of interest, but not really who we were."[2] Iona Stroman and her friends in South Philadelphia watched *American Bandstand* almost every day and were especially excited to see their favorite local teenage singers perform on the show.[3] When one such group, Weldon McDougal's Philadelphia Larks, performed on *American Bandstand*, he remembers that his neighbors gathered to watch the performance:

> There weren't many families that owned televisions, but the guy who lived directly next door to me did have a television. And he would let us sit on the porch and he would open the window so we could look in and see it. And when I was on television on *American Bandstand*, he went next door and got my mother and the other neighborhood kids so they could see it.[4]

Outside of Philadelphia, Julian Bond remembered watching *American Bandstand* after growing up in Atlanta, Georgia. Bond, who went on to become the Student Nonviolent Coordinating Committee's (SNCC) communications director and the chairman of the NAACP, writes that before being inspired by the civil rights work of black students, "My role models—although we did not call them that then—were white teenagers, mostly Italian American youngsters who danced five afternoons a week on ABC's *American Bandstand*. I was a rural, small-town kid . . . these youngsters were big-city sophisticates to me, and I aped their clothes and style."[5] In addition to these individual black teenagers, black newspapers in Chicago, New York, Atlanta, and Philadelphia noted when black artists appeared on *American Bandstand*.[6] While black viewers saw many of the top black recording artists on *American Bandstand*, they almost never saw any black teenagers among the show's dancers or studio audience.

As noted in chapter one, while several black teenagers attended *Bandstand* in the show's first two years as a local program (1952–53), the program soon adopted admission policies that, while not explicitly whites only, had the effect of discriminating against black teenagers.[7] Among the black teenagers who protested this discrimination, Walter Palmer engineered a plan to get membership cards for black teens by giving the applications Irish, Polish, and Italian last names, and teens from William Penn high school in North Philadelphia wrote to the Commission on Human Relations asking the city's discrimination watchdog group to investigate *Bandstand*'s segregation.[8] None of these efforts changed the show's admission policies, and, by the time Clark took over the show in 1956, it was primarily a space for white teenagers.

Shortly after Clark became the host of the show, the *Philadelphia Tribune* ran its first front-page story on *Bandstand*. Citing a "flood" of "complaints of racial segregation" by black teenagers who sought admission to the show, the front page story declared "No Negroes on Bandstand Show, TV Boss Says They're Welcome."[9] In response to the *Tribune* reporter's questions, James Felix, a WFIL program manger, insisted that the show admitted teens on a "first-come, first-served basis." Felix also said he suspected that few black teens "showed up at the station because they didn't 'feel welcome.' But ... that does not mean that we (the station) do not want them to participate on bandstand."[10]

The following year, a group of black teens from South Philadelphia tested the contention that *American Bandstand* held a color-blind admission policy. Young community activist Vivian Brooker organized the test in early October 1957. Brooker later recalled that the Little Rock school integration crisis, and rise of racial tensions in Philadelphia that followed Little Rock, started the planning that led to the protest of *American Bandstand*. Brooker and her peers were among the many Americans who examined what political theorist Danielle Allen calls local "habits of citizenship" in the wake of Little Rock.[11] The teens who participated in the test were part of a fan club who wanted to see South Philadelphia teen singer Bobby Brookes perform on *American Bandstand*. They wrote to the show a week in advance to request tickets and, after receiving no reply, arrived at the show early to wait in line. They continued to wait as the studio door guard admitted white teenagers, and they pleaded with the guard for over an hour to allow them into the studio. The guard finally admitted the teenagers after a reporter from the *Philadelphia Tribune*, the city's largest black newspaper, asked to speak with the station manager.

Iona Stroman, who was one of the teens who challenged the show's segregation that day, remembered that while the door guard used racial slurs, "once we got in things were fine. We grew up around a lot of those [white] kids, so there wasn't any tension there." Asked about what motivated their test of *American Bandstand*'s segregation, Stroman recalled: "It wasn't like we set out to change history or anything. We just thought that this is unfair. It's right here in Philadelphia, and we can't even go to it."[12] Despite their efforts, the barrier that Vivian Brooker, Iona Stroman, and the other teenagers cracked in October 1957 remained in place. Without an explicit policy of segregation to protest, the teens and the city's civil rights advocates lacked the leverage to overturn *American Bandstand*'s discriminatory policies. Although they were not able to change the show's policies, these black teens used a national civil rights story as motivation to challenge discrimination in their own city.

In addition to these teenagers, several contemporary press accounts outside of Philadelphia questioned the policy of racial segregation at *American Bandstand*. In September 1958, the *New York Post* ran a series of articles about the program and quoted an anonymous veteran of the show who claimed that it was WFIL-TV's "practice [to admit] only eight or nine" black teenagers per day, "and not to focus the camera on them." When asked about the lack of representation of black teenagers, Ted Fetter, an ABC executive, said the network's decision was influenced by the controversy that erupted over deejay Alan Freed's television program showing black teenage R&B singer Frankie Lymon dancing with a white teenage girl a year earlier.[13] Clark refused to comment about the camera shots of the studio audience, but held that the show's "doors are open to anyone who wants to attend."[14]

In the midst of the payola scandal in 1959, the black newspaper *New York Age* also raised the question of segregation on *American Bandstand*. "[W]e are concerned about another matter which has never seemed to bother many people," the article offered. "This is the question of Negro participation on the various TV bandstand programs." After praising the "quiet, but effective" efforts of Alan Freed to address racial prejudice in the music business and to welcome black teenagers in his concert audiences, the article asked, "Have you ever seen Negro kids on Dick Clark's program? Perhaps, a few times, but the unspoken rule operates—Negro kids simply have been quietly barred from the 'American Bandstand.'"[15] Los Angeles musician, deejay, and antiracism activist Johnny Otis penned one of the strongest critiques of *Bandstand*'s racial policies in his *Los Angeles Sentinel* column. "There's something about Dick Clark that I consider more objectionable than all of [the payola charges] put together," Otis wrote. "I'm talking about the obvious and apparently deliberate discrimination against Negro people on his programs. I've never seen a colored face in his studio audience and Negro youngsters are rejected as dancers on stage." Otis quoted a report from an *American Bandstand* staff member who said: "'We are instructed to screen all applicants to the show by their last names . . . we select people whose last names sound Italian, Jewish, or foreign . . . less chance of picking Negroes that way.'" Masco Young, a *Philadelphia Tribune* columnist, noted Otis's critique of Clark for "emceeing one of the most famous jim crowed shows on TV."[16]

Several of the white teenagers who danced on *American Bandstand* in the late 1950s support the contention that participation of black teenagers did not increase substantially after Clark took over the program. Arlene Sullivan, a regular on the show from 1957 to 1959, remembered that black teens "had their own show [*The Mitch Thomas Show*]," and that while "nobody ever kept anybody out," only a few black teens ever came to the show.[17] When asked about the racial or ethnic composition of the audience, Joe Fusco, who attended South Philadelphia High School and danced on the show every day from 1957 through 1959, was more suspicious:

> It was very, very white, that's what it was. At that time, I would watch people who were black, or not white, Puerto Rican, I don't care what they were, they wouldn't let them in. . . . To this day, Dick Clark takes credit for the few times black kids got in there, but he never wanted them in there. And that was very disgusting to me. I had no control over something like that. That was about the most disgusting thing, to see that is very heartbreaking, as a kid and knowing what they're actually doing and doing it in a sneaky way. Because no matter how long those kids waited in that line, somehow someway they didn't get in, because I used to look to see if they got in later. And in my time going to that show, I only saw two black kids that got in and sat in the bleachers, and he [Dick Clark] paid no attention to them. . . . Not many [black teens] even tried to get in there. That I really want to stress. You'd never see that many try to get in there, but when you did, and you knew that they were not going to get in, it bothered you.[18]

Ray Smith, who was not a regular, but who attended the show enough that classmates at West Philadelphia's Bartram High School called him "Mr. Bandstand," remembered that the threat of violence also limited the number of black teens who attended the show. "I don't remember one" black teenager who regularly attended the show, Smith recalled.

> It may have been an integrated show but black kids didn't go. . . . I also think that when blacks came to the show they were very often beat up afterwards. I only saw it once, and that could have been the only time it ever happened, but knowing the mindset of a lot of those [white] kids, I don't think that was the only time. . . . But from the years between, I started in 1956 and left in '59, I don't think I ever saw black kids there. I saw them in line one day, and that's where I saw kids beat up in the parking lot.[19]

In addition to these recollections, black teens continued to report to the *Philadelphia Tribune* that *American Bandstand*'s staff was turning them away from the studio. The circumstances of these complaints in

1959 and 1961 resembled earlier cases. The show's producers denied that they had a white-only policy, but the black teenagers who tried to get into the studio were always excluded for some reason. Some were told that they lacked a membership card, others that they did not meet the dress code, and others that the studio was full.[20] Between 1958 and 1963, the *Philadelphia Tribune* also published seven editorials or letters to the editor regarding *American Bandstand*'s exclusion of black teens. A December 1958 column sent Christmas greetings to "Dick Clark of Bandstand," wishing him a "new attitude toward Negro children which will permit them to be welcomed to his show." A 1960 letter to the editor conveyed similar feelings: "I am a songwriter and a school teacher and I can't understand why our youngsters don't appear on American Bandstand. American Bandstand is a Nation wide program coming from a northern state, but it is segregated." Finally, in 1963, *American Bandstand*'s last year in Philadelphia, a letter writer suggested that black deejay Jocko Henderson "approach one of the local TV stations about starting a Negro bandstand-type program" to challenge the "white teenagers who dance on Dick Clark's show."[21] Henry Gordon, who grew up in the Cobbs Creek Section of West Philadelphia and attended West Philadelphia High School in 1963 and 1964, agreed that black teens remained unwelcome on *American Bandstand*: "It was all white. It didn't bother us, we just know our, I don't want to say knew our place, but that's what it basically boils down to."[22]

In theory, the issue of *American Bandstand*'s segregation should be an empirical question: How many black teenagers made it into the show's studio between 1957 and 1964? The question, unfortunately, is not this simple. Establishing definitive evidence of *American Bandstand*'s studio audience in these years is difficult because dick clark productions, Inc., holds almost all of the existing video footage of the program. In June 2010, however, the company launched an online licensing portal, the "dick clark media archives." The Web site includes more than 130 short clips of *American Bandstand* from 1957 to 1963, all of which feature white teenagers.[23] Additionally, the archive at the Paley Center for Media in New York has two full episodes of *American Bandstand* from 1957 and three anniversary specials, and neither the episodes nor the clips from the anniversary specials show any black teenagers.[24] Similarly, all publicly available visual evidence of *American Bandstand*'s audience in these years supports the view that the audience was not regularly integrated. Several hundred photos from the show in the late 1950s and early 1960s are available in *American Bandstand* souvenir yearbooks (1957–59), '*Teen* magazines (1957–1963), Clark's autobiography *Rock, Roll, and Remember* (1976), Clark's two coauthored histories of the show, *The History of American Bandstand* (1985) and *Dick Clark's American Bandstand* (1997), and the *Dick Clark's American Bandstand 50th Anniversary* booklet (2007). Among the images of thousands of teens in the studio, only two pictures include any black teenagers, a pair of girls seated in the bleachers in each photo.[25] All of the evidence, including contemporary press accounts, the recollections of regulars on the show and those excluded from the show, and available pictures and video material, suggest that *American Bandstand* remained a space for white teenagers until it moved to Los Angeles in 1964.

THE MEMORY OF INTEGRATION ON *AMERICAN BANDSTAND*

How then do we understand Dick Clark's claim that he integrated *American Bandstand* by the late 1950s? His first chronicle of the show's history, the 1973 *Dick Clark 20 Years of Rock 'n' Roll Yearbook*, makes no mention of integration.[26] Clark first commented on the program's integration in his 1976 autobiography, *Rock, Roll, and Remember*. Clark recalled:

> "Bandstand" was a segregated show for years. It became integrated in 1957 because I elected to make it so. . . . I was aware of [the Freed controversy]. I was also aware that rock 'n' roll and "Bandstand" owed their existences to black music and the black artists who sang it. By the time I had the show a year I knew it had to be integrated. Tony [Mammarella] and I made sure we had black representation which increased as the years went by.[27]

Here, Clark refers to *American Bandstand*'s "integration" and the increase in "black representation," emphasizing black musical artists rather than the presence of black teenagers in the studio audience. By calling attention to the visibility *American Bandstand* provided to black artists twenty years earlier, Clark sought to absolve the show and himself of charges of appropriating black music. Clark's memory of integrating the show responded to music historians and critics who, writing in the wake of the civil rights movement, raised awareness of the frequent exploitation of black music artists by white producers.[28]

By the mid-1970s, moreover, *American Bandstand* ratings were in decline and faced a challenge from *Soul Train*. Created by black deejay

Don Cornelius as a black dance show, *Soul Train* started in Chicago in 1970 before being picked up by stations across the country the following year. By 1973, the show drew many of the top R&B performers and competed with *American Bandstand* for viewers on Saturday afternoons. To compete with *Soul Train*, Clark developed *Soul Unlimited*, hosted by black Los Angeles deejay Buster Jones, that broadcast in place of *American Bandstand* every fourth Saturday on ABC. Cornelius felt that *Soul Unlimited* was a blatant attempt to push *Soul Train* off the air and, with the help of the Reverend Jesse Jackson and Operation PUSH, took his case to the vice president of ABC. For his part, Clark felt that *Soul Train* was encroaching on his turf, telling *Rolling Stone* reporter Ben Fong-Torres, "that's my time period" and if ABC "wants to put a black *Bandstand* on, then I'll do it."[29] ABC, however, persuaded Clark to drop *Soul Unlimited* before summer 1973.[30] *American Bandstand* and *Soul Train*, however, remained rival shows throughout the 1970s and 1980s. Aiming to shore up *American Bandstand*'s reputation, Clark's 1976 memory of integrating *American Bandstand* emphasized the show's role as a champion of black performers but did not extend to the exclusion of black teenagers from the studio audience.

Clark first addressed the integration of the studio audience in his 1978 record collection celebrating the show's twenty-fifth anniversary. The enclosed booklet includes an entry for each year from 1952 to 1975, featuring tidbits on *American Bandstand* and current events. The entry for 1960 includes a reference to the show's integration:

> The civil rights movement captured the conscience of America as the first wave of "sit-ins" spread throughout the South while sympathetic boycotts were organized in the North. I'm proud to say "Bandstand" was already by then one of the first integrated shows on national television. After all, there would've been no rock 'n' roll without black music. And despite the fears of sponsors, we never received a single protest over the appearance of black couples on the show.[31]

The themes seen here—the reference to the national civil rights context and the *American Bandstand*'s place as a groundbreaking television show—would continue to inform Clark's memory of the show. Clark returned to the topic of integration in a 1990 *Rolling Stone* interview. Clark told journalist Henry Schipper the first time he ever spoke to a black teenager on the air in 1957 he was "terrified" because he "didn't know what the reaction was going to be" among southern viewers. Since there was no outpouring of protest from southern affiliates, Clark continued, "From that day forward, nobody ever called, and it just happened."[32] In a 1994 interview with historian John Jackson, Clark offered a history of the integration of the show's audience, while downplaying the nobleness of his intentions. Producer Tony Mammarella and "[I] alone decided that we had to get more [blacks] on the air," Clark told Jackson, "because we knew as we went on with the show and it got to be seen nationally, [segregation] couldn't be. It wasn't anything that we did as do-gooders or [that] we were politically inclined, or anything other than the fact, 'this made sense.'" When asked about the timing of this decision, Clark told Jackson that after the show went national in 1957, "there was never a rule not to show blacks on *American Bandstand*," and "as the years went by—'58, '59—more black kids attended. They didn't turn up in great numbers because they hadn't been welcome for so many years."[33]

Clark offered a more detailed version of this memory in the introductory essay to his 1997 book, *Dick Clark's American Bandstand* (a similar version of this story appears in *Dick Clark's American Bandstand 50th Anniversary*, published in 2007). After retelling the story of the first time he spoke to a black teen on the air, Clark describes *American Bandstand*'s integration in the context of television history:

> There was one important change that [Producer] Tony [Mammarella] and I made in 1957. Up until that time, the dancers on *Bandstand* had one thing in common—they were all white. You didn't see a lot of black people on TV in the fifties, or other minorities either. This was eight years before Bill Cosby starred with Robert Culp in *I Spy*, nine years before Nichelle Nichols was cast as Lieutenant Uhura in *Star Trek*, and eleven years before Diahann Carroll played *Julia*, all pioneering roles for black actors. Even in 1968, when Petula Clark kissed Harry Belafonte on the cheek, there was an uproar among advertisers and stations in the South. So in 1957, we were charting new territory. I don't think of myself as a hero or civil rights activist for integrating the show; it was simply the right thing to do.[34]

Here, Clark situates *American Bandstand* as a pioneering show in terms of racial representations and brings civil rights into the discussion of the show's history. Clark elaborated on the integration of *American Bandstand* as a television breakthrough in a 2003 magazine for fans of the show:

> [W]hen we integrated the studio audience in the early days, we were truly going where no television show had gone before. Black kids and white kids would not only be sitting together in the bleachers, but out on the same floor *dancing*. We weren't even sure what the reaction would be in our conservative hometown, Philadelphia, much less on ABC affiliates through the Deep

South. Perhaps because we didn't boast about what we were doing, or announce it, or talk about it in any way—we just *did* it—it went virtually unnoticed.[35]

Finally, when asked about the show's racial policies in a *New York Times* interview in 2011, Clark answered simply: "As soon as I became the host, we integrated."[36]

In these interviews and popular histories from 1978 to 2011, Clark became progressively bolder in his retelling of how he integrated *American Bandstand*'s studio audience. In this memory, Clark took the initial risk of upsetting viewers, affiliates, and sponsors by integrating the show. When no backlash emerged, Clark expanded the show's integration. In the process, *American Bandstand* made television history and contributed to civil rights. As outlined earlier, however, these memories run counter to the historical record. *American Bandstand* continued to discriminate against black teenagers, and black teenagers continued to protest this discrimination during the show's tenure in Philadelphia.

Part of the problem with the memories in these popular histories of *American Bandstand* is that Clark fails to address the antiblack racism, both locally and nationally, that motivated the show's exclusion of black teens. The introductory essay in *Dick Clark's American Bandstand* (1997) is illustrative in this regard. Here, Clark's memories of *American Bandstand* are nested in an overview of important events in U.S. history from the 1950s and 1960s. The first page of the essay, for example, features a full-page picture of black protestors in 1962 in Times Square carrying signs reading "End Segregation in Birmingham, Ala." and "End Segregation Across the Nation."[37] Subsequent pages offer pictures and captions related to other events and development from the 1950s: *Brown v. Board of Education*, Little Rock, the red scare, the increase in television set sales, the postwar demographic boom, and the expansion of suburbia.[38] Aligning *American Bandstand* with this checklist of important national events encourages readers to see the program as an important part of U.S. history. At the same time, this approach makes it difficult to address the topic of *American Bandstand*'s segregation in a way that is not simplistic and uplifting.

As the proceeding chapters have demonstrated, *American Bandstand*'s racially discriminatory admission policies need to be understood in the context of local struggles over education, housing, public space, and media, as well as national developments in music, radio, television, and civil rights. While *American Bandstand* did not "chart new territory" in integration, as Clark remembers, the racial policies of other institutions in Philadelphia in this era were not much better. Black workers seeking jobs in the city's retail, banking, food production, and unionized construction industries confronted employment discrimination.[39] Racially exclusionary housing policies in the suburbs restricted the housing choices of black families, and white homeowners' groups in neighborhoods across the city met the prospect of integration with threats of violence and mob intimidation.[40] In youth spaces, managers of roller skating rinks and swimming pools held separate "white" and "sepia" days or excluded black teens altogether through membership policies.[41] In sports, the Philadelphia Phillies were the last National League baseball team to integrate, and their first black star, Dick "Richie" Allen, was openly taunted by their fans and ridiculed in the press in the mid-1960s.[42] The city's public schools grew more racially segregated due to the school board's construction and zoning policies, while at the same time the school board adopted the rhetoric of intercultural education to deflect charges of discrimination.[43]

Civil rights advocates worked to uproot racial discrimination in the city, but they faced vocal opposition from the many white Philadelphians who mobilized to support segregation, as well as a city government that lacked the political will and resources to take on discrimination in employment, housing, education, or public facilities. Moreover, recent postwar histories of Charlotte, Atlanta, Detroit, Oakland, Chicago, and New York show many similarities to Philadelphia. While the local details differ, cities across the country witnessed vocal opposition to civil rights and integration, abetted by local and federal officials who actively and tacitly supported this opposition. In short, there was not widespread support, either locally or nationally, for the racial integration of a youth space like *American Bandstand*.

On television, commercial broadcasters strove to reach large numbers of consumers without offending anyone. By the late 1950s, historian James Baughman notes, television programming "narrowed largely to whatever (morally mainstream) productions appeared likely to reach the largest number of viewers."[44] Most relevant for *American Bandstand* was the question of showing interracial dancing on television. Alan Freed's television show served as a warning on this front. As noted earlier, an ABC executive told the *New York Post* that the network's decision not to feature black teenagers on *American Bandstand* was influenced by the controversy that erupted over deejay Alan Freed's television program showing black teenage R&B singer Frankie Lymon dancing with a white teenage girl a year earlier.[45] Freed's program, which started broadcasting nationally on ABC in July 1957, was canceled shortly after the controversy. Like integrated schools and other forms of cross-racial association, interracial dancing violated the deeply held orthodoxy against interracial sex.

During *American Bandstand*'s years in Philadelphia, more than twenty states had laws prohibiting interracial marriage, including the neighboring states of Delaware and Maryland.[46] Historians Peggy Pascoe, Fay Botham, and Jane Dailey have shown how these prohibitions were frequently rooted in religious ideas about racial separation and served as a pillar of white supremacy.[47] This was far from being a view held only by extremists; Dailey's study of southern fears of race mixing in the wake of the *Brown* decision shows that the "argument that God was against sexual integration was articulated across a broad spectrum of education and respectability, by senators and Ku Klux Klansmen, by housewives, sorority sisters, and Rotarians, and, not least of all, by mainstream Protestant clergymen."[48] The fears of integration and interracial dancing influenced the admission policies of teen dance shows. For example, the studio audiences of Baltimore's *Buddy Deane Show* and Washington, D.C.'s *Milt Grant Show* were completely segregated, with black teenagers welcome only for a specific day each month. Among the dozens of *Bandstand*-era televised teen dance shows, I have found no evidence that any were regularly integrated before 1964.[49] This widespread and deeply rooted animus to interracial coupling fueled much of the opposition to rock and roll and would have been impossible for the producers of *American Bandstand* to ignore.

Viewing *American Bandstand* in these local and national contexts does not let Dick Clark off the hook. Rather, it makes clear that the decision to maintain racially discriminatory admission policies flowed logically from neighborhood and school segregation, the commercial pressures of national television, and deeply held beliefs about the dangers of racial mixing. Absent this local and national context, Clark's memory takes the presence of black musical entertainers and the very infrequent entry of black teenagers on *American Bandstand* as evidence of consistent integration of the show's studio audience, and then takes this "integration" as evidence of the program's historical importance. Clark's claims of integrating the show not only overstate *American Bandstand*'s role as a force for social good; they also obscure the very reasons why integrating the show would have been noteworthy.

In the context of local and national mobilization in favor of segregation, underscored by widespread antiblack racism, integrating *American Bandstand* would have been a bold move and a powerful symbol. Broadcasting daily evidence of Philadelphia's vibrant interracial teenage culture would have offered viewers images of black and white teens interacting as peers at a time when such images were extremely rare. Clark and *American Bandstand* did not choose this path. One of Clark's contemporaries, Johnny Otis, noted this missed opportunity in a 1960 article: "As a result of the tremendous impression he made on the youth of American, Dick Clark had a golden opportunity to advance the cause of democracy in a wonderful way. But, instead, he and/or the TV network he works with chose to travel the lily-white Jim Crow route!"[50]

When Clark first discussed the integration of *American Bandstand* in the mid-1970s, twenty years after he took over the program, he did so to cast his show in a favorable light with respect to *Soul Train*. While focused on a contemporary competitor, Clark also used the topic of integration to establish *American Bandstand* as an important site of interracial exchange in the early years of television and rock and roll. In his attempt to ensure that *American Bandstand*'s 1957 national debut be remembered as a milestone, Clark's published memories of the show in the 1990s and 2000s have expanded on these integration claims, casting *American Bandstand* as a breakthrough television program that should be remembered alongside pivotal moments from the civil rights era. The historical record, however, contradicts these memories and shows that rather than being a fully integrated program that welcomed black youth, *American Bandstand* continued to discriminate against black teens throughout the show's Philadelphia years.

In his popular histories of the show, Clark presents the question of *American Bandstand*'s segregation as a simple moral question of right or wrong, rather than a deeply entrenched system of policies and customs with material consequences. He presents himself as the brave individual who broke down *American Bandstand*'s racial barriers, rather than describing the immense economic and social pressures that made segregation the safe course of action. Clark's memories are instructive because they exhibit the selective memory that historian Jacquelyn Dowd Hall and others have identified in the dominant narratives of the civil rights era. Against the distortions in many of these narratives, Hall suggests making civil rights "[h]arder to celebrate as a natural progression of American values. Harder to cast as a satisfying morality tale. Most of all, harder to simplify, appropriate, and contain."[51] One place to take up Hall's challenge is with the popular narratives of the *American Bandstand* era. Whereas Clark elides the complex histories of civil rights, race relations, television, and rock and roll of which *American Bandstand* was a part, the next chapter examines two productions from the 2000s, *American Dreams* and *Hairspray*, that take up these questions more directly.

CHAPTER 8

Still Boppin' on *Bandstand*

American Dreams, Hairspray, *and*
American Bandstand *in the 2000s*

It was fifty years ago today that *American Bandstand*
changed the way a generation listened to music and brought
rock and roll into American living rooms. . . . Even today the
show is influencing pop culture, changing people's lives.
American Bandstand may not be on the air now, but it's in
our hearts forever.

—*Good Morning America*, August 5, 2007

For a show that left television in 1989, *American Bandstand* was very busy in the 2000s. In 2007, Time Life promoted "Dick Clark's American Bandstand 50th Anniversary Collection" through television infomercials.[1] This twelve-CD box set, like the dozens of other compilations over the past half-century, marketed the history of rock and roll under the *American Bandstand* and Dick Clark brands. Numerous media outlets also paid tribute to *American Bandstand*'s fiftieth anniversary, including *Good Morning America*, which described *Bandstand* as a generation-defining show for baby boomers and traced *Bandstand*'s influence on the contemporary reality television program *American Idol*.[2] Two months before this anniversary attention, Washington Redskins football team owner Daniel Snyder bought dick clark productions, including the rights to the *American Bandstand* name and over eight hundred hours of footage, for $175 million. Snyder, whose private equity firm also owns Johnny Rockets, a 1950s-themed hamburger chain, told *USA Today*: "[w]e feel there's an Americana synergy between Johnny Rockets and American Bandstand and can visualize a video box system in our locations featuring our content."[3] Snyder is also the chairman of the board of Six Flags amusement parks, and the company's chief executive officer told the *Washington Post* that he "envisions the 877 hour-long 'American Bandstand' reruns being broadcast on plasma screens across Six Flags parks."[4] Given these developments, the commercial profitability and longevity of *American Bandstand* will extend well past its fiftieth anniversary year.

While it is impossible to predict how future visitors to Johnny Rockets or Six Flags will understand the history of the *American Bandstand* era, two recent productions take up these questions directly. The Emmy award-winning television drama *American Dreams* explores race relations in early 1960s Philadelphia on and around *American Bandstand*. And the musical film *Hairspray* tells the story of the struggle over segregation on Baltimore's version of *American Bandstand*. As commercial productions, the stories of the past presented in *American Dreams* and *Hairspray* have reached, and continue to reach, millions of viewers in dozens of countries. During its three seasons, *American Dreams* drew an audience of 8 to 13 million viewers each week, and the first season of the show is available on DVD.[5] The 2007 film version of *Hairspray*, meanwhile, grossed over $110 million in the United States and $80 million internationally and earned another $100 million in U.S. DVD sales, and the USA network paid $13 million for the cable rights to the film.[6] Although *Hairspray* does not mention *American Bandstand* by name, many film critics described *Hairspray*'s *Corny Collins Show* as an "*American Bandstand*-style" program.[7] Even the *American Bandstand 50th Anniversary Collection* booklet notes that "*Hairspray* . . . chronicles the integration of a fictional Baltimore-based *Bandstand*-type TV series."[8]

Whereas the link between *Hairspray* and *American Bandstand* was obvious for several reviewers, for younger viewers who were drawn to the film by teen stars Zac Effron (*High School Musical*) and Amanda Bynes (*The Amanda Show*), *Hairspray* might be the first introduction to *American Bandstand*–era dance shows. Likewise, *American Dreams* appealed to young viewers with cameo performances by contemporary popular music stars portraying artists from the 1960s. For this younger generation, the history of *American Bandstand* starts not with the images of the show itself, but with representations of the era in *American Dreams* and *Hairspray*. As such, these recent productions are crucial to understanding how the popular history of the *American Bandstand* era is being articulated in the 2000s.

There is much to recommend both *American Dreams* and *Hairspray*. While selected images from *American Bandstand* have long circulated in popular media, *American Dreams* and *Hairspray* provide narrative context to show how televised teenage dance shows became historically important for young people in particular times and places. Both productions use historically informed representations to tell stories in which television plays a central role. This is not to argue that these productions rely strictly on verifiable data or aim for the level of accuracy that one expects of written history. Rather, *American Dreams* and *Hairspray* juxtapose familiar televisual themes from the *American Bandstand* era with fictionalized characters, dialogue, and televisual representations. The resulting narratives present the history of the *American Bandstand* era in a way that inextricably links the subjects that are central to my project: teenage television, music, youth culture, urban space, racial discrimination, and civil rights. Although *American Dreams'* and *Hairspray's* respective methods of historical storytelling are tuned to commercial audiences, both productions use moving images, music, and dancing to celebrate and critique the mediated history of *American Bandstand* in ways that are not possible in written history.[9] At their best, *American Dreams* and *Hairspray* approach the history of televised teen dance shows with more nuance and complexity than Dick Clark's popular histories of *American Bandstand*. At the same time, however, *American Dreams* and *Hairspray* frequently use this nuance and complexity in the service of comforting narratives about interracial unity and white innocence.

The producers of both *American Dreams* and the Broadway version of *Hairspray* cited September 11 as the event that made their nostalgic stories of interracial unity and white innocence in the *American Bandstand* era relevant in the 2000s. In his commentary on the pilot episode, *American Dreams'* creator Jonathan Prince reflected on the connections between September 11 and the 1960s:

> When I wrote the pilot and I turned it in in August, a month later I got a phone call from one of the guys at NBC who had been helping me develop [the show]. . . . [He] called me and said, "are you watching TV?" . . . And I turned on the TV, and its September 11th, and I'm watching buildings in flames, and he said, "I think your show just got a lot more relevant." Because there was a generation of people who didn't know what it felt like to lose President Kennedy. This is, where were you when you [sic] walked on the moon? Where were you when President Kennedy was killed? Where were you when Martin Luther King was shot? . . . We have a generation who lived pretty much without that . . . but this was epic, the tragedy of losing President Kennedy was epic . . . there are these moments that unify us as a people and often they're tragedy, sadly. And this was one of them.[10]

The pilot episode of *American Dreams* shows characters reacting to news of the assassination of President Kennedy before closing with black-and-white footage of NBC's live coverage of the event from 1963. Here, *American Dreams* shows people unified across racial and generational lines in the face of a tragedy, and this historical narrative offers a "relevant" model for viewers after September 11. Jeff Zucker, NBC's president, agreed that while the series "was not developed in response to what happened [on September 11] it resonates with what happened."

David Rockwell offered similar comments regarding his work as a set designer on the Broadway production of *Hairspray*: "The heart of *Hairspray*—both the movie and the musical—encompasses John Waters's belief in racial, sexual, class and body-type tolerance. Although it went unspoken, as a result of September 11, 2001, every member of the *Hairspray* family realized the significance of transferring John's vision of empowerment and hopefulness to the stage."[11]

Critics also reviewed *American Dreams* and *Hairspray* in the context of post-September 11 entertainment. When *American Dreams* debuted in fall 2002, it was joined by another show on the 1960s (the comedy *Oliver Beene)*, remakes of three 1950s and 1960s era programs (*Dragnet, Twilight Zone*, and *Family Affair)*, two shows about men reliving their high school days in the 1980s (the comedy *Do Over* and the drama *That Was Then)*, and retrospective specials on Lucille Ball, Jackie Gleason, Jerry Lewis, and Ozzie and Harriet Nelson. Commenting on this fall schedule, *New York Times* critic Caryn James wrote:

> What we'll be watching in the fall suggests that programmers believe the mood to be overwhelmingly nostalgic and backwardlooking. . . . One after the other the networks—rarely adventurous to begin with—wrapped themselves in the flag, offered schedules dripping with nostalgia and announced shows that will play it safer than ever.

Even in this context of nostalgic television programming, *American Dreams'* promotional material stood out. NBC promoted *American Dreams* heavily during its 9/11 anniversary coverage, encouraging viewers to "Remember the innocence. Remember the music."[12] As part of the first television season developed after September 11, *American Dreams* was part of what media studies scholar Lynn Spigel describes as an effort to channel "the nation back to normalcy—or at least to the normal flows of television and consumer culture." "The return to normal," Spigel argues, "was enacted not just through the narrative frames of news stories but also through the repositioning of audiences back into television's fictive time and places."[13] Michiko Kakutani, writing in the *New York Times*, noted that this emphasis on nostalgia and a comforting return to normalcy extended to both Hollywood and Broadway, where

> producers have decided Americans want . . . nostalgia—the logic being that people in times of trouble will gravitate toward entertainment that reminds them of simpler, happier times [such as] the candy-colored Broadway musical 'Hairspray' and the much hyped new NBC show 'American Dreams [which] draw on fond remembrances of the 'American Bandstand' era.[14]

One of the interesting things about the renewed attention to the *American Bandstand* era in the 2000s is that both producers and critics of *American Dreams* and *Hairspray* took it as self-evident that stories about race relations in the 1960s would be comforting and nostalgic for viewers in the years after 9/11. Left unsaid in the promotion and reception of these productions was that both *American Dreams* and *Hairspray* looked to the familiar domestic black-white racial binary at a time when the dimensions of race in the United States had become increasingly multiethnic and transnational. Viewed in this light, the narratives of innocence and interracial unity featured prominently in *American Dreams* and *Hairspray* can be seen as comforting because they are not about the geopolitics of the contemporary United States. As media studies scholar Marita Sturken argues,

> American national identity, and the telling of American history, has been fundamentally based on a disavowal of the role played in world politics by the United States not simply as a world power, but as a nation with imperialist policies and aspirations to empire. This disavowal of the United States as an empire has allowed for the nation's dominant self-image as perennially innocent.[15]

Similarly, with narratives that solve the problem of black-white racial tensions in the 1960s through interracial cooperation, *American Dreams* and *Hairspray* could also be comforting because they were not about the political and cultural citizenship struggles of Muslims and Muslim-Americans. Focusing on these citizenship struggles in the context of 9/11 and U.S. imperialism, scholars like Sunaina Maira, Evelyn Alsultany, and Malini Johar Schueller have reiterated the "problems of imagining the nation as [a] singular community."[16] The racial profiling and detention of Muslims and Muslim-Americans may seem far removed from the *American Bandstand* era, but that, in some ways, is the point. More research is needed to understand how civil rights narratives are being used after 9/11, but at a time when other racial dimensions were emerging, *American Dreams* and *Hairspray* located their narratives of national unity and innocence safely in domestic black-white racial tensions in the 1960s.

While both *American Dreams* and *Hairspray* portray racial conflicts to raise the dramatic tensions, both productions manage these racial conflicts so as not to offend the "fond remembrances" of contemporary viewers. *American Dreams* cuts between overlapping story lines to present multiple perspectives on racial conflicts, but refuses to criticize white racism. *Hairspray,* meanwhile, locates racism within a single villainous character. Both productions, moreover, are organized around the coming of age stories of teenage protagonists. Encouraging viewers to identify with these innocent characters, *American Dreams* and *Hairspray* make a virtue out of historical naivety regarding race. Presented in this way, the *American Bandstand* era becomes part of a simplistic history in which changing racial attitudes in the 1960s produced a color-blind and fully equal society.

In this respect, *American Dreams* and *Hairspray* are part of a much larger struggle over how the history of the civil rights era is remembered. As media studies scholar Herman Gray argues, "the civil rights subject performs important cultural work since it helps construct the mythic terms through which many Americans can believe that our nation has now transcended racism."[17] These popular histories of the civil rights era, Gray notes, say as much (or more) about the present as the past, producing raced subjects "who fit the requirements of contemporary circumstance."[18] For viewers in the 2000s, *American Dreams* and *Hairspray* provide narrative proof that individual racial prejudice existed "back then," but was overcome through the racial tolerance of whites and the successful assimilation of African Americans. Scholars like Jacquelyn Dowd Hall, Paula Moya, Hazel Rose Markus, and Eduardo Bonilla-Silva have described how narratives such as this provide the foundation for claims that in the post–civil rights era, the United States is a color-blind or post-racial society. Hall traces the logic and implications of this narrative:

> In the absence of overtly discriminatory laws and with the waning of conscious bias, American institutions became basically fair. Free to compete in a market-driven society, African Americans thereafter bore the onus of their own failure and success. If stark group inequalities persisted, black attitudes, behavior, and family structure were to blame.[19]

With limited consideration of the structural aspects of racism, the narratives of interracial unity in *American Dreams* and *Hairspray* too easily bleed into narratives that take color-blindness to have been the singular objective and most important legacy of the civil rights era. My point here is not that *American Dreams* and *Hairspray* are bad history. Rather, I am most interested in the ways *American Dreams* and *Hairspray* look to the *American Bandstand* era to tell stories about the past and present, and how these productions foreground narratives of white innocence and interracial unity that work against structural understandings of racism.

AMERICAN DREAMS

In looking to the music, television, youth culture, and race relations of the *American Bandstand* era, *American Dreams*' producers offered the show to advertisers and viewers as a series that could be both entertaining and educational. In a speech at a broadcasters' meeting, *American Dreams* producer Jonathan Prince said that in addition to commercial success in ratings and advertisements, "what we want is to make a difference. What we want is to know that people are watching. And not merely watching, but talking about it."[20] Unlike *I'll Fly Away* or *Homefront*, early 1990s civil rights dramas that earned critical praise as "quality television" but failed to draw large popular audiences, *American Dreams* promised to be serious enough to prompt conversations regarding race relations while remaining commercially viable.[21] As part of this commercial appeal, Prince gained Dick Clark's permission to use old clips from *American Bandstand*.[22] Prince and Clark became co-executive producers of *American Dreams*, although Prince led the day-to-day series production. *American Dreams* also featured contemporary musical artists portraying historical performances on *American Bandstand* (e.g., Usher as Marvin Gaye, Vanessa Carlton as Dusty Springfield, and Kelly Rowland as Martha Reeves).

Through historical footage and recreated performances, *American Dreams* established the importance of *American Bandstand*, and television more broadly, to the social life of the 1960s. Television, moreover, is central to the social and economic dreams of several of the show's characters. The program examines the lives of a white family (the Priors) and a black family (the Walkers) in early 1960s Philadelphia. The social life of the show's teenage protagonist, Meg Prior (Brittany Snow), revolves around *American Bandstand*. The economic well-being of both families, meanwhile, hinges on the success of Jack Prior's (Tom Verica) television store, where Henry Walker (Jonathan Adams) also works. By making television central to how the show's characters have fun, earn a living, and learn about the news of their city and the nation, *American Dreams* fused television history and local race relations in a provocative way. Regardless of how different viewers interpret *American Dreams* or the show's portrayal of *American Bandstand,* the program demands that these interpretations account for television as a medium that mediates, records, and reenacts history.

Unlike Dick Clark's popular histories of *American Bandstand,* which detached the show from the social history of postwar Philadelphia, *American Dreams* offers a more nuanced history of *American Bandstand* by situating its story line in the context of early 1960s Philadelphia. The first scene in the pilot episode, for example, opens with a caption reading "Philadelphia, 1963" and immediately shows teens waiting to be admitted to *American Bandstand*. Next, the program shows two of its teenage protagonists, Meg Prior and Roxanne Bojarski (Vanessa Lengies), running home to watch *American Bandstand* on television. As these teens race home, the camera cuts to Meg's mother and sister in the living room watching a locally broadcast cooking show. The scene moves through the television, from the living room to the WFIL studio, where a camera crew is shooting the cooking show. This television-as-portal shot is used a second time, to move from the WFIL studio to Jack Prior's television store, where kids are gathering to watch *American Bandstand*. The scene then returns to show Meg and Roxanne running home as the crew of *American Bandstand* counts down to airtime inside the WFIL studio. The reenactment of *American Bandstand* opens with a soft focus on the actor playing Dick Clark in the background, and a hard focus on the black-and-white historical footage of Dick Clark on the television monitor. After the "historical" Clark introduces Martha and the Vandellas, the scene shifts among three sets of dancers: Meg and Roxanne dancing at home, kids dancing in Meg's father's television store, and teens dancing in the *American Bandstand* studio. Within the first six minutes of the debut episode, *American Dreams* portrays the complexity of the production and consumption of *American Bandstand* through this range of televisual representations.

American Dreams, unlike Clark's histories, downplays the question of integration on *American Bandstand*'s. *American Dreams*' version of *American Bandstand* occasionally includes two or three black teenagers in the crowd, but all of the regular dancers are white. The racial demographics of *American Bandstand*'s studio audience are noted in the third episode of *American Dreams*. During a scene in the *American Bandstand* studio, Meg learns a new dance from a black teenager. The camera pans to the right to show that this interracial pair is dancing in front of the WFIL studio camera, which is presumably broadcasting the image to television affiliates across the country. The camera pans further to the right to find two middle-aged white men in suits watching the couple on the WFIL studio monitor. The show identifies the two men by signs on their chairs that read "sponsor." Gesturing toward the monitor featuring the image of the interracial couple, one of the men asks "Are we on the air here?"[23] This concerned sponsor is assured by his partner that the show is broadcasting a commercial and not the studio image. These two sponsors, portrayed by present-day NBC television executives, are identified in the credits as the "Ad Guys" and do not appear in any other episodes of *American Dreams*.[24] Their brief appearance in this episode is the most direct reference *American Dreams'* producers make to *American Bandstand*'s racial representations. This scene implies that sponsors exercised a great deal of control over the images *American Bandstand* broadcast and blames these sponsors, rather than Dick Clark or the rest of *American Bandstand*'s production staff, for the show's racial segregation.

While this "blame the sponsors" trope is familiar, this scene is interesting because it presents a more historically accurate picture of the "integration" of *American Bandstand*, one that casts Dick Clark's claims about ending the show's racial segregation in a different light. Rather than "charting new territory" or "going where no television show had gone before," as Clark has previously contended, this scene suggests that one or two black teens very occasionally made it into the studio and that producers consciously kept black teens off camera. In this view, *American Bandstand* reluctantly practiced token integration, and through selective camera work, even this token integration would have been invisible to television viewers. This definition of integration is a far more modest claim about *American Bandstand*'s role as a "force for social good," but it helps explain how Dick Clark could believe that he integrated *American Bandstand* while the show continued to discriminate against black teenagers.[25]

Although *American Dreams* does not address *American Bandstand*'s racially discriminatory admission policies, by portraying *American Bandstand* amid the racial discrimination and tensions in Philadelphia,

American Dreams encourages its audience to consider the role television played in mediating daily life in the 1960s. To bolster the show's historical accuracy, *American Dreams* employed two full-time researchers to find specific details of Philadelphia in this era.[26] This research is most evident in the show's portrayal of the riot in North Philadelphia in the summer of 1964. The climactic riot scene in the first season's final episode opens with historical *American Bandstand* footage of Dick Clark introducing Mitch Ryder and the Detroit Wheels. The scene moves from this black-and-white footage to the recreated *American Bandstand* studio, where the band portraying the group performs a rock and roll version of "C.C. Ryder." The scene then cuts repeatedly between the studio and a street in North Philadelphia, while the song plays continuously in the background. In the street scene, a middle-aged black man and woman are arguing, first with each other and then with two police officers. The police forcibly arrest them for being drunk and disorderly while a number of black motorists and passersby watch the incident unfold. The show's producers packed this scene with historical details, using the real names of the woman who was arrested and the police officer who arrested her.[27] The scene is shifting, therefore, between two historical reenactments. The first is a reenactment of a musical performance that originally broadcast on *American Bandstand* in 1966 and resembles the musical reenactments featured in almost every episode of *American Dreams*.[28] The reenactment of the altercation and arrest that sparked the Philadelphia riots, in contrast, portrays a moment that happened outside the view of television cameras in the summer of 1964. The latter reenactment is the show's most specific portrayal of a historical event in Philadelphia other than *American Bandstand*. The juxtaposition of these reenactments is important because it asks viewers to watch and remember *American Bandstand* in the context of Philadelphia's simmering racial tensions.

As the riots develop, the episode continues to move between reenactments of *American Bandstand* and dramatizations of the different interpretations and implications of the riots. The scene immediately following the arrest cuts among the *American Bandstand* studio, a group of young black men in North Philadelphia talking about the arrest, and a group of white police officers in a diner doing the same. While the police jokingly recount how the drunken woman hit one of the officers on the scene, the black men express anger and frustration at what they see as police brutality. One of the men, Willie Johnson (Nigel Thatch), appeared in earlier episodes encouraging his peers to develop intra-racial solidarity, using language that resonates with the rhetoric of black nationalism popularized by Malcolm X.[29] Henry Walker's nephew Nathan (Keith Robinson), who is drawn to the racial consciousness encouraged by Willie Johnson, gets the last word in the street corner exchange:

> Ain't nothing right about this. Up in Harlem, police killed that boy James Powell. You think that boy deserved to die? What for? They ain't got no reason. None. We're supposed to just stand back until they murder one of us? That's in Harlem, that's in St. Augustine, it's Rochester, it's Chicago, it's North Philly. Ain't never gonna change.[30]

This scene grounds the anger and frustration of these young black men in historically specific incidents of racial violence. Regarding the place of this scene in the series, Prince added, "[f]rom the very beginning, I told NBC that I wanted the final episode to be the riots. . . . The idea of the end of episode 25 was to show how one event, the riots, brought everybody together, white, black, old, young."[31] More specifically, *American Dreams* uses the riots to bring its characters together in a common story line, but the show does not attempt to resolve what the riots mean for the characters, or how viewers might interpret either the historical riots or their fictional portrayal.

Televisual representations are the primary way *American Dreams* links different characters without erasing their different perspectives on the riots. Willie Johnson and Nathan are the only characters who see the riots start in person, whereas all of the other characters learn about the riots via black-and-white footage on television (the actual footage is of the Watts riots, but the events are here described as taking place in North Philadelphia).[32] *American Dreams* uses these televised images of the riots as a way to locate the show's characters in relation to the event. Meg's mother and younger siblings watch the riots unfold on television from the safety of their living room. In *American Bandstand*'s studio, the show's producer watches the riots on a monitor in the control room and makes plans to send the studio audience home. Jack Prior and Henry Walker see footage of the riots in the television store, and leave the televised riots behind to find their teenage children, Meg and Sam, in the streets of North Philadelphia. Riot images are also on the televisions in the North Philadelphia store, where Meg and Sam (Arlen Escarpeta) are boarding up the windows in anticipation of the riots reaching their block. For *American Dreams*' characters, these historical television images convey both the reality and proximity of the riots. For the show's television audience, this scene also links *American*

Bandstand as one of several sites with an emotional and geographic relationship to the riot.

The final riot scene also threatens the burgeoning interracial friendship between Sam and Meg. Sam is last shown with his cousin Nathan, kneeling over Willie Johnson who has been shot by a police officer. While Sam stays with Willie, Meg's uncle removes her from the riots. The first season closes with Meg looking back at Sam from the back window of her uncle's police car. Of this ending, Prince suggests, "[t]o end the first season with Meg in the back of a cop car, staring out, that's a different girl than the girl who was watching *Bandstand* in that first pilot episode, filed with nothing but hope."[33] Although this link between *American Bandstand* and the riots is not, in fact, historically accurate (*American Bandstand* moved to California several months before the Philadelphia riots in 1964), by portraying *American Bandstand* in a racially charged local context, *American Dreams* encourages viewers to see *American Bandstand* as part of the social history of Philadelphia.

This riot scene, however, also highlights how *American Dreams* seeks to manage racial tensions to avoid offending contemporary viewers. Producer Jonathan Prince has suggested that, by cutting between the different stories of the event that sparked the riot, he intended to leave the interpretation of the scene open to the viewer. In his DVD commentary on the episode, Prince said, "When I wrote it I just thought, I want to hear both people's point of view, because somewhere in the middle lay the truth."[34] By giving *American Dreams'* representations of history an air of uncertainty, Prince suggests, he intended for viewers to engage more closely with the history and memory of this era.

More simply, however, *American Dreams'* narrative ambiguity supports the show's broad appeal as a commercial network television program. *American Dreams* pursues the widest possible audience by presenting an array of different characters with whom viewers could identify or not on the basis of age, race, gender, class, religion, or political opinion. The show attempts to appeal across these marketing demographics without offending anyone. The challenge of trying to sell to all of these demographic groups is that viewers' reactions to the riot scene and the series would vary based on each viewer's memory, knowledge, and interpretation of what happened before, during, and after the summer of 1964. This is important, especially for a show called *American Dreams*, because as political scientist Jennifer Hochschild has shown, race and class shape how people understand the American dream. "African

Americans increasingly believe that racial discrimination is worsening and that it inhibits their race's ability to participate in the American dream," Hochschild argues. "[W]hites increasingly believe that discrimination is lessening and that blacks have the same chance to participate in the dream as whites."[35] Similar to the survey data Hochschild analyzed, a 2002 Gallop poll found that members of different racial groups have very different views of police and the criminal justice system. Eighty-four percent of whites said that the criminal justice system respects the civil rights of black citizens, compared to only 33 percent of blacks.[36] This opinion poll, from the same year *American Dreams* debuted, is indicative of the different ways of seeing race, crime, and policing that viewers would bring to the riot episode. In short, *American Dreams* approaches race in terms of marketing demographics (e.g., accumulating different viewers from different racial groups), without consideration for the ways race shapes how viewers understand the show's narratives and even the show's title.[37]

American Dreams' strategy of narrative ambiguity frequently introduces different points of view, but refuses to criticize white racism, even when it takes place "back then" in the diegetic past of the 1960s. The intersecting story lines in the riot scene, for example, present police brutality and black nationalism as equivalents. Willie and Nathan are cast as the dangerous black characters who jeopardize Henry and Sam's efforts at integration. These representations, Herman Gray notes, look back to portrayals of black people in the civil rights era as either "decent but aggrieved blacks who simply wanted to become a part of the American dream, or as threats to the very notion of citizenship and nation."[38] Setting the "bad" black characters against the "good" black characters presents viewers with a simplistic view of black opinions regarding integration and racial equality.

Closing the season finale with Meg being rescued from North Philadelphia, moreover, reemphasizes the show's commitment to the innocence of white characters and viewers. Whether Meg has learned anything about race relations or racism in her city is, in the narrative, less important than the fact that she is a "different girl than the girl who was watching *Bandstand* in that first pilot episode, filed with nothing but hope."[39] Meg's loss of innocence, marked by her inability to be a carefree teenage consumer, receives more emphasis in the finale than the police brutality and economic, social, and political inequality that precipitated the riots in Philadelphia. Focusing on the danger Meg faces during the riot also echoes the use of urban riots by conservatives as evidence of the failure of liberal antipoverty programs and of the dangers posed by urban communities of color. In response to these perceived dangers, "law and order" became a favorite slogan of conservative politicians during and after the 1960s. U.S. Senator Barry Goldwater, for example, articulated this argument in the speech that launched his 1964 presidential campaign:

> It is on our streets that we see the final, terrible proof of a sickness which not all the social theories of a thousand social experiments has even begun to touch. Crime grows faster that population, while those who break the law are accorded more consideration than those who try to enforce the law. Law-enforcement agencies—the police, the sheriffs, the F.B.I.—are attacked for doing their jobs. Law breakers are defended. Our wives, all women, feel unsafe on our streets.[40]

This prospect of urban spaces being unsafe for white wives and daughters was a recurring theme in the law and order rhetoric and is evident when Meg is in danger in the riots. Since viewers are encouraged to identify with Meg's dreams and fears throughout the series, the image of her, clearly scared, driving away from North Philadelphia and looking back at riots is a powerful one. The power of this image, however, draws on ideas about black lawlessness and white innocence that shape *American Dreams*' story of the riots.

Similarly, Prince's suggestion that *American Dreams* was looking for the truth among multiple viewpoints also underestimates the cultural meanings viewers are likely to ascribe to the idea of urban riots generally. The use of television footage of the Watts riots is important here. This historical footage, appearing on television screens in the Priors' home and stores, connects the different characters and the audience to the immediacy of the "live" riot. Presumably, Prince elected to use coverage from the Watts riots, the most famous urban rebellion of the decade, because this footage was more plentiful and visceral than similar footage from the Philadelphia riots. *American Dreams*' substitution of Watts for Philadelphia, however, is suggestive of the ways in which viewers would bring their own cultural knowledge of urban riots, and urban space more generally, to this episode.

As historian Gerald Horne has shown, the Watts riots became a cultural symbol of urban crisis and influenced the way politicians and citizens talked about race, poverty, and cities in the following decades. Similarly, media studies scholar Steve Macek argues that film, television, magazines, and newspapers have promoted images of "economically depressed urban centers like Philadelphia, Baltimore, St. Louis, and Detroit" as "vast landscapes of fear."[41] Rather than asking viewers to engage critically with their own assumptions about urban riots and, more broadly, race, poverty, and cities, *American Dreams'* riot episode presents both "point[s] of view, because somewhere in the middle lay the truth."

Alternatively, *American Dreams* might have provided more context for viewers to understand why the show's black and white characters held different opinions of relevant issues, such as police surveillance and brutality. In his foreword to R&B musician and civil rights activist Johnny Otis's history of the Watts riots, for example, American studies scholar George Lipsitz writes:

> Otis asks his readers to view the destruction in Watts in August 1965 as a product of pressures built up over centuries. Rather than viewing the riots as the product of deranged or criminal elements in the community, Otis depicts the uprising as a political statement by people deprived of any other meaningful way of getting their grievances heard.[42]

Rather than offering a comforting story, Otis's *Listen to the Lambs* challenges readers to understand the everyday realities that produced urban uprisings in places like Watts and Philadelphia. Without this historical context, *American Dreams* praises its audience for engaging with a serious and dramatic historical moment, but ultimately uses the riots as stage dressing for a story of lost innocence that reinforces what viewers already think about the riots and the *American Bandstand* era.

HAIRSPRAY

Like *American Dreams*, *Hairspray* focuses on music, television, youth culture, and race relations in the *American Bandstand* era. *Hairspray* revolves around the *Corny Collins Show*, a fictionalized version of the *Buddy Deane Show*, which broadcast in Baltimore from 1957 to 1963. Like the film's fictional *Corny Collins Show*, the *Buddy Dean Show* was segregated. The station allowed only white teens to attend the weekday broadcasts, with the exception of one Monday each month when black teenagers filled the studio.[43] Unlike *American Bandstand*, whose producers insisted that their racially discriminatory admission policies were color-blind, the *Buddy Deane Show's* policy of segregation was explicit. In 1963, the Civic Interest Group, an integrationist group founded at

Morgan State University and made up of college and high school students from Baltimore, challenged this policy by obtaining tickets for black and white teens to attend the show on a day reserved for black teenagers. After the surprise interracial broadcast, the television station received bomb and arson threats, hate mail, and complaints from parents of white teenagers.[44] Facing controversy over the possibility of more integrated broadcasts, the station canceled the *Buddy Deane Show* in the fall of 1963.

John Waters, who grew up in Baltimore and was a devoted fan of the *Buddy Deane Show*, drew on this history to write and direct the original film version of *Hairspray* in 1988. Waters's earlier films, low-budget camp comedies like *Pink Flamingoes*, earned him a following among independent movie fans. Waters brought a milder version of his deadpan camp aesthetic to *Hairspray*, which had a $2.7 million budget and was his first film to receive a family-friendly PG rating.[45] The *Wall Street Journal*'s film critic commented that "the strangest thing about [Waters's] latest picture, 'Hairspray,' is how very sweet and cheerful it is."[46] In Waters's film a fat teenage girl, Tracy Turnblad (Ricki Lake), dreams of being a regular dancer on the *Corny Collins Show*.[47] After achieving her goal, Tracy realizes that the show's policy of segregation is unfair and joins with the black teens who have befriended her to integrate the program. Unlike the tensions that followed the real protest and integration of the *Buddy Deane Show*, Waters's *Hairspray* ends with the protesters succeeding triumphantly. The television news reporter covering the *Corny Collins Show*'s integration in the film sums up the scene: "You're seeing history being made today. Black and white together on local TV. The *Corny Collins Show* is now integrated!"[48]

Before making *Hairspray*, Waters helped to publicize the history of the *Buddy Deane Show*'s segregation in an essay on the program in his 1986 book *Crackpot: The Obsessions of John Waters*. Commenting on the film's revisionist history, Waters freely admitted that "I gave it a happy ending that it didn't have."[49] In a 1988 interview Waters said he believed a major Hollywood production would have downplayed the show's segregation. "I felt that to ignore that fact would be really inauthentic," Waters argued. "[I]f Hollywood would have made this movie, they would have had blacks on the show and just ignored the fact that none of the shows . . . did then."[50] While Waters imagined a happy ending contrary to historical events, his film is clear about segregation on the *Buddy Deane Show*.

Hairspray's happy ending also gave the story a narrative arc that appealed to Broadway and Hollywood producers. Broadway producer Margo Lion, who also grew up watching the *Buddy Deane Show* as a teenager in Baltimore, approached Waters in 1999 about making a musical from his film. Lion brought in a team of musical composers, lyricists, and writers to bring the show to Broadway. The resulting show maintained the basic structure of Waters's story, but fitting its transition to Broadway, the new *Hairspray* featured over a dozen original songs that conveyed the show's narrative.[51] This stage production earned eight Tony Awards, including best musical, and paved the way for a second film version, a musical comedy closely modeled on the Broadway version.[52] The 2007 film version of *Hairspray* is indebted to Waters's original, but it differs in two important respects. First, with a larger budget, wider distribution, and a well-known cast, the new *Hairspray*'s commercial goals went well beyond those of Waters's film. As Michael Lynne, CEO of New Line Cinema noted of translating *Hairspray* into a big budget Broadway musical and film, "you take a film that was a cult film and you translate it to a medium where it must be a blockbuster if it's going to succeed. There is no cult version of a Broadway musical."[53] Second, the new *Hairspray* makes greater use of music, dance, and reconstructions of historical television programs to appeal to a larger audience.[54] The way the 2007 version of *Hairspray* navigates between these commercial aspirations while remaining faithful to Waters's story makes it the focus of my analysis. The resonance between the *Corny Collins Show* and *American Bandstand*, moreover, makes *Hairspray* a part of the mediated history of *American Bandstand*.

Hairspray raises the topic of racial segregation early in the film while introducing the *Corny Collins Show* (unless otherwise noted, all reference to *Hairspray* in the rest of this chapter are to the 2007 version). Like *American Dreams*, the scene opens with Tracy (Nikki Blonsky) and her best friend Penny (Amanda Bynes) rushing home from school. As the girls run home, the scene cuts to the *Corny Collins Show* dancers and crew getting ready for the start of the program. The two girls arrive in the living room and turn on the television in time for Corny Collins's (James Marsden) opening monologue, "Hey there teenage Baltimore. Don't change that channel, because it's time for *The Corny Collins Show*."[55] As the film's audience joins Tracy and Penny in watching the black-and-white recreation of Baltimore's local teenage dance program, Corny opens the show by singing "The Nicest Kids in Town." The song's lyrics introduce the television program and slyly reference the show's segregation:

Every afternoon you turn your TV on
And we know you turn the sound up when your parents are gone
And then you twist and shout for your favorite star
And once you've practiced every step that's in your repertoire
You better come on down and meet the nicest kids in town
Nice *white* kids who like to lead the way
And once a month we have our *Negro Day!*[56] (emphasis added)

The film calls attention to its use of anachronistic racial terminology by having Corny sing "white" clearly and sharply, and by having all eighteen of the teenage *Corny Collins Show* dancers join in to sing "Negro Day." During the song, the film cuts from the *Corny Collins Show*'s studio where the song is being performed to the living room where Tracy and Penny are dancing along with the show, and to Tracy's television broadcasting black-and-white images of the *Corny Collins Show*. Tracy and Penny dance throughout the scene, and the lyrics about the show's segregation do nothing to break them out of their afternoon routine. In his comments on the film, producer Neil Meron suggests that this normalcy was intended to stand out to the film's viewers:

> I think young people have a really eye opening experience when they're watching this movie, just in terms of the racial divide that existed then and about how shocking things were then that aren't anymore. They want to know if these things actually existed. . . . There is a truth to *Hairspray* that really tells young people what it was like, and how far we may have come on certain issues.[57]

The lyrics about segregation in "The Nicest Kids in Town" are intended to be both humorous and educational for the film's audience, but they are presented as part of the everyday order of things for Tracy, Penny, and the teenagers on the *Corny Collins Show*.

The film's audience learns more about the segregation of the *Corny Collins Show* in the next scene, where Tracy and Penny watch the program on several televisions displayed in the window of an electronics store. As the girls look on, Corny introduces Motormouth Maybelle (Queen Latifah), the host of the one day a month when the show opens its studio to black teenagers. "I'm Motormouth Maybelle," she says, "reminding [sic] the last Tuesday of the month is rhythm and blues day. That's right, Negro Day will be coming your way."[58] Before Maybelle can finish her pitch, the camera drifts to Amber Von Tussle (Brittany Snow), the film's blonde teenage antagonist. Maybelle says "ah, over here," reminding the cameraman to refocus on her. In this scene, as in "The Nicest Kids in Town" sequence, the film moves among images of Maybelle on the set of the *Corny Collins Show*, Tracy and Penny watching Maybelle on the television, and close-ups of the televised picture of Maybelle. The shifts between scenes of the *Corny Collins Show* being produced and scenes of the film's characters watching and dancing to the program establish the "liveness" of television within the film's narrative. The film situates television as central to the lives of the characters even when they are not in the television studio. In turn, the importance of television to the characters' lives helps to explain their protests against segregation on the *Corny Collins Show*.

The musical number "New Girl in Town" highlights the stakes of protesting segregation on the *Corny Collins Show*. This montage scene contrasts the whiteness of the *Corny Collins Show* with the show's segregated Negro Day. "New Girl in Town" also introduces an interracial romance subplot between Maybelle's son, Seaweed (Elijah Kelley), and Tracy's friend Penny. Producer Neil Meron described these intersecting story lines in his commentary on the film: "so much happens during this song, which is one of the beautiful things about doing movie musicals that you can't do on stage . . . you can accomplish so much during a song visually, storytelling wise."[59] The visual and musical storytelling in "New Girl in Town" starts with Amber and two other white teens performing the song on the set of the *Corny Collins Show*. Halfway through the song, the scene cuts to a black female trio, the fictional Dynamites, singing the song on Negro Day. This transition, coproducer Craig Zadan noted, "shows you the difference between a vanilla version of the song, with the white girls, and then the soulful version of the song, the sassy version of the song, on Negro Day."[60] In highlighting this change in musical styles, this scene juxtaposes reenactments of the *Buddy Deane Show*'s segregated white and black days. Unlike the one Monday a month when black teenagers were allowed on the real *Buddy Deane Show*, *Hairspray* presents the performances on Negro Day as being more dynamic and original than those on the *Corny Collins Show*.

While Waters's film both accentuated and satirized the distinction between "square" white teenagers and "hip" black youth, *Hairspray* (2007) uses the different dancing and singing styles to highlight the *Corny Collins Show*'s appropriation of black culture. Unlike Waters's film and the Broadway play, which mentioned but never showed Negro Day, this scene is the audience's first glimpse of Motormouth Maybelle presiding over the black teen dance telecast. After the Dynamites finish singing, the camera focuses on Maybelle as she reads a promotion for a fictional hair care product, "Nap-away" ("Every kink will be gone in a blink"). Queen Latifah plays the Maybelle character with the confidence and energy she displayed in her career as a hip-hop artist, but in this scene she registers disappointment as she reads the advertisement. Zadan argues that in the scene viewers "get to see how much Motormouth Maybelle is happy to be hosting Negro Day, but at the same time how demeaning it is to be doing this ad for this hair product."[61] Maybelle's negotiation of the limited opportunities offered by this segregated television program is made explicit in the exchange between Maybelle and the program manager, Velma Von Tussle (Michelle Pfeiffer), that closes the scene:

> VVT: How dare you pick the same song ["New Girl in Town"]!
>
> MM: They [The Dynamites] wrote it.
>
> VVT: You watch yourself. You are one inch from being canceled. You know what your demographic is? Cleaning ladies and lawn jockeys. (Velma walks off)
>
> MM (to her teenage son): A foot in the door, that's all it is. One toe at a time.[62]

This exchange explicates the montage scenes during "New Girl in Town." Maybelle's matter-of-fact line, "they wrote it," identifies the Dynamites as the writers of "New Girl in Town" and references the numerous historical examples of white artists reaping financial gains by covering black rhythm and blues songs.[63] This scene is also the film's most explicit confrontation regarding racism. Director Adam Shankman called Velma's "cleaning ladies and lawn jockeys" statement "the most dangerous line" in the film, and Zadan said that they wanted the characters in this scene to go "very, very far with the racism issue."[64] Through this unsubtle exchange, the film reveals Velma to be a racist character and exposes the segregated *Corny Collins Show* to be a site of racial discrimination. This exchange also establishes the film's approach to racism. In treating racism as an attitude and locating racial prejudice in a single character, *Hairspray* makes it possible for the narrative to fix racism through interracial cooperation.

"Welcome to the Sixties," a song at the film's midpoint, foreshadows the resolution of these racial tensions. The Dynamites are integral to the visual and musical composition of the scene, which focuses on Tracy's convincing her agoraphobic mother, Edna Turnblad (John Travolta), to leave the house and embrace the future. Tracy starts the song, singing

"Hey mama, hey mama, look around / Everybody's groovin' to a brand new sound," before turning on the family's television set to reveal the Dynamites performing dance steps in time with the song.[65] As Tracy delivers the title of the song, "Hey mama, welcome to the sixties," she points toward the television, and her mother's face registers surprise at the black-and-white image of the Dynamites on the television. While Tracy cajoles her mother, the film returns to the televised image of the Dynamites twice more, and the singers join the vocal track of the song.

The Dynamites' visibility is heightened when Tracy finally gets her mother to leave the house. The Dynamites take on a more prominent role in the vocal track, and, through special effects, still images of the group come to life from advertisements on a building, a bus stop, and a billboard. The group also appears on several television screens in a store's display window. Throughout "Welcome to the Sixties," the Dynamites get the top billing, which the *Corny Collins Show* denied them just minutes earlier during the Negro Day segment of "New Girl in Town." The extreme visibility of this black singing group on television and in public advertisements represents, in the film's narrative, the progressive changes that await the characters in "the sixties." Tracy, who initiated these changes, emerges as the integrationist hero to counter the racist villain, Velma.

The film further establishes television as a site of struggle for racial equality, and Tracy as a champion of integration, through a protest march on the station that broadcasts the *Corny Collins Show*. The scene opens on a neighborhood street where Maybelle and dozens of black community members are gathering with picket signs reading "Integration, Not Segregation," "TV Is Black and White," and "Let Our Children Dance."[66] Tracy emerges from the crowd and tells Maybelle she wants to join the march. The two characters have a brief exchange that establishes what Tracy, the only white person at the rally, stands to lose by challenging segregation:

MM: You're going to pay a heavy price.

TT: I know.

MM: You'll never dance on TV again.

TT: If I can't dance with Seaweed and Little Inez [Maybelle's son and daughter], then I don't want to dance on TV at all. I just want tomorrow to be better.[67]

Given the importance the film assigns to Tracy's dream of dancing on the *Corny Collins Show,* she risks a lot by joining the protest. Although the film does not portray who organized this protest, Maybelle is heard giving directions and encouragement as the camera pans across the crowd. Maybelle is clearly established as the protest leader when she sings "I Know Where I've Been."

Producer Craig Zadan describes Maybelle's ballad as "[t]he emotional core of the movie" and "the number that moves people the most."[68] There is no equivalent song in Waters's film, which eschews sentimentality in favor of camp humor. "I Know Where I've Been" draws instead on the stage version of *Hairspray,* which raises the story's emotional stakes in order to make the successful resolution in the final act more joyous. *Hairspray* (2007) encourages this emotional reaction by presenting the song in a serious tone without any of the verbal or visual jokes found in the film's other songs. The film also links the song with a protest march that gives the scene a visual component resembling historical images of civil rights marches. In contrast to the dance numbers in the rest of the film, Maybelle delivers a slow and soulful version of "I Know Where I've Been," with backup vocals by an off-screen gospel choir.[69] As Maybelle leads the crowd to the television station, dozens of black Baltimoreans join the protestors, and these marchers lip-sync the choirs' part. At several points in the scene, moreover, the camera films the crowd from the front so that Maybelle and the protestors are singing and marching directly toward the screen. Through the growth of the crowd and the rising emotion of the song, the film further establishes the protest against segregation on television as a major civil rights issue for the film's characters.

This scene also differentiates the film's segregation theme from the main character's struggle to become popular as a fat teenage girl.[70] Waters's film, which satirizes discrimination against black and fat teenagers, does not clearly distinguish between the two. In the DVD commentary for the new film, moreover, Waters suggests: "If we're making a movie about outsiders, black people and integration, then what's even further? I think a fat girl gets more hassle than a black girl. If you ask any really fat people, they say they walk down the street and nobody looks at them."[71] In contrast to Waters's suggestion, *Hairspray* (2007) does not treat racial discrimination and anti-fat prejudice as equivalents. While *Hairspray* (2007) also uses Tracy's weight to universalize her outsider appeal, the film assigns more emotional power to the segregation subplot and to Queen Latifah's character than to Tracy's pursuit of acceptance and popularity. Rather than suggesting that all outsiders face similar struggles as Waters's film sometimes implies, *Hairspray* (2007) focuses more attention on the injustice of racial segregation and discrimination.

Hairspray (2007) also downplays the provocative gender casting decisions in Waters's film. Whereas *Hairspray* (1988) cast Divine, best known for playing drag queens in Waters's earlier films, as both Tracy's mother and the racist (and male) television station owner, *Hairspray* (2007) toned down these challenging gender representations by casting John Travolta to play Tracy's mother. Director Adam Shankman noted that *Hairspray*'s (2007) producers cast Travolta with an eye on the film's commercial prospects:

> In the tradition of "Hairspray," which started with John [Waters], obviously, casting Divine, it's one of my favorite things that Edna's played by a man because it's anarchistic. And when [the producers] told me that they were talking to John [Travolta], I strangely immediately understood, because knowing that they were wanting to make a big, commercial hit movie out of this, and it's a musical, what man are you going to go to that's the biggest musical star that we have? And because of "Grease" and "Saturday Night Fever," it is John Travolta.[72]

Here again, *Hairspray* (2007) smoothed away the transgressive edges of Waters's film to appeal to the largest possible mainstream audience. As a result, the new film foregrounds the segregation story line more so than the original. By using a civil rights story as a commercial attraction, *Hairspray* is the latest in what filmmaker and media studies scholar Allison Graham and media studies scholar Jennifer Fuller have identified as the long line of civil rights–themed films and television shows since the late 1980s.[73]

While "I Know Where I've Been" is *Hairspray*'s most serious portrayal of civil rights, the film's concluding song resolves the issue of segregation on the *Corny Collins Show* with an upbeat and humorous dance number. Tracy kicks off "You Can't Stop the Beat" with her performance in the *Corny Collins Show*'s "Miss Teen Hairspray" competition. Tracy's performance fulfills her dream of being the lead dancer on the *Corny Collins Show* and sets the program's integration in motion. Tracy's dance partner, Link Larkin (Zac Efron), invites Maybelle's daughter, Little Inez (Taylor Parks), out to dance. As Little Inez holds center stage, becoming the first black teenager on the *Corny Collins Show*, the film cuts between her dancing and a table of telephone operators who tally votes on the dance contest from the show's viewers. After Inez's performance, the film's interracial couple, Seaweed and Penny, pick up the song.

After the two teens finish singing, they kiss, and the scene shifts from the *Corny Collins Show*'s studio to the show's image on a television in Penny's mother's living room. Penny's mother tries to wipe the black-and-white image of the interracial kiss off television screen with a handkerchief while Corny intones to the camera, "Live television, there's nothing like it."[74] Penny's mother's resistance to her daughter's interracial relationship and televised kiss is portrayed as a comically retrograde viewpoint. Her viewpoint, moreover, is not shared by the viewers of the *Corny Collins Show*. Unlike the real *Buddy Deane Show*, which received hate mail and bomb threats after its sudden integration, Inez receives a "tidal wave of calls" of support from the film's Baltimoreans.[75] After Inez is named the winner of the "Miss Teen Hairspray" dance contest and the lead dancer on the show, Corny declares: "Ladies and gentlemen, the *Corny Collins Show* is now and forever officially integrated!"[76] The film depicts public support for this integration with a shot of an interracial audience watching the show on television at a clothing store, and a second shot of a television reporter breaking the news outside of the studio. In front of a mostly white group of teenagers celebrating on the sidewalk, the reporter announces: "Interracial dancing has broken out at the WYZT stage. Just look at the crowd reaction."[77] By cutting among these scenes, the film uses three televisual representations to reimagine the historical struggle over the *Buddy Deane Show*'s segregation. The film shows the integration inside of the *Corny Collins Show*'s studio, how different viewers reacted to the televised image of the show's integration, and how the show's integration itself became a television news event.

The finale of "You Can't Stop the Beat" closes on a similarly triumphant note. In contrast to the stark division of black and white dancing styles in "New Girl in Town," the teenage backup dancers perform steps that producer Neil Meron suggests are meant to reference the show's integration:

> What's great about [Adam Shankman's] choreography [in "You Can't Stop the Beat"] is that, subtly, the black dancers and the white dancers have the same choreography. When all the choreography in the movie prior to this was segregated by race, and now it's all together, which is a very, very subtle reference to the theme of this movie.[78]

In the musical film's diegetic world, this integrated choreography is as important as the successful visual integration of the television program. The film's teenage characters not only overturn segregation on the *Corny Collins Show*; they immediately erase the film's earlier distinctions between "square" white teens and "hip" black teens. The film reinforces this subtle reference moments later when Corny Collins invites Maybelle out to sing the final verse of the song. Corny declares "this is the future" and tells Maybelle that "this is your time."[79] Maybelle sings: "You can't stop today as it comes speeding down the track / Child, yesterday is hist'ry and it's never coming back / 'Cause tomorrow is a brand new day and it don't know white from black."[80] In the film's narrative, this utopian vision of a color-blind future solves the problem of segregation and racial injustice. Unlike the narrative ambiguity at the end of *American Dreams'* first season, *Hairspray*'s narrative is fully revolved and unequivocally happy. *Hairspray* also uses the *Corny Collins Show*'s television camera to expose Velma Von Tussle's attempt to switch the tallies so that her daughter, and not Inez, would win. As the camera captures Velma's confession, the film cuts to an interracial group watching the program on a set of televisions in a store's display window. The film's protagonists, therefore, not only succeed in integrating the television show; they use the medium to prove the dishonesty of the show's racist producer.

This happy ending, of course, runs counter to historical events. The television station that broadcast *The Buddy Deane Show* canceled it shortly after civil rights activists successfully integrated a single episode. *Hairspray*'s ending resembles the utopian sensibility that film scholar Richard Dyer has identified as fundamental to musical films.[81] *Hairspray* presents a utopian version of early 1960s Baltimore that is more racially integrated and fair than the real era's history. John Waters created this particular vision, but more commercially minded producers and their audiences have shared in this ideal. Like Waters's film and the stage show, *Hairspray*'s (2007) historical representations and utopian conclusion have the potential to mislead viewers about the level of racism in the early 1960s, the rate of success for civil rights activists, and the integration of televised teenage dance programs like *American Bandstand*. Viewed in this way, *Hairspray* endorses a view of the civil rights era in which an innocent white teen (Tracy) joins forces with a progressive medium (television) to vanquish racism, located, in the end, in the attitudes of a single character (Velma).

Without minimizing the dangers of this film to promote a simplistic view of history, it is important to differentiate *Hairspray* from films like *Mississippi Burning* (1988), which erases the grassroots local activism of black Mississippians, and *Forrest Gump* (1994), which intervenes in major historical events of the 1960s and 1970s in order to emphasize the innocence of the United States.[82] *Hairspray*, in contrast, does not ask its audience to view it as historically accurate (like *Mississippi Burning*), nor does it trivialize the historical era it celebrates and satirizes (like *Forrest Gump*). In other words, *Hairspray* encourages viewers to take the struggles over segregation on teenage television shows seriously, without claiming to be a historically true civil rights story. While *Hairspray* also foreground narratives of interracial unity and innocence, this utopian vision of the *American Bandstand* era is ultimately more successful than the narrative ambiguity of *American Dreams*. Unlike the narrative ambiguity of *American Dreams*, which encourages viewers to embrace what they already think, *Hairspray*'s utopian vision of the *American Bandstand* era is less likely to encourage viewers to see the film as a completely accurate representation. Along these lines, producer Craig Zadan suggests that

> the wonderful thing about the movie . . . is the fact that while we are dealing with some very serious subject matter, we're doing it in such a highly comic and entertaining way. So you never feel like we're on a soap box, or we're preaching to you, or we're saying this is the lesson you need to learn. You're laughing and you're smiling and you're enjoying all of it, and yet, hopefully, you come away from it with something serious to talk about afterwards.[83]

There is no guarantee that viewers of *Hairspray* will discuss the film's serious subject matter as Zadan suggests. The film, however, makes it difficult to overlook racism with regard to historical television dance shows, and, at the very least, provides a starting point for viewers to learn more about the *American Bandstand* era.

A 2008 production by the World Performance Project at Yale University offers a final example of the relevance of *American Bandstand* in the 2000s, one that engages more critically with the *American Bandstand* era than either *American Dreams* or *Hairspray*. Developed through a seminar-studio course taught by dramaturges and professional dancers, *Don't Look Back! A Rock 'n' Roll Orpheus* used televised teen dance shows and popular music and dance from the 1950s and 1960s to create and perform a multimedia version of the Greek myth of Orpheus and Eurydice. As the basis for this production, students conducted research on *American Bandstand*, Baltimore's *Buddy Deane Show*, Washington, D.C.'s *The Milt Grant Show* and *Teenarama*, and *Hairspray*, as well as rock and roll and civil rights. What is interesting about *Don't Look Back!* is that it used historical media and representations from the *American Bandstand* era without suggesting that the problem of race was solved in the 1960s. One way *Don't Look Back!* did this was by directly engaging with the idea of the 2000s as a post-racial era. "As rehearsals and scriptwriting began," the producers note,

> it became clear that creating a frame through which the modern post-racial identification of students could enter the past would be as necessary as keeping our audience mindful of the present. The success of the piece depended on our ability to transport the audience and the student-performers back to the 1950s . . . without fully obscuring the time/space reality of the [present].[84]

The play tried to accomplish this by having the teen performers portray both *American Bandstand* dancers and modern actors using camcorders to send live feeds to projection screens above the stage. The resulting production mixed period media from the 1950s and 1960s (including footage from *American Bandstand*), live portrayals of *American Bandstand* era dancing, and live present-day commentary on both of the former. This approach encouraged the teen performers and audiences to move back and forth between the *American Bandstand* era and the present, using each as a lens to examine the other. This helped *Don't Look Back!* avoid the easy nostalgia for national innocence of *American Dreams* and tempered the utopian interracial unity of *Hairspray*. Finally, recognizing the complexities and dangers of representing historical race relations in an era when many of the teen performers and audience members viewed themselves as post-racial, *Don't Look Back!* used a mix of historical and contemporary media to directly address and challenge these viewpoints. Perhaps because it was not a major commercial production like *American Dreams* and *Hairspray*, *Don't Look Back!* encouraged its teen performers and audiences to do more than remember the innocence of the *American Bandstand* era.

My focus in this chapter has been on how *American Dreams* and *Hairspray* engage with the history of the *American Bandstand* era. Despite their limitations, both *American Dreams* and *Hairspray* present the history of the *American Bandstand* era with more nuance than did previous popular histories of the show published by Dick Clark. For my undergraduate students, *Hairspray* and, to a lesser extent, *American Dreams* are primary points of reference for this era. I view this as an opportunity rather than a handicap. Similar to my project, both *American Dreams* and *Hairspray* encourage viewers to examine the histories of television, music, youth culture, and civil rights concurrently and in relation to specific urban spaces. I hope, however, that my students will be suspicious of the narratives of innocence and interracial unity at play in both productions. These narratives can too easily be taken as endorsements of a color-blind racial ideology in which racism is strictly a problem of individual prejudice and in which this prejudice has disappeared since the 1960s. Still, suspicion of these narratives can also provide the basis for critical analysis of the *American Bandstand* era and a more nuanced understanding of race and racism in a supposedly post-racial era.

Conclusion

Everybody Knows about American Bandstand

While Nina Simone never performed on *American Bandstand,* her song "Mississippi Goddam" offers a lens through which to examine the issues at the heart of this book. In her autobiography, Simone recalled that she wrote "Mississippi Goddam" in response to two tragic events that shocked the nation:

> I was sitting there in my den . . . when news came over the radio that somebody had thrown dynamite into the 16th Street Baptist Church in Birmingham, Alabama while black children were attending a Bible study class. . . . It was more than I could take, and I sat struck dumb in my den like St. Paul on the road to Damascus: all the truths that I had denied to myself for so long rose up and slapped my face. The bombing of the little girls in Alabama and the murder of Medgar Evers were like the final pieces of a jigsaw that made no sense until you had fitted the whole thing together. I suddenly realized what it was to be black in America in 1963.[1]

The lyrics of "Mississippi Goddam" express Simone's indignation at the repeated acts of racial terror in the United States: "Alabama's got me so upset / Tennessee made me lose my rest / And everybody knows about Mississippi Goddam." With "everybody knows," Simone captures the fact that, with national media coverage of the assassination of Medgar Evers and the Birmingham church bombing, it would have been difficult for anyone not to be aware of these events. Still, Simone makes it clear that this awareness does not equal a commitment or sense of urgency to fight for racial equality: "Why don't you see it? / Why don't you feel it? /

I don't know / I don't know."[2] Simone described "Mississippi Goddam" as "my first civil rights song," and this work remains useful for thinking about the history of the civil rights movement more broadly.[3]

Knowing about the nationally visible tragedies of 1963 was not the same as understanding these murders as part of a larger system of state-sanctioned violence that maintained the political disenfranchisement of blacks in the South and blocked the passage of meaningful civil rights legislation at the federal level. This gap between an awareness of bad things happening to individual black people and the systemic allocation of resources away from black communities is important because, as historian Thomas Sugrue argues, "the ways that we recount the history of racial inequality and civil rights—the narratives that we construct about our past—guide our public policy priorities and our lawmaking and, even more fundamentally, shape our national identity."[4] Absent an understanding of the civil rights movement's ambitious economic, political, legal, and social goals, the legacy of the movement can be defined narrowly as a call to embrace racial color-blindness. This ideology of racial color-blindness focuses on overcoming individual racial prejudice and takes the decline in overt racism since the civil rights era as evidence of the end of racism. This view of civil rights ignores the histories of systematic discrimination, such as the public policies that maintained school and residential segregation, as well as how the long-term legacies of these policies disadvantaged black communities. To paraphrase Simone, everybody knows about the civil rights movement, but not everyone understands the movement as a decades-long fight to uproot structures of white supremacy.

Philadelphia was not Mississippi, and the history of *American Bandstand* is not equivalent to the racial violence that motivated "Mississippi Goddam." Still, Simone's song suggests an approach to history that has motivated this book. Everybody knows about *American Bandstand*, but like narrow views of civil rights, this awareness can obscure more than it reveals. The dominant memory of *American Bandstand*'s effect on society is that it took a bold and progressive stance on racial integration. Rather than making clear how race influenced nearly every facet of life in the postwar era—where people lived and worked, where young people went to school, and what images viewers saw on television—this dominant memory suggests that the country, led by commercial media industries in the liberal North, was well on its way to overcoming racism by the late 1950s. This rhetoric of progress and innocence is not unique to *American Bandstand*, but as the show was one of the most popular television programs of all time, this memory offers a barometer of how far the nation has come with regard to race.

To complicate this memory, this book has shown how *American Bandstand* became a site of struggle over racial segregation and how the show influenced and was influenced by racial discrimination and civil rights activism in the city's neighborhoods and schools. For those who watched *American Bandstand* during its heyday in the 1950s and early 1960s, this book has provided stories that were not part of the show's afternoon broadcasts. Understanding how the local *Bandstand* developed into a national phenomenon, how *American Bandstand* constructed a vision of national youth culture, and how *American Bandstand* drew from black popular culture while excluding black teenagers adds depth and nuance to popular memories of *American Bandstand*. For those who know the early years of the program only through vintage black-and-white clips, this book has provided local and national context to make it clear that *American Bandstand* was more than the background images seen in 1950s-themed montages. Understanding how white homeowners organized to maintain segregation in the neighborhoods around *American Bandstand*'s studio, how *American Bandstand*'s producers and school board officials opposed meaningful integration while claiming to hold color-blind policies, and how black teenagers and civil rights activists protested racially discriminatory policies on *American Bandstand* and in Philadelphia's schools and neighborhoods shows that far from being a relic from a more innocent age of popular culture, *American Bandstand* was at the center of local and national struggles over segregation and representations of race.

Through *American Bandstand* and postwar Philadelphia, this book has brought together topics that, while closely related, are typically dealt with separately in urban history, civil rights history, media studies, and youth history. My analysis of the tensions around *American Bandstand*'s West Philadelphia studio builds on the work of historians like Robert Self, David Freund, and Eric Avila who have examined the political, economic, and sociospatial transformations of postwar metropolitan areas.[5] Like the work of historians Thomas Sugrue, Jeanne Theoharis, Komozi Woodard, and Martha Biondi, my book also makes it clear that de facto segregation and civil rights activism flourished in the urban North.[6] At the same time, as a history of urban popular culture, this project builds on the work of media scholars like Lynn Spigel, Anna McCarthy, Steven Classen, Mark Williams, and Victoria Johnson who have explored the spatial relationships engendered by television in postwar cities, suburbs, and rural areas.[7] My analysis of the history of *American Bandstand* and struggles over school segregation in postwar Philadelphia is also coupled with a concern for the popular presentations of this history. Building on the work of George Lipsitz, Mimi White, Jennifer Fuller, and Herman Gray, my book examines the parameters and implications of television's engagements with race, history, and popular memory.[8] I build on the work of these historians and media scholars to offer a new perspective on the history of youth culture that contributes to work by Kelly Schrum, Susan Douglas, Aniko Bodroghkozy, and Matt Garcia.[9]

The importance of this interdisciplinary approach is that it brings together themes of postwar history that are usually examined discretely, including the emergence of youth culture, the development of television as a local and national medium, the growth of rock and roll as a dominant musical genre, white resistance to school and residential desegregation in the North, the grassroots activism that made each of the former battlegrounds over civil rights and racial equality, and the ongoing struggle over how these important themes in postwar history are remembered. These key strands of postwar history were lived simultaneously and need to be studied simultaneously. This book has synthesized these themes through *American Bandstand* because the teenagers who danced on, watched, or protested *American Bandstand* did so not just as media consumers, but also as students and citizens who experienced struggles over racial segregation in schools and neighborhoods.

By examining *American Bandstand* in the context of postwar Philadelphia, this book also contributes to the excellent histories of the city by Matthew Countryman, Lisa Levenstein, James Wolfinger, and Guian McKee.[10] When I started this project, Philadelphia had received relatively less attention than other major cities like Chicago, Los Angeles, and New York, but thankfully scholars have started to fill in this gap. Matthew Countryman has shown Philadelphia's importance to the postwar history of civil rights and to the development of black power politics. Countryman's work makes it clear that de facto segregation was entrenched in northern cities like Philadelphia, and I build on this work by exploring how white mobilization for segregated housing and the development of television programming that accommodated these sentiments shaped how people saw the city in racialized ways. Lisa Levenstein demonstrates how working-class black women played leading roles in grassroots activism. While different from the public institutions that Levenstein highlights, *Bandstand* was an important part of the everyday youth culture of which young black women were a part. Among the black teenagers who protested their exclusion from *Bandstand*, young working-class women from William Penn High School were the first to ask the city's Commission on Human Relations to address the show's discrimination, and after the show debuted nationally as *American Bandstand*, young black women continued to push for equal access to the program. My analysis of white homeowners' groups builds on James Wolfinger's detailed study of everyday fights over work and housing and contributes a new perspective on how these efforts to defend white privilege resonated via television across neighborhood, city, and regional levels. Finally, Guian McKee shows that Philadelphia city leaders recognized the problem of deindustrialization earlier than most and developed regional responses to counteract these declines. The "WFIL-adelphia" marketing campaign, developed by Walter Annenberg's Triangle Publications to appeal to advertisers, shows that media corporations also had a stake in, and profited from, this regional growth.

Everybody knows about *American Bandstand*, but this awareness means little if it is not connected to the local and national contexts that made the show important, influential, and controversial. *American Bandstand* brought teenagers together every day in the 1950s and early 1960s at an unprecedented national level. Several black musicians profited from exposure on television and surely broadened the outlooks of many viewers regarding race relations. To call *American Bandstand* a force for social good, however, obscures the ways the show reinforced, rather than challenged, segregationist attitudes locally and nationally. *American Bandstand*'s producers made choices with regard to the show's segregation and racial representations that, while not unique in their historical context, fell far short of the social good for which the city's civil rights advocates fought. Everybody knows about *American Bandstand*. My hope is that this book will connect this awareness to the historical, and still unfinished, struggles for racial equality in which *American Bandstand* was a highly visible site.

Notes

INTRODUCTION

1. Fred Bronson, *Dick Clark's American Bandstand 50th Anniversary* (New York: Time Life, 2007), 9.

2. This quotation is included in the two *American Bandstand* popular histories coauthored by Dick Clark and Fred Bronson; see Dick Clark and Fred Bronson, *Dick Clark's American Bandstand* (New York: Collins Publishers, 1997), 19; Bronson, *Dick Clark's American Bandstand 50th Anniversary*, 9.

3. Jacquelyn Dowd Hall, "The Long Civil Rights Movement and the Political Uses of the Past," *Journal of American History* 91 (March 2005): 1235.

4. Robert Self, *American Babylon: Race and the Struggle for Postwar Oakland* (Princeton, NJ: Princeton University Press, 2003), 267.

CHAPTER I

1. *The Official 1955 Bandstand Yearbook* [no publication information listed], 13.

2. Margaret Weir, "Urban Poverty and Defensive Localism," *Dissent*, Summer 1994, 337–42; Thomas Sugrue, *The Origins of the Urban Crisis: Race and Inequality in Postwar Detroit* (Princeton, NJ: Princeton University Press, 1996), 210. On the fights over open housing in other cities, see Robert Self, *American Babylon: Race and the Struggle for Postwar Oakland* (Princeton, NJ: Princeton University Press, 2003), 159–70; Becky Nicolaides, *My Blue Heaven: Life and Politics in the Working-Class Suburbs of Los Angeles, 1920–1965* (Chicago: University of Chicago Press, 2002); David Freund, *Colored Property: State Policy and White Racial Politics in Suburban America* (Chicago: University of Chicago Press, 2007); Arnold Hirsch, "Massive Resistance in the Urban North: Trumbull Park, Chicago, 1953–1966," *Journal of American History*, 82 (September, 1995), 522–50.

3. Freund, *Colored Property*, 13.

4. Charles Abrams, *Forbidden Neighbors: A Study of Prejudice in Housing* (Port Washington, NY: Kennikat Press, 1955), ix.

5. Anna McCarthy, *Ambient Television: Visual Culture and Public Space* (Durham, NC: Duke University Press, 2001), 16.

6. "WFIL, WFIL-TV Now Operating From Integrated New Quarters," *Philadelphia Inquirer*, October 13, 1952.

7. Commission on Human Relations (CHR), "Philadelphia's Negro Population: Facts on Housing," October 1953, CHR collection, box A-620, folder 148.4, Philadelphia City Archives (PCA).

8. Ibid.

9. Ibid.

10. CHR, "Philadelphia's Non-White Population 1960, Report no.1, Demographic Data," box A-621, folder 148.4, PCA.

11. Davis McAllister, "Between the Suburbs and the Ghetto: Racial and Economic Change in Philadelphia, 1933–1985" (Ph.D. diss., Temple University, 2006), 151. Original quotation in Clarence Cave, "Equal Housing Opportunity: Real Estate Dilemma," *Realtor* 41 (May 1960): 4.

12. Abrams, *Forbidden Neighbors*, 171.

13. CHR, "Philadelphia's Negro Population: Facts on Housing."

14. CHR, "A Report on the Housing of Negro Philadelphians," 1953, CHR collection, box A-620, folder 148.4, PCA; ibid.

15. Beryl Satter, *Family Properties: Race, Real Estate and the Exploitation of Black Urban America* (New York: Metropolitan Books, 2009), 6.

16. CHR, "Annual Report, 1953," 1953, CHR collection, box A-620, folder 148.4, PCA; Matthew Countryman, *Up South: Civil Rights and Black Power in Philadelphia* (Philadelphia: University of Pennsylvania Press, 2006), 58.

17. On the CHR's response to employment discrimination cases, see Countryman, *Up South*, 58–68.

18. Ibid., 92–95.

19. On white homeowners' groups, see Hirsch, "Massive Resistance in the Urban North," 522–50; Sugrue, *The Origins of the Urban Crisis*, 210–29; Abrams, *Forbidden Neighbors*, 181–90; Herman Long and Charles Johnson, *People vs. Property? Race Restrictive Covenants in Housing* (Nashville: Fisk University Press, 1947), 39–55; 73–85.

20. Luigi Laurenti, *Property Values and Race: Studies in Seven Cities* (Berkeley: University of California Press, 1960), 184.

21. Angora Civic Association (ACA), "To Residents of This Section of West Phila.," March 1955, Fellowship Commission (FC) collection, Acc 626, box 61, folder 34, Temple University Urban Archives (TUUA).

22. ACA, "Do you like your home?" November 18, 1954, FC collection, Acc 626, box 61, folder 34, TUUA.

23. ACA, "Help!! Help!!" May 19, 1955, FC collection, Acc 626, box 61, folder 34, TUUA.

24. West Philadelphia Fellowship Commission, "Angora Civic Association Meeting," May 19, 1955, FC collection, Acc 626, box 61, folder 34, TUUA.

25. Mary Constantine, "Memo re: Angora Civic Association," [n.d., ca. 1954], FC collection, Acc 626, box 61, folder 34, TUUA.

26. Ibid.

27. Angora Civic Association, "Help!! Help!!"

28. James Wolfinger, *Philadelphia Divided: Race and Politics in the City of Brotherly Love* (Chapel Hill: University of North Carolina Press, 2007), 170–71.

29. Ibid., 188.

30. West Philadelphia Fellowship Commission, "Angora Civic Association," November 18, 1954, Acc 626, box 61, folder 34, TUUA.

31. Freund, *Colored Property*, 337.

32. Daniel Martinez HoSang, *Racial Propositions: Ballot Initiatives and the Making of Postwar California* (Berkeley: University of California Press, 2010), 20–21.

33. Ibid.

34. Ibid.

35. On the practices of blockbusting real estate agents, see Sugrue, *The Origins of the Urban Crisis*, 194–97.

36. "Go West Young Man," *Philadelphia Tribune*, September 9, 1952; "Race Realty" and "West Phila. Specials," *Philadelphia Tribune*, July 5, 1952.

37. Historians of blockbusting note that brokers who accelerated racial change were cast as scapegoats of the "legitimate" real estate industry, but they could not have functioned without the industry's commitment to maintaining segregated housing markets. On blockbusting, see W. Edward Orser, *Blockbusting in Baltimore: The Edmondson Village Story* (Lexington: University of Kentucky Press, 1994); Kevin Fox Gotham, *Race, Real Estate, and Uneven Development: The Kansas City Experience, 1900–2000* (Albany: State University of New York Press, 2002), 91–119; Satter, *Family Properties*, 111–16.

38. "Let's All Pull Together," November 8, 1954, FC collection, Acc 626, box 61, folder 37, TUUA. On the Fellowship Commission and CHR's attempts to reach out to the homeowners' groups, see Dennis Clark, memo to Maurice Fagan, December 16, 1954, FC collection, Acc 626, box 61, folder 37, TUUA; Anna McGarry, letter to Mary Constantine, November 30, 1954, FC collection, Acc 626, box 61, folder 37, TUUA; Rev. Donald Ottinger, letter to Arthur Cooper, November 1, 1954, FC collection, Acc 626, box 61, folder 37, TUUA.

39. Fellowship Commission, Committee on Community Tensions meeting minutes, January 12, 1955, National Association for the Advancement of Colored People, Philadelphia branch (NAACP) collection, URB 6, box 4, folder 104, TUUA; Maurice Fagan, letter to Nicholas Petrella, February 2, 1955, FC collection, Acc 626, box 61, folder 37, TUUA.

40. On this effort, see CHR, "What to Do Kits: A Program for Leaders in Changing Neighborhoods," 1958, CHR collection, Box A-620, folder 148.4, PCA. On the CHR's failed neighborhood stabilization plan, see Countryman, *Up South*, 71–75.

41. Fellowship Commission, Report to the Community, October 1952, FC collection, Acc 626, box 53, folder 9, TUUA; Fellowship Commission, Report to the Community, May 1953, FC collection, Acc 626, box 53, folder 10, TUUA.

42. "Tensions Committee Notes Rise in Biased Groups," Fellowship Commission, Report to the Community, January 1955, FC collection, Acc 626, box 53, folder 12, TUUA.

43. Fellowship Commission, Report to the Community, February 1955, FC collection, Acc 626, box 53, folder 12, TUUA.

44. Countryman, *Up South*, 92–95.

45. Satter, *Family Properties*, 136–41.

46. Wolfinger, *Philadelphia Divided*, 7.

47. Thomas Edsall and Mary Edsall, *Chain Reaction: The Impact of Race, Rights, and Taxes on American Politics* (New York: W.W. Norton, 1991), 139.

48. Self, *American Babylon,* 168.

49. Phil Ethington, "Segregated Diversity: Race-Ethnicity, Space, and Political Fragmentation in Los Angeles County, 1940–1994," Final Report to the John Randolph Haynes and Dora Haynes Foundation (September 13, 2000), 43.

50. Oliver Williams et al., *Suburban Differences and Metropolitan Policies: A Philadelphia Story* (Philadelphia: University of Pennsylvania Press, 1965), 217–19. Survey cited in Michael Danielson, *The Politics of Exclusion* (New York: Columbia University Press, 1976), 28; and Sheryll Cashin, *The Failures of Integration: How Race and Class Are Undermining the American Dream* (New York: Public Affairs, 2004), 265.

51. Jill Quadagno, *The Color of Welfare: How Racism Undermined the War on Poverty* (New York: Oxford University Press, 1994), 99.

52. George Lipstiz, The Possessive Investment in Whiteness: How White People Profit from Identity Politics (Philadelphia: Temple University Press, 1998), 27–33; Douglas Massey and Nancy Denton, American Apartheid: Segregation and the Making of the Underclass (Cambridge, MA: Harvard University Press, 1993), 186–216.

53. Quadagno, *The Color of Welfare,* 98.

54. Educational Equality League, "Notes on the Meeting with the Board of Education," October 26, 1951, NAACP collection, URB 6, box 6, folder 137, TUUA.

55. *West Philadelphia High School Record,* June 1951, West Philadelphia High School.

56. "Angry Parents Resent Remarks by Principal," *Philadelphia Tribune,* October 23, 1951.

57. Walter Palmer, interviewed by author, June 29, 2007.

58. Weldon McDougal, interviewed by author, March 27, 2006.

59. *West Philadelphia High School Record,* 1954–60 editions, West Philadelphia High School.

60. "Investigation of Skating Rink: Interim Report," 1952, NAACP collection, URB 6, box 20, folder 383, TUUA; Spence Coxe, letter to Joseph Barnes, December 12, 1952, NAACP collection, URB 6, box 20, folder 383, TUUA.

61. CHR, "Recommendation for Closing Case: Concord Skating Rink," January 11, 1955, CHR collection, Box A-2860, folder 148.2 "Minutes 1953–1957," PCA.

62. Commission of Human Relations, Meeting Minutes, September 21, 1953, CHR collection, Box A-2860, folder 148.2 "Minutes 1953–1957," PCA.

63. "NAACP Radio Report on WCAM," September 27, 1953, NAACP collection, URB 6, box 21, folder 421, TUUA; West Philadelphia Fellowship Council, Minutes, October 27, 1953, FC collection, Acc 626, box 61, folder 36, TUUA; CHR, "Minutes of Meeting on Skating Rink Project," March 30, 1954, NAACP collection, URB 6, box 21, folder 421, TUUA.

64. CHR, "Minutes of Meeting on Skating Rink Project," March 30, 1954, NAACP collection, URB 6, box 20, folder 383, TUUA.

65. CHR, "Recommendation for Closing Case: Crystal Palace Roller Skating Rink," January 19, 1955, CHR collection, Box A-2860, folder 148.2 "Minutes 1953–1957," PCA; "Recommendation for Closing Case: Concord Skating Rink"; CHR, Annual Report, 1954, CHR collection, Box A-620, folder 148.1, PCA.

66. Mitzi Jacoby, letter to Mabel Queens, January 20, 1955, Fellowship House (FH) collection, Acc 723, box 14, folder "Mitzi Jacoby correspondence 1955 #2," TUUA; Mitzi Jacoby, letter to Milo Manly, July 21, 1955, FH collection, Acc 723, box 14, folder "Mitzi Jacoby correspondence 1955 #2," TUUA; Mitzi Jacoby, letter to Ira D. Reid, March 24, 1958, FH collection, Acc 723, box 14, folder "Mitzi Jacoby correspondence 1958–9," TUUA.

67. "You Have a Stake in Delaware, Valley, U.S.A.," *Philadelphia Inquirer*, October 12, 1952. On nineteenth-century boosterism, see Williams Cronin, *Nature's Metropolis: Chicago and the Great West* (New York: W.W. Norton & Company, 1991).

68. "Raw Materials," *Philadelphia Inquirer*, October 13, 1952.

69. "You Have a Stake in Delaware, Valley, U.S.A."

70. WFIL-TV, "For Advertisers . . ."

71. WFIL-TV, "WFIL-adelphia, the MAIN STREET of Delaware Valley, U.S.A.," *Philadelphia Inquirer*, October 13, 1952.

72. Alison Isenberg, *Downtown America: A History of the Place and the People Who Made It* (Chicago: University of Chicago Press, 2004), 3.

73. Ibid., 2.

74. Ibid., 42–77.

75. Ibid., 43.

76. On Disneyland, see Eric Avila, *Popular Culture in the Age of White Flight: Fear and Fantasy in Suburban Los Angeles* (Berkeley: University of California Press, 2004), 106–44; George Lipsitz, "Consumer Spending as State Project: Yesterday's Solutions and Today's Problems" in *Getting and Spending: European and American Consumer Society in the Twentieth Century*, ed. Susan Strasser, Charles McGovern, and Matthias Judt (Washington, DC: Cambridge University Press, 1998), 136–40.

77. Howell Baum, *Brown in Baltimore: School Desegregation and the Limits of Liberalism* (Ithaca, NY: Cornell University Press, 2010); Orser, *Blockbusting in Baltimore*, 84–130; Brett Gadsden, "Victory without Triumph: The Ironies of School Desegregation in Delaware, 1948–1978," (Ph.D. diss., Northwestern University, 2006); Peter Irons, *Jim Crow's Children: The Broken Promise of the Brown Decision* (New York: Viking, 2002), 107–17.

78. Maryland repealed its antimiscegenation law shortly before the Supreme Court's *Loving* decision in 1967, while Delaware did not repeal its statue until 1986. On the history of miscegenation law, see Peggy Pascoe, *What Comes*

Naturally: Miscegenation Law and the Making of Race in America (New York: Oxford University Press, 2009).

79. E. S. Bankes, "Financial Basis of Expansion," *Philadelphia Inquirer*, October 13, 1952, 79–80.

80. Abrams, *Forbidden Neighbors*, 102, 172.

81. Lynn Spigel, *Welcome to the Dreamhouse: Popular Media and Postwar Suburbs* (Durham, NC: Duke University Press, 2001), 35.

82. William Boddy, *Fifties Television: The Industry and Its Critics* (Urbana: University of Illinois Press, 1993), 51.

83. Federal Communication Commission, Annual Report, 1955. On the FCC's policies and practices in the years surrounding the television freeze, see Hugh Slotten, *Radio and Television Regulation: Broadcast Technology in the United States, 1920–1960* (Baltimore: The Johns Hopkins University Press, 2000), 145–88; ibid., 28–64, 113–31; James Baughman, *Same Time, Same Station: Creating American Television* (Baltimore: The Johns Hopkins University Press, 2007), 56–81.

84. Michael Stamm, "Mixed Media: Newspaper Ownership of Radio in American Politics and Culture, 1920–1952," (Ph.D. diss., University of Chicago, 2006), 19.

85. Baughman, *Same Time, Same Station*, 74–79.

86. Christopher Ogden, *Legacy: A Biography of Moses and Walter Annenberg* (Boston: Little, Brown and Company, 1999), 322–23.

87. Ibid., 322.

88. Glenn Altschuler and David Grossvogel, *Changing Channels: America in TV Guide* (Urbana: University of Illinois Press, 1992), 4–6.

89. Gaeton Fonzi, *Annenberg: A Biography of Power* (New York: Weybright and Talley, 1969), 24.

90. John Jackson, *American Bandstand: Dick Clark and the Making of a Rock 'n' Roll Empire* (New York: Oxford University Press, 1997), 14–15.

91. Ibid., 7–13.

92. On the radio stars who moved to television in the late 1940s and early 1950s, see Susan Murray, *Hitch Your Antenna to the Stars: Early Television and Broadcast Stardom* (New York: Routledge, 2005).

93. Dick Clark and Richard Robinson, *Rock, Roll and Remember* (New York: Popular Library, 1976), 60.

94. A 1951 survey of 250 students at Philadelphia's Northeast High School, for example, found that the *950 Club* was their favorite radio program. Paul Duffield, "The 'Teen-Ager's' Taste in Out-of-School Music," *Music Educators Journal*, 37 (June-July 1951): 19–20. On the *950 Club*, see Jackson, *American Bandstand*, 9–12.

95. Jackson, *American Bandstand*, 14–16.

96. Ibid., 16–19.

97. *The Official 1955 Bandstand Yearbook*, 4–7; ibid., 19.

98. Jerry Blavat, interviewed by author, July 25, 2006.

99. Jackson, *American Bandstand*, 24.

100. Ibid., 20–24.

101. The Official 1955 Bandstand Yearbook.

102. Ibid., 26.

103. Richard Peterson, "Why 1955? Explaining the Advent of Rock Music," *Popular Music* 9 (January 1990): 97–116.

104. Richard Peterson and David Berger, "Cycles in Symbol Production: The Case of Popular Music," *American Sociological Review* 40 (April 1975): 160, 165; Christopher Sterling, *Stay Tuned: A History of American Broadcasting* (Mahwah, NJ : Lawrence Erlbaum Associates, 2002), 365–70.

105. Sterling, *Stay Tuned*, 365–70.

106. Alan Freed was a white deejay who helped to popularize black R&B and popularized the term *rock and roll*. See John A. Jackson, *Big Beat Heat: Alan Freed and the Early Years of Rock and Roll* (New York: Schirmer Books, 1991). On WDIA, see Louis Cantor, *Wheelin' on Beale: How WDIA-Memphis Became the Nation's First All-Black Radio Station and Created the Sound That Changed America* (New York: Pharos Books, 2002). On the large number of independent record companies that developed the national market for R&B and rock and roll, see Steve Chapple and Reebee Garofalo, *Rock 'n' Roll Is Here to Pay: The History and Politics of the Music Industry* (Chicago: Nelson-Hall, 1977), 27–49; Charlie Gillet, *The Sound of the City: The Rise of Rock and Roll* (New York: Outerbridge & Dienstfrey, 1970), 79–134. For a useful study of one of the companies, see Donald Mabry, "The Rise and Fall of Ace Records: A Case Study in the Independent Record Business," *The Business History Review* 64 (Autumn 1990): 411–50.

107. Among studies of the interracial exchanges in rock and roll, see Glenn Altschuler, *All Shook Up: How Rock 'n' Roll Changed America* (New York: Oxford University Press, 2003), 3–66; Brian Ward, *Just My Soul Responding: Rhythm and Blues, Black Consciousness, and Race Relations* (Berkeley: University of California, 1998), 123–69; George Lipsitz, "Land of a Thousand Dances: Youth, Minorities, and the Rise of Rock and Roll," in *Recasting America: Culture and Politics in the Age of the Cold War*, ed. Lary May (Chicago, University of Chicago Press, 1989), 267–84; Matt Garcia, "'Memories of El Monte:' Intercultural Dance Hall in Post-World War II Greater Los Angeles," in *Generations of Youth: Youth Cultures and History in Twentieth-Century America*, ed. Joe Austin and Michael Nevin Willard (New York: New York University Press, 1998), 157–72. On the working-class roots of rock and roll and the appeal of these values and traditions across class lines to listeners in urban, suburban, and rural areas, see George Lipsitz, *Time Passages: Collective Memory and American Popular Culture* (Minneapolis: University of Minnesota Press, 1990), 99–132; Medovoi, *Rebels: Youth and the Cold War Origins of Identity* (Durham, NC: Duke University Press, 2005), 91–134.

108. Jackson, *American Bandstand*, 20.

109. Quoted in Murray Forman, "'One Night on TV Is Worth Weeks at the Paramount': Musicians and Opportunity in Early Television, 1948–55," *Popular Music* 3 (2002): 257.

110. Tom McCourt and Nabeel Zuberi, "Music on Television," The Museum of Broadcast Communications, http://www.museum.tv/archives/etv/M/htmlM/musicontele/musicontele.htm (accessed October 25, 2006).

111. McDougall interview.

112. Jackson, *American Bandstand*, 21–22.

113. Ibid., 24.

114. Wolfinger, *Philadelphia Divided*, 189.

115. Palmer interview. Palmer went on to be an important community activist in West Philadelphia. On Palmer's work in addressing educational inequality and racism, see Countryman, *Up South*, 191–99, 225–68.

116. CHR, "Present Status of Current 'C' Cases," May 4, 1954, CHR collection, Box A-2860, folder 148.2 "Minutes 1953–1957," PCA.

117. Pricilla Penn, "Social Notes of Interest in the Quaker City Whirl," *Philadelphia Tribune*, June 1, 1954.

118. CHR, "Intergroup Tensions in Recreation Facilities," March 7, 1955, NAACP collection, URB 6, box 4, folder 104, TUUA. On William Penn High School and the work of black educator Ruth Wright Hayre in improving the educational offerings at the school, see chapter four.

119. Jackson, *American Bandstand*, 23.

120. Ibid., 57.

121. Blavat interview.

122. "Arrest TV Em Cee as Drunken Driver," *Philadelphia Tribune*, June 23, 1956.

123. On rock and roll music and dance halls as spaces for intercultural exchange, see Lipsitz, "Land of a Thousand Dances"; Garcia, "'Memories of El Monte'"; Ward, *Just My Soul Responding*.

CHAPTER 2

1. The Fellowship Commission formed in October 1941 with representatives from the Jewish Community Relations Council, Fellowship House, Friends Committee on Race Relations, and Philadelphia Council on Churches. The Philadelphia branch of the NAACP joined in 1942, and by 1955 the Fellowship Commission included nine community agencies.

2. Maurice Fagan, "Fellowship Commission Annual Dinner Meeting, Report by Executive Director," February 6, 1952, Jewish Community Relations Council (JCRC) collection, box 007, folder 012, Philadelphia Jewish Archives Center (PJAC).

3. Anna McCarthy, *The Citizen Machine: Governing by Television in 1950s America* (New York: The New Press, 2010), 4–9.

4. Ibid., 7.

5. Ien Ang, *Desperately Seeking the Audience* (New York: Routledge), 32.

6. On *Americans All, Immigrants All*, see Barbara Savage, *Broadcasting Freedom: Radio, War, and the Politics of Race, 1938–1948* (Chapel Hill: University of North Carolina Press, 1999), 21–62.

7. "Report to the Community," October 1948, FC collection, Acc 626, box 53, folder 5, TUUA; "Within Our Gates: List of Profiles" [n.d.], [ca. 1950], FC collection, Acc 626, box 43, folder 62, TUUA; Ruby Smith, "Lesson in Race Relations Brought Philadelphia Weekly via Radio," *The Philadelphia Afro-American*, February 14, 1948.

8. Max Franzen, "Film Discussion," in "Report to the Community," December 1948, FC collection, Acc 626, box 53, folder 5, TUUA; Mary Constantine,

"Film + Discussion=Action" [n.d.], [ca. 1949], FC collection, Acc 626, box 43, folder 43, TUUA.

9. Fellowship Commission, "Report to the Community," October 1952, FC collection, Acc 626, box 53, folder 9, TUUA.

10. Helen Trager and Marian Yarrow, *They Learn What They Live: Prejudice in Young Children* (New York: Harper & Brothers, 1952).

11. On the Early Childhood Project, see Catherine Mackenzie, "Prejudice Can Be Unlearned," *New York Times*, July 25, 1948; Barbara Barnes, "Prejudices Can Be Un-Learned, Experiments Conducted Here Show," *Philadelphia Evening Bulletin*, October 11, 1951; "Report of the Committee on Evaluations," July 8, 1949, Fellowship House (FH) collection, Acc 723, box 30, folder "Early Childhood," TUUA; "Minutes: Committee on Program Priorities," November 12, 1951, Jewish Community Relations Council (JCRC) collection, box 003, folder 015, PJAC; "Annual Meeting," February 20, 1950, FC collection, Acc 626, box 1, folder 5, TUUA.

12. On the broad intellectual history of intercultural education (also called intergroup education by some educators), see Cherry McGee Banks, "Intercultural and Intergroup Education, 1929–1959: Linking Schools and Communities," in *Handbook of Research on Multicultural Education*, 2nd ed., ed. James Banks (San Francisco: Jossey-Bass, 2004), 753–69; Nicholas Montalto, *A History of the Intercultural Educational Movement, 1924–1941* (New York: Garland Publishing, 1982); Ronald Goodenow, "The Progressive Educator, Race, and Ethnicity in the Depression Years: An Overview," *History of Education Quarterly* 15 (Winter 1975): 365–94; Patricia Graham, *Progressive Education: From Arcady to Academe: A History of the Progressive Education Association, 1919–1955* (New York: Teachers College Press, 1967); O. L. Davis Jr., "Rachel Davis DuBois: Intercultural Education Pioneer," in *Bending the Future to Their Will: Civic Women, Social Education, and Democracy*, ed. Margaret Smith Crocco and O. L. Davis Jr. (New York: Rowman & Littlefield, 1999), 169–84; Daryl Michael Scott, "Postwar Pluralism, *Brown v. Board of Education*, and the Origins of Multicultural Education," *Journal of American History* 91 (June 2004): 69–82.

13. Jennie Callahan, *Television in School, College, and Community* (New York: McGraw-Hill, 1953), 46. On the cooperation between the Philadelphia's commercial television stations and the schools, see Philadelphia Board of Education, "Report of Television-Radio Activities," 1953, Division of Radio and TV, box 76, Philadelphia School District Archive (PSDA). For contemporary articles citing Philadelphia as a leader in the field of educational television, see Belmont Farley, "Education and Television," *Music Educators Journal* 39 (November-December 1952): 18–20; Burton Paulu, "The Challenge of the 242 Channels: II," *The Quarterly of Film, Radio, and Television* 7 (Winter 1952): 140–49. On the development of public television more broadly, see Laurie Ouellette, *Viewers Like You: How Public TV Failed the People* (New York: Columbia University Press, 2002).

14. Max Franzen, letter to Herbert Jaffa, April 7, 1953, FC collection, box 43, folder 59, TUUA; Philadelphia Fellowship Commission, "Report to the Community," February 1953, FC collection, box 53, folder 10, TUUA.

15. For more on the Fellowship Clubs, see Fellowship House collection, Acc 723, boxes 13, 14, 32, 33, TUUA.

16. Max Franzen, letter to Maury Glaubman, January 19, 1953, FC collection, box 43, folder 59, TUUA.

17. Maurice Fagan, letter to Erma Cunningham, February 10, 1953, box 43, folder 59, TUUA.

18. While car ownership rates by race are unavailable, a 1957 survey of eighteen thousand high school students in Philadelphia found that 27 percent of their families did not own cars. Since this survey included a large number of higher-income college-bound white students, the rate was likely closer to 50 percent for black families. In 1952, then, the question of hot-rodding was probably an academic one for most black teenagers and many white teenagers. On this survey, see Philadelphia Commission on Higher Educational Opportunities, "Educational and Vocational Plans Survey," June 1957, Philadelphia Commission on Higher Educational Opportunity (PCHEO) collection, box A-300, folder 60-13, PCA.

19. Maurice Fagan, letter to Herbert Miller, February 3, 1953, FC collection, box 43, folder 59, TUUA.

20. John W. Adams, letter to Maurice Fagan, May 11, 1953, FC collection, box 43, folder 59, TUUA.

21. Maurice Fagan, "Intercultural Education Is a Process," *Education* 68 (November 1948): 182–87.

22. Fagan, letter to Erma Cunningham, February 10, 1953.

23. Fagan, letter to Herbert Miller, February 3, 1953.

24. *Brotherhood of Man* (1946), an animated film promoting racial tolerance, was based on anthropologist Ruth Benedict's book *The Races of Mankind. Home of the Brave* (1949) told the fictional story of a black Army private in World War II who suffered from a nervous breakdown and psychosomatic paralysis brought on by racism in society. On these and other postwar liberal films, see Thomas Cripps, *Making Movies Black: The Hollywood Message Movie from World War II to the Civil Rights Era* (New York: Oxford University Press, 1993), 151–73.

25. Franzen, letter to Herbert Jaffa, April 7, 1953.

26. Ibid.

27. McCarthy, *The Citizen Machine*, 93.

28. In the late 1940s and early 1950s, a number of radio performers and personalities began to experiment with televised talk shows. For a general overview of these and other national television talk shows in the 1950s, see Bernard Timberg, *Television Talk: A History of the TV Talk Show* (Austin: University of Texas Press, 2002), 1–55.

29. Megan Pincus Kajitani, "A Product of Its Time: *Youth Wants to Know*, Postwar Teenagers, and 1950s Network Television," paper delivered at annual meeting of National Communication Association, 2003.

30. Herbert Miller, letter to WCAU-TV, January 19, 1952, FC collection, box 43, folder 59, TUUA.

31. Fagan, letter to Herbert Miller, February 3, 1953.

32. Herbert Miller, letter to Maurice Fagan, February 4, 1953, FC collection, box 43, folder 59, TUUA.

33. Franzen, letter to Herbert Jaffa, April 7, 1953.

34. Maurice Fagan, letter to Nancy Thorp, November 11, 1952, FC collection, box 43, folder 59, TUUA.

35. While this ideal family type was already evident in *The Adventures of Ozzie and Harriet* in 1952, it became more prevalent in the late 1950s with programs such as *Leave it To Beaver* (1957) and *The Donna Reed Show* (1958). On the spatial relationship among living rooms, televisual images of nuclear families, and television viewers, see Lynn Spigel, *Welcome to the Dreamhouse: Popular Media and Postwar Suburbs* (Durham: Duke University Press, 2001), 31–106; Mary Beth Haralovich, "Sit-Coms and Suburbs: Positioning the 1950s Homemaker," in *Private Screenings: Television and the Female Consumer*, ed. Lynn Spigel and Denise Mann (Minneapolis: University of Minnesota Press, 1992), 111–41; Lynn Spigel, *Make Room for TV: Television and the Family Ideal in Postwar America* (Chicago: University of Chicago Press, 1992); Cecelia Tichi, *Electronic Hearth: Creating an American Television Culture* (New York: Oxford University Press, 1991); Ella Taylor, *Prime-Time Families: Television Culture in Postwar America* (Berkeley: University of California Press, 1989).

36. Among the works on television and "liveness," see Jane Feuer, "The Concept of Live Television: Ontology as Ideology," in *Regarding Television: Critical Approaches—An Anthology*, ed. E. Ann Kaplan (Frederick, MD: University Publication of America, 1983), 12–22; Rhona Berenstein, "Acting Live: TV Performance, Intimacy, and Immediacy (1945–1955)," in *Reality Squared: Televisual Discourse on the Real*, ed. James Friedman (New Brunswick, NJ: Rutgers University Press, 2004), 25–49.

37. Franzen, letter to Herbert Jaffa, April 7, 1953.

38. Lois Labovitz, letter to Maurice Fagan, January 14, 1953, FC collection, box 43, folder 59, TUUA.

39. Thomas Breslin, letter to Maurice Fagan, [n.d.] [ca. February 1953], box 43, folder 59, TUUA.

40. Fagan, letter to Herbert Miller, February 3, 1953.

41. Helen Bradley, letter to Maurice Fagan, November 6, 1952, FC collection, box 43, folder 59, TUUA.

42. Max Franzen, letter to Helen Bradley, November 14, 1952, FC collection, box 43, folder 59, TUUA.

43. Max Franzen, letter to Herbert Jaffa, April 20, 1953, FC collection, box 43, folder 59, TUUA.

44. Maurice Fagan, letter to Lois Labovitz, February 10, 1953, FC collection, box 43, folder 59, TUUA.

45. Maurice Fagan, letter to Margaret M. Kearney, September 2, 1953, FC collection, box 43, folder 59, TUUA.

46. *The Official 1955 Bandstand Yearbook* [no publication information listed], 30.

47. On the ways in which television producers and commentators classify viewer identities in terms related to gender, work, and daypart, see Haralovich, "Sit-Coms and Suburbs: Positioning the 1950s Homemaker"; Kristen Hatch, "Daytime Politics: Kefauver, McCarthy and the American Housewife," in *Reality Squared*, ed. Friedman, 75–91.

48. *The Official 1957 Bandstand Yearbook* [no publication information listed].

49. Franzen, letter to Herbert Jaffa, April 20, 1953.

50. Clarence Pickett, letter to Donald W. Thornburgh, June 29, 1953, box 43, folder 59, TUUA. On the Fellowship Commission's hope that the program would resume in the fall of 1953, see "Report to the Community," May 1953, FC collection, box 53, folder 10, TUUA.

51. Fagan, letter to Margaret Kearney, September 2, 1953.

52. Callahan, *Television in School, College, and Community*, 263.

53. Ibid., 46, 262; Philadelphia Board of Education, "Report of Television-Radio Activities," 1953, Division of Radio and TV, box 76, PSDA.

54. Lizbeth Cohen, *A Consumers' Republic: The Politics of Mass Consumption in Postwar America* (New York: Vintage Books, 2004); Charles McGovern, *Sold American: Consumption and Citizenship, 1890–1945* (Chapel Hill: University of North Carolina Press, 2006).

55. Lizabeth Cohen, "The New Deal State and Citizen Consumers," in *Getting and Spending: European and American Consumer Society in the Twentieth Century*, ed. Susan Strasser, Charles McGovern, and Matthias Judt (Washington, DC: Cambridge University Press, 1998), 114.

56. Cohen, *Consumers' Republic*, 403–404.

57. Following Jürgen Habermas's study of the social sites where meanings are articulated and contested, sociologists and media studies scholars have applied the concept of a public sphere to television talk shows, where the everyday experiential knowledge of "ordinary people" competes with, and is often privileged over, expert knowledge. Jürgen Habermas, *The Structural Transformation of the Public Sphere: An Inquiry into a Category of Bourgeois Society* (Cambridge, MA: MIT Press, 1991). Among scholars who have examined the concept of public spheres in relation to television, see Andrew Tolson, ed., *Television Talk Shows: Discourse, Performance, Spectacle* (Mahwah, NJ: Lawrence Erlbaum, 2001), 7–30; Jane Shattuc, *The Talking Cure: TV Talk Shows and Women* (New York: Routledge, 1997); James Friedman, "Attraction to Distraction: Live Television and the Public Sphere," *Reality Squared: Televisual Discourse on the Real*, ed. Friedman, 138–54.

CHAPTER 3

1. On de facto school segregation in the North in the 1950s and early 1960s, see Adina Beck, "Exposing the 'Whole Segregation Myth': The Harlem Nine and New York City's School Desegregation Battles," and Jeanne Theoharis, "'I'd Rather Go to School in the South': How Boston's School Desegregation Complicates the Civil Rights Paradigm," in *Freedom North: Black Freedom Struggles outside the South, 1940–1980*, ed. Jeanne Theoharis and Komozi Woodard (New York: Palgrave Macmillan, 2003), 65–92, 125–52; Davison Douglas, *Jim Crow Moves North: The Battle over Northern School Segregation, 1865–1954* (New York: Cambridge University Press, 2005), 219–73; Jack Dougherty, *More Than One Struggle: The Evolution of Black School Reform in Milwaukee* (Chapel Hill: University of North Carolina Press, 2004); Jeffrey Mirel, *The Rise and Fall of an Urban School System: Detroit, 1907–81* (Ann Arbor: University of Michigan Press, 1993), 217–92; John Rury, "Race, Space, and the Politics of Chicago's Pub-

lic Schools: Benjamin Willis and the Tragedy of Urban Education," *History of Education Quarterly* 39 (Summer 1999): 117–42; John Rury and Jeffrey Mirel, "The Political Economy of Urban Education," *Review of Research in Education* 22 (1997): 49–110; Alan Anderson and George Pickering, *Confronting the Color Line: The Broken Promise of the Civil Rights Movement* (Athens: University of Georgia Press, 1986), 44–102.

2. See Matthew Lassiter, *The Silent Majority: Suburban Politics in the Sunbelt South* (Princeton: Princeton University Press, 2006); Kevin Kruse, *White Flight: Atlanta and the Making of Modern Conservatism* (Princeton: Princeton University Press, 2005); Joseph Crespino, *In Search of Another Country: Mississippi and the Conservative Counterrevolution* (Princeton: Princeton University Press, 2007); Joseph Crespino, "The Best Defense Is a Good Offense: The Stennis Amendment and the Fracturing of Liberal School Desegregation Policy, 1964–72," *Journal of Policy History* 18 (no. 3, 2006); Robert Pratt, *The Color of Their Skin: Education and Race in Richmond Virginia, 1954–89* (Charlottesville: University of Virginia Press, 1992); Matthew Lassiter and Joseph Crespino, eds., *The Myth of Southern Exceptionalism* (New York: Oxford University Press, 2010).

3. Lassiter, *Silent Majority*, 137.

4. George Lipsitz, "Getting around Brown: The Social Warrant of the New Racism," in *Remembering Brown at Fifty: The University of Illinois Commemorates Brown v. Board of Education*, ed. Orville Vernon Burton and David O'Brien (Urbana: University of Illinois Press, 2009), 48.

5. On anti-prejudice work by Jewish organizations, see Stuart Svonkin, *Jews against Prejudice: American Jews and the Fight for Civil Liberties* (New York: Columbia University Press, 1997).

6. On the lack of attention given to educational issues in the city's newspapers and political debates, see Peter Binzen, interviewed by Walter Philips, 1979, The Walter Phillips Oral History Project file, TUUA.

7. For studies that examine the power of elites in the history of urban schools, see Samuel Bowles and Herbert Gintis, *Schooling in Capitalist America: Educational Reform and the Contradictions of Economic Life* (New York: Basic Books, 1976); David Tyack, *The One Best System: A History of Urban Education in the United States* (Cambridge, MA: Harvard University Press, 1974).

8. Albert Blaustein, *Civil Rights U.S.A.: Cities in the North and West, 1962* (New York: Greenwood Press, 1968), 121–22;

9. Marilyn Gittell and T. Edward Hollander, *Six Urban School Districts: A Comparative Study of Institutional Response* (New York: Frederick Praeger Publishers, 1968), 25.

10. Ibid., 28; Binzen interview, 11–12.

11. On the Commission on Human Relations' lack of authority with regard to the public schools, see "Commission on Human Relations (CHR) Minutes," June 9, 1955, CHR collection, box A-2860, folder 148.2 "Minutes 1953–1957," PCA; "CHR Minutes," September 19, 1955, CHR collection, box A-2860, folder 148.2 "Minutes 1953–1957," PCA; CHR, "1957 Annual Report," CHR collection, box A-620, folder 148.1, PCA; "1959 Achievements in Terms of the Program Goals for the Year," 1960, CHR collection, box A-2823, folder 148.2, "Agenda & Minutes 1959," PCA; "Minutes of Meeting of the Commission on Human Relations,"

December 8, 1959, CHR collection, box A-2823, folder 148.2, "Agenda & Minutes 1959," PCA; Christopher Edley, letter to George Schermer, January 18, 1961, FL collection, Acc 469, box 2, folder 19, TUUA; Edley, letter to Logan, January 31, 1961, FL collection, Acc 469, box 2, folder 19, TUUA.

12. Blaustein, *Civil Rights U.S.A.*, 123.

13. Greater Philadelphia Movement, *A Citizens Study of Public Education in Philadelphia* (Philadelphia: Greater Philadelphia Movement, 1962). Quoted in Michael Clapper, "The Constructed World of Postwar Philadelphia Area Schools: Site Selection, Architecture, and the Landscape of Inequality" (Ph.D. diss, University of Pennsylvania, 2008), 33–34.

14. "What Is the Fellowship Commission?" [n.d.] [ca. 1946], FC collection, Acc 626, box 1, folder 3, TUUA.

15. Helen Trager and Marian Yarrow, *They Learn What They Live: Prejudice in Young Children* (New York: Harper & Brothers, 1952), 3.

16. The Bureau on Intercultural Education's work during this period at the national level, such as "Americans All—Immigrants All," a nationally broadcast intercultural radio program, incorporated aspects of both cultural pluralist and assimilationist perspectives. On "Americans All—Immigrants All" and the use of radio for intercultural education, see Barbara Dianne Savage, *Broadcasting Freedom: Radio, War, and the Politics of Race, 1938–1948* (Chapel Hill: University of North Carolina Press, 1999). On the Bureau of Intercultural Education within the intellectual history of intercultural education, see Cherry McGee Banks, "Intercultural and Intergroup Education, 1929–1959: Linking Schools and Communities," in *Handbook of Research on Multicultural Education, 2nd edition*, ed. James Banks (San Francisco: Jossey-Bass, 2004), 753–69.

17. Barbara Barnes, "Prejudices Can Be Un-learned, Experiments Conducted Here Show," *Philadelphia Evening Bulletin*, October 11, 1951.

18. Catherine Mackenzie, "Prejudice Can Be Unlearned," *New York Times*, July 25, 1948. For more information on the early childhood project, see "Report of the Committee on Evaluations," July 8, 1949, FH collection, Acc 723, box 30, folder "Early Childhood," TUUA; "Minutes: Committee on Program Priorities," November 12, 1951, JCRC collection, box 003, folder 015, PJAC; "Annual Meeting," February 20, 1950, FC collection, Acc 626, box 1, folder 5, TUUA.

19. George Trowbridge, "Fellowship Commission Annual Meeting, Report of Chairman," February 18, 1947, FC collection, Acc 626, box 1, folder 5, TUUA.

20. Maurice Fagan, letter to Clarence Pickett, October 11, 1951, PFC collection, MSS 115, sec 1, box 002, folder 005, PJAC; "Report on the Meeting at Fellowship Farm," September 26, 1952, PFC collection, MSS 115, sec 1, box 002, folder 005, PJAC. On *They Shall Be Heard*, see chapter 2.

21. "Proposal to the Ford Foundation," September 1953, FC collection, Acc 626, box 57, folder 13, TUUA. On the Fellowship Commission's proposal to the Ford Foundation, see PFC collection, MSS 115, Sec 1, folders 002-005, PJAC; FC collection, Acc 626, box 57, folder 13, TUUA; FC collection, Acc 626, box 43, folder 31, TUUA.

22. Walter Jackson, *Gunnar Myrdal and America's Conscience: Social Engineering and Racial Liberalism, 1938–1987* (Chapel Hill: University of North

Carolina Press, 1990), 26–28; John Stanfield, *Philanthropy and Jim Crow in American Social Science* (Westport, CT: Greenwood Press, 1985), 140–42.

23. Jackson, *Gunnar Myrdal and America's Conscience*, 17, 20, 34.

24. Frederick Keppel to Gunnar Myrdal, August 12, 1937, quoted in Stanfield, *Philanthropy and Jim Crow in American Social Science*, 149

25. Stephen Steinberg, *Turning Back: The Retreat from Racial Justice in American Thought and Policy* (Boston: Beacon Press, 1995), 49.

26. Rayford Logan, ed., *What the Negro Wants* (1944; New York: Agathon Press, 1969), xxxiii.

27. Ibid., 14.

28. On the influence of *An American Dilemma*, see David Southern, *Gunnar Myrdal and Black-White Relations: The Use and Abuse of An American Dilemma, 1944–1969* (Baton Rouge: Louisiana State University Press, 1987); Steinberg, *Turning Back*, 65–67; Steinberg, "An American Dilemma: The Collapse of the Racial Orthodoxy of Gunnar Myrdal," *Journal of Blacks in Higher Education* 10 (Winter 1995–96) 64–70; Sugrue, *Sweet Land of Liberty*, 59–62.

29. Maurice Fagan, letter to Clarence Pickett, July 21, 1952, PFC collection, MSS 115, sec 1, box 002, folder 005, PJAC. For a critique of Fagan's faith in social science methods to address prejudice, see Isaiah Minkoff, letter to Fagan, January 5, 1953, PFC collection, MSS 115, sec 1, box 002, folder 005, PJAC.

30. Fellowship Commission, "Comments on the October 6th Discussion Memorandum on the Proposal to the Ford Foundation," November 1952, FC collection, Acc 626, box 43, folder 31, TUUA; Gordon Allport, letter to Clarence Pickett, October 12, 1952, FC collection, Acc 626, box 43, folder 31, TUUA. For more on Fagan's correspondence with these social scientists, see FC collection, Acc 626, box 57, folder 13, TUUA.

31. Fellowship Commission, "Report on the Meeting at Fellowship Farm," September 26, 1952, JCRC collection, box 002, folder 005, PJAC.

32. "Educational Equality League (EEL) History Highlights: 1932–1960" [n.d.], [ca. 1960], FL collection, Acc 469, box 1, folder 1, TUUA. On school segregation in Philadelphia before 1950, see Vincent Franklin, *The Education of Black Philadelphia: The Social and Educational History of a Minority Community, 1900–1950* (Philadelphia: University of Pennsylvania Press, 1979).

33. One of the teachers for whom Floyd Logan advocated was Ruth Wright Hayre, the first black high school teacher in Philadelphia. On Hayre's work, see Matthew Delmont, "The Plight of the 'Able' Student: Ruth Wright Hayre and the Struggle for Equality in Philadelphia's Black High Schools, 1955–1965," *History of Education Quarterly* 50 (May, 2010), 204–230.

34. "EEL History Highlights: 1932–1960"; Doris Wiley, "Letter-Writer Logan Often Scores Where Pickets Don't in Rights Fight," *Philadelphia Evening Bulletin*, June 6, 1965; Acel Moore, "A Civil Rights Fighter Deserved More, *Philadelphia Evening Bulletin*, August 7, 1980; "Floyd Logan Dies; Crusader for Equality," *Philadelphia Evening Bulletin*, February 12, 1979.

35. Floyd Logan, letter to Louis Hoyer, December 2, 1948, FL collection, Acc 469, box 2, folder 9, TUUA; Floyd Logan, letter to Walter Biddle Saul, March 3, 1949, FL collection, Acc 469, box 2, folder 9, TUUA; Anne Phillips,

"The Struggle for School Desegregation in Philadelphia, 1945–1967" (Ph.D. diss., University of Pennsylvania, Philadelphia, 2000), 65–67.

36. *Digest of Education Statistics,* 2004, National Center for Education Statistics, http://nces.ed.gov/programs/digest/d04/tables/dt04_056.asp and http://nces.ed.gov/programs/digest/d04/tables/dt04_102.asp (accessed November 16, 2006). On the development of high schools in the first half of the twentieth century, see Edward Krug, *The Shaping of the American High School* (New York, Harper & Row, 1964).

37. Jack Balkin, ed., *What "Brown v. Board of Education" Should Have Said* (New York: New York University Press, 2002), 65–66.

38. Harrison Fry, "Teachers Advised on Ex-G.I. Pupil," *Philadelphia Evening Bulletin,* March 6, 1946; Joseph Nolan, "Franklin Course Aids 5000 Vets," *Philadelphia Evening Bulletin,* December 29, 1947; Joseph Nolan, "Vet Courses at Franklin Win Acclaim," *Philadelphia Evening Bulletin,* December 30, 1947; Joseph Nolan, "Vets Praise Curricula at Franklin," *Philadelphia Evening Bulletin,* December 31, 1947; "City High School Has Three Names," *Philadelphia Evening Bulletin,* September 5, 1948; Harrison Fry, "Veterans Complete Courses in Two Years; Point Way to High School of Future," *Philadelphia Evening Bulletin,* January 23, 1949; "Franklin High Tailors Courses," *Philadelphia Evening Bulletin,* April 29, 1949.

39. Middle States Association of Schools and Colleges, "Report of the Visiting Committee on the Evaluation of the Benjamin Franklin High School," May 25, 1951, FL collection, Acc 469, box 20, folder 26, TUUA.

40. The Redevelopment Authority and the Citizen's Council on City Planning (CCCP) were watchdog agencies that oversaw the activities of the Philadelphia Housing Association (later the Housing Association of Delaware Valley), the leading urban planning authority in postwar Philadelphia. John Bauman writes that in reality the CCCP "became both a sounding board and an advertising agent for the planners' vision of the postwar city." John Bauman, *Public Housing, Race, and Renewal: Urban Planning in Philadelphia, 1920–1974* (Philadelphia: Temple University Press, 1987), 99.

41. Barbara Barnes, "Pupils Learn Lessons in Alley Classroom," *Philadelphia Evening Bulletin,* November 2, 1950. For similar comments by a teacher at the school, see Martin Rosenberg, "A School Helps to Improve Its Neighborhood," *School News and Views,* January 1, 1951.

42. On the founding and goals of the life adjustment education movement, see Harl Douglass, ed., *Education for Life Adjustment: Its Meanings and Implementation* (New York: Ronald Press Company, 1950); Diane Ravitch, *Troubled Crusade: American Education, 1945–1980* (New York: Basic Books, 1983), 64–68. For a contemporary analysis of the relationship between high school curriculum tracks and students' class status, see August Hollingshead, *Elmstown Youth: The Impact of Social Classes on Adolescents* (New York: Wiley, 1949).

43. Herbert Kliebard, *The Struggle for the American Curriculum: 1893–1958,* 3rd ed. (New York: Routledge Falmer, 2004), 250–70.

44. Floyd Logan, letter to J. Harry LaBrum, May 20, 1963, FL collection, Acc 469, box 2, folder 21, TUUA; Walter Reeder, letter to Floyd Logan, May 13, 1963, FL collection, Acc 469, box 7, folder 12, TUUA; School District of

Philadelphia, "Department of Business Statement," September 19, 1961, FL collection, Acc 469, box 30, folder 5, TUUA; "Jim Crow's Sweetheart Contract," *Greater Philadelphia Magazine*, 58 (February 1963).

45. "Survey Recommends That Building Be Totally Demolished," *Philadelphia Tribune*, October 6, 1951; Joseph V. Baker, "'Segregation' Hit At Benjamin Franklin High," *Philadelphia Inquirer*, October 7, 1951.

46. "Report on the Proceeding of the Conference on 'Democratization of the Philadelphia Public Schools,'" October 15, 1951, National Association for the Advancement of Colored People, Philadelphia Branch (NAACP) collection, URB 6, box 6, folder 138, TUUA.

47. "Angry Parents Resent Remarks by Principal," *Philadelphia Tribune*, October 23, 1951; "Negro Baiting Assembly Talk Angers Parents," *Pittsburgh Courier*, October 27, 1951. For the case that precipitated the principal's comments, see "3 Boys Confess in Taxi Slaying," *Philadelphia Inquirer*, October 17, 1951.

48. W. E. Morton, letter to NAACP office, October 21, 1951, NAACP collection, URB 6, box 6, folder 135, TUUA.

49. EEL, "Notes on the Meeting with the Board of Education."

50. "Slurs Create Incident," *Teacher Union News*, Vol. 6, No. 2, January 1952, NAACP collection, URB 6, box 6, folder 137, TUUA.

51. EEL, "A Six-Point Program for the West Philadelphia High School," January 10, 1952, NAACP collection, URB 6, box 6, folder 137, TUUA.

52. "Conference of Educational Equality League and Supporting Organization with Members of Board of Public Education in Executive Session," June 10, 1952, FL collection, Acc 469, box 1, folder 4, TUUA. Throughout the 1950s, Logan coupled his praise for democratic education with anticommunist rhetoric. On the anticommunist rhetoric of many civil rights activists during this period, see Mary Dudziak, *Cold War Civil Rights: Race and the Image of American Democracy* (Princeton, NJ: Princeton University Press, 2000); Penny Von Eschen, *Race against Empire: Black Americans and Anticolonialism, 1937–1957* (Ithaca, NY: Cornell University Press, 1997); Shana Bernstein, *Bridges of Reform: Interracial Civil Rights Activism in Twentieth-Century Los Angeles* (New York: Oxford University Press, 2010).

53. "Conference of Educational Equality League and Supporting Organization with Members of Board of Public Education in Executive Session." On the materials the EEL presented to the school board, see "Suggestions for Policy on Democratization of Philadelphia Public Schools," June 10, 1952, FL collection, Acc 469, box 1, folder 4, TUUA; "Some Pertinent Facts about Philadelphia Schools" [n.d.], [ca. October 1951], FL collection, Acc 469, box 8, folder 27, TUUA; "History Highlights: Educational Equality League: 1932–1960."

54. "Conference Report: Meeting with Walter Biddle Saul" [n.d.], [ca. October 4, 1952], FL collection, Acc 469, box 4, folder 30, TUUA. For examples of the school boundary information on which Logan based his claims about racial gerrymandering, see Louis Hayer, letter to Floyd Logan, February 19, 1952, FL collection, Acc 469, box 26, folder 8, TUUA.

55. Ibid.

56. Ibid.

57. "School Board Denies Charge of Jim-Crow," *Philadelphia Tribune*, July 18, 1953.

58. "Report: Review of Meetings with Board," July 9, 1953, FL collection, Acc 469, box 1, folder 4, TUUA.

59. "Report: Educational Policies Special Committee," June 24, 1953, FL collection, Acc 469, box 19, folder 1, TUUA.

60. Floyd Logan, letter to Mrs. John Frederick Lewis, September 19, 1953, FL collection, Acc 469, box 2, folder 13, TUUA.

61. Ibid.

62. Gary Orfield, "Segregated Housing and School Resegregation" in *Dismantling Desegregation: The Quiet Reversal of Brown v. Board of Education*, Gary Orfield, Susan Eaton, and the Harvard Project on School Desegregation (New York: The New Press, 1996), 312–13. On the adoption of the de facto explanation of residential segregation, see Lipsitz, "Getting around *Brown*," 51–54.

63. Jeanne Theoharis, "Hidden in Plain Sight: The Civil Rights Movement outside the South," in *The Myth of Southern Exceptionalism*, ed. Matthew Lassiter and Joseph Crespino (New York: Oxford University Press, 2010), 49–73; Martha Biondi, *To Stand and Fight: The Struggle for Civil Rights in Postwar New York City* (Cambridge, MA: Harvard University Press, 2003), 246–48; Kathryn Neckerman, *School Betrayed: Roots of Failure in Inner-City Education* (Chicago: University of Chicago Press, 2007), 81–106; Sugrue, *Sweet Land of Liberty*, 194–96; Adina Back, "Up South in New York: The 1950s School Desegregation Struggles" (Ph.D. diss., New York University, 1997).

64. See, for example, "Conference Report: Meeting with Walter Biddle Saul" [n.d.]; "School Board Denies Charge of Jim-Crow;" "Report: Review of Meetings with Board;" "Report: Educational Policies Special Committee."

65. David L. Ullman, memo to Members of Fellowship Commission Executive Committee, December 31, 1952, JCRC collection, box 007, folder 006, PJAC; "Fellowship Commission Fair Educational Opportunities Committee minutes," February 6, 1953, FL collection, Acc 469, box 37, folder 24, TUUA.

66. David Ullman, memo to Members of Fellowship Commission Executive Committee, April 22, 1955, NAACP collection, URB 6, box 16, folder 318, TUUA. On the educational issues addressed by the Fellowship Commission, see "Fellowship Commission Fair Educational Opportunities Committee Minutes 1953–56," JCRC collection, box 007, folders 005–006, PJAC.

67. Maurice Fagan, letter to Clarence E. Pickett and Leon J. Obermayer, September 16, 1955, FC collection, Acc 626, box 57, folder 13, TUUA.

68. Michael Clapper, "School Design, Site Selection, and the Political Geography of Race in Postwar Philadelphia," *Journal of Planning History* 5 (August 2006): 247–49.

69. CHR, "Philadelphia's Negro Population: Facts on Housing."

70. Charles Neville, "Origin and Development of the Public High School in Philadelphia," *The School Review* 35, no. 5 (May 1927): 367–68. On the history of Central High School of Philadelphia, see David Labaree, *The Making of an American High School: The Credentials Market and the Central High School of Philadelphia, 1838–1939* (New Haven, CT: Yale University Press, 1988).

71. The Alumni Association of Northeast High School, "75th Anniversary Record," 1965, Northeast High School file, Philadelphia School District Archives (PSDA).

72. Robert Wayne Clark, "To the Young Men of Edison," http://www.philsch.k12.pa.us/schools/edison/hstclark.html (accessed October 1, 2006); Helen Oakes, "The Oakes Newsletter," December 14, 1973, Thomas Edison High School file, PSDA. On the importance of alumni to the school, see "Northeast High Parents, Alumni Library Drive," *Philadelphia Evening Bulletin*, January 22, 1960.

73. Fellowship Commission, "Summary Statement of the Northeast," December 6, 1957, NAACP collection, URB 6, box 2, folder 33, TUUA;

74. David McAllister, "Between the Suburbs and the Ghetto: Racial and Economic Change in Philadelphia, 1933–1985" (Ph.D. diss, Temple University, 2006), 160–61.

75. Guian McKee, *The Problem of Jobs: Liberalism, Race, and Deindustrialization in Philadelphia* (Chicago: University of Chicago Press, 2008), 59.

76. Jeannie Oakes, *Keeping Track: How Schools Structure Inequality* (New Haven, CT: Yale University Press, 2005), 226–27, 247–48.

77. "Number of Negro Teachers and Percentage of Negro Students in Philadelphia Senior High Schools, 1956–1957" [n.d.], FL collection, Acc 469, box 14, folder 10, TUUA. On the intercultural education program implemented at Northeast High School, see "Intergroup Education, Northeast High School," 1960–61, Northeast High School file, PSDA.

78. On the construction of the new Northeast High School, see "Northeast High Opens Monday," *Philadelphia Inquirer*, February 7, 1957; George Riley, "Northeast to Open as City's Newest Public High School," *Philadelphia Evening Bulletin*, February 10, 1957; "Noted Alumni Attend Rites at New Northeast High," *Philadelphia Inquirer*, May 2, 1957; "New School Buildings Provide for Growing City's Needs," *School News and Views*, February 28, 1957, Northeast High School files, PSDA; "New Northeast High School Occupies 43-Acre Site," *Philadelphia Evening Bulletin*, May 1, 1957; Harrison Fry, "Northeast High Will Dedicate New School," *Philadelphia Evening Bulletin*, April 28, 1957; "All-Day Program to Dedicate New Northeast High May 1," *Philadelphia Evening Bulletin*, April 14, 1957. On the new schools being built in the 1950s in the suburban Delaware Valley, see "New Schools for Newcomers," *Philadelphia Inquirer*, September 24, 1957; Peter Binzen, "Cheltenham Twp. Prepares to Open $6,390,000 High School and Pool," *Philadelphia Evening Bulletin*, August 17, 1959; Clapper, "School Design, Site Selection, and the Political Geography of Race in Postwar Philadelphia," 247.

79. Robert Wayne Clark, "To the Young Men of Edison."

80. The Alumni Association of Northeast High School, "75th Anniversary Record."

81. Blaustein, *Civil Rights U.S.A.*, 138.

82. For examples of Logan's correspondence with Superintendent Allen Wetter and Business Manager Add Anderson, see "Notes on telephone conversation with Add Anderson," May 29, 1958, FL collection, Acc 469, box 8, folder 7, TUUA; "Notes on telephone conversation with Allen Wetter," June 7, 1958, FL collection, Acc 469, box 8, folder 7, TUUA.

83. Philadelphia Board of Education, Division of Research, "A Ten-Year Summary of the Distribution of Negro Pupils in the Philadelphia Public Schools, 1957–1966," December 23, 1966, FL collection, Acc 469, box 23, folder 6, TUUA; "Number of Negro Teachers and Percentage of Negro Students in Philadelphia Senior High Schools, 1956–1957" [n.d.], FL collection, Acc 469, box 14, folder 10, TUUA.

84. On the curriculum options at Edison High School, see Robert Wayne Clark, "The Occupational Practice Shop," *Clearing House Magazine*, April 1961, Urban League (UL) collection, URB 1, box 9, folder 145, TUUA; Philadelphia Advisory Council for Vocational Education, "Minutes of Meeting," April 25, 1961, UL collection, URB 1, box 9, folder 145, TUUA.

85. "Educational League Wins Fight for New Franklin High," *Philadelphia Tribune*, March 8, 1955; Floyd Logan, letter to Allen Wetter, September 19, 1956, FL collection, Acc 469, box 9, folder 2, TUUA.

86. In the late 1950s, the Reverend Leon Sullivan organized an employment agency for black teenagers in his North Philadelphia neighborhood. In the early 1960s, he was a leader among the four hundred ministers who organized several successful selective patronage campaigns against private employers to improve job opportunities for black workers. Matthew Countryman, *Up South: Civil Rights and Black Power in Philadelphia* (Philadelphia: University of Pennsylvania Press, 2006), 83–119.

87. "Meeting Minutes: Conference with the Board of Superintendents and District Superintendents," September 21, 1959, FL collection, Acc 439, box 9, folder 2, TUUA.

88. Floyd Logan, letter to Dr. Carl Seifert, December 3, 1957, FL collection, Acc 469, box 11, folder 6, TUUA; Floyd Logan, "Petition to Members of the Board of Public Education," [n.d.] [ca. 1957], FL collection, Acc 469, box 6, folder 27, TUUA; Floyd Logan, "Script for WDAS Radio Discussion of Integration in the Philadelphia Public Schools," FL collection, Acc 469, box 9, folder 22, TUUA.

89. William Odell, "Educational Survey Report for the Philadelphia Board of Public Education," February 1965, PSDA; School District of Philadelphia Curriculum Report, May 1963 cited in Helen Oakes, "The School District of Philadelphia" [n.d.] [ca. 1968], FL collection, Acc 469, box 24, folder 33, TUUA. For Logan's work on behalf of parents whose children were tracked into lower-level courses based on IQ scores, see FL collection, Acc 469, box 8, folder 12, TUUA.

90. Floyd Logan, letter to Allen Wetter, February 19, 1960, FL collection, Acc 469, box 9, folder 2, TUUA.

91. Peter Binzen, "Class at Franklin High Drops from 151 to 21 in 3 Years," *Philadelphia Evening Bulletin*, January 10, 1961. On the Philadelphia school board's construction program in these years, see Clapper, "School Design, Site Selection, and the Political Geography of Race in Postwar Philadelphia."

92. "Their Three Best Years," *Philadelphia Evening Bulletin*, January 14, 1961.

93. Floyd Logan, letter to Allen Wetter, March 8, 1961, FL collection, Acc 469, box 9, folder 2, TUUA.

94. Allen Wetter, letter to Elias Wolf, January 30, 1961, box 34, "Greater Philadelphia Movement" folder, PSDA.

95. Oakes, *Keeping Track*, 173.

96. James Conant, The American High School Today: A First Report to Interested Citizens (New York: McGraw-Hill, 1959); James Conant, Slums and Suburbs: A Commentary on Schools in Metropolitan Areas (New York: McGraw-Hill, 1961).

97. Stephen Preskill, "Raking from the Rubbish: Charles W. Eliot, James B. Conant, and the Public Schools" (Ph.D. diss., University of Illinois at Urbana-Champaign, 1984), 280–82.

98. On the "great debate" regarding education in the United States in the cold war era and the influence of Conant's reports, see David Gamson, "From Progressivism to Federalism: The Pursuit of Equal Educational Opportunity, 1915–1965," in *To Educate a Nation: Federal and National Strategies of School Reform*, ed. Carl Kaestle and Alyssa Lodewick (Lawrence: University of Kansas Press, 2007), 177–201; Steven Tozer, Paul Violas, and Guy Senese, *School and Society: Educational Practice as Social Expression* (New York: McGraw-Hill, 1993), 24–33, 187–211; and Preskill, "Raking from the Rubbish," 264–317.

99. Conant, *Slums and Suburbs*, 31.

100. Ibid., 7, 145–47.

101. Ravitch, *The Troubled Crusade*, 152.

102. On the influence of cultural deprivation research on educational policies and practices, see James Banks, "Multicultural Education: Historical Development, Dimensions, and Practice," *Review of Research in Education*, 19 (1993): 28–30; Ravitch, *The Troubled Crusade*, 145–81; Maris Vinovskis, *The Birth of Head Start: Preschool Education Policies in the Kennedy and Johnson Administrations* (Chicago University of Chicago Press, 2005).

103. Riessman's reference to "one in three" young people being culturally deprived was influenced by the Ford Foundation's Great Cities School Improvement Studies, published in 1960. Frank Riessman, *The Culturally Deprived Child* (New York: Harper, 1962), 9.

104. Ibid., 8, 80.

105. Ibid., 1–9. On the influence of Riessman's book, see Ravitch, *The Troubled Crusade*, 154–60.

106. Philadelphia School Board, "The Story of the Philadelphia Public Schools in 1962 and in a Few Prior Years, with, Here and There, a Comment about the Future," October 1, 1962, FL collection, Acc 469, box 25, folder 14, TUUA.

107. Wetter, "For Every Child: The Story of Integration in the Philadelphia Public Schools." For Logan's critique of Wetter's position on integration, see "Dr. Wetter Hit for Stand on Mixing Schools," *Philadelphia Tribune*, May 21, 1960; Floyd Logan, letter to Members of Board of Public Education, November 23, 1960, FL collection, Acc 469, box 2, folder 20, TUUA.

CHAPTER 4

1. Jeanne Theoharis, "Introduction" in *Freedom North: Black Freedom Struggles Outside the South, 1940–1980*, ed. Jeanne Theoharis and Komozi Woodard (New York: Palgrave Macmillan, 2003), 2.

2. Thomas Sugrue, *Sweet Land of Liberty: The Forgotten Struggle for Civil Rights in the North* (New York: Random House, 2008), xiv.

3. "Urge State Action on School Bias," *Philadelphia Tribune*, June 1, 1954; Floyd Logan, letter to Governor John Fine, May 19, 1954, FL collection, Acc 469, box 3, folder 22, TUUA. On Logan's attempts to promote integration in Philadelphia in the wake of *Brown*, see Floyd Logan, letter to Mercedes and William Dodds, May 18, 1955, FL collection, Acc 469, box 2, folder 14, TUUA.

4. On the importance of information networks to civil rights, see Sugrue, *Sweet Land of Liberty*, 541. For examples of Floyd Logan's raising the profile of school segregation in Philadelphia through the *Philadelphia Tribune*, see "Desegregation in School," *Philadelphia Tribune*, September 18, 1954; "School Board Asked to Redistrict for Full Integration," *Philadelphia Tribune*, March 8, 1955; "Gov. Leader to Submit Logan School Plan to Commission," *Philadelphia Tribune*, May 7, 1955; "Separate Schools in Penna.," *Philadelphia Tribune*, May 17, 1955; "Fate of Integration in Local Courts," *Philadelphia Tribune*, June 4, 1955; "Logan Sparks Drive to Learn Extent of School Bias in Pa.," *Philadelphia Tribune*, November 24, 1956; "Race Segregation in Pennsylvania Schools Appears Doomed," *Philadelphia Tribune*, February 26, 1957; Floyd Logan, letter to John Saunders, [n.d.] [ca. 1956], FL collection, Acc 469, box 2, folder 14, TUUA; Floyd Logan, letter to Eustace Gay, July 21, 1956, FL collection, Acc 469, box 4, folder 9, TUUA. For examples of Floyd Logan's efforts to make Philadelphia's school segregation a story in the mainstream press, see Floyd Logan, letter to Frank Ford, August 30, 1957, FL collection, Acc 469, box 2, folder 15, TUUA; Floyd Logan, letter to Editor of *Evening Bulletin*, September 7, 1957, FL collection, Acc 469, box 10, folder 4, TUUA; Floyd Logan, letter to Adam Clayton Powell, January 24, 1956, FL collection, Acc 469, box 2, folder 14, TUUA; Floyd Logan, letter to Editor of *Look Magazine*, June 23, 1956, FL collection, Acc 469, box 4, folder 9, TUUA.

5. For examples of the coverage of Little Rock in the mainstream Philadelphia newspapers, see Robert Roth, "U.S. Probes Arkansas' Use of Troops to Bar Integration; President Criticises [sic] Governor," *Philadelphia Evening Bulletin*, September 3, 1957; "Guardsmen Bar Negroes from Arkansas School," *Philadelphia Evening Bulletin*, September 4, 1957; "Hate for Elizabeth," *Philadelphia Evening Bulletin*, September 6, 1957; "Faubus Warns against Force; Negroes Ejected at 2d School," *Philadelphia Evening Bulletin*, September 9, 1957; "Eisenhower Warns He'll Use Troops if Little Rock Terror Continues," *Philadelphia Inquirer*, September 24, 1957; "1000 Troops Ring Little Rock School; Fighting 'Anarchy,' Eisenhower Says," *Philadelphia Inquirer*, September 25, 1957; "Bayonets Impose Arkansas Peace," *Philadelphia Inquirer*, September 26, 1957; "9 in School, All Quiet in Little Rock," *Philadelphia Inquirer*, September 27, 1957; "Eisenhower Rejects Pledge by Faubus as Insufficient; Little Rock Troops to Stay," *Philadelphia Inquirer*, October 2, 1957; "President, Faubus Locked in Troop Removal Impasse; Little Rock Pupils Harass 9," *Philadelphia Inquirer*, October 3, 1957; "Little Rock 'Walkout' Fails, Guards Bar Rowdy Pupils; President Hits Faubus' Acts," *Philadelphia Inquirer*, October 4, 1957.

6. For examples of the coverage of southern school segregation fights outside of Little Rock in the mainstream Philadelphia newspapers, see "Two Sisters

Barred from High School in Virginia," *Philadelphia Evening Bulletin*, September 5, 1957; "Score of Men Attack Minister Leading Children into Alabama School," *Philadelphia Evening Bulletin*, September 9, 1957; "Dynamiters Wreck Nashville Schools," *Philadelphia Evening Bulletin*, September 10, 1957; Thomas Stokes, "Demonstrations in South Painting Ugly Picture of U.S.," *Philadelphia Evening Bulletin*, September 11, 1957; Payton Gray Sr., "Blame Arkansas for Riots Here: School Authorities Acting to Prevent Mass Panic in City," *Philadelphia Tribune*, October 1, 1957.

7. "Exclusive! (WCAU advertisement)," *Philadelphia Evening Bulletin*, September 11, 1957.

8. David Halberstam, *The Fifties* (New York: Villard Books, 1993), 679.

9. Taylor Branch, *Parting the Waters: America in the King Years, 1954–63* (New York: Simon and Schuster, 1988), 223.

10. On television news coverage of the civil rights movement, see Sasha Torres, *Black, White, and in Color: Television and Black Civil Rights* (Princeton, NJ: Princeton University Press, 2003), 135; Julian Bond, "The Media and the Movement" in *Media, Culture, and the Modern African American Freedom Struggle*, ed. Brian Ward (Gainesville: University Press of Florida, 2001), 16–40; University of Virginia Center for Digital History "Television News of the Civil Rights Era 1950–1970," http://www.vcdh.virginia.edu/civilrightstv/ (accessed November 15, 2007).

11. On the southern campaign of massive resistance, see Numan Bartley, *The Rise of Massive Resistance: Race and Politics in the South during the 1950's* (Baton Rouge: Louisiana State University Press, 1969); James Ely Jr., *The Crisis of Conservative Virginia: The Byrd Organization and the Politics of Massive Resistance* (Knoxville: University of Tennessee Press, 1976); Matthew Lassiter and Andrew Lewis, eds., *The Moderates Dilemma: Massive Resistance to School Desegregation in Virginia* (Charlottesville: University of Virginia Press, 1998); Clive Webb, ed., *Massive Resistance: Southern Opposition to the Second Reconstruction* (New York: Oxford University Press, 2005). For a similar campaign of violence in the North related to housing, see Arnold Hirsch, "Massive Resistance in the Urban North: Trumbull Park, Chicago, 1953–1966," *Journal of American History* 82 (September 1995): 522–50.

12. Peter Irons, *Jim Crow's Children: The Broken Promise of the Brown Decision* (New York: Viking, 2002), 179.

13. Saul Kohler, "Police Commissioner Gibbons Talks on Delinquency," *Philadelphia Inquirer*, October 4, 1957; "1000 Pupils Riot on S. Broad St.; 15 Are Arrested," *Philadelphia Inquirer*, September 25, 1957; "Schoolgirls Protected from S. Phila. Crowd," *Philadelphia Inquirer*, September 27, 1957; "Youth Fights Erupt Anew," *Philadelphia Evening Bulletin*, September 25, 1957; "Residents Air Racial Tension," *Philadelphia Evening Bulletin*, October 1, 1957.

14. Art Peters, "Negroes Break Barrier of TV Bandstand Show," *Philadelphia Tribune*, October 5, 1957. On this protest of *American Bandstand*, see chapter 7.

15. On the influence of Little Rock on white newspapers outside the South, see Gene Roberts and Hank Klibanoff, *Race Beat: The Press, the Civil Rights*

Struggle, and the Awakening of a Nation (New York: Vintage Books, 2006), 213–14.

16. Saul Kohler, "A Discussion on Integration Problem in Phila. Schools," *Philadelphia Inquirer*, October 13, 1957. For similar statements by school officials praising Philadelphia's antidiscrimination efforts, see Allen Wetter, letter to Floyd Logan, June 3, 1958, FL collection, Acc 469, box 3, folder 10, TUUA; "Phila. Moving to Fore in School Integration," *Philadelphia Tribune*, October 31, 1959; Commission on Human Relations, "A Statement of Concern for Public Education in Philadelphia," May 17, 1960, FL collection, Acc 469, box 40, folder 19, TUUA.

17. Floyd Logan, letter to Carl Morneweck, October 14, 1957, FL collection, Acc 469, box 11, folder 6, TUUA.

18. For examples of the *Philadelphia Tribune*'s coverage of struggles over southern school segregation after Little Rock, see "The 'Desegregation Front,' " *Philadelphia Tribune*, August 30, 1958; "Ceaseless Fight for School Desegregation Highlight of 1958," *Philadelphia Tribune*, January 3, 1959; "New Orleans Police Official: 'The Worst Is Yet to Come,' " *Philadelphia Tribune*, November 18, 1960; "Further Delay Would Only Worsen Climate for Ending Segregation," *Philadelphia Tribune*, December 3, 1960.

19. "Brief Supporting Petition to Board of Public Education of the School District of Philadelphia," February 10, 1959, FL collection, Acc 469, box 3, folder 10, TUUA.

20. Albert Blaustein, "Philadelphia, Pennsylvania," in *Civil Rights U.S.A.: Public Schools, Cities in the North and West, 1962*, United States Commission on Civil Rights (New York: Greenwood Press, 1968), 125; also quoted in Phillips, "The Struggle for School Desegregation in Philadelphia, 1945–1967" (Ph.D. diss., University of Pennylvania, 2000), 68–70.

21. "Minutes of October 5, 1959 Meeting," October 5, 1959, FL collection, Acc 439, box 1, folder 5, TUUA.

22. Theodore Graham, "Educational Equality League Sparked Fight to Halt School Discrimination," *Philadelphia Tribune*, July 11, 1959.

23. On the resistance to the Fellowship Commission's work on housing discrimination, see West Philadelphia Fellowship Commission, "Angora Civic Association," November 18, 1954, Acc 626, box 61, folder 34, TUUA.

24. Fellowship Commission, "The Philadelphia Childhood Relations Seminar: Three Years of Action-Research in Intergroup Education," November 1956, NAACP collection, URB 6, box 5, folder 107, TUUA.

25. Fellowship Commission Committee on Community Tensions meeting minutes, January 13, 1960, JCRC collection, box 002, folder 008, PJAC.

26. "Commission Asks School Survey," *Jewish Exponent*, February 19, 1960; David Horowitz, letter to Maurice Fagan, February 29, 1960, FC collection, Acc 626, box 39, folder 22, TUUA; Emma Bolzau, Assistant to Associate Superintendent, letter to David Horowitz, April 12, 1960, FC collection, Acc 626, box 39, folder 22, TUUA; Irving Shull, letter to friend, June 23, 1960, JCRC collection, box 003, folder 021, PJAC.

27. Curriculum Office, Philadelphia Public Schools, "A Guide to the Teaching of American History and Government," 1960, FL collection, Acc 469, box 12, folder 16, TUUA.

28. Curriculum Office, Philadelphia Public Schools, "A Guide to the Teaching of American History and Government."

29. Maurice Fagan, letter to David Horowitz, May 18, 1960, FC collection, Acc 626, box 39, folder 22, TUUA; Jules Cohen, letter to Maurice Fagan, May 13, 1960, PFC collection, box 002, folder 010, PJAC.

30. Fellowship Commission, "Meeting of Social Studies Department Heads and Fellowship Commission Representatives," June 30, 1960, Acc 626, box 39, folder 22, TUUA; Maurice Fagan, letter to Jules Cohen, July 18, 1960, FC collection, Acc 626, box 39, folder 22, TUUA; Maurice Fagan, letter to Charles Benham, July 15, 1960, FC collection, Acc 626, box 39, folder 22, TUUA; Peter Binzen, "Social Studies Textbooks in Public School Assailed," *Philadelphia Evening Bulletin*, July 5, 1960; "Dateline: Delaware Valley U.S.A.," *Philadelphia Inquirer*, July 5, 1960; "Fellowship Group Demands More Spunk in School Texts," *Philadelphia Daily News*, July 5, 1960; "Fellowship Unit's Probe Attacks School Textbooks," *Jewish Times*, July 8, 1960; "The Fellowship Survey of Textbooks," *Jewish Exponent*, July 8, 1960.

31. Peter Binzen, "Phila. Schools to Add Course about Bigotry," *Philadelphia Evening Bulletin*, July 6, 1960. While later articles in the *Philadelphia Tribune* and the *Jewish Exponent* quoted Fagan and Horowitz, respectively, regarding this course, Peter Binzen's article in the *Evening Bulletin* did not cite a source for his story on the new school units. For these related stories, see "Public School Anti-bigotry Courses Set," *The Philadelphia Tribune*, July 9, 1960; "Public Schools to Implement Textbook Work," *Jewish Exponent*, July 15, 1960.

32. "Indoctrination Course," *Philadelphia Evening Bulletin*, July 10, 1960.

33. Allen Wetter, "Public Schools vs. Bigotry," *Philadelphia Evening Bulletin*, July 17, 1960.

34. "Less Puritanical Approach," *Philadelphia Evening Bulletin*, July 17, 1960.

35. "By What Authority?" and "Free-Thinking Migrants," *Philadelphia Evening Bulletin*, July 17, 1960.

36. See chapter one for a discussion of defensive localism in relation to housing.

37. On the social warrant of consumer citizenship that underwrites this language of privatization, see George Lipsitz, "Getting around Brown: The Social Warrant of the New Racism," in *Remembering Brown at Fifty: The University of Illinois Commemorates Brown v. Board of Education*, ed. Orville Vernon Burton and David O'Brien (Urbana: University of Illinois Press, 2009), 54–59.

38. Maurice Fagan, "Controversy Leads to Exploration of Views," *Philadelphia Evening Bulletin*, July 24, 1960.

39. On the Fellowship Commission's community college public relations campaign, see "Junior College in Phila. Urged," *Philadelphia Inquirer*, November 4, 1960; "McBride Announces Start of Campaign to Establish Junior College in Philly," *Sons of Italy Times*, November 7, 1960; "Fellowship Commission Spurs Move for Junior College in Philadelphia," *Philadelphia Dispatch*, November 13, 1960; "Drive Is Started to Set Up Community College Here," *Philadelphia Evening Bulletin*, April 5, 1961; "Fellowship Conference to Discuss City College," *Jewish Exponent*, March 31, 1961; "Fellowship Commission Sparks

Drive for Junior Colleges," *Philadelphia Evening Bulletin*, April 5, 1961; "Phila. AFL-CIO Endorses Plan for Junior College Here," *Philadelphia Evening Bulletin*, June 15, 1961; Fellowship Commission, "Report to the Community," November 1960, FC collection, Acc 626, box 53, folder 17, TUUA; "Report to the Community," February 1961, FC collection, Acc 626, box 53, folder 18, TUUA; "Report to the Community," April 1961, FC collection, Acc 626, box 53, folder 18, TUUA; Maurice Fagan, letter to Charles Sunstein, February 1, 1962, FC collection, Acc 626, box 26, folder 5, TUUA; Maurice Fagan, letter to Georges Carousso, July 27, 1962, FC collection, Acc 626, box 27, folder 13, TUUA; Maurice Fagan, letter to Edmund Glazer, July 17, 1962, FC collection, Acc 626, box 27, folder 13, TUUA.

40. E. Washington Rhodes, "The Man of the Year," *Philadelphia Tribune*, January 2, 1960.

41. On the NAACP's limited role in educational issues in the 1950s, see "The Philadelphia Branch in Retrospect for the Past Three and a Half Years," 1957, NAACP collection, URB 6, box 6, folder 151, TUUA; "Annual Report of the Phila. Branch of the NAACP for 1959," 1960, NAACP collection, URB 6, box 30, folder 37, TUUA.

42. Floyd Logan, "Statement to the Governor's Committee on Education," May 24, 1960, FL collection, Acc 469, box 2, folder 18, TUUA.

43. Phillips, "The Struggle for School Desegregation in Philadelphia, 1945–1967," 75. On Logan's efforts to ensure that these policies were implemented, see Floyd Logan, letter to Charles Boehm, January 9, 1961, FL collection, Acc 469, box 3, folder 10, TUUA; Floyd Logan, letter Charles Boehm, April 27, 1962, FL collection, Acc 469, box 3, folder 26, TUUA; EEL, "Report on Meeting with Charles Boehm," February 7, 1961, FL collection, Acc 469, box 3, folder 26, TUUA.

44. Charles Beckett, "Report of the Education Committee for the Months of January and February 1961," March 1961, FL collection, Acc 469, box 29, folder 1, TUUA.

45. Floyd Logan, letter to Allen Wetter, April 20, 1961, Acc 469, box, 4, folder 7, TUUA.

46. Ibid.

47. Cecil Moore, letter to Dr. Charles Boehm, May 29, 1961, FL collection, Acc 469, box 4, folder 7, TUUA.

48. On the New Rochelle case, see Sugrue, *Sweet Land of Liberty*, 190–99; John Kaplan, "New Rochelle, New York," in *Civil Rights U.S.A.: Public Schools, Cities in the North and West, 1962*, United States Commission on Civil Rights (New York: Greenwood Press, 1968), 33–103. On the lawsuits filed against school districts in the North and West after New Rochelle, see Gary Orfield, *Must We Bus? Segregated Schools and National Policy* (Washington, DC: Brookings Institution, 1978), 363–87.

49. Phillips, "The Struggle for School Desegregation in Philadelphia, 1945–1967," 86. On the NAACP's approach to *Chisholm v. Board of Public Education*, see Blaustein, *"Philadelphia, Pennsylvania,"* 111–73; "School Board OKs $15 Million Bond Sale for Construction; Objects to Answering 75 Questions in NAACP Bias Suit," *Philadelphia Evening Bulletin*, January 9, 1963.

50. Orfield, *Must We Bus?* 364.

51. Gittell and Hollander, Six Urban School Districts: A Comparative Study of Institutional Response—Baltimore, Chicago, Detroit, New York, Philadelphia, St. Louis (New York: Praeger, 1968), 26.

52. Phillips, "The Struggle for School Desegregation in Philadelphia, 1945–1967," 117.

53. William Lee Akers, letter to Cecil B. Moore, January 9, 1963, FL collection, Acc 469, box 29, folder 1, TUUA.

54. Phillips, "The Struggle for School Desegregation in Philadelphia, 1945–1967," 118.

55. Matthew Countryman, *Up South: Civil Rights and Black Power in Philadelphia* (Philadelphia: University of Pennsylvania Press, 2006), 149.

56. Ibid., 134.

57. "Summary of the Fifth Meeting of Discussion Group on Negro-Jewish Relationships," June 10, 1963, JCRC collection, box 012, folder 005, PJAC; Philadelphia Fellowship Commission AGEX meeting minutes, January 25, 1954, JCRC collection, box 002, folder 001, PJAC. On the grassroots protests that challenged this educational and employment discrimination, see Thomas Sugrue, "Affirmative Action from Below: Civil Rights, the Building Trades, and the Politics of Racial Equality in the Urban North, 1945–1969," *Journal of American History* 91 (June 2004): 145–73; Countryman, *Up South*, 130–48.

58. Bonaparte, "'Average Joes' Star in Demonstrations."

59. "The Only Thing That We Did Wrong Was to Let Segregation Stay So Long," *Philadelphia Tribune*, May 28, 1963.

60. Countryman, *Up South*, 138–39.

61. "Education Is Vital to Solution of Explosive Civil Rights Struggle," *Philadelphia Tribune*, June 18, 1963.

62. "School Board Doubts Duty in Promoting Integration," *Philadelphia Evening Bulletin*, January 8, 1963; Peter Binzen, "School Board Won't File Plan on Integration," *Philadelphia Evening Bulletin*, July 17, 1963; "School Decision to Contest Suit Vexes Judge," *Philadelphia Inquirer*, July 18, 1963; Peter Binzen, "Facing the Issue: Can the Schools Offset Housing Segregation?" *Philadelphia Evening Bulletin*, July 21, 1963; Lawrence O'Rourke, "School Board to Get Formal Biracial Plan," *Philadelphia Evening Bulletin*, September 8, 1963; Lawrence O'Rourke, "Secret Integration Plan for Schools Disclosed: NAACP Aide OKd It," *Philadelphia Evening Bulletin*, September 12, 1963; Mark Bricklin, "School Board Members Wonder Who's Running Things," *Philadelphia Tribune*, September 14, 1963; Philadelphia Coordinating Council on School Integration, "School Integration Bulletin," September 1963, FL collection, Acc 469, box 37, folder 12, TUUA.

63. Lawrence O'Rourke, "400 Ministers Start 'Direct Action' on Schools," *Philadelphia Evening Bulletin*, September 9, 1963; "Negro Pastors Begin Secret School Action," *Philadelphia Evening Bulletin*, September 10, 1963; Floyd Logan, "Statement on Judge Raymond Pace Alexander's Plea to the 400 Negro Ministers," September 14, 1963, FL collection, Acc 469, box 29, folder 1, TUUA. On Logan's opposition to Walter Biddle Saul's refusal to file the desegregation

plan, see Floyd Logan, letter to Member of the Board of Public Education, August 23, 1963, FL collection, Acc 469, box 29, folder 1, TUUA.

64. Mark Bricklin, "NAACP Wins as School Board Bows to Demands," *Philadelphia Tribune*, September 28, 1963.

65. Mark Bricklin, "NAACP Pickets Continue Despite Bd. Surrender," *Philadelphia Tribune*, October 22, 1963.

66. Mark Bricklin, "Meade School Boycott Spearheads NAACP Victory," *Philadelphia Tribune*, October 22, 1963.

67. Bill Alexander, "Denial of NAACP Pact by Saul Shocks Judge, Moore into Disbelief," *Philadelphia Tribune*, November 9, 1963. On the community meetings to discuss school integration, see Urban League of Philadelphia, "Report on School Integration Forum," October 28, 1963, FL collection, Acc 469, box 43, folder 13, TUUA.

68. "96 School Borders Face Revision to Foster Integration," *Philadelphia Inquirer*, April 1, 1964; "Crippins Calls Boundary Plan 'Not Detailed,'" *Philadelphia Evening Bulletin*, April 2, 1964; Peter Binzen, "Board Discloses New Boundaries for City Schools," *Philadelphia Evening Bulletin*, April 7, 1964; "Boundary Plan Called 'Farce,' 'A Fine Start,'" *Philadelphia Evening Bulletin*, April 8, 1964; School District of Philadelphia, "Is There Room for Me?" [n.d.] [ca. April 1964], FL collection, Acc 469, box 37, folder 22, TUUA; Philadelphia Public School, "Press Release," April 7, 1964, FL collection, Acc 469, box 27, folder 31, TUUA.

69. Bill Alexander, "2 Adversaries Blast Edict as Fraud, Disgrace," *Philadelphia Tribune*, January 14, 1964.

70. "Set Feb 3 Deadline for Pennell Desegregation," *Philadelphia Tribune*, January 25, 1964; Mark Bricklin, "Pennell School Parents to Picket Board of Education," *Philadelphia Tribune*, February 8, 1964; Henry Benjamin, "School Board Has Emergency Meet," *Philadelphia Tribune*, February 1, 1964; Mark Bricklin, "Board of Education Refuses to Take Students from Gaston Church Classes," *Philadelphia Tribune*, March 14, 1964; Coordinating Council on School Integration, "Meeting Minutes," December 9, 1964, FL collection, Acc 469, box 37, folder 12, TUUA; Florence Cohen, open letter, January 2, 1964, FL collection, Acc 469, box 39, folder 5, TUUA; Ogontz Area Neighborhood Association, "Statement on Integration of the Pennell School," November 12, 1963, FL collection, Acc 469, box 39, folder 5, TUUA.

71. Phillips, "The Struggle for School Desegregation in Philadelphia, 1945–1967," 184. On these busing protests, see "Wetter Hears 100 Protest Busing Pupils," *Philadelphia Evening Bulletin*, January 24, 1964; "Crowd Heckles Dr. Wetter on Busing Program," *Philadelphia Inquirer*, February 8, 1964; "School Busing Problem," *Philadelphia Evening Bulletin*, May 31, 1964; Floyd Logan, "Problems in Democracy of Philadelphia Public Schools," August 2, 1965, FL collection, Acc 469, box 15, folder 4, TUUA.

72. Chris Perry, "Episcopal Pastor Blasts D'Ortona's Two-Way Position," *Philadelphia Tribune*, June 6, 1964.

73. Gaeton Fonzi, "Crisis in the Classroom," *Greater Philadelphia Magazine,* January 1964, 30.

74. Ibid., 31, 64.

75. Ibid., 64, 73. On the intersection of gender and race in postwar attacks on welfare, see Jennifer Mittelstadt, *From Welfare to Workfare: The Unintended Consequences of Liberal Reform, 1945–1965* (Chapel Hill: University of North Carolina Press, 2005).

76. Ibid., 64.

77. Ibid., 77.

78. Floyd Logan, "Answer to 'Crisis in the Classroom,'" January 21, 1964, FL collection, Acc 469, box 9, folder 16, TUUA. For the *Philadelphia Tribune*'s coverage of the controversy surrounding the article, see Mark Bricklin, "Educational Equality League Says Article Libels All Tan Youth," *Philadelphia Tribune*, January 14, 1964; Floyd Logan, "Answer to 'Crisis in the Classroom,'" January 28, 1964. On Floyd Logan's opposition to the cultural deprivation paradigm, see Floyd Logan, "Urban Reconstruction: Human Resources," January 1963, RWH collection, box 11, folder 20, AAMP.

79. Phillips, "The Struggle for School Desegregation in Philadelphia, 1945–1967," 138.

80. Floyd Logan, letter to James Tate, July 13, 1964, FL collection, Acc 469, box 2, folder 22, TUUA.

81. Mark Bricklin, "'Negroes Can't Wait for Neighborhoods to Be Integrated,'" *Philadelphia Tribune*, May 16, 1964.

82. Fred Bonaparte, "'Neighborhood Rights Northern Version of States Rights'—NAACP," *Philadelphia Tribune*, May 26, 1964. For similar critiques of neighborhood school groups as segregationists, see "Negro Likens Parents' Group to Racist Unit," *Philadelphia Evening Bulletin*, May 13, 1964.

83. On these white homeowners associations and housing discrimination, see chapter 1.

84. Matthew Lassiter, *The Silent Majority: Suburban Politics in the Sunbelt South* (Princeton: Princeton University Press, 2006), 122–23. On the use of the "freedom of choice" strategy in the South, see Charles Bolton, *The Hardest Deal of All: The Battle over School Integration in Mississippi, 1870–1980* (Jackson: University Press of Mississippi, 2005), 117–66; Kevin Kruse, "The Fight for 'Freedom of Association': Segregationist Rights and Resistance in Atlanta," in *Massive Resistance: Southern Opposition to the Second Reconstruction,* ed. Clive Webb (New York: Oxford University Press, 2005), 99–116.

85. Phillips, "The Struggle for School Desegregation in Philadelphia, 1945–1967," 143.

86. For example, 78 percent of the students were the first generation in their families to pursue post–high school education, and 54 percent of students came from families that were below the city's median income level. And whereas less than 1 percent of students at the University of Pennsylvania and Temple University were black students from Philadelphia high schools, black students made up 23 percent of the community college student body, and Puerto Rican students composed another 2 percent. Community College of Philadelphia, "Progress and Self-Evaluation Report Prepared for the Commission on Institutions of Higher Education, Middle States Association of College and Secondary Schools,

November 1, 1967, Community College (CC) collection, Acc 378.154 C734s1, Community College of Philadelphia Archives (CCPA); Fellowship Commission, "Joint Meeting of the Committee on Opportunities for Higher Education minutes," July 8, 1964, FC collection, Acc 626, box 28, folder 39, TUUA; Community College of Philadelphia, *Civitas, A Yearbook*, June 1967, CC collection, Acc A378.748 C734ci, CCPA.

87. James Clay, "West Philadelphia School's New Gym to Be Named after Floyd Logan," *Philadelphia Tribune*, January 30, 1979.

88. On the Girard College protest, see Countryman, *Up South*, 168–78; Art Peters, "NAACP Girds for Girard College Battle," *Philadelphia Tribune*, January 5, 1965; Mark Bricklin, "1000 Police 'Protect' Girard College from 50 NAACP Pickets," *Philadelphia Tribune*, May 4, 1965; Mark Bricklin and Fred Bonaparte, "Girard College Operating Illegally Leading Constitutional Atty. Says," *Philadelphia Tribune*, May 8, 1965; Mark Bricklin, "No Settlement of Girard College Demonstration in Sight," *Philadelphia Tribune*, May 15, 1965; Ray McCann, "Moore, Woods Lead 1000 on Girard College, *Philadelphia Tribune*, January 5, 1965; Jim Magee, "AMEs Stage 22-Block Girard March," *Philadelphia Tribune*, June 22, 1965; "Experts See City Plan to Integrate Girard Doomed," *Philadelphia Tribune*, September 18, 1965; Jacob Sherman, "NAACP Calls off Girard College Picketing as Lawsuit for 7 N. Phila. Boys Is Filed," *Philadelphia Tribune*, December 18, 1965.

89. On these school protests, see Countryman, *Up South*, 223–57.

90. On Rizzo's opposition to school desegregation efforts, see Orfield, *Must We Bus?* 160, 172, 191–95; Countryman, *Up South*, 255; Fred Hamilton, *Rizzo* (New York: Viking, 1973), 14, 106–10.

91. Orfield, *Must We Bus?* 172.

92. On the Philadelphia school desegregation case, see Orfield, *Must We Bus?* 172–75; Malik Morrison, "An Examination of Philadelphia's School Desegregation Litigation," *Penn GSE Perspectives on Urban Education* 3 (no. 1, 2004); School District of Philadelphia, "News Release: School Desegregation Case Almost 40 Years Old, Comes to End," July 13, 2009, www.phila.k12.pa.us/desegregation/rel-deseg-case-7-09.pdf (accessed August 15, 2010); Valerie Russ, "Today: Hearing to Fight Jim Crow Education in Philly Schools: Officials Agree to Make Improvement Changes in 'Racially Isolated' Schools," *Philadelphia Daily News*, July 13, 2009.

93. Danielle Allen, *Talking to Strangers: Anxieties of Citizenship since Brown v. Board of Education* (Chicago: University of Chicago Press, 2004), 5.

CHAPTER 5

1. Barlow, *Voice Over*, 211. On the importance of radio deejays in black communities, see Brian Ward, *Radio and the Struggle for Civil Rights in the South* (Gainesville: University Press of Florida, 2004); Mark Newman, *Entrepreneurs of Profit and Pride: From Black-Appeal to Radio Soul* (New York: Praeger, 1988); Johnny Otis, *Upside Your Head! Rhythm and Blues on Central Avenue* (Hanover, NH: Wesleyan University Press, 1993); Johnny Otis, *Listen to the Lambs* (1968;

Minneapolis: University of Minnesota Press, 2009); George Lipsitz, *Midnight at the Barrelhouse: The Johnny Otis Story* (Minneapolis: University of Minnesota Press, 2010); Magnificent Montague, *Burn Baby! BURN! The Autobiography of Magnificent Montague* (Urbana: University of Illinois Press, 2003); Richard Stamz, *Give 'Em Soul, Richard! Race, Radio, and Rhythm and Blues in Chicago* (Urbana: University of Illinois Press, 2010); Louis Cantor, *Wheelin' on Beale: How WDIA-Memphis Became the Nation's First All-Black Radio Station and Created the Sound That Changed America* (New York: Pharos Books, 2002).

2. On the development of black-appeal radio, see Barlow, *Voice Over*, 108–33; Newman, *Entrepreneurs of Profit and Pride*, 79–92; Robert Weems, Jr., *Desegregating the Dollar: African American Consumerism in the Twentieth Century* (New York: New York University Press, 1998), 42–55.

3. Jeanne Theoharis and Komozi Woodard, "Introduction," in *Groundwork: Local Black Freedom Movements in America*, ed. Jeanne Theoharis and Komozi Woodard (New York: New York University Press, 2005), 3.

4. Quoted in Barlow, *Voice Over*, 124.

5. Philadelphia deejay Georgie Woods used *rock and roll* to describe the artists who performed at his concerts and the music he played on his radio show. While this music can also be described as rhythm and blues, throughout this chapter I use *rock and roll* because it was the term preferred by Woods and the common term used by the *Philadelphia Tribune*. For example, see Georgie Woods, "Rock and Roll with Georgie Woods," *Philadelphia Tribune*, January 25, 1955; "The George Woods Rock "n Roll Show," *Philadelphia Tribune*, April 23, 1955; "Rock "n Roll," *Philadelphia Tribune*, July 30, 1955.

6. James Spady, *Georgie Woods: I'm Only a Man* (Philadelphia: Snack-Pac Book Division, 1992), 15–19, 40–41; Chris Perry III, "Leading Philly D-J's Writing for Tribune," *Philadelphia Tribune*, January 22, 1955.

7. Georgie Woods, "Rock and Roll with Georgie Woods," *Philadelphia Tribune*, January 25, 1955.

8. "The George Woods Rock 'N Roll Show," *Philadelphia Tribune*, April 23, 1955; "In Person George Woods Rock 'N Roll," *Philadelphia Tribune*, October 8, 1955; Archie Miller, "Fun and Thrills in Philly," *Philadelphia Tribune*, November 29, 1955; "Big Rock and Roll Show at Mastbaum," *Philadelphia Tribune*, December 10, 1955; "All New Rock 'N Roll Show," *Philadelphia Tribune*, December 13, 1955.

9. John Albert, "Georgie Woods' 'Rock and Roll Show' Draws 5,000 at Academy," *Philadelphia Tribune*, October 18, 1955.

10. "Mystery Shrouds Rift between DeeJay George Woods and WHAT," *Philadelphia Tribune*, October 15, 1955; "'King' Woods on New Throne," *Philadelphia Tribune*, January 14, 1956.

11. "Georgie Woods Takes over Top Spot at Station WDAS," *Philadelphia Tribune*, January 24, 1956.

12. Spady, *Georgie Woods*, 94–95.

13. Quoted in John Roberts, *From Hucklebuck to Hip-Hop: Social Dance in the African American Community in Philadelphia* (Philadelphia: Odunde Inc., 1995), 46–47.

14. Guthrie Ramsey Jr., *Race Music: Black Cultures from Bebop to Hip-Hop* (Berkeley: University of California Press, 2003), 4. On dance spaces in Philadelphia, see Benita Brown, "'Boppin' at Miss Mattie's Place': African-American Grassroots Dance Culture in North Philadelphia from the Speakeasy to the Uptown Theater during the 1960s" (Ph.D. diss, Temple University, 1999).

15. "Teen-Agers Welcome Disc Jockeys," *Philadelphia Tribune*, October 12, 1954.

16. "Crediting the Philadelphia Tribune" [Re-Vels picture], *Philadelphia Tribune*, August 2, 1955; "Smiles of Appreciation" [Re-Vels picture], *Philadelphia Tribune*, May 19, 1956; Art Peters, "Huge Crowd Sees Talent Contest at Allen Homes Auditorium," *Philadelphia Tribune*, December 14, 1957; "Guest Artists," *Philadelphia Tribune*, December 17, 1957; "If You're Confused," *Philadelphia Tribune*, June 7, 1958; Dolores Lewis, "Philly Date Line," *Philadelphia Tribune*, October 4, 1958.

17. Weldon McDougal, interviewed by author, March 27, 2006.

18. Anthony Gribin and Matthew Schiff, *Doo-Wop: The Forgotten Third of Rock 'N Roll* (Iola, WI: Krause Publications, 1992)

19. On the development of vocal harmony groups, see Stuart Goosman, *Group Harmony: The Black Urban Roots of Rhythm and Blues* (Philadelphia: University of Pennsylvania Press, 2005); Robert Pruter, *Doowop: The Chicago Scene* (Urbana: University of Illinois Press, 1996); Philip Groia, *They All Sang on the Corner: A Second Look at New York City's Rhythm and Blues Vocal Groups* (New York: Phillie Dee Enterprises, 1983); Montague, *Burn Baby! BURN!* 67.

20. On the *Philadelphia Tribune*'s coverage of local singing groups, see "Appearing in Tribune Home Show" [Guytones picture], *Philadelphia Tribune*, May 22, 1956; "Quintet Hailed by Rock and Roll Fans," *Philadelphia Tribune*, June 9, 1956; "Winners of Talent Show" [the Satellites photo], *Philadelphia Tribune*, March 19, 1957; "Dynatones," *Philadelphia Tribune*, September 11, 1956; "Teen-Age 'Superiors' Debut on M.T. Show," *Philadelphia Tribune*, November 19, 1957; Laurine Blackson, "Penny Sez," *Philadelphia Tribune*, December 3, 1957; Art Peters, "Rosen Homes Teenage Vocal Group Gets Recording Contract," December 21, 1957; "Lee Andrews and the Hearts" [photo], *Philadelphia Tribune*, April 19, 1958; Gil Zimmerman, "Person to Person," *Philadelphia Tribune*, May 3, 1958; "Lee Andrews and the Hearts" [photo], *Philadelphia Tribune*, June 7, 1958; "Fast Rising Vocal Group" [the Five Sounds photo], *Philadelphia Tribune*, February 10, 1959; "The Decisions," *Philadelphia Tribune*, May 5, 1959; "Their Big Day" [Dee Jays photo], *Philadelphia Tribune*, January 12, 1960; Malcolm Poindexter, "Local Vocal Group Sets Their Sights on Stardom," *Philadelphia Tribune*, November 15, 1960; "'The Presidentials' Set Sights on Instrumentals and Vocal Success," *Philadelphia Tribune*, November 29, 1960; "The Da'prees" [photo], *Philadelphia Tribune*, March 25, 1961; "Chirpers" [Joyettes photo], *Philadelphia Tribune*, April 2, 1963; "Big Sound" [the Supremes photo], *Philadelphia Tribune*, April 6, 1963; "The Exceptions," *Philadelphia Tribune*, June 16, 1964; "Members of One of Philly's Swingingest Young Groups" [Bobby and the Lovetones photo], *Philadelphia Tribune*, June 23, 1964.

21. On the recreation activities sponsored by black community centers and religious institutions, see V. P. Franklin, "Operation Street Corner: The Wharton Centre and the Juvenile Gang Problem in Philadelphia," in *W. E. B. Du Bois, Race, and the City: The Philadelphia Negro and Its Legacy,* ed. Michael Katz and Thomas Sugrue (Philadelphia: University of Pennsylvania Press, 1998), 195–215; "Sigma Iota Gamma Sorority" [photo], *Philadelphia Tribune,* November 9, 1957; Theodore Graham, "300 Youths Enjoying St. Matthew's Program," *Philadelphia Tribune,* November 16, 1957; Muriel Bonner, "St. Monica's Teens Have Active Program," *Philadelphia Tribune,* November 23, 1957; Theodore Graham, "300 Youths, Adults Hail Program at Zion Church," *Philadelphia Tribune,* November 30, 1957; Theodore Graham, "Youth Recreation Haven at Tasker Street Church," *Philadelphia Tribune,* December 3, 1957; Theodore Graham, "Program of St. Charles Parish Asset to Youths," *Philadelphia Tribune,* December 10, 1957; Theodore Graham, "Zion Community Center Meeting Youth Challenge," *Philadelphia Tribune,* December 21, 1957; Graham, "Wharton Center Program Has Aided Over 55,000," *Philadelphia Tribune,* December 21, 1957; "Rho Phi Omega Fraternity" [photo], *Philadelphia Tribune,* December 31, 1957; Jack Saunders, "I Love a Parade," *Philadelphia Tribune,* January 14, 1958; Charles Layne, "St. Rita's Rock 'n' Roll Revival a Real Swingeroo," *Philadelphia Tribune,* September 26, 1961.

22. Weldon McDougal interview.

23. Eustace Gay, "Pioneer in TV Field Doing Marvelous Job Furnishing Youth with Recreation," *Philadelphia Tribune,* February 11, 1956; Gary Mullinax, "Radio Guided DJ to Stars," *The News Journal Papers* (Wilmington, DE), January 28, 1986, D4.

24. "The NAACP Reports: WCAM (Radio)," August 7, 1955, NAACP collection, URB 6, box 21, folder 423, TUUA.

25. Otis Givens, interviewed by author, June 27, 2007.

26. Quoted in Roberts, *From Hucklebuck to Hip-Hop,* 37.

27. On the *Philadelphia Tribune*'s "Teen-Talk" coverage of Mitch Thomas's show, see "They're 'Movin' and Groovin,'" *Philadelphia Tribune,* July 31, 1956; Dolores Lewis, "Talking with Mitch," *Philadelphia Tribune,* November 9, 1957; Dolores Lewis, "Stage Door Spotlight," *Philadelphia Tribune,* November 9, 1957; "Teen-Age 'Superiors' Debut on M.T. Show" *Philadelphia Tribune,* November 19, 1957; Laurine Blackson, "Penny Sez," *Philadelphia Tribune,* December 7, 1957; Dolores Lewis, "Philly Date Line," *Philadelphia Tribune,* December 7, 1957; "Queen Lane Apartment Group" [photo], *Philadelphia Tribune,* December 7, 1957; Jimmy Rivers, "Crickets' Corner," *Philadelphia Tribune,* January 21, 1958; Edith Marshall, "Current Hops," *Philadelphia Tribune,* March 1, 1958; Edith Marshall, "Current Hops," *Philadelphia Tribune,* March 8, 1958; Edith Marshall, "Talk of the Teens," *Philadelphia Tribune,* March 22, 1958; Edith Marshall, "Current Hops," *Philadelphia Tribune,* March 22, 1958; Edith Marshall, "Current Hops," *Philadelphia Tribune,* April 5, 1958; Jimmy Rivers, "Crickets' Corner," *Philadelphia Tribune,* April 22, 1958; "Presented in Charity Show" [Mitch Thomas photo], *Philadelphia Tribune,* April 22, 1958; Laurine Blackson, "Penny Sez," *Philadelphia Tribune,* April 26, 1958; Jimmy Rivers, "Crickets' Corner," *Philadelphia Tribune,* April 29, 1958.

28. Art Peters, "Negroes Crack Barrier of Bandstand TV Show," *Philadelphia Tribune*, October 5, 1957; "Couldn't Keep Them Out" [photo], *Philadelphia Tribune*, October 5, 1957; Delores Lewis, "Bobby Brooks' Club Lists 25 Members," *Philadelphia Tribune*, December 14, 1957.

29. On the crossover appeal of black-oriented radio, see Ward, *Radio and the Struggle for Civil Rights in the South*; Barlow, *Voice Over*; Susan Douglas, *Listening In*, 219–55.

30. As noted in chapter one, *The Grady and Hurst Show* was a televised version of Joe Grady and Ed Hurst's *950 Club*. The teens who danced during the *950 Club* radio broadcast influenced WFIL's decision to develop *Bandstand*. On *The Grady and Hurst Show*, see John Jackson, *American Bandstand: Dick Clark and the Making of a Rock 'n' Roll Empire* (New York: Oxford University Press, 1997), 28, 48.

31. "Black Philadelphia Memories," dir. Trudi Brown (WHYY-TV12, 1999).

32. "Teen-Age 'Superiors' Debut on M.T. Show," *Philadelphia Tribune*, November 19, 1957.

33. On Mitch Thomas's concerts, see Archie Miller, "Fun and Thrills," *Philadelphia Tribune*, December 4, 1956; "Rock 'n Roll Show and Dance," *Philadelphia Tribune*, April 19, 1958; "Swingin' the Blues," *Philadelphia Tribune*, August 5, 1958; "Mitch Thomas Show Attracts over 2000," *Philadelphia Tribune*, August 18, 1958; "Don't Miss the Mitch Thomas Rock and Roll Show," *Philadelphia Tribune*, July 2, 1960.

34. Mullinax, "Radio Guided DJ to Stars."

35. Ray Smith, interviewed by author, August 10, 2006.

36. Herbert Howard, *Multiple Ownership in Television Broadcasting* (New York: Arno Press, 1979), 142–47.

37. Ibid.

38. Barlow, *Voice Over*, 129; Giacomo Ortizano, "On Your Radio: A Descriptive History of Rhythm-and-Blues Radio during the 1950s" (Ph.D. diss, Ohio University , 1993), 391–423.

39. Art Peters, "Mitch Thomas Fired from TV Dance Party Job," *Philadelphia Tribune*, June 17, 1958.

40. Howard, Multiple Ownership in Television Broadcasting, 146.

41. Gerry Wilkerson, Broadcast Pioneers of Philadelphia, http://www.geocities.com/broadcastpioneers/whyy1957.html (accessed March 1, 2007).

42. Mullinax, "Radio Guided DJ to Stars."

43. J. Fred MacDonald, *Blacks and White TV: Afro-Americans in Television Since 1948* (Chicago: Nelson-Hall Publishers, 1983), 17–21, 57–64; Jannette Dates, "Commercial Television," in *Split Image: African Americans and the Mass Media*, ed., Jannette Dates and William Barlow (Washington, DC: Howard University Press, 1993), 267–327; Christopher Lehman, *A Critical History of Soul Train on Television* (Jefferson, NC: McFarland & Company, 2008), 28; Stamz, *Give 'Em Soul, Richard!*, 62–63, 77–78; Barlow, *Voice Over*, 98–103; Clarence Williams, "JD Lewis Jr., A Living Broadcasting Legend," *ACE Magazine*, October 2002, http://www.cbc-raleigh.com/capcom/news/2002/corporate_02/williams_lewis_story/williams_lewis_story.htm (accessed August 15, 2010).

44. Jackson, *American Bandstand*, 2–7.

45. Ibid., 30–32.

46. On the protests against rock and roll, see Brian Ward, *Just My Soul Responding: Rhythm and Blues, Black Consciousness, and Race Relations* (Berkeley: University of California, 1998), 90–113; Glenn Altschuler, *All Shock Up: How Rock 'n' Roll Changed America* (New York: Oxford University Press, 2003), 39, 72–77; Linda Martin and Kerry Seagrave, *Anti-Rock: The Opposition to Rock 'n' Roll* (New York: Da Capo Press, 1993), 41–43; "Segregation Wants Ban on 'Rock and Roll,'" *New York Times*, March 30, 1956; George Leonard, "Music or Madness?" *Look*, June 26, 1956, 48; "Rock 'n' Roll," *Time*, July 23, 1956, 34; "White Council vs. Rock and Roll," *Newsweek*, April 23, 1956. On white citizens' councils, see Neil McMillen, *The Citizens' Council: Organized Resistance to the Second Reconstruction, 1954–64* (Urbana: University of Illinois Press, 1994).

47. On the moral panic over juvenile delinquency, see James Gilbert, *A Cycle of Outrage: America's Reaction to the Juvenile Delinquent in the 1950s* (New York: Oxford University Press, 1986); Thomas Doherty, *Teenagers and Teenpics: The Juvenilization of American Movies in the 1950s* (Philadelphia: Temple University Press, 2002), 54–82; David Hadju, *The Ten-Cent Plague: The Great Comic-Book Scare and How It Changed America* (New York: Farrar, Straus and Giroux, 2008). On moral panics and youth more broadly, see Joel Best, *Threatened Children: Rhetoric and Concern about Child-Victims* (Chicago: University of Chicago Press, 1990); Gerard Jones, *Killing Monsters: Why Children Need Fantasy, Super Heroes, and Make-Believe Violence* (New York: Basic Books, 2003); John Springhall, *Youth, Popular Culture, and Moral Panics* (New York: Palgrave Macmillan, 1999).

48. Dick Clark and Richard Robinson, *Rock, Roll and Remember* (New York: Popular Library, 1976), 71.

49. Jackson, *American Bandstand*, 40.

50. Clark, *Rock Roll and Remember*, 71.

51. Ibid., 82.

52. Jackson, *American Bandstand*, 41.

53. Ibid., 50.

54. Christopher Anderson, "Disneyland," in *Television: The Critical View*, 6th ed., ed. Horace Newcomb (New York: Oxford University Press, 2000), 20.

55. Quoted in ibid.," 21; Herman Land, "ABC: An Evaluation," *Television* magazine, December 1957, 94.

56. *The Official Bandstand Yearbook 1957*, [no publication information listed].

57. Jackson, *American Bandstand*, 52.

58. Harry Harris, "WFIL's 'Bandstand' Goes National—Not without Some Strain," *Philadelphia Inquirer*, August 6, 1957; Jackson, *American Bandstand*, 66.

59. Bob Bernstein, "'Bandstand' Sociology but Not Entertainment," *Billboard*, August 12, 1957, 48.

60. J. P. Shanley, "TV: Teen-Agers Only," *New York Times*, August 6, 1957, 42.

61. Lawrence Laurent, "If It's Keen to Teens It Goes on Television," *The Washington Post*, August 10, 1957.

62. George Pitts, "TV's 'American Bandstand' a Noisy Menagerie!" *Pittsburgh Courier*, July 12, 1958.

63. Jackson, *American Bandstand*, 67–68.

64. Richard Peterson, "Why 1955? Explaining the Advent of Rock Music," *Popular Music* 9 (January 1990): 97–116.

65. Jon Hartley Fox, *King of Queen City: The Story of King Records* (Urbana: University of Illinois Press, 2009), 59.

66. On the importance of *American Bandstand* to record sales, see John Broven, *Record Makers and Breakers: Voices of Independent Rock ' n' Roll Pioneers* (Urbana: University of Illinois Press, 2009); Anthony Musso, *Setting the Record Straight: The Music and Careers of Recording Artists from the 1950s and early 1960s . . . in Their Own Words* (Bloomington, IN: Author-House, 2007).

67. Joe Smith, *Off the Record: An Oral History of Popular Music* (New York: Warner Books, 1988), 103; Jackson, *American Bandstand*, 85.

68. On the history of payola, see Kerry Segrave, *Payola in the Music Industry: A History, 1880–1991* (Jefferson, NC: McFarland & Company, 1994).

69. Quoted in David Szatmary, *Rockin' in Time: A Social History of Rock-and-Roll* (Upper Saddle River, NJ: Prentice Hall, 2000), 59.

70. "Newest Music for a New Generation: Rock 'n' Rolls On 'n' On," *Life*, April 18, 1958, 166–68.

71. Quoted in John Jackson, *Big Beat Heat: Alan Freed and the Early Years of Rock & Roll* (New York: Schirmer Books, 1991), 288.

72. Quoted in Jackson, *American Bandstand*, 179.

73. Clark and Robinson, *Rock, Roll and Remember*, 268.

74. Jackson, *American Bandstand*, 182. On the payola hearings, see Segrave, *Payola in the Music Industry*, 100–58; Jackson, *Big Beat Heat*, 238–327; Ward, *Just My Soul Responding*, 161–69.

75. Anthony Lewis, "Dick Clark Denies Receiving Payola; Panel Skeptical," *New York Times*, April 30, 1960, 1.

76. Pete Martin, "I Call on Dick Clark," *Saturday Evening Post*, October 10, 1959, 70.

77. Bill Davidson, "The Strange World of Dick Clark," *Redbook*, March 1960, 111.

78. Jackson, *American Bandstand*, 153–96; Ward, *Just My Soul Responding*, 165; "Guilty Only of Success," *TV Guide*, September 10–16, 1960.

79. Steve Chapple and Reebee Garofalo, *Rock 'n' Roll Is Here to Pay: The History and Politics of the Music Industry* (Chicago: Nelson-Hall, 1977), 57–60; Jackson, *American Bandstand*, 197–98.

80. Chapple and Garofalo, *Rock 'n' Roll Is Here to Pay*, 51.

81. Clark and Robinson, *Rock, Roll and Remember*, 140; Jim Dawson, *The Twist: The Story of the Song and Dance that Changed the World* (Boston: Faber and Faber, 1995), 21–29; Jackson, *American Bandstand*, 170–71, 218.

82. Chapple and Garofalo, *Rock 'n' Roll Is Here to Pay*, 49.

83. Ibid.; Peter Guralnick, *Feel Like Going Home: Portraits in Blues and Rock 'n' Roll* (1971; New York: Little, Brown and Company, 1999), 20.

84. Michael Shore and Dick Clark, *The History of American Bandstand* (New York: Ballantine Books, 1985), 81–84, 127–32.

85. Jackson, *American Bandstand*, 225.

86. On the economics of television reruns in the 1950s and 1960s, see Phil Williams, "Feeding Off the Past: The Evolution of the Television Rerun," in *Television: The Critical View*, 6th ed., ed. Horace Newcomb (New York: Oxford University Press, 2000),, 52–72.

87. Jackson, *American Bandstand*, 227–87.

88. Office of City Representative Division of Public Information Board of Trade and Conventions, The Song of Philadelphia [n.d.] [ca. 1962] (MacDonald and Associates, Chicago).

89. Georgie Woods hosted dozens of concerts from 1956 through 1965 at the Uptown and elsewhere. For a sample of these concerts, see "Disc Jockey's Rock and Roll Show Attracts 4500 Teenagers," *Philadelphia Tribune*, September 11, 1956; "The Biggest Show of Stars for '58," *Philadelphia Tribune*, April 1 and 12, 1958; "Georgie Woods Rock, Roll Show Lures 80,000 Fans to Uptown," *Philadelphia Tribune*, June 10, 1958; "40,000 Teenagers Await Big Uptown Theater Show," *Philadelphia Tribune*, April 18, 1959; "Georgie Woods Presents a Gala Holiday Rock 'n Roll Show at the Uptown Theater," *Philadelphia Tribune*, November 21, 1959; "Georgie Woods Presents 5th Anniv. Rock 'n Roll Show," *Philadelphia Tribune*, November 22, 1960; "Georgie Woods of WDAS Presents All-Star Show," *Philadelphia Tribune*, June 20, 1961; "Georgie Woods 8th Anniversary Rock 'n' Roll Show," *Philadelphia Tribune*, November 20, 1962; "Georgie Woods Presents 9th Anniversary Show," *Philadelphia Tribune*, November 19, 1963; Lucille Alexander, "Pips, Tops, Impressions Impressive in Georgie Woods' Show at Uptown," *Philadelphia Tribune*, June 9, 1964; "Georgie Woods Presents His Rock 'n Roll Convention," *Philadelphia Tribune*, August 25, 1964; "Uptown," *Philadelphia Tribune*, August 28, 1965.

90. Art Peters, "Woods' Rock, Roll 'Thriller' Lures 60,000 to Uptown Theatre," *Philadelphia Tribune*, March 1, 1958.

91. "40,000 Teenagers Await Big Uptown Theater Show," *Philadelphia Tribune*, April 18, 1959.

92. On the record hops that Georgie Woods and Mitch Thomas hosted, see "Teen-Agers Welcome Disc Jockeys," *Philadelphia Tribune*, October 12, 1954; Jimmy Rivers, "Mitch Thomas at Skating Rink," *Philadelphia Tribune*, January 7, 1958; Tommy Curtis, "Elmwood Teenagers," *Philadelphia Tribune*, January 18, 1958; Billy Johnson, "Teen Social Whirl," *Philadelphia Tribune*, January 25, 1958; Jimmy Rivers, "Crickets' Corner," *Philadelphia Tribune*, April 1, 1958; Jimmy Rivers, "Crickets' Corner," *Philadelphia Tribune*, May 6, 1958; Jimmy Rivers, "Crickets' Corner," *Philadelphia Tribune*, May 10, 1958; Gil Zimmerman, "Person to Person," *Philadelphia Tribune*, May 10, 1958; Jimmy Rivers, "Crickets' Corner," *Philadelphia Tribune*, May 13, 1958; Edith Marshall, "Current Hops," *Philadelphia Tribune*, May 17, 1958; Jimmy Rivers, "Crickets' Corner," *Philadelphia Tribune*, May 20, 1958; Jimmy Rivers, "Crickets' Corner,"

Philadelphia Tribune, August 18, 1958; Laurine Blackson, "Penny Sez," *Philadelphia Tribune*, October 4, 1958; Laurine Blackson, "Penny Sez," *Philadelphia Tribune*, December 6, 1958; Jimmy Rivers, "Crickets' Corner," *Philadelphia Tribune*, January 6, 1959; "Fortieth Street Youth Committee Entertained 1200 Children," *Philadelphia Tribune*, January 6, 1959; "'Mobbed by Teenagers,'" *Philadelphia Tribune*, April 18, 1959. On other record hops for black teenagers in the Philadelphia area, see Billy Johnson, "Teen Social Whirl," *Philadelphia Tribune*, April 26, 1958; Muriel Bonner, "Teen Chatter," *Philadelphia Tribune*, September 20, 1958; Veronica Hill, "Jamming with Ronnie," *Philadelphia Tribune*, November 1, 1958; Veronica Hill, "Jamming with Ronnie," *Philadelphia Tribune*, November 22, 1958; Veronica Hill, "Jamming with Ronnie," *Philadelphia Tribune*, January 31, 1959.

93. On these local youth programs, see V. P. Franklin, "Operation Street Corner," in *W. E. B. Du Bois, Race, and the City: The Philadelphia Negro and Its Legacy*, ed. Michael Katz and Thomas Sugrue (Philadelphia: University of Pennsylvania Press, 1998), 195–215.

94. Georgie Woods, "Geo. Woods Says," *Philadelphia Tribune*, September 19, 1959.

95. Ibid.

96. Georgie Woods, "Geo. Woods Says," *Philadelphia Tribune*, October 3, 1959.

97. Georgie Woods, "Geo. Woods Says," *Philadelphia Tribune*, October 10, 1959.

98. Ibid.

99. Woods, "Geo. Woods Says," October 3, 1959.

100. Mark Bricklin, "DJ's Georgie Woods, Reggie Lavong Join Local Businessmen to Establish New Commercial TV Station for Philadelphia, *Philadelphia Tribune*, August 22, 1964; "City's New TV Station Seeks Huge Juice Boost," *Philadelphia Tribune*, January 30, 1965; "Georgie Woods Seventeen Canteen," *Philadelphia Tribune*, October 30, 1965; Masco Young, "The Notebook," *Philadelphia Tribune*, December 14, 1965; Masco Young, "Notebook," *Philadelphia Tribune*, March 1, 1966.

101. Spady, *Georgie Woods*, 114, 120, 162.

102. Quoted in Barlow, *Voice Over*, 206.

103. Art Peters, "'Sermons,' Songs Blend into Revival Atmosphere," *Philadelphia Tribune*, May 18, 1963.

104. Ibid.

105. Ibid.

106. Fred Bonaparte, "'Average Joes' Star in Demonstrations," *Philadelphia Tribune*, May 28, 1963.

107. "NAACP Slates Saturday Rally for Slain Birmingham Girls," *Philadelphia Tribune*, September 21, 1963.

108. Mark Bricklin, "14,000 Jam NAACP Convention Hall Freedom Show; $30,000 Raised," *Philadelphia Tribune*, March 21, 1964; Mark Bricklin, "$16,000 Given to Four Groups at Mon. Lunch," *Philadelphia Tribune*, March 24, 1964. On Leon Sullivan and the Opportunities Industrialization Center, see

Matthew Countryman, *Up South: Civil Rights and Black Power in Philadelphia* (Philadelphia: University of Pennsylvania Press, 2006), 112–19.

109. "Freedom Show of '64" [concert ad], *Philadelphia Tribune*, March 7, 1964.

110. Bricklin, "14,000 Jam NAACP Convention Hall Freedom Show; $30,000 Raised."

111. "Snipers Wound 2 Marchers in Selma Vigil," *Philadelphia Tribune*, March 16, 1965.

112. Mark Bricklin and Jim Magee, "12,000 Ring City Hall in Protest Demonstration," *Philadelphia Tribune*, March 16, 1965.

113. Ibid.

114. Jack Saunders, "Georgie Woods: Disc Jockey, Rights Fighter, Humanitarian," *Philadelphia Tribune*, March 23, 1965.

115. Barlow, *Voice Over*, 207–11. See also Ward, *Radio and the Struggle for Civil Rights in the South*.

116. Countryman, *Up South*, 170. On the concurrent development of the New Left on Philadelphia area college campuses, see Paul Lyons, *The People of This Generation: The Rise and Fall of the New Left in Philadelphia* (Philadelphia: University of Pennsylvania Press, 2003).

117. Ibid., 171.

118. On the Girard College protest, see Countryman, *Up South*, 168–78; Art Peters, "NAACP Girds for Girard College Battle," *Philadelphia Tribune*, January 5, 1965; Mark Bricklin, "1000 Police 'Protect' Girard College from 50 NAACP Pickets," *Philadelphia Tribune*, May 4, 1965; Mark Bricklin and Fred Bonaparte, "Girard College Operating Illegally Leading Constitutional Atty. Says, *Philadelphia Tribune*, May 8, 1965; Mark Bricklin, "No Settlement of Girard College Demonstration in Sight," *Philadelphia Tribune*, May 15, 1965; Ray McCann, "Moore, Woods Lead 1000 on Girard College, *Philadelphia Tribune*, January 5, 1965; Jim Magee, "AMEs Stage 22-Block Girard March," *Philadelphia Tribune*, June 22, 1965; "Experts See City Plan to Integrate Girard Doomed," *Philadelphia Tribune*, September 18, 1965.

119. Jacob Sherman, "NAACP Calls off Girard College Picketing as Lawsuit for 7 N. Phila. Boys Is Filed," *Philadelphia Tribune*, December 18, 1965.

120. John A. Jackson, *A House on Fire: The Rise and Fall of Philadelphia Soul* (New York: Oxford University Press, 2004), 14–16.

121. Kenny Gamble, "Introduction," in James Spady, *Georgie Woods: I'm Only a Man* (Philadelphia: Snack-Pac Book Division, 1992), iii.

122. Ward, *Just My Soul Responding*, 418.

123. Jackson, *A House on Fire*, 92–151; Ward, *Just My Soul Responding*, 418.

124. Gamble, "Introduction," iii.

CHAPTER 6

1. Dick Clark and Richard Robinson, *Rock, Roll and Remember* (New York: Popular Library, 1976), 81.

2. Josh Kun, *Audiotopia: Music, Race, and America* (Berkeley: University of California Press, 2005), 2.

3. Benedict Anderson, *Imagined Communities: Reflections on the Origin and Spread of Nationalism*, rev. ed. (New York: Verso, 1991), 35.

4. Diana Mutz, Impersonal Influence: How Perceptions of Mass Collectives Affect Political Attitudes (Cambridge, UK: Cambridge University Press, 1998), xvi. Quoted in Sarah Igo, The Averaged American: Surveys, Citizens, and the Making of a Mass Public (Cambridge, MA: Harvard University Press, 2007), 12.

5. On the locally televised teenage dance programs that competed with *American Bandstand*, see Tom McCourt and Nabeel Zuberi, "Music on Television," Museum of Broadcast Communications, http://www.museum.tv/archives /etv/M/htmlM/musicontele/musicontele.htm (accessed July 1, 2007); Laura Wexler, "The Last Dance," *Style: Smart Living in Baltimore* magazine, September/ October 2003, 130–35, 166–69; Gary Kenton, "Cool Medium Hot," *Television Quarterly* 36 (Winter 2006): 36–41; Clay Cole, *Sh-Boom! The Explosion of Rock ' n' Roll 1953–1968* (New York: Morgan James Publishing, 2009), 26, 43, 46, 72; Jake Austen, *TV a-Go-Go: Rock on TV from American Bandstand to American Idol* (Chicago: Chicago Review Press, 2005), 42; Matt Schudel, "Milt Grant: Dance Host, TV Station Entrepreneur," *Washington Post*, May 3, 2007; Richard Harrington, "Before Dick Clark, Washington Had Boogied on Milt Grant's Show," *Washington Post*, May 2, 2007; "J. D. Lewis Jr. obituary," *News and Observer* (Raleigh, NC), February 20, 2007; "Bud Davies obituary," *Detroit News*, October 28, 2006; "Bill Craig Jr. obituary," *Star Press* (Muncie, IN), March 23, 2006; "Clark Race Popular Radio DJ and Host of KDKA-TV's 'Dance Party,' " *Pittsburgh Post-Gazette*, July 28, 1999; "David Hull, 66, Host of 'Chicago Band Stand," *Chicago Tribune*, May 4, 1999; "KPTV Premieres High Time, Portland's First Music Show for Teenagers, with Host Ed Gilbert," KPTV (Portland, OR) Timeline, http://home.comcast.net/~kptv/timeline/timeline.htm (accessed July 1, 2007).

6. "Milt Grant Pitches His Show to Sponsors," May 27, 1957, http://www. youtube.com/watch?v=CJLTQ-3Mgik (accessed, October 15, 2010).

7. Michael Shore and Dick Clark, *The History of American Bandstand: It's Got a Great Beat and You Can Dance to It* (New York: Ballantine Books, 1985), 13.

8. "American Bandstand," December 17, 1957 (video recording), Acc T86:0318, Museum of Radio and Television (MTR).

9. Ibid.

10. "American Bandstand," December 18, 1957 (video recording).

11. On the concept of imagined communities, see Anderson, *Imagined Communities*. On the production strategies through which television constructs its national audience, see Victoria Johnson, *Heartland TV: Prime Time Television and the Struggle for U.S. Identity* (New York: New York University Press, 2008); Sasha Torres, *Black, White, and in Color: Television and Black Civil Rights* (Princeton, NJ: Princeton University Press, 2003); Marita Sturken, "Television Vectors and the Making of a Media Event," in *Reality Squared: Televisual Discourse on the Real*, ed. James Friedman (New Brunswick, NJ: Rutgers University Press, 2004), 185–202. For related studies of imagined communities

with respect to radio, see Susan Douglas, *Listening In: Radio and the American Imagination* (Minneapolis: University of Minnesota Press, 2004); Jason Loviglio, *Radio's Intimate Public: Network Broadcasting and Mass-Mediated Democracy* (Minneapolis: University of Minnesota Press, 2005);.

12. *American Bandstand Yearbook, 1958* [no publication information listed].

13. "American Bandstand," December 2, 1957 (video recording), Acc T86:0317, MTR; "American Bandstand," December 17, 1957; "American Bandstand," December 18, 1957.

14. On the development of teenage girls' consumer culture in decades before World War II, see Kelly Schrum, *Some Wore Bobby Sox: The Emergence of Teenage Girls' Culture, 1920–1945* (New York: Palgrave Macmillan, 2006).

15. Louis Kraar, "Teenage Customers: Merchants Seek Teens' Dollars, Influence Now, Brand Loyalty Later," *Wall Street Journal*, December 6, 1956, 1, 11.

16. Schrum, *Some Wore Bobby Sox*, 2. On Eugene Gilbert, see Dwight MacDonald, "A Caste, A Culture, and A Market—I," *New Yorker*, November 22, 1958; James Gilbert, *A Cycle of Outrage: America's Reaction to the Juvenile Delinquent in the 1950s* (New York: Oxford University Press, 1986, 205–10; Eugene Gilbert, *Advertising and Marketing to Young People* (Pleasantville, NY: Printers' Ink Books, 1957); Grace Palladino, *Teenagers: An American History* (New York: Basic Books, 1996), 96–115.

17. Gilbert, Advertising and Marketing to Young People, 4.

18. Igo, *The Averaged American*, 4, 18.

19. "Challenging the Giants," *Newsweek*, December 23, 1957, 70.

20. *American Bandstand*, December 18, 1957.

21. On interpolated television advertising in this era, see Lawrence Samuel, *Brought to You By: Postwar Television Advertising and the American Dream* (Austin: University of Texas Press, 2001); Susan Murray, *Hitch Your Antenna to the Stars: Early Television and Broadcast Stardom* (New York: Routledge, 2005); and Lynn Spigel, *Make Room for TV: Television and the Family Ideal in Postwar America* (Chicago: University of Chicago Press, 1992).

22. Clark, *Rock, Roll and Remember*, 112–13.

23. Melvin Maddocks, "Television," *Christian Science Monitor*, May 29, 1958.

24. "American Bandstand: Review," *TV Guide*, October 19, 1957, 3; John Jackson, *American Bandstand: Dick Clark and the Making of a Rock 'n' Roll Empire* (New York: Oxford University Press, 1997), . 69

25. On the construction of women as the ideal consumers in the 1950s, see Haralovich, "Sit-Coms and Suburbs: Positioning the 1950s Homemaker," in *Private Screenings: Television and the Female Consumer*, ed. Lynn Spigel and Denise Mann (Minneapolis: University of Minnesota Press, 1992), 111–41.

26. "American Bandstand: Review," 22–23.

27. Arlene Sullivan, interviewed by author, July 7, 2006.

28. Pat Molittieri, "My Farewell to Bandstand," *Teen*, June 1959. For other *American Bandstand* coverage, see *Teen Magazine Presents—My Bandstand Buddies*, 1959; *Teen Magazine Presents—My Bandstand Blast!* 1960; *Teen* magazine, August 1958, November 1958, February 1959, June 1959, October 1959, December 1960.

29. "Meet 'Bandstand's Dance Queen," 'Teen, June 1959.

30. American Bandstand Yearbook, 1958

31. Ray Smith, interviewed by author, August 10, 2006. In a documentary about the dance the Twist, Jimmy Peatross and Joan Buck tell a related story about learning how to do the Strand from black teenagers. Twist, dir. Ron Mann (Sphinx Productions, 1992).

32. Gary Mullinax, "Radio Guided DJ to Stars," The News Journal Papers (Wilmington, DE), January 26, 1986.

33. "Black Philadelphia Memories," dir. Trudi Brown (WHYY-TV12, 1999).

34. On the black dance cultures out of which dances like the Stroll emerged, see Katrina Hazzard-Gordon, Jookin': The Rise of Social Dance Formations in African-American Culture (Philadelphia: Temple University Press, 1990); Lynne Fauley Emery, Black Dance from 1619 to Today, 2nd rev. ed. (Hightstown, NJ: Princeton Book Company, 1988); Barbara Glass, African American Dance (Jefferson, NC: McFarland & Company, 2006). On teen dances like the Stroll, see Tim Wall, "Rocking around the Clock: Teenage Dance Fads from 1955 to 1965" in Ballroom, Boogie, Shimmy Sham, Shake: A Social and Popular Dance Reader, ed. Julie Malnig (Urbana: University of Illinois Press, 2009).

35. Quoted in Jackson, American Bandstand, 211. Clark also discusses the Stroll in his autobiography, see Clark and Robinson, Rock, Roll, and Remember, 133–36.

36. American Bandstand, December 17, 1957.

37. Mullinax, "Radio Guided DJ to Stars."

38. On ethnicity in early and mid-1950s network television, see George Lipsitz, Time Passages: Collective Memory and American Popular Culture (Minneapolis: University of Minnesota Press, 1990), 39–75.

39. Arlene Sullivan interview.

40. Frank Spagnuola, interviewed by author, July 27, 2006.

41. Shore and Clark, The History of American Bandstand, 39.

42. Francis Ianni, "The Italo-American Teen-Ager," Annals of the American Academy of Political and Social Science, 338 (November 1961): 78.

43. Thomas Guglielmo, White on Arrival: Italians, Race, Color, and Power in Chicago, 1890–1945 (New York: Oxford University Press, 2004), 6–13.

44. Thomas Guglielmo, "'No Color Barrier': Italians, Race, and Power, in the United States," in Are Italians White? How Race Is Made in America, ed. Jennifer Guglielmo and Salvatore Salerno (New York: Routledge, 2003), 41.

45. Jordan Stanger-Ross, Staying Italian: Urban Change and Ethnic Life in Postwar Toronto and Philadelphia (Chicago: University of Chicago Press, 2009); Stefano Luconi, From Paesani to White Ethnics: The Italian Experience in Philadelphia (Albany: State University of New York Press, 2001); Carmen Teresa Whalen, From Puerto Rico to Philadelphia: Puerto Rican Workers and Postwar Economies (Philadelphia: Temple University Press, 2001); Matthew Countryman, Up South: Civil Rights and Black Power in Philadelphia (Philadelphia: University of Pennsylvania Press, 2006).

46. Anita Messina, interviewed by author, June 29, 2006.

47. Carmella Gullon (Mulloy), interviewed by author, July 24, 2006.

48. Christopher Small, *Musicking: The Meanings of Performance and Listening* (Hanover, NH: Wesleyan University Press, 1998), 13.

49. Darlina Burkhart (McCormick), interviewed by author, June 14, 2006.

50. Anita Messina interview.

51. Ray Smith interview; Anita Messina interview; Carmella Gullon (Mulloy) interview; Dick Clark and Fred Bronson, *Dick Clark's American Bandstand* (New York: Collins Publishers, 1997), 27; Francis Burke, "Stonehurst Priest's Social Center Marks 3 Years of Success in Youth Guidance," *Philadelphia Evening Bulletin*, December 6, 1959.

52. Carmella Gullon (Mulloy) interview.

CHAPTER 7

1. My approach to the study of historical memory is influenced by Renee Romano and Leigh Raiford, eds., *The Civil Rights Movement in American Memory* (Athens: University of Georgia Press, 2006).

2. Joan Cannady (Countryman), interviewed by author, February 27, 2006.

3. Iona Stroman (Billups), interviewed by author, July 16, 2007.

4. Weldon McDougal, interviewed by author, March 27, 2006.

5. Julian Bond, "The Media and the Movement," in *Media, Culture, and the Modern African American Freedom Struggle*, ed. Brian Ward (Gainesville: University Press of Florida, 2001), 27.

6. On the coverage of *American Bandstand* in the black press, see "Dick Clark 'Bandstand' Spotlights Sepia Aces," *Chicago Defender*, August 8, 1959; "TV Guide," *New York Amsterdam News*, February 28, 1959; "Television Program," *Atlanta Daily World*, November 21, 1957; "Tonight's Pix-Viewing," *Chicago Daily Defender*, May 12, 1959; "Dick Clark Spotlight James Brown's Flames," *Chicago Defender*, October 29, 1960; "Dick Clark TV Guests 'Names,'" *Chicago Defender*, January 14, 1961; "TV Guide," *New York Amsterdam News*, February 18, 1961; "Bobby Bland Set for 'American Bandstand,'" *Chicago Daily Defender*, March 15, 1961; "TV Guide," *New York Amsterdam News*, March 25, 1961; "TV Tapes," *Chicago Daily Defender*, August 7, 1961; "What's on TV?" *New York Amsterdam News*, December 9, 1961; "TV Hi-Lites," *Philadelphia Tribune*, March 13, 1962; "TV Hi-Lites," *Philadelphia Tribune*, March 17, 1962; "TV Hi-Lites," *Philadelphia Tribune*, June 28, 1962.

7. Walter Palmer, interviewed by author, June 29, 2007.

8. Ibid.; CHR, "Present Status of Current 'C' Cases," May 4, 1954, CHR collection, Box A-2860, folder 148.2 "Minutes 1953–1957," PCA; CHR, "Intergroup Tensions in Recreation Facilities," March 7, 1955, NAACP collection, URB 6, box 4, folder 104, TUUA. On these efforts to integrate *Bandstand* in the early 1950s, see chapter one.

9. Art Peters, "No Negroes on Bandstand Show, TV Boss Says They're Welcome," *Philadelphia Tribune*, September 22, 1956.

10. Ibid.

11. Danielle Allen, *Talking to Strangers: Anxieties of Citizenship since Brown v. Board of Education* (Chicago: University of Chicago Press, 2004), 4.

12. Stroman (Billups) interview.

13. On the controversy of interracial dancing on Alan Freed's show, see John A. Jackson, *Big Beat Heat: Alan Freed and the Early Years of Rock and Roll* (New York: Schirmer Books, 1991), 168–69. On the related concerns over interracial themes in film, see Susan Courtney, *Hollywood Fantasies of Miscegenation: Spectacular Narratives of Gender and Race, 1903–1967* (Princeton: Princeton University Press, 2005).

14. Gael Greene, "Dick Clark," *New York Post*, September 24, 1958.

15. "Mr. Clark and Colored Payola," *New York Age*, December 5, 1959, 6.

16. Johnny Otis, "Johnny Otis Says Let's Talk," *Los Angeles Sentinel*, January 28, 1960; Masco Young, "They're Talking About," *Philadelphia Tribune*, February 20, 1960.

17. Arlene Sullivan, interviewed by author, July 6, 2006.

18. Joe Fusco, interviewed by author, August 8, 2006.

19. Ray Smith, interviewed by author, August 10, 2006.

20. "Teen Agers Claim Discrimination on Clark's Band Stand," *Philadelphia Tribune*, September 8, 1959; "Girl, 14, Says She, Friends Were Barred from Dick Clark TV Show," *Philadelphia Tribune*, October 21, 1961.

21. Dorthy Anderson, "Strictly Politics," *Philadelphia Tribune*, December 23, 1958; "Readers Say: 'All the Uncle Toms Have Moved up North,'" *Philadelphia Tribune*, July 12, 1960; "Teenagers Talented," *Philadelphia Tribune*, April 2, 1963; E. Washington Rhodes, "Where Are the Parents of 'Bandstand's' Youth?" *Philadelphia Tribune*, January 14, 1958; "Tribune Readers Say: Stop Imitating Others' Errors," *Philadelphia Tribune*, February 4, 1958; "Tribune's Open Forum," *Philadelphia Tribune*, January 2, 1960; "Readers Say: Protests Same Old White Faces on Dick Clark TV Show," *Philadelphia Tribune*, June 17, 1961.

22. Henry Gordon, interviewed by author, June 6, 2006.

23. "dick clark media archives," http://www.dickclarklicensing.com (accessed October 15, 2010).

24. The list of available clips from *American Bandstand* in this era include "American Bandstand," December 2, 1957 (video recording), Acc T86:0317, Museum of Television and Radio (MTR); "American Bandstand," December 17, 1957 (video recording), Acc T86:0318, MTR; "American Bandstand: 25th Anniversary," February 4, 1977 (video recording), Acc T79:0274, MTR; "American Bandstand: 40th Anniversary," May 13, 1992 (video recording), Acc B:25885, MTR; "American Bandstand: 50th Anniversary," May 3, 2002 (video recording), Acc B:71426, MTR; *Twist*, dir. Ron Mann (Sphinx Productions, 1992); *Bandstand Days* (Teleduction, 1997); *American Dreams*, dir. Jonathan Prince (Universal Studios, 2004; DVD, 7 discs). The "Bandstand Moments" DVD included with the 50th Anniversary boxed set only includes footage from the period after the show moved to Los Angeles.

25. One of the pictures appears in both of Dick Clark's histories of the show, see Michael Shore and Dick Clark, *The History of American Bandstand: It's Got a Great Beat and You Can Dance to It* (New York: Ballantine Books, 1985), 46; Dick Clark and Fred Bronson, *Dick Clark's American Bandstand* (New York: Collins Publishers, 1997), 56–57. The second picture is in the 50th

Anniversary boxed set booklet; see Bronson, *Dick Clark's American Bandstand 50th Anniversary*, 40.

26. Richard Robinson and Dick Clark, *Dick Clark 20 Years of Rock 'n' Roll Yearbook* (New York: Buddah Records, Inc., 1973).

27. Clark, *Rock, Roll, and Remember*, 110–12.

28. Lawrence Redd, *Rock Is Rhythm and Blues: The Impact of Mass Media* (Lansing: Michigan State University, 1974); Peter Guralnick, *Feel Like Going Home: Portraits in Blues and Rock 'n' Roll* (New York: Vintage Book, 1971); Steve Chapple and Reebee Garofalo, *Rock 'n' Roll Is Here to Pay: The History and Politics of the Music Industry* (Chicago: Nelson-Hall, 1977), 231–69; Stephen Walsh, "Black-Oriented Radio and the Civil Rights Movement," in *Media, Culture, and the Modern African American Freedom Struggle*, ed. Brian Ward, 67–81; Brian Ward, *Just My Soul Responding: Rhythm and Blues, Black Consciousness, and Race Relations* (Berkeley: University of California, 1998), 339–450.

29. Ben Fong-Torres, "'Soul Train' vs. Dick Clark; Battle of the Bandstands," *Rolling Stone*, June 7, 1973, 10.

30. Stanley Williford, "Don Cornelius, Dick Clark Feud Ends," *Los Angeles Sentinel*, June 7, 1993. On the competition between *American Bandstand* and *Soul Train*, see Christopher Lehman, *A Critical History of Soul Train on Television* (Jefferson, NC: McFarland & Company, 2008); John Jackson, *American Bandstand: Dick Clark and the Making of a Rock 'n' Roll Empire* (New York: Oxford University Press, 1997), 255–80; Christine Acham, *Revolution Televised: Prime Time and the Struggle for Black Power* (Minneapolis: University of Minnesota Press, 2004), 54–84.

31. Dick Clark with Allen Daniel Goldblatt, *Dick Clark Remembers 25 Years of Rock 'n' Roll, Happy Days, and American Bandstand* (Hopkins, MN: Imperial House, 1979), 11.

32. Henry Schipper, "Dick Clark," *Rolling Stone*, April 19, 1990, 126

33. Jackson, *American Bandstand*, 140–41.

34. Clark and Bronson, *Dick Clark's American Bandstand*, 19, 21. Clark's coauthor, Fred Bronson, repeats parts of this quotation in *Dick Clark's American Bandstand 50th Anniversary* (2007).

35. Dick Clark, "Behind the Scenes at Bandstand" in *American Bandstand the Rock 'n' Roll Years: 1956–1962* (New York: AMI Specials, Inc., 2003).

36. Andrew Goodman, "Dick Clark, Still the Oldest Living Teenager," *New York Times*, March 25, 2011.

37. Clark and Bronson, *Dick Clark's American Bandstand*, 10.

38. Ibid., 10–24.

39. Matthew Countryman, *Up South: Civil Rights and Black Power in Philadelphia* (Philadelphia: University of Pennsylvania Press, 2006).

40. On the racial discrimination in housing and neighborhood housing fights, see CHR, "A Report on the Housing of Negro Philadelphians," 1953, CHR collection, box A-620, folder 148.4, PCA; ACA; "To Residents of This Section of West Phila.," March 1955, FC collection, Acc 626, box 61, folder 34, TUUA; ACA, "Help!! Help!!" May 19, 1955, FC collection, Acc 626, box 61, folder 34, TUUA.

41. On the racial discrimination in youth recreation, see "Investigation of Skating Rink: Interim Report," 1952, NAACP collection, URB 6, box 20, folder 383, TUUA; Spence Coxe, letter to Joseph Barnes, December 12, 1952, NAACP collection, URB 6, box 20, folder 383, TUUA; CHR, "Recommendation for Closing Case: Concord Skating Rink," January 11, 1955, CHR collection, Box A-2860, folder 148.2 "Minutes 1953–1957," PCA; Commission of Human Relations, Meeting Minutes, September 21, 1953, CHR collection, Box A-2860, folder 148.2 "Minutes 1953–1957," PCA; "NAACP Radio Report on WCAM," September 27, 1953, NAACP collection, URB 6, box 21, folder 421, TUUA; West Philadelphia Fellowship Council, Minutes, October 27, 1953, FC collection, Acc 626, box 61, folder 36, TUUA; CHR, "Minutes of Meeting on Skating Rink Project," March 30, 1954, NAACP collection, URB 6, box 21, folder 421, TUUA; CHR, "Minutes of Meeting on Skating Rink Project," March 30, 1954, NAACP collection, URB 6, box 20, folder 383, TUUA; CHR, "Recommendation for Closing Case: Crystal Palace Roller Skating Rink," January 19, 1955, CHR collection, Box A-2860, folder 148.2 "Minutes 1953–1957," PCA; "Recommendation for Closing Case: Concord Skating Rink;" CHR, Annual Report, 1954, CHR collection, Box A-620, folder 148.1, PCA.

42. Matthew Frye Jacobson, "'Richie' Allen, Whitey's Ways, and Me: A Political Education in the 1960s," in *In the Game: Race, Identity, and Sports in the Twentieth Century*, ed. Amy Bass (New York: Palgrave Macmillan, 2005), 19–46; William Kashatus, *September Swoon: Richie Allen, the '64 Phillies, and Racial Integration* (University Park: Penn State University Press, 2004).

43. On school segregation in Philadelphia, see Philadelphia Board of Education, Division of Research, "A Ten-Year Summary of the Distribution of Negro Pupils in the Philadelphia Public Schools, 1957–1966," December 23, 1966, FL collection, Acc 469, box 23, folder 6, TUUA; "Number of Negro Teachers and Percentage of Negro Students in Philadelphia Senior High Schools, 1956–1957" [n.d.], FL collection, Acc 469, box 14, folder 10, TUUA.

44. James Baughman, *Same Time, Same Station: Creating American Television, 1948–1961* (Baltimore: Johns Hopkins University Press, 2007), xiii.

45. Jackson, *Big Beat Heat*, 168–69.

46. Miscegenation laws remained in place in seventeen southern states until they were overturned by the U.S. Supreme Court's decision in *Loving v. Virginia* (1967). Additionally, a number of other states repealed their laws before *Loving*, but after *American Bandstand* started broadcasting nationally: California (1959), Nevada (1959), Idaho (1959), Arizona (1962), Nebraska (1963), Utah (1963), Indiana (1965), and Wyoming (1965).

47. On miscegenation laws, see Peggy Pascoe, *What Comes Naturally: Miscegenation Law and the Making of Race in America* (New York: Oxford University Press, 2009); Fay Botham, *Almighty God Created the Races: Christianity, Interracial Marriage, and American Law* (Chapel Hill: University of North Carolina Press, 2009); Jane Dailey, "Sex, Segregation, and the Sacred after Brown," *Journal of American History* 91 (June 2004), 119–44.

48. Dailey, "Sex, Segregation, and the Sacred after Brown," 125.

49. New York deejay Clay Cole suggests that his locally broadcast *Clay Cole Show* (1959–68) was racially integrated, but he does not indicate when this in-

tegration began, and I was unable to verify his memory with other sources. See Clay Cole, *Sh-Boom: The Explosion of Rock 'n' Roll, 1953–1968* (New York: Morgan James, 2009), 55, 186.

50. Otis, "Johnny Otis Says Let's Talk."

51. Jacquelyn Dowd Hall, "The Long Civil Rights Movement and the Political Uses of the Past," *Journal of American History* 91 (March 2005): 1235.

CHAPTER 8

1. *Dick Clark's American Bandstand 50th Anniversary* (12 compact discs; Time Life; 2007); "Dick Clark's American Bandstand 50th Anniversary," http://www.timelife.com/webapp/wcs/stores/servlet/ProductDisplay?catalogId =10001&storeId=1001&langId=-1&productId=10506 (accessed January 10, 2008).

2. On the fiftieth anniversary coverage of *American Bandstand*, see Ken Emerson, "The Spin on 'Bandstand,'" *Los Angeles Times*, August 5, 2007, M9; David Hinckley, "50 Years Ago, Show Put Rock Squarely in the Mainstream," *New York Daily News*, August 4, 2007, 67.

3. David Lieberman, "Dan Snyder Buys Dick Clark's TV, Music Company," *USA Today*, June 19, 2007, 2B.

4. Thomas Heath and Howard Schneider, "Snyder Adds a TV Icon to His Empire," *Washington Post*, June 20, 2007, D01.

5. Rick Kissell, "Peacock 'Dreams' up Powerful Sunday Perf," *Daily Variety*, October 8, 2002, 4; Stephen Battaglio, "CBS Pulls out a Narrow Nielsen Victory: NBC Still Leads Youth Market," *New York Daily News*, November 6, 2002, 99; Gail Shister, "Competition May Kill 'Dreams,' Despite Critics' Acclaim," *Philadelphia Inquirer*, February 7, 2004, C5.

6. *Hairspray* box office data, http://www.the-numbers.com/movies/2007/ HAIRS.php (accessed October 15, 2010); Pamela McClintock, "'Hairspray' Sings Its Way to Top 5 Overseas," *Variety*, September 30, 2007, 16; John Dempsey, "'Hairspray' Gets USA All Lathered Up," *Daily Variety*, October 5, 2007, 5; Susan King, "If You Want Some More 'Hairspray,'" *Los Angeles Times*, November 5, 2007, E2; Cristoph Mark, "'Hairspray' Cast Gels in New Production," *The Daily Yomiuri* (Tokyo), October 19, 2007, 14; Ong Sor Fern, "Hairspray Has Heart," *The Straits Times* (Singapore), August 22, 2007; Karen Price, "Major New Role for Ball as Broadway Smash 'Hairspray' Prepares to Hit London's West End," *The Western Mail* (London), June 23, 2007, 3; "Bit of Bounce," *The Irish Times*, July 13, 2007, 10; Fiona Byrne, "Hairspray Premiere—South Yarra," *Sunday Herald Sun* (Australia), 177.

7. For a selection of the film reviewers who likened the *Corny Collins Show* to *American Bandstand*, see Susan King, "If You Want Some More *Hairspray*," *Los Angeles Times*, November 20, 2007, E2; David Ansen, "'Hairspray' Is a Plus-Size Pleasure," *Newsweek*, July 23, 2007, http://www.newsweek.com/id /33063 (accessed September 15, 2007); Randy Cordova, "Hairspray," *The Arizona Republic*, July 20, 2007, http://www.azcentral.com/ent/movies/articles /0720hairspray0720.html (accessed September 15, 2007); Dana Stevens, "Not a Drag," *Slate.com*, July 19, 2007, http://www.slate.com/id/2170730/nav/tap3/

(accessed September 15, 2007); Steve Persall, "'Hairspray' Sticks with Success," *St. Petersburg Times* (Florida), July 19, 2007, 22W.

8. Fred Bronson, *Dick Clark's American Bandstand 50th Anniversary* (New York: Time Life, 2007), 9.

9. My use of the term *mediated history* is influenced by Steve Anderson, "Loafing in the Garden of Knowledge: History TV and Popular Memory" *Film and History* 30, no.1 (March 2000): 14–23; Gary Edgerton, ed., *Television Histories: Shaping Collective Memory in the Media Age* (Lexington: University Press of Kentucky, 2001); Derek Kompare, *Rerun Nation: How Repeats Invented American Television* (New York: Routledge, 2005); George Lipsitz, *Time Passages: Collective Memory and American Popular Culture* (Minneapolis: University of Minnesota Press, 1990); Robert Rosenstone, *History on Film/Film on History* (Harlow, UK: Pearson, 2006); Lynn Spigel, "From the Dark Ages to the Golden Age: Women's Memories and Television Reruns," *Screen* 36, no.1 (Spring 1995): 16–33.

10. "'Pilot' Commentary with Executive Producer Dick Clark and Creator and Executive Producer Jonathan Prince," in *American Dreams*, dir. Jonathan Prince (Universal Studios, 2004) (DVD, 7 discs), disc 1.

11. Quoted in Mark O'Donnell et. al., *Hairspray: The Roots* (New York: Faber and Faber, 2003), 92.

12. Caryn James, "For Fall, TV Looks Back, and Back," *New York Times*, May 18, 2002, B7-8; Jeff Giles, "American Dreams," *Newsweek*, September 16, 2002.

13. Lynn Spigel, "Entertainment Wars: Television Culture after 9/11," *American Quarterly* 56, no. 2 (June 2004).

14. Michiko Kakutani, "And Now, Back to Our Regularly Scheduled Programming," *New York Times*, September 11, 2002, 35.

15. Marita Sturken, *Tourists of History: Memory, Kitsch, and Consumerism from Oklahoma City to Ground Zero* (Durham, NC: Duke University Press, 2007), 7.

16. Malini Johar Schueller, "The Borders and Limits of American Studies: A Picture from Beirut," *American Quarterly* 6,. no. 4 (December 2009): 843; Sunaina Maira, *Missing: Youth, Citizenship, and Empire after 9/11* (Durham, NC: Duke University Press, 2009); Evelyn Alsultany, "Selling American Diversity and Muslim American Identity through Nonprofit Advertising Post-9/11," *American Quarterly* 59, no. 3 (September 2007): 593–622; Ashley Dawson and Malini Johar Schueller, eds., *Exceptional State: Contemporary U.S. Culture and the New Imperialism* (Durham, NC: Duke University Press, 2007).

17. Herman Gray, "Remembering Civil Rights: Television, Memory, and the 1960s," in *The Revolution Wasn't Televised: Sixties Television and Social Conflict*, ed. Lynn Spigel and Michael Curtin (New York: Routledge, 1997), 356.

18. Ibid., 353.

19. Jacquelyn Dowd Hall, "The Long Civil Rights Movement and the Political Uses of the Past," *Journal of American History* 91, no. 4 (March 2005): 1237. Among other studies on the use of color-blind rhetoric to justify racial inequality, see Hazel Rose Markus and Paula Moya, "Doing Race: An Introduction," in *Doing Race: 21 Essays for the 21st Century*, ed. Hazel Rose Markus

and Paul Moya (New York: W.W. Norton & Company, 2010); Eduardo Bonilla-Silva, *Racism without Racists: Color-Blind Racism and the Persistence of Racial Inequality in the United States* (New York: Rowman & Littlefield Publishers, 2010).

20. Jonathan Prince, "National Association of Broadcasters Keynote Address," April 18, 2005. See also Carla Hay, "Music and Showbiz," *Billboard*, September 7, 2002; Carla Hay, "Sound Tracks," *Billboard*, October 26, 2002.

21. On *I'll Fly Away* and *Homefront*, see Mimi White, "'Reliving the Past Over and Over Again,': Race, Gender, and Popular Memory in Homefront and I'll Fly Away," in *Living Color: Race and Television in the United States*, ed. Sasha Torres (Durham, NC: Duke University Press, 1998), 118–39. On other television civil rights dramas in this era, see Jennifer Fuller, "Recovering the Past: Race, Nation, and Civil Rights Drama in the Nineties" (Ph.D. diss., University of Wisconsin-Madison, 2004).

22. John Levesque, "'American Dreams' Strikes Timely Chord," *Seattle Post-Intelligencer*, July 26, 2002.

23. "New Frontier," in *American Dreams*, disc 1.

24. Ibid.

25. On the struggle over the memory of segregation on *American Bandstand*, see chapter 7.

26. Jonathan Storm, "Philadelphia Dreamin' (out in L.A.)," *Philadelphia Inquirer*, January 4, 2004, H1.

27. On the North Philadelphia riot, see Leonora Berson, *Case Study of a Riot: The Philadelphia Story* (New York: Institute of Human Relations Press, 1966); Matthew Countryman, *Up South: Civil Rights and Black Power in Philadelphia* (Philadelphia: University of Pennsylvania Press, 2006), 154–64.

28. The original performance of "Jenny Take a Ride" by Mitch Ryder and the Detroit Wheels took place in January 1966. Michael Shore and Dick Clark, *The History of American Bandstand: It's Got a Great Beat and You Can Dance to It* (New York: Ballantine Books, 1985), 135.

29. "Past Imperfect," in *American Dreams*, disc 5; "The Carpet Baggers," in *American Dreams*, disc 5.

30. "City on Fire," in *American Dreams*, disc 7.

31. "'City on Fire' Commentary with Executive Producer Dick Clark and Creator and Executive Producer Jonathan Prince," in *American Dreams*, disc 7.

32. Ibid.

33. Ibid.

34. Ibid.

35. Jennifer Hochschild, *Facing Up to the American Dream: Race, Class, and the Soul of the Nation* (Princeton, NJ: Princeton University Press, 1995), 55.

36. Darren K. Carlson, "Civil Rights: A Profile in Profiling," *Gallop*, July 9, 2002, http://www.gallup.com/poll/6361/civil-rights-profile-profiling.aspx (accessed October 15, 2010).

37. On how race and class shaped ways of seeing the 1992 Los Angeles riots, see Darnell Hunt, *Screening the Los Angeles 'Riots': Race, Seeing, and Resistance* (New York: Cambridge University Press, 1997).

38. Gray, "Remembering Civil Rights," 351.

39. "'City on Fire' Commentary with Executive Producer Dick Clark and Creator and Executive Producer Jonathan Prince," in *American Dreams*, disc 7.

40. Barry Goldwater, "Peace through Strength: Private Property, Free Competition, Hard Work," *Vital Speeches of the Day* 30 (October 1, 1964): 746.

41. Gerald Horne, *The Fire This Time: The Watts Uprising and the 1960s* (Charlottesville: University of Virginia Press, 1995); Steve Macek, *Urban Nightmares: The Media, the Rights, and the Moral Panic over the City* (Minneapolis: University of Minnesota Press, 2006), xii.

42. George Lipsitz, "Foreword," in *Listening to the Lambs*, Johnny Otis (1968; Minneapolis: University of Minnesota Press, 2009), ix.

43. Laura Wexler, "The Last Dance," *Style: Smart Living in Baltimore*, September/October 2003, 130–35; 166–69; John Waters, *Crackpot: The Obsessions of John Waters* (New York: Macmillan Publishing Company, 1986), 97; "The Roots of Hairspray," in *Hairspray*, dir. Adam Shankman (New Line, 2007; DVD, 2 discs), disc 2; "Buddy Dean, 78, TV Host and Inspiration of 'Hairspray,'" *New York Times*, July 27, 2003, N30.

44. Wexler, "The Last Dance," 167.

45. Aljean Harmetz, "John Waters Cavorts in the Mainstream," *New York Times*, February 21, 1988, 84.

46. *Hairspray* was reviewed more widely and, in general, more favorably than Waters's earlier films. On these reviews, see Julie Salamon, "On Film: 'Hairspray' and 'Frantic,'" *Wall Street Journal*, February 1988, 24; Alan Bell, "'Hairspray' Settles on 60s Integration," *Los Angeles Sentinel*, March 10, 1988, B8; Janet Maslin, "Film: 'Hairspray,' Comedy from John Waters," *New York Times*, February 26, 1998, C17; Rita Kempley, "'Hairspray': John Waters' Baldly Comic Look Back," *Washington Post*, February 26, 1988, B1; David Sterritt, "Two Films Dealing Unconventionally with Concerns of Blacks," *Christian Science Monitor*, February 26, 1988, 21.

47. My use of *fat* rather than *overweight* is influenced by *The Fat Studies Reader*. Marilyn Wann, writes: "Currently in mainstream U.S. society, the O-words, 'overweight' and 'obese,' are considered more acceptable, even more polite, than the F-word, 'fat.' In the field of fat studies, there is agreement that the O-words are neither neutral nor benign.... In fat studies, there is respect for the political project of reclaiming the word *fat*, both as the preferred neutral adjective (i.e., short/tall, young/old, fat/thin) and also the preferred term of political identity. There is nothing negative or rude in the word *fat* unless someone makes the effort to put it there; using the word *fat* as a descriptor (not a discriminator) can help dispel prejudice." Marilyn Wann, "Foreword," in *The Fat Studies Reader*, ed. Esther Rothblum and Sondra Solovay (New York: New York University Press, 2009), xii.

48. *Hairspray*, dir. John Waters (New Line Cinema, 1988; DVD; New Line Home Entertainment; 2002).

49. "John Waters Commentary," in *Hairspray* (1988); "The Roots of Hairspray," in *Hairspray* (2007), disc 2; O'Donnell et. al., *Hairspray: The Roots*, 11. On John Waters's revision of the history of the *Buddy Deane Show*, see Renee

Curry, "Hairspray: The Revolutionary Way to Restructure and Hold Your History," *Literature Film Quarterly* 24 no. 2 (1996): 165–68.

50. "John Water interview with Terry Gross," *Fresh Air* (NPR, 1988), July 19, 2007, transcript available on Lexis-Nexis Academic Universe.

51. O'Donnell et. al., *Hairspray: The Roots*, 6–13.

52. Jesse McKinley, "Baltimore Embraces Its Offbeat Child, 'Hairspray,' " *New York Times*, September 18, 2003.

53. "The Roots of Hairspray," in *Hairspray* (2007), disc 2.

54. On the use of music to increase the commercial potential of popular films, see Jeff Smith, *The Sounds of Commerce: Marketing Popular Film Music* (New York: Columbia University Press, 1998); Jonathan Romney and Adrian Wootton, ed., *Celluloid Jukebox: Popular Music and the Movies since the 50s* (London: British Film Institute, 1995).

55. *Hairspray* (2007), disc 1.

56. Ibid; O'Donnell et. al., *Hairspray: The Roots*, 22–26. On the comic uses of music in film, see Jeff Smith, "Popular Songs and Comic Allusion in Contemporary Cinema," in *Soundtrack Available*, ed. Pamela Robertson Wojcik and Arthur Knight (Durham, NC: Duke University Press, 2001), 407–30.

57. "Commentary with Producers Craig Zadan and Neil Meron," in *Hairspray*, dir. Adam Shankman (New Line, 2007; DVD, 2 discs), disc 1.

58. Ibid.

59. "Commentary with Producers Craig Zadan and Neil Meron," in *Hairspray* (2007), disc 1.

60. Ibid.

61. Ibid.

62. *Hairspray* (2007), disc 1.

63. On the financial exploitation of black musicians, see Redd, *Rock Is Rhythm and Blues*; Guralnick, *Feel Like Going Home*; Chapple and Garofalo, *Rock 'n' Roll Is Here to Pay*, 231–69; Walsh, "Black-Oriented Radio and the Civil Rights Movement," 67–81; Brian Ward, *Just My Soul Responding: Rhythm and Blues, Black Consciousness, and Race Relations* (Berkeley: University of California, 1998), 339–450.

64. "Commentary with Director Adam Shankman," in *Hairspray* (2007), disc 1; "Commentary with Producers Craig Zadan and Neil Meron," in *Hairspray* (2007), disc 1.

65. *Hairspray* (2007).

66. Ibid.

67. Ibid.

68. "Commentary with Producers Craig Zadan and Neil Meron," in *Hairspray* (2007), disc 1.

69. "You Can't Stop the Beat: The Long Journey of Hairspray," in *Hairspray* (2007), disc 2.

70. See note 48.

71. "The Roots of Hairspray," in *Hairspray* (2007), disc 2.

72. "Adam Shankman Interview with Terry Gross," *Fresh Air* (NPR), July 19, 2007, transcript available on Lexis-Nexis Academic Universe.

73. Allison Graham, "Reclaiming the South: Civil Rights Films and the New Red Menace," in Brian Ward, ed., *Media, Culture, and the Modern African American Freedom Struggle* (Gainesville: University Press of Florida, 2001), 82–103; Fuller, "Recovering the Past."

74. *Hairspray* (2007), disc 1.

75. Ibid.

76. Ibid.

77. Ibid.

78. "Commentary with Producers Craig Zadan and Neil Meron," in *Hairspray* (2007), disc 1.

79. *Hairspray* (2007), disc 1.

80. Ibid.

81. Richard Dyer, "Entertainment and Utopia," in *Hollywood Musicals, The Film Reader*, ed. Steven Cohan (New York: Routledge, 2002), 19–29.

82. On *Mississippi Burning* and *Forrest Gump*, see Robert Rosenstone, *Visions of the Past: The Challenges of Film to Our Idea of History* (Cambridge, MA: Harvard University Press, 1995), 72–73; Sumiko Higashi, "Walker and *Mississippi Burning*: Postmdernism versus Illusionist Narrative," in *The Historical Film: History and Memory in Media*, ed. Marica Landy (New Brunswick, NJ: Rutgers University Press, 2001), 218–31; Vincent Rocchio, *Reel Racism Confronting Hollywood's Construction of Afro-American Culture* (Boulder: Westview Press, 2000), 95–113; Robert Burgoyne, *Film Nation: Hollywood Looks at U.S. History* (Minneapolis: University of Minnesota Press, 1997), 104–19.

83. "Commentary with Producers Craig Zadan and Neil Meron," in *Hairspray* (2007).

84. Joseph Cermatori, Emily Coates, Kathryn Krier, Bronwen MacArthur, Angelica Randle, and Joseph Roach, "Teaching African American Dance / History to a 'Post-Racial' Class: Yale's Project O," *Theatre Topics* 19, no. 1 (2009): 11.

CONCLUSION

1. Nina Simone with Stephen Cleary, *I Put a Spell on You: The Autobiography of Nina Simone* (New York: Da Capo Press, 1993), 89.

2. Nina Simone, "Mississippi Goddam," 1964, *Nina Simone: Anthology*, disc 1 (compact disc; RCA/BMG; 2003).

3. Simone, *I Put a Spell on You*, 90.

4. Thomas Sugrue, *Not Even Past: Barack Obama and the Burden of Race* (Princeton, NJ: Princeton University Press, 2010), 4.

5. Robert Self, *American Babylon: Race and the Struggle for Postwar Oakland* (Princeton, NJ: Princeton University Press, 2003); David Freund, *Colored Property: State Policy and White Racial Politics in Suburban America* (Chicago: University of Chicago Press, 2007); Becky Nicolaides, *My Blue Heaven: Life and Politics in the Working-Class Suburbs of Los Angeles, 1920–1965* (Chicago: University of Chicago Press, 2002); Eric Avila, *Popular Culture in the Age of White Flight: Fear and Fantasy in Suburban Los Angeles* (Berkeley: University of California Press, 2004).

6. Thomas Sugrue, *Sweet Land of Liberty: The Forgotten Struggle for Civil Rights in the North* (New York: Random House, 2008); Jeanne Theoharis and Komozi Woodard, eds., *Freedom North: Black Freedom Struggles outside the South, 1940–1980* (New York: Palgrave Macmillan, 2003); Jeanne Theoharis and Komozi Woodard, eds., *Groundwork: Local Black Freedom Movements in America* (New York: New York University Press, 2005); Martha Biondi, *To Stand and Fight: The Struggle for Civil Rights in Postwar New York City* (Cambridge, MA: Harvard University Press, 2003).

7. Lynn Spigel, *Welcome to the Dreamhouse: Popular Media and Postwar Suburbs* (Durham, NC: Duke University Press, 2001); Lynn Spigel, *Make Room for TV: Television and the Family Ideal in Postwar America* (Chicago: University of Chicago Press, 1992); Anna McCarthy, *Ambient Television: Visual Culture and Public Space* (Durham, NC: Duke University Press, 2001); Steven Classen, *Watching Jim Crow: The Struggles over Mississippi TV, 1955–1969* (Durham, NC: Duke University Press, 2004); Mark Williams, "Entertaining 'Difference': Strains of Orientalism in Early Los Angeles Television," in *Living Color: Race and Television in the United States,* ed. Sasha Torres (Durham NC: Duke University Press, 1998), 12–34; Victoria Johnson, *Heartland TV: Prime Time Television and the Struggle for U.S. Identity* (New York: NYU Press, 2008).

8. George Lipsitz, *Time Passages: Collective Memory and American Popular Culture* (Minneapolis: University of Minnesota Press, 1990); Mimi White, "'Reliving the Past Over and Over Again': Race, Gender, and Popular Memory in *Homefront* and *I'll Fly Away*," in *Living Color: Race and Television in the United States,* ed. Sasha Torres (Durham, NC: Duke University Press, 1998), 118–39; Jennifer Fuller, "Recovering the Past: Race, Nation, and Civil Rights Drama in the Nineties" (Ph.D. diss., University of Wisconsin-Madison, 2004); Herman Gray, "Remembering Civil Rights: Television, Memory, and the 1960s," in *The Revolution Wasn't Televised: Sixties Television and Social Conflict,* ed. Lynn Spigel and Michael Curtin (New York: Routledge, 1997), 349–58.

9. Kelly Schrum, *Some Wore Bobby Sox: The Emergence of Teenage Girl's Culture, 1920–1945* (New York: Palgrave Macmillan, 2004); Susan Douglas, *Where the Girls Are: Growing up Female with the Mass Media* (New York: Three Rivers Press, 1994); Aniko Bodroghkozy, *Groove Tube: Sixties Television and the Youth Rebellion* (Durham, NC: Duke University Press, 2001); Matt Garcia, "'Memories of El Monte': Intercultural Dance Halls in Post-World War II Greater Los Angeles," in *Generations of Youth: Youth Cultures and History in Twentieth-Century America,* ed. Joe Austin and Michael Nevin Willard (New York: New York University Press, 1998), 157–72.

10. Matthew Countryman, *Up South: Civil Rights and Black Power in Philadelphia* (Philadelphia: University of Pennsylvania Press, 2006); Matthew Countryman, "'From Protest to Politics': Community Control and Black Independent Politics in Philadelphia, 1965–1984," *Journal of Urban History* 32 (September 2006): 813–61; James Wolfinger, *Philadelphia Divided: Race and Politics in the City of Brotherly Love* (Chapel Hill: University of North Carolina Press, 2007); James Wolfinger, "The Limits of Black Activism: Philadelphia's Public Housing in the Depression and World War II," *Journal of Urban*

History 35 (September 2009): 787–814; Guian McKee, *The Problem of Jobs: Liberalism, Race, and Deindustrialization in Philadelphia* (Chicago: University Chicago Press, 2008); Guian McKee, "'I've Never Dealt with a Government Agency Before': Philadelphia's Somerset Knitting Mills Project, the Local State, and the Missed Opportunities of Urban Renewal," *Journal of Urban History* 35 (March 2009): 387–409; Lisa Levenstein, *A Movement without Marches: African American Women and the Politics of Poverty in Postwar Philadelphia* (Chapel Hill: University of North Carolina Press, 2009).

Index

AMERICAN CROSSROADS

Edited by Earl Lewis, George Lipsitz, George Sánchez, Dana Takagi, Laura Briggs, and Nikhil Pal Singh